PERSPECTIVES IN POLITICAL SOCIOLOGY

Edited by Andrew Effrat

The Bobbs-Merrill Company, Inc.
Indianapolis   New York

Library of Congress Cataloging in Publication Data
Main entry under title:
Perspectives in political sociology.
Articles which originally appeared in Sociological inquiry, v. 42, no. 3 and
    4, 1972.
1. Political sociology—Addresses, essays, lectures.
   I. Effrat, Andrew, ed.   II. Sociological inquiry.
JA76.P44   301.5'92   73-4329
ISBN 0-672-51746-9
ISBN 0-672-61322-0 (pbk)
Printed in the United States of America
First Printing

PERSPECTIVES IN
POLITICAL SOCIOLOGY

List of Contributors

ANDREW EFFRAT is associate professor of sociology in education at The Ontario Institute for Studies in Education. He is also the editor of *Sociological Inquiry*.

PETER M. HALL is professor of sociology and department chairman at the University of Missouri at Columbia.

ROSABETH MOSS KANTER is associate professor of sociology at Brandeis University.

SIDNEY R. WALDMAN is associate professor of political science at Haverford College.

DAVID EASTON, professor of political science at the University of Chicago, is generally recognized as one of the leading contemporary political theorists.

ROBERT J. WERLIN is associate professor of sociology at the University of California at Santa Cruz.

DANIEL ROSSIDES is professor of sociology at Bowdoin College and chairman of that department.

COLEMAN ROMALIS is assistant professor of sociology at York University, Atkinson College, in Toronto, Canada.

SEYMOUR MARTIN LIPSET is professor of sociology at Harvard University and has been a major figure in political sociology for a number of years.

TERRY N. CLARK is professor of sociology at the University of Chicago and is perhaps best known for his work on community decision-making.

TALCOTT PARSONS is professor of social relations at Harvard University. He enjoys an international reputation as scholar and teacher.

Contents

PERSPECTIVES IN
POLITICAL SOCIOLOGY

Power to the Paradigms:
An Editorial Introduction

The Ontario Institute for Studies in Education

"Power to the Paradigms" might seem like a strange, even reactionary, call at the present time. I reject that reading. This is a call not only for greater recognition of the scientific utility of paradigms or theoretical perspectives and greater conscious reliance on them as analytical tools. This is also an effort to suggest that paradigms in social science have been, in many ways, the slaves of ideologies. I wish to explore ways they might be liberated to realize more fully their de-alienated potential.

Frankly, I am not certain such liberation is possible. Attributes of the perspectives that I see as fortuitous or as the result of a particular historical development may actually be inherent in these schemes, but I do want to raise some questions and suggest some directions that might at least to some extent de-alienate them. It is probably impossible to resolve a number of these and related issues in this space. Nor do I think there are any easy, clear-cut answers—especially when the questions are so complex, ambiguous, and poorly formulated. But I will try to be openly and fruitfully uncertain.

The paradigms on which this work focuses are some of the principal theoretical perspectives for the analysis of political phenomena, particularly as developed in the field of political sociology. This field has grown quite rapidly in the past decade or so. During this period, a large number of empirical studies and some important general and middle-range theoretical works have appeared. Given this relatively rapid and perhaps sudden burst of activity, it is to be expected that gaps, discontinuities, and the like would arise within and among the various approaches. Further, it is fairly well agreed that we are living through a time of paradigm crisis—of dissatisfaction with existing paradigms, of open clashes among approaches, and of relatively serious search for new ones.[1] It seems particularly important in such a time to reconsider and compare the distinctive nature of these perspectives.

I wish to express my gratitude to Robert Baker, Paul Paschke, and Phillip Stone of OISE and Marcia Effrat of York University for their very helpful comments in regard to this paper.

[1] However, as I shall indicate below, it is quite problematic whether there are any "paradigms" in sociology as yet and whether it is actually in "crisis" in the rigorous senses of these terms.

Hence, this collection of essays, critiques, and rejoinders is addressed to the needs of several different audiences within this field, including sociologists and political scientists, those more theoretically and those more empirically oriented, and introductory-level students as well as more technically sophisticated scholars. This work is also intended to be of use to those interested in general theory *per se* in that it examines relatively fundamental features of the perspectives.

More specifically, the collection is intended to provide (a) overviews of the nature of some of the principal contemporary perspectives in political analysis—particularly their distinctive notions, basic assumptions, and major propositions; (b) clearer pictures of the present state of work on these perspectives—both conceptual and empirical; and (c) assessments of major strengths and weaknesses, important gaps, and an indication of work that is particularly needed now in these perspectives. The confrontations that we have arranged among proponents of different paradigms is intended to tease out assumptions and provide a balanced assessment of the perspectives. Some indication should emerge as to what are major criticisms of the paradigms and how they might be dealt with. Perhaps such open conflict and exchange may also result in some further liberation and a clearer picture of what is accidental and what essential in a given paradigm.

In this chapter, I will discuss the scope of political sociology, the nature and components of paradigms in general and some of the principal types of paradigms in political sociology. I will attempt to provide a general framework in terms of which a systematic comparison of the paradigms could be made. The comparison of the perspectives that follows will be at best only a skeleton of what seem to be the principal features of the paradigms that I hope the reader will find fruitful to alter, refine, and flesh out. This chapter concludes with a preview of some of the other essays in the book and a consideration of where these perspectives might go from here.

THE SCOPE OF POLITICAL SOCIOLOGY

I doubt that any simple definition could be offered that would adequately encompass the scope of political sociology or that would satisfy the range of different political sociologists, and that would provide a clear and lasting boundary vis-à-vis political science. For those who like capsule formulations, however, the following seem to be some of the better characterizations available:

> "Political sociology is that branch of sociology which is concerned with the social causes and consequences of given power distributions within or between societies, and with the social and political conflicts that lead to changes in the allocation of power." (Coser, 1966: 1)

"Political sociology may be said to comprise several lines of inquiry as well as several methods of investigation:

1. Voting behavior in communities and in the nation (attitude and opinion research);
2. Concentration of economic power and political decision-making (documentary evidence, mathematical models);
3. Ideologies of political movements and interest groups (documentary evidence, content analysis);
4. Political parties, voluntary associations, the problem of oligarchy and the psychological correlates of political behavior (documentary evidence, attitude and opinion research, psychological testing, etc.);
5. Government and the problem of bureaucracy (documentary evidence, attitude and opinion research, etc.)" (Bendix & Lipset, 1966: 10)

"Broadly conceived, political sociology is concerned with the social basis of power in all institutional sectors of society . . . with patterns of social stratification and their consequences in organized politics. . . . In narrower terms, political sociology focuses on the organizational analysis of political groups and political leadership . . . the study of both formal and informal party organization, with its linkages to the governmental bureaucracy, the legal system, interest groups and the electorate at large." (Janowitz, 1968: 298)

These conceptions tend to focus on *concrete* political activities that would be largely associated with relatively traditional governmental and political institutions. A more *analytical* conception[2] of the nature and scope of the field would crosscut the various types of concrete institutions and societies and the various levels of social organization and focus on their common analytical features, such as centralization of authority, bases of legitimacy, and internal cleavages. Thus, one might conceive of political sociology as concerned with the causes, patterns, and consequences of the distribution and processes of power and authority in all social systems—ranging from small groups and families to educational, religious, etc., institutions as well as in regard to governmental or political institutions. Unfortunately, relatively little of this sort of work has been done by political sociologists, although one does find specialists in these other fields very much concerned with diverse political aspects.

The concerns of the field might be summarized somewhat more systematically in terms of a series of overlapping circles—some circles containing others completely and some only partially. The smallest and innermost circle would represent the smallest unit of analysis usually focused on and what many see as the basic unit of societies—namely, the *individual* or a *role*. Substantive questions usually dealt with at this level concern the ways individuals or role incumbents bargain and communicate with each other in regard to political issues, the nature and sources of an individual's (or

---

[2] For a more careful discussion of the distinction between concrete and analytical, see Levy, 1952: 35–36.

collection of individuals) political attitudes or ideology (e.g., in regard to foreign policy, party identification or governmental centralization) and behavior (e.g., voting, and other forms of participation).

The next larger circle might represent small scale *primary groups* in which individuals interact largely on an informal, face-to-face basis such as families, friendship groups, and perhaps small-scale neighborhood clusterings. Another circle, not necessarily completely encompassing this one, would be larger aggregates of individuals that are also not formally organized, such as social classes, religious, ethnic and regional groupings and the like. Some of the major substantive questions in regard to these sectors usually concern their impact on individual attitudes and behavior, for example, how social class or friendship networks affect voting or party identification or how families socialize their members into political information and opinions. It is also common to analyze the larger scale groups in regard to the concentration or distribution of various types of attitudes and behavior to make generalizations about, for example, what types of groups support what types of ideologies.

Another overlapping circle would be more *formal organizations* such as political parties, business firms, governmental agencies, ethnic associations and the like. Substantive questions dealt with at this level would concern the nature of the decision-making structures and processes in these organizations and what differences these make for organizational support and effectiveness. Other questions would concern the interaction of these organizations with each other—what inputs they make to each other, how they bargain and exchange resources, whether there are various interlocking elites that seem to govern them, how powerful they are, etc. Other sets of concerns would be how entities at this level (1) articulate "down"—for example, to influence individuals' attitudes and participation, (2) articulate "across" to other intermediate-level types of groups—for example, to relate to ethnic or religious cleavages, and (3) articulate "up"— to be influenced by societal and institutional norms and processes.

The next larger or more macro-level that is traditionally identified would be the *institutional*. This term refers, roughly, to functionally related complexes of roles, norms, and organizations such as the economy, the polity, or the religious sector. A still more inclusive level would be the *societal*.[3] The substantive questions usually dealt with at these macro-levels concern the sources and consequences of political development or modernization, the conditions promoting or inhibiting various types of distribution of power and political structures such as democracy, the composition and change of

---

[3] One could distinguish still other levels such as international groupings, regions, and the like, but the above distinctions should suffice for illustrative purposes.

elites, the nature, extent and sources of conflict and consensus among groups, etc.

Several of the "Grand Classical Questions" that are often dealt with at all of these levels concern the nature of political and social order—what the principal processes are and how the diverse individual and collective interests succeed—or fail—in regulating and coordinating their activities. A second complex of problems concerns the phenomena of political and social change—what are its principal types, sources, and consequences.[4] I think it will be particularly instructive to consider how the different perspectives deal with these central questions.

The distinction between political sociology and political science seems to be an increasingly difficult one to make, particularly in the last decade when there has been a growing exchange across the disciplinary boundaries. If one had to make such a distinction, however, one might stress, among other things, the following different emphases in approaches. First, political sociologists have tended to pay more attention than political scientists to the social structural or societal context of political phenomena and to be more concerned with society as a whole and the interaction of its parts—of which the political aspect is only one set. For example, in approaching a phenomenon such as political parties or communities, political sociologists might concern themselves more with how these entities relate to other non-political associations, institutions, and norms in society or to unofficial and informal practices. Second, political sociologists have tended to be more analytically oriented. That is, in analyzing political phenomena, they have sought to use more general conceptual tools and to formulate propositions that might apply to a large range of different political activities in different societies, whereas political scientists have tended to focus more on the historical particularity of given situations and events.

Of course, both of these statements are very general characterizations that are not applicable to all sociologists or all political scientists by any means and are probably decreasingly accurate characterizations. Further, they are the opinions of one perhaps imperialistic sociologist.

This collection includes representatives of seven major perspectives in political sociology: Marxism, structural functional analysis, systems theory, the Weberian approach, Parsonian theory, symbolic interactionism, and exchange theory. Why these and not others? And how might they be more systematically related to each other?

I have chosen to focus on certain of these perspectives—the first five

---

[4] Rather than attempt a frustratingly brief history that traces the development and differentiation of political sociology in a sweeping "Plato to Parsons fashion," I would refer the interested reader to Eisenstadt, 1971: 3–24; Lipset, 1969; and Parsons, et al., eds., 1961: 85–97.

named above—because they are the ones on which the most work in contemporary political sociology seems to rest. I have included the latter two—
exchange theory and symbolic interactionism—because they have not been
applied particularly extensively to political phenomena and yet they seem
quite rich and promising.

A PERSPECTIVE ON PERSPECTIVES:
THE NATURE AND FUNCTIONS OF PARADIGMS

In approaching the question of how these theoretical perspectives or
paradigms might be more systematically compared, let us first consider what
a paradigm is supposed to be and to do. The popularity of the term "paradigm" and the viewpoint associated with it owes much to the work of
Thomas Kuhn (see particularly *The Structure of Scientific Revolutions,*
1970). Kuhn's book can be seen as revolutionary in its own right. Essentially, Kuhn argues against the empiricist-positivist position that science
progresses primarily through the linear accumulation and refinement of facts
and the steady revision of generalizations based on the dispassionate consideration of data. Instead, Kuhn suggests paradigms play a central role in
structuring scientific activity and are far more the focus of science than are
facts.

While Kuhn does not provide a particularly clear-cut definition, "paradigm" seems to refer to a theoretical system or perspective that includes:
(1) an indication of what are important and researchable questions or problems, (2) general explanatory principles or answers to these questions,
(3) "praxis-oriented exemplars"[5] and models[6] for conceptualizing and
solving scientific puzzles, (4) criteria for what are appropriate data, methodologies, and instruments, and (5) an axiology (or value orientations[7]),
epistemology and ontology that underlie and ground all the above.

---

[5] Exemplars seem to be the most central components of paradigms for Kuhn. The
term refers primarily to "the concrete problem-solutions that students encounter from
the start of their scientific education, whether in laboratories, on examinations, or at
the end of chapters in science texts" (Kuhn, 1970: 187). In physics for example,
exemplars would be classic problems or experiments such as the inclined plane, the
conical pendulum and Keplerian orbits as well as the relatively standard ways of solving these problems. Exemplars function to socialize the potential scientist into the
praxis (the actions and action-oriented knowledge) of his field. They provide him
with concrete examples of what is relevant information and how he can apply
symbolic generalizations or raw-schemas to diverse specific situations.

[6] Models seem to be a summary term for conceptions of what are useful orienting
notions (for example, that "all perceptible phenomena are due to the interaction of
qualitatively neutral atoms in the void, or, alternatively, to matter and force, or to
fields" [Kuhn, 1970: 184]) or basic analogies and metaphors (for example, that the
molecules of a gas behave like elastic billiard balls in random motion).

[7] This term also refers to general norms and criteria concerning important scientific
activities, such as, that predictions should be accurate and quantitative (as opposed to

Thus, it is a paradigm that structures the scientist's activities—his particular conceptualizations, specific problems he chooses to focus on, concrete ways he selects to solve these problems, what he regards as true, probable, or fruitful. It is a paradigm then that not only makes sense of facts, but enables one to perceive or conceptualize a fact or a phenomenon in the first place. For example, one might consider the following data:

Figure 1.   *Illustration from Hanson, 1958:13.*

When asked to state what this is some people regard it as a type of bird with its beak open, others as some sort of horned animal such as an antelope. When pressed further they might respond that it is a series of lines on paper, a picture, or even a deliberately ambiguous projective test! Of course, the point is not only that these identical sense data can be and are interpreted in a number of different ways that vary at least with the different (albeit crude) paradigms that one brings to bear on the phenomena but also that the data would be essentially meaningless without criteria for perceiving and processing it. The history of science holds many more interesting and complex examples of these points. Many of the great controversies in science are essentially clashes between different perspectives or paradigms in their interpretation of the meaning, validity, or reliability of particular data.[8]

Kuhn identifies a number of stages through which sciences tend to pass. (1) First, there is a "pre-paradigmatic phase" during which a number of theoretical approaches or schools, often fused with much broader philosophical concerns, are in competition with each other with no one of them com-

---

loose or qualitative), that theories should be simple, consistent, and plausible, that science should (or should not) be socially useful and relevant.

[8] See the Copernican vs. Ptolemaic conceptions in astronomy, the Phlogiston controversy in chemistry, Einsteinian vs. Newtonian physics, etc. The various confrontations in this book are quite representative of basic differences in the social sciences.

manding the respect and allegiance of the relevant scientific community.[9]

(2) When some paradigm develops sufficient sophistication and support to be widely recognized and used by scientists as their principal framework, then the field in question has emerged into a "paradigmatic phase." In this stage, scientists engage in "normal science" in which they are largely employing the reigning paradigm to conceptualize and solve problems, develop instruments, make theoretical specifications, etc. The paradigm is relatively safe and the scientist proceeds to solve puzzles with it rather than to challenge assumptions or develop fundamental revisions.

(3) A "crisis phase" is entered when significant anomalies, inelegances, challenges, and the like accumulate to the point where the reigning paradigm is increasingly felt to be failing or discredited in the eyes of a significant proportion of the relevant scientific community. New paradigms may be developed or revived and there is likely to be a period of dissensus and competition among the various perspectives perhaps comparable to the pre-paradigmatic phase.

(4) There is then likely to occur a "scientific revolution"—a relatively discontinuous leap or shift to a significantly different paradigm that usually involves a radical reconstruction of the field's basic criteria and conceptualizations.

Throughout all of this, the adage seems to hold that theories never die—just those who believe in them. And the believers do not readily die generally because, with some syllogistic agility, a good theorist can make a rich paradigm account for apparently disconfirming or anomalous data.[10] It would seem, then, that theories tend to fall less due to their being proven wrong than because of their increasing inelegance, loss of "heuristicity," credibility gaps, and the like.[11]

None of this is to suggest that theories "die" forever. I am inclined to

---

[9] The distinction between paradigm and theoretical school or approach and the question of when a school becomes a paradigm are important issues. There seems to be two main criteria of "paradigmness": (1) The degree of acceptance in the "relevant scientific community." However, it is a complex question as to how broadly this community should be defined and what is the magic percentage of adherents or level of institutionalization for a school to be regarded as having taken over a particular field and thus become a paradigm. (2) The extent of "development" of the theoretical system itself. This might concern whether it has developed quite explicit paradigmatic questions and answers, some moderately sophisticated methods, relatively solid empirical grounding or support, is relatively well integrated and internally consistent, and the like.

[10] It is in this sense that it has been suggested that a truly "crucial experiment" is extremely difficult to design. See Toulmin, 1957.

[11] The criteria of elegance and heuristicity are difficult to pin down. They encompass a paradigm's power to organize data and propositions, to conceptualize phenomena, to suggest further insight, to solve "neatly" what are defined as crucial problems, and much more. In his article included here, Easton seems to rely to an important extent on these criteria in discussing exchange theory.

see the history of a science as a struggle among a few fundamental positions —e.g., an atomistic one and a holistic or systemic one—that reoccur, hold sway for a period, and then are overthrown by a more sophisticated version of an opposing position. The "defeated" paradigm may even be partially incorporated or taken over by the new synthesis. The basic positions take different specific forms throughout history in regard to different particular problems and they perhaps become generally more sophisticated over time as they attempt to deal with anomalies and, in general, respond to and coopt or compete with opposing positions. This process might be summarized as a pattern of dialectical evolution—of theses competing with antitheses leading to new syntheses.

I find Kuhn's perspective among the most useful on science and theory; however, I would want to go beyond it in certain respects (or at least develop some directions in which he is moving when he emphasizes that paradigms are based in a scientific *community*). Kuhn's perspective strikes me as still too rational, his revolutions still too bloodless. I think it is useful to emphasize that scientific schools seem more akin to ideological movements than is generally recognized, that scientific discourse and activity is more like ideological polemics and efforts to "maneuver for high ground," in effect, that scientific conflict is a form of ideological warfare. I think this is particularly the case in "crisis" phases such as the one into which sociology has entered.[12]

What are some of the implications of this approach to paradigms and scientific activity? First, I think this view argues for a radical skepticism vis-à-vis all theoretical schools. It suggests a concern that scientists may want to seem right at least as much as be right and an awareness that important factors in a given theoretical school's popularity may relate more to public relations and institutional power bases than the inherent truth or even beauty of the theory.

Second, this view suggests that one should examine a paradigm or theoretical perspective for its core values and philosophical roots in order to gain insight into the perspective and perhaps to develop an ability to see the implications of the theory that the theory itself may not yet have come to.

Finally, what are some of the implications of this view for what is desirable scientific activity? It might seem cynical to suggest that one implication

[12] Certainly a rigorous application of the criteria mentioned in footnote 9 would lead to the conclusion that sociology is still in a pre-paradigm phase—the vast bulk of sociologists throughout the world do not seem to have ever reached consensus on a particular paradigm and no paradigm seems to have become sufficiently well developed. Considerably looser and more generous use of the criteria (as I have been making) might suggest that there have been a number of reigning paradigms at least in the U.S. such as the Chicago school and structural functionalism and that sociology is now in a crisis phase. (See also Gouldner, 1970, and Kuklick, in press.)

is that one should be intensely committed to "pushing" one's theoretical school—that one should seek to develop it as far as possible logically and empirically, to co-opt or subsume other theoretical positions, to identify "politically effective persuaders" such as doing exciting studies that capture people's (and particularly graduate students') imagination or that solve some particularly visible anomaly. However, this view might also help to liberate scientists from a peculiar and perhaps debilitating kind of ambivalence and mystification that has perhaps inhibited scientific discourse and kept it from progressing as rapidly as it might. In other words, if one takes an evolutionary view relatively seriously, one can see a fairly open and honest conflict situation as enabling the useful components of paradigms to prosper and survive and the paradigms to evolve more rapidly and sophisticatedly.

It may well be the case that sociology will continue for quite some time in "crisis"—having a number of competing and non-integratable paradigms. This situation of perpetual conflict could even be to the advantage of the "search for truth" and a healthier situation than "normal science" where a given paradigm would be the reigning orthodoxy.

TOWARDS A TYPOLOGY OF PARADIGMS
IN POLITICAL SOCIOLOGY

Let us now turn to the question of how we might systematically conceptualize and interrelate the paradigms in political sociology (and, by implication, sociology in general).

One of the implications of the above, more conflict-oriented conception of paradigms is that we should look to the major controversies and conflicts that have divided and differentiated political sociologists. Two major sets of factors could be focused on in this regard. The first concerns the *level of analysis and organization* of social phenomena on which the paradigm tends to focus. Let us call the two polar positions "micro-level" and "macro-level." Other terms for the micro-level are "atomistic" or "reductionist," while other terms for the macro-level are "holistic" and "emergentist." The distinction often made by political scientists between behavioral and systemic or institutional approaches would also parallel ours.

The micro-level paradigms are primarily concerned with the behavior of particular actors, small-scale social systems, face-to-face interactions and their properties, and intra-personal factors. Thus, for example, exchange theorists tend to focus on interpersonal exchanges in small group or face-to-face settings, while more psychoanalytically oriented analysts of political phenomena (e.g., Lasswell, 1930) focus on such intra-psychic factors as anxieties, private motives, and defense mechanisms. One gets the impression that many micro-level theorists regard individuals as in some sense "more real" than groups or structural properties. Contrast this to Rossides's summary of Weber's position on "human nature" (p. 193).

The macro-level paradigms tend to treat as their principal explanatory factors more large-scale properties of social phenomena such as general cultural milieux, socio-economic classes, institutional and other social structural arrangements—aspects of social systems that it claims are not the properties of any one individual or small-scale element. The macro-level approach emphasizes that individuals or more elementary particles can only be understood in relation to larger systemic contexts, and is concerned to a much greater extent with the functioning of systems as a whole and relationships among their major substructures.[13]

Most actual macro-level theorists do try to "reach down" and account for micro-level phenomena, just as micro-level theorists try to generalize or aggregate "up" from the acts of individuals to system properties. However, our classification is based on the primary focus of analysis and elements emphasized in explanations or accounts. Clearly the macro-level analysts offer a much richer array of terms for conceptualizing, tools for measuring, and propositions to account for macro-level phenomena such as organizational, collective, and structural factors—as do micro-level analysts for micro-level phenomena.

The second basis for classification concerns the *substantive factors* that the paradigm treats as the principal independent variables or explanatory agents. I have found it useful to distinguish four main types in this regard: material, affective or cathectic, interactional or conative, and ideal or symbolic. The meaning of these terms should become clear as we discuss the phenomena associated with each of the approaches. Essentially, material factors would refer to physical sanctions and resources, technology, economic interests and the like; affective to intra-psychic feelings and their related processes; interactional and conative to various patterns of activities or performances; and ideal or symbolic to normative or evaluative components such as values and ideologies.[14]

Cross-cutting these foci yields an eight-fold table in which I would classify the principal paradigms as indicated in Table I.

---

[13] One formulation of this distinction has been that micro-level theorists emphasize the elements of social systems while macro-level theorists are concerned with the system as a whole. This is a useful formulation with the understanding that the macro-level theorists would also see relatively large-scale properties, such as social classes or norms, as also being important elements of social systems.

[14] I shall pass over the question of whether there is a general dimension here running from "materialfaktoren" to "idealfaktoren"—each step being, in some sense, more symbolic (or cybernetically higher in information than energy) as it moves toward the idealfaktoren. Also, any resemblance of these four factors to a Parsonian AGIL scheme is not coincidental. However, both of these questions would involve us in more technical issues than is appropriate for this introduction.

Table I

A CLASSIFICATION OF SOME PARADIGMS FOR POLITICAL ANALYSIS

Substantive Component Emphasized	*Level of Analysis*	
	Macro-level	Micro-level
Material	Marxists	Exchange theorists Utilitarians
Affective	Culture & Personality School	Freudians
Interactional	Durkheimians or French Social Collectivists	Symbolic Interactionists Activities Theory (à la Dreeben)
Idealist or Symbolist	Weberians and German Idealists Parsonians Cyberneticists	Phenomenologists Ethnomethodologists

Let me make several general comments before explicating this scheme. First the classification is of course an attempt at abstraction or distillation. That is, any particular theorist or theoretical school may use a number of different components as explanatory factors, nevertheless, I would suggest that the paradigms rely *primarily* upon the sets of factors and the level of analysis into which they have been classified. Second, this scheme would of course be expandable to distinguish a more middle-range level in which indeed one is likely to find a great many sociologists.[15]

Of course, the development of a useful typology is a theoretical task in itself and reflects a theorist's paradigmatic biases. I have chosen to focus on the apparently major points of theoretical (and in a sense ideological) dispute among the paradigms. Other approaches might emphasize the language or metaphor of the paradigm, the social and economic biases that the perspective seems to reflect, etc. I would certainly not claim that my classification is complete or without problems since it is only the second generation of the scheme. Nevertheless, it should facilitate a more systematic comparison and identification of the theoretical highlights of the paradigms to be considered as well as a consideration of potential points of complementarity and conflict.

---

[15] Another way of representing this scheme would be in the form of a matrix with the vertical axis representing the level of analysis or organization ranging from macro through middle-range to micro or even sub-social and the horizontal axis ranging from materialist through affectivist and interactionist to idealist. This might allow for a more sensitive plotting or representation of the various theorists' positions.

COMPARING THE PERSPECTIVES

Our comparison of the paradigms and explication of the above classification will be in terms of what we see as the main components of paradigms. In our attempt to deal with the material in a relatively introductory fashion, we shall not seek to be exhaustive and shall focus on: (1) the focal problems or dependent variables of the paradigm in question, (2) the primary determinants, causal agents or independent variables and propositions that the paradigm tends to emphasize, (3) the principal exemplars and models, (4) the methodologies or strategies of data gathering, and (5) the apparent value orientations of those using the paradigm.

Given the scope of the task at hand, we shall just focus on those paradigms dealt with in this issue. Our treatment is not intended to provide a detailed or complete introduction to the theories, but rather an impressionistic sketch of some of their principal highlights. Our discussion will obviously need to be fleshed out much further and is subject to considerable revision—something we trust the reader will do in light of the articles to follow and consultation of other primary and secondary sources.

Finally, the following summary is certainly an oversimplified characterization of the richness and complexity (and, indeed, the vagueness and contradictoriness) of a large number of different people who have used these paradigms. Given the ambiguity of this material, then, it is unlikely that I have succeeded in keeping my own biases out of the attempt to discuss and identify the apparent emphases of the theories. I have certainly not intended to put any value on, for example, being more macro- or more micro-level, more material, or symbolic. Clearly the paradigms as they have developed to date all have their distinctive strengths and limitations as far as I am concerned, although I would be less than candid not to say that my sympathies lie largely with the macro-level analysts, especially some sort of synthesis of the Parsonian and Marxist approaches.

First let us take up symbolic interactionism. This perspective tends to treat the following as the focal questions or problems to be explained: whether and how a negotiated order or joint action is created, maintained, and disrupted in a given social setting; the sources of particular behaviors or symbolic gestures in particular contexts and how they function to influence definitions and perceptions; the process of everyday interactions, particularly the outcomes of interpersonal bargaining and communication; and the process of socialization, especially the acquisition of culture and the determinants of self concepts.

The primary determinants that this perspective is likely to emphasize are subjective or internal and shared orientations, symbols, meanings, self-concepts, and definitions of situation.[16] Often these subjective meanings are analyzed in the form of "internalized others" and significant reference groups. The bases for these subjective meanings or "mind" more generally are treated as being in various interpersonal interactions (particularly role playing and role taking leading to the internalization of significant others[17]), overt activities and cues, and gestural exchanges or negotiations—although of course meanings and definitions influence what activities are performed and how they are interpreted. Symbolic interactionists vary among themselves in how much emphasis they give in their causal interpretations to activity or interaction components as opposed to more symbolic, informational components. Generally, they seem to fuse these components such that they are focusing on symbolic or meaning-carrying activity. The concept of "gesture" would be particularly focal or exemplary for this perspective.

Probably the principal exemplars and models of this paradigm would be of society and social life as a network of interactional games or dramas. (These images would be particularly useful in capturing both the relative autonomy of individuals' particular performances as well as their interdependence and role complementarity.) There is a decided emphasis in this approach on social and political *processes* (see, for example, Hall's "power in action") and the non-institutionalized aspects of society. The political and social order is seen as being in considerable flux and as a creation of actors who are constantly adapting to and negotiating in concrete and specific situations. Socialization, shared symbols, and bargaining help solve the problem of order, but the order is still highly problematic and quite fragile. Much of the content of the political process involves overt and often dramatic actions, confrontations, or gestures that manipulate symbols, influence information flow, alter definitions of situations, mobilize support through impression management and the like. Change may come about through successful bargaining, redefinitions of situations, and more or less temporary reconstructions of reality. Leadership, particularly of a relatively personal or charismatic sort, would also play an important role in the political process and change. In sum, the symbolic interactionist would approach most social phenomena as problematic negotiated syntheses (or potential syntheses or breakdowns) of separate, diverse, and competing subjectivities. This view certainly does not go as far as Leibniz's "windowless monads"— at least the monads seem to have windows and unlockable doors.

The methodology relied upon seems to be particularly the study of individ-

---

[16] One oft-cited summary statement is W. I. Thomas's to the effect that, if men define things as real, they are real in their consequences.

[17] Cf. my fourteen-month-old daughter saying to herself as she holds back from touching some forbidden object "No, no, Elana!" Personal communication, September 1972.

uals in specific role performances or small groups in relatively "natural settings," often through participant observation or open-ended interviewing in order to fathom actors' meanings and definitions of the situation. An attempt is generally made to analyze gestural exchanges or acted-out meanings in order to get at actors' goals and means and to capture the processes of interaction. There is also an emphasis on sensitive, flexible, and exploratory "inspection" of phenomena, sometimes relying on well-informed observers to attempt to transcend sociological preconceptions.

While I would not say that the basic values inherent in this perspective are "liberal" (especially given Hall's disclaimers), the perspective has traditionally taken a basically benign view of social life emphasizing democratic and cooperative aspects and tending to see people as relatively free to negotiate and create their own courses of action. Of course, a more Marxist influence might share this as a potential ideal for society while emphasizing, as a careful symbolic interactionist analysis might, structural factors that constrain individuals and that limit freedom. This seems to be the direction in which Hall is moving when he de-emphasizes consensus factors in his analysis and points to a future theoretical synthesis of Lukacs and Blumer.

The classification of this perspective as micro-level is not to deny Hall's effort to show that symbolic interactionism can deal with and has dealt with more macro-level issues and forms of organization. Rather, it is to stress both that the focal questions have tended to be more at the micro-level and that the answers and conceptualizations on which symbolic interactionism focuses are more micro-level elements, such as individual actors' subjective perspectives and activities. The individual is treated as a more basic acting unit as opposed to a more macro-level perspective that treats collective entities such as social classes, organizations, institutions, and culture as equally if not more effective. This emphasis strikes me as resting at least in part on certain epistemological and ontological assumptions that most micro-level theories seem to have in common. That is, they seem to regard at least implicitly the individual (or properties of the individual such as the mind) as in some sense more "real" than groups or group properties (witness Hall, page 42, quoting Strauss et al. with approval "that the very idea of 'nation' or 'society' is only a fiction . . . "). There is an emphasis on individual symbolizations and the actor as more voluntaristic than one often finds in the more macro-level theories which tend to focus on more collective symbolizations such as general cultural and normative constraints and which often give more explanatory and constraining power to these macro-level factors.[18]

---

[18] Even symbolic interactionists' concern with such macro-level phenomena as mass communications and collective behavior does not refute these points. These phenomena tend to be the more individually created and institutionally unregulated macro-level

I have suggested in Table I that most symbolic interactionists would be classified in or near the conative or activity-focused set of substantive independent variables. This is perhaps going too far given the heavy emphasis on symbolic or meaningful components. However, I did want to give emphasis to the activity variables that sociologists have tended to neglect or conceptualize poorly. (Perhaps the most exciting and explicit work of this sort can be found in Dreeben, 1968; Bidwell, in press, and most of Goffman's work.) Essentially, I am giving heavy weight to what seems to be the focus of symbolic interactionist's concerns—what people actually do, the conceptualization of the self as a way of acting, the bases of meaning, symbolization and pluralistic values in the activities and roles that actors must perform, etc. It would probably be most appropriate to classify this approach as somewhere between a more pure activity-based one and a symbolist one. This synthesis is rather neatly summarized in Blumer's definition of symbolic interaction ". . . as activity in which human beings interpret each other's gestures and act on the basis of the meaning yielded by that interpretation" (1969: 65–66).

Turning now to exchange theory we would identify the focal problems as a concern to account for: (a) an individual's learning a given belief or developing a propensity to perform particular overt behaviors (such as according legitimacy to the state or participating in certain types of political activities), (b) who interacts with whom for what, (c) continuities and changes in activities primarily of individuals but also of organizations and other sub-structures of society.

The independent variables or causal factors that the theory focuses on are primarily micro-level material incentives (such as material goods, physical force, or personal approval) that is, the nature, amount, schedule, etc. of rewards and punishments or costs and benefits that individuals receive. Individuals are seen as acting *as if* they sought to maximize or satisfice profit in interactions.[19] Thus, the theory relies heavily on the Skinnerian operant conditioning paradigm that emphasizes the importance of a specific individual's particular reinforcement history and the immediate stimulus situation. Stability and change in political behavior would be accounted for in terms of the continuation or alteration of the reward structure or profitability of behaviors. Political order is seen as arising out of the similarity of interests, rewards for cooperation, punishment for noncooperation, bargaining, and the like. Power is conceptualized as based essen-

---

ones. Of course, symbolic interactionists suggest that institutional behavior is not quite as "institutional" or rule-governed as many macro-level theorists seem to believe.

[19] The central "laws" concerning the relationships among stimulus, reward, and behavior that the theory emphasizes are well summarized by Waldman on pp. 103–104. Of course, even "satisficing" can be seen as a way of maximizing profits—that is, it minimizes costs of cognitive searching, anxiety in seeking the very best deal, etc.

tially on the ability to provide scarce rewards and political processes—such as rendering political support, making demands for particular policies, and selecting various policy options—are seen as essentially oriented to the allocation or attainment of various positive sanctions or avoidance of negative ones.

Perhaps the principal model would be the conception of groups as market places with individuals as various sorts of entrepreneurs and salespeople trying to exchange their various wares. The primary analytical thrust is to seek out what particular actors are getting in exchange for what and with what consequences. Some of the main conceptual tools relied on are drawn from Skinnerian learning theory and economics—cost/benefit analysis, supply/demand curves, stimulus-response conditioning, and the like.

The favored methodology tends to be relatively rigorous and quantified observation and analysis of overt behavior, often through non-participatory observation or experimental manipulation. While actors' expectations are regarded as important to be aware of, they are generally treated as capable of being inferred from direct observation of stimulus and response interchanges.

The value orientations of those employing this approach often seem to be those of laissez faire individualism, emphasizing a free and efficient market and the maximizing of individual rational pursuit of self interest.

Exchange theory obviously has a number of important theoretical aspects in common with symbolic interactionism. Although there are of course macro-level aspects to the theories (as, for example, exchange theory's emphasis on political market structures), they are both predominantly micro-level in their focus on individual actors and on the more elementary particles of social organization and in their attempt to build up from individual pay-offs, orientations, interactions, and other elements an account of the behavior of societies and their sub-structures. Waldman puts his stance clearly (p. 154) in stating that "The real issue, of course, is not that system properties differ from the properties of individuals, but whether the former can be derived from or explained in terms of the latter."[20] Exchange theory obviously differs from symbolic interactionism in its considerably lesser emphasis on and less developed treatment of symbolic and informational components.[21]

---

[20] Also see Homans's effort (1964: 816–817) to show the generality of his propositions and their ability to subsume macro-level phenomena. His treatment might be criticized by macro-level analysts as taking as givens and in effect leaving unexplained most of the important macro-level variables (such as the high demand for cotton textiles, the low productivity of labor, the existing state of technology, and other socio-political constraints, in his attempted revision of Smelser's explanation of technical innovation in cotton manufacturing). The reader should probably be particularly watchful for the taken-for-granted assumptions in the essays that follow.

[21] The other principal sets of elements for which exchange theory provides a significant place are affective components (e.g., individual needs and wants) as well

Let us now turn to a consideration of two macro-level positions—the Marxist and the idealist. One prior question is where in our scheme we would place the structural functionalists and the systems theorists whose work is represented in this collection particularly by Easton, Kanter, and Clark.

As I see it, these two positions are at a more general or inclusive level than the substantive theories with which we have been dealing. In many ways, what is fundamental to both structural functionalism and systems theory would be essentially what we mean by macro-level theory. For example, the focal questions concern the social system as a whole and its principal large-scale structures and processes, such as social classes, value orientations, integration, equilibrium, etc. The determinants that these approaches emphasize are also considerably more at a cultural or social structural level than the above two micro-level approaches. The specific substantive factors emphasized would depend on which type of structural functionalism or systems theory is being employed. These approaches also tend to rely on what Easton calls "methodological holism" which attempts "to understand the relationship of the component subsystems to the full organized entity" (p. 144; see also his p. 146). These approaches are particularly interested in and seek to develop analytical tools for conceptualizing and measuring the distinctive properties of collectivities and are often quite sensitive to "contextual effects" on individual attitudes and performance.

Thus, more substantive theories such as Marxist, Parsonian theory, and Easton's perspective, can be seen as particular "brands" of structural functionalism and/or of systems theory. The materialist brand as represented by Marx would tend to emphasize material factors as the primary determinants of social phenomena while the Parsonians would tend to emphasize such ideal factors as value orientations and existential beliefs. Nevertheless, these theories seem to share important aspects of their analysis. For example, the Marxist perspective can be seen as functionalist or systems theoretical in that, like Parsonian or Durkheimian perspectives, it emphasizes the functional interdependence and interchange among system parts, the functional differentiation among structures and their contributions to systemic functioning, the consequences (eufunctional and dysfunctional) of particular structures for the fulfillment or lack of fulfillment of societal and personal functions, the sources of system equilibrium and disequilibrium, etc.[22]

The Durkheimian or French social collectivist brand of functionalism seems to be the closest to a relatively pure macro-level activities or inter-

---

as individual activities or overt behavior—although the material rewarding significance of the content of these activities is the focus of theoretical concern.

[22] In fairness, I would speculate that Marxists might react by agreeing that these general theoretical features are shared, but countering that they are not that central to their concerns and that they lack the important critical substance (to be discussed below) that is distinctive of Marxist theory.

actionist perspective. The focus is on such interactive patterns or organizational properties as systemic solidarity, the division of labor, cohesion, differentiation, social density, centralization, group cleavages, and the like. Most sociologists labelled as functionalists (such as Robert Merton, Wilbert Moore, Kingsley Davis, Talcott Parsons, and S. M. Lipset) often rely on both interactionist and symbolic components, although with a considerably heavier emphasis on the latter.

It is when we come to the exemplars and models that the differences between the structural functionalists and systems theorists emerge most clearly. The former tend to use more of an organic conception of society (drawn apparently to an important extent from biological theory and using such terms as structures, functions, homeostatic mechanisms, equilibrium, and evolution) while the systems theorists seem to have more of a mechanistic conception (relying heavily on computer and engineering images such as input, conversion, output, and feedback).[23]

Next let us turn to the Marxist perspective. The focal problems and dependent variables that this perspective is concerned to explain are essentially (1) the sources and nature of exploitation, oppression, alienation, false consciousness and the like both in the relationships among classes in a society and among nations; (2) aspects and functions of the "super-structure" such as the state, laws, religion, etc.; (3) the class structure and relationships in society, particularly the relationship of the ruling class to the ruled; and (4) the sources of and obstacles to radical change in social structures. A number of these, as with the other approaches, become explanatory factors in their own right as the analysis unfolds. For example, the bases of the state, religion, or entertainment may be analyzed and then their functions or consequences may be indicated.[24]

---

[23] I find it difficult to agree with Easton's characterization of functionalism as relatively fruitless and static (although he may be correct about its usage and development to date in political science). First, structural functionalists have analyzed change, evolution, and revolution in social systems quite extensively. Even if one hypothesizes that systems tend to maintain themselves, one can still ask (and functionalists have asked) under what conditions systems will not maintain themselves or will change into what other types of systems. Further, the organic analogy clearly has built into it the concept of growth and evolution as well as the possibility of quite radical changes as in, for example, the importance it gives to "mutations." Second, just as biological functionalists have not been limited to one general issue, sociological functionalists have certainly gone beyond the concern to specify requisites to consider other questions suggested by the perspective—the mechanisms and processes of how various structures fulfill various systemic functions, the implications for the "health" or disorganization of the various patterns of interaction among the structures, the evolutionary potential of various societal forms, etc. Of course, it would take a much longer discussion to demonstrate adequately that functionalism's content is not really taken over from systems or other theories.

[24] These consequences may be of a temporarily integrative or false-consciousness-maintaining sort as suggested in the dictum that religion is the opiate of the masses.

The principal determinants or independent variables for this perspective are the "sub-structures": the material conditions and direct relationships to such, primarily the means or forces and relations of economic production. Emphasis is also given to dialectical patterns and forces, particularly to conflict among classes and contradictions in society—especially between the forces and relations of production. Thus, the sub-structure is seen as the prime determinant of the super-structure. Order and integration in pre-communist societies are seen as resulting from the oppression by the ruling class of the lower classes. The "normal" state of society is essentially one of conflict and cleavage. The principal political processes (as all history) consist in various forms of class struggle or maneuvering by the ruling class to avoid or contain various forms of class conflict. The state operates as a governing board of the ruling class and laws are instruments of oppression or manipulation.[25] With respect to change, non-communist systems are seen as containing the seeds of their own destruction—classes become increasingly polarized, contradictions, alienation and conflict become increasingly overt and it is only a matter of time before a revolutionary consciousness takes hold and an oppressed class seizes power. Only when the final polarization of the proletariat and the capitalists is overcome does the egalitarian and collectivist mode of societal organization come into being.

Some non-material components also figure heavily in a Marxist analysis such as the importance of man's nature—his interests (although they are material to an important extent in base and content), his false consciousness, his subjective responses to alienating conditions in the sub-structure, etc.

I have difficulty identifying any simple or clearcut exemplar or model for this paradigm. A relatively static one might be a "stalagmite" image of the super-structure being built upon the material foundation and grounding of the substructure (as opposed to a "stalactite" image that might represent the symbolist position). However, this does not seem adequate for capturing the dialectical evolving nature of society and politics in the Marxian vision. A "steam engine" model of pressures building up and exploding when the contradictions develop sufficiently might be better, but this still does not seem to capture the evolving nature of the conflict such that out of the clash between thesis and antithesis a new synthesis arises.

With respect to methodological procedures, the approach often relies on historical analysis focusing on economic and political conditions and exploitation. Marxists often range from the analysis of large-scale structural relationships to quite detailed events in the everyday political arena.[26] Sub-

---

[25] In Mills's somewhat more pluralistic and Weberian version, government, business, and the military tend to form an interlocking network to promote their interests—in effect forming a power elite if not a ruling class.

[26] Marx's "The Eighteenth Brumaire of Louis Bonaparte" is a classic example. Also see Molotch, 1970.

stantively, there is a constant probing into the superstructure in order to expose false consciousness, exploitation, and the like, and to show its base in and protection of vested interests.

The value position of the approach is relatively clear and explicit. There is a strong commitment to the search for individual and collective liberation from material and political constraints particularly in the form of inequality and exploitation, a concern for the liberation or de-alienation of people so that they could fulfill themselves in a free, fraternal, and egalitarian society. "Scientism" or value neutrality would be seen as a suspension of one's critical and normative faculties, a limitation of oneself to solving technical problems, an abandonment of power to the forces of the status quo—in short, a cop-out. Marxism values quite explicitly a critical and praxis-fused theory—one that constantly measures the actual against ideals and that is based on and oriented to working in and changing the world.

Let us now turn to a consideration of the idealist or symbolist perspective. We are treating here a number of theorists, such as Max Weber, Talcott Parsons, Neil Smelser, David Easton, Karl Deutsch, and S. M. Lipset, who, although they have some important and interesting differences among them, seem for our purposes to have more that joins them together than separates them.

One formulation of the focal problems of this perspective that pulls much together is how do "informational" or cultural components function or fail to function in guiding and regulating lower-level informational components or other components such as social structure and personality. This question is often manifested in a variety of ways: what are the conditions maintaining and altering a moving or stable social equilibrium, how do institutionalized patterns (such as legitimate authority or free enterprise) influence individual and organized collective activity, and what are the relations between culture, social system, and personality.

The primary determinants generally stressed are normative and, in a very general sense, cognitive components—values, meanings, norms, generalized existential beliefs (such as that humans can master nature), collective commitments, and the like. The social and political order is seen largely as an expression and specification of the ideals and value orientations that are institutionalized in society.[27] The leading proponents of this approach such as Parsons and Easton analyze quite extensively the very complex conversion, interchange and combinatorial processes concerning the specification and generalization of orientations and their interaction with other sorts of components (see particularly Easton, 1965, and Parsons and Smel-

---

[27] The approach would emphasize that even individual freedom and discretion are institutionally based and structurally patterned. See Parsons's discussion of Clark as well as Lipset's response to Romalis.

ser, 1956). While the approach seeks to systematically include other factors, the primary substance of values are seen as the primary shapers of the form of institutions and of political activity (see, for example, Lipset's discussion of American foreign policy or the oppression of Blacks, Rossides's discussion of U.S. liberalism, etc.). Particularly apt here is Rossides's characterization of Weber's work as treating ". . . human behavior as a system of relationships energized by meanings (values, norms, culture)" (p. 199).[28] This perspective also tends to perceive the political order as a highly pluralistic one (as opposed to elitist) with the pluralism based to an important extent on value differences (religion, language, ethnicity, life style). The principal sources of change and instability that are stressed tend to be value conflict and contradictions[29] as well as the working out and implementation of the implications of various value orientations that may have latent or ironic consequences (see, for example, Weber's analysis of the Protestant Ethic and the development of rational bourgeois capitalism as well as Rossides's discussion of other Weberian ironies). Thus, major political changes such as revolutions might be seen to arise from the differential institutionalization and resultant conflict of opposing ideologies in a given society. Another set of factors that this approach emphasizes would be responses to various dissatisfactions and inadequate functioning in society. The perceptions of these dissatisfactions and the types of responses selected are treated as resulting from the meaning system and value orientations adhered to.[30]

I should add that, as with sophisticated versions of all of the other perspectives, this is in no way a mono-causal approach. For example, Rossides (p. 191) points up Weber's multi-causal position as would a close reading of Lipset's essay. Further, in many ways the Parsonian perspective attempts to

---

[28] Also consider other aspects of Weber's work: his analysis of the importance of religious beliefs, his less material conception of class and emphasis on the notion of status groups, his concern with the process of rationalization (that is, how the cultural system is restructured along certain lines and restructures social systems), and even his treatment of bureaucracy (which can be seen as a form of rationalization of collective activities) more as a specific cultural system—focusing on its distinctive norms and bases of authority. Also see Parsons's statement to the effect that social systems consist in patterns of institutionalized normative culture (Parsons, et al. 1961: 30). Further, see Easton's (1965) emphasis on the importance of such factors as legitimacy and demands (which he conceives in good cybernetic fashion as messages or units of information).

[29] As opposed to, for example, the Marxist emphasis on material contradictions and conflicts. I find unacceptable the usual equation between Marxism and conflict theory on the one hand and Parsonian theory and a consensus model on the other. Marxists can be seen as emphasizing consensus (of course based on a false identity of objective interests) as much as Parsonian and functionalists more generally have discussed various forms of value conflict.

[30] For fuller explications of this theory and discussions of such notions as evolution, adaptive upgrading, value generalization, structural differentiation, etc., see Parsons, 1961 and 1964, and Smelser, 1959 and 1962.

be quite systematically comprehensive with regard to other components of social action. For example, while the notion of "hierarchy of control" (Parsons, 1968: 5–29) gives the peak regulatory position to highly generalized normative and symbolic components, it also permits to be systematically included in the scheme interactional, affective or personality, and energy or material components and their interchanges. Parsonians also attempt to indicate the conditions under which other components besides the symbolic ones may play a more controlling or determining role.

Again, no simple and clear-cut exemplars suggest themselves. The basic model for the symbolist perspective seems to be essentially that of the culture as a more or less loosely integrated language or axiomatic system specified to and institutionalized in social systems and internalized in personality systems.[31] A stalactite image suggests itself—the more generalized, higher level information components (such as generalized conceptions of the desirable) being specified to, influencing, or regulating ever more specific aspects of the culture, collective and interpersonal interactions, and so on. Of course, the stalactite model does not really capture the dynamic and evolving conception of social action sufficiently. Most of those who use this approach at least implicitly seem to employ a cybernetic notion of causality (as opposed to a more materialist one) and I think this has been one of the major sources of confusion and criticism in the field. This conception of causality is difficult to capture and is perhaps best conveyed by considering the way a grammar guides, regulates, and provides elements for the combinatorial process but does not in a material sense "cause" linguistic output.[32] Table II from Smelser (1962: 44) might help pull together a number of these themes concerning the hierarchical structuring of cultural and social systems, the relationships of specification and generalization among components, the notion of cybernetic regulation of energy components by higher level information components, etc.

In general, the principal distinctive methodologies attempt to identify the basic or underlying patterns of meanings or values in a given system and then to demonstrate how these are manifested in or shape process and change

---

[31] As should be apparent by now, these approaches draw heavily on biological, economic, and linguistic analogies and models. It would carry us into more technical ground than can be adequately covered here to explicate the Parsonian conception of power as a generalized medium of exchange analogous to money (and other media) and operating like a specialized language. Another important aspect of his conceptualization of power is its non-zero sum nature such that the general amount of power in a system can expand or one individual's growing power need not imply another's declining power—similar to the situation in regard to a system's or individual's state of wealth. See particularly Parsons, 1963.

[32] The distinction in Aristotle between material and final causes may be useful here. This suggestion is based on remarks by Charles Ackerman a number of years ago concerning striking parallels between Aristotle's four types of causes and Parsons's AGIL scheme.

Table II

LEVELS OF SPECIFICITY OF THE COMPONENTS OF SOCIAL ACTION

Level	Values	Norms	Mobilization of motivation for organized action	Situational facilities
1	Societal values	General conformity	Socialized motivation	Preconceptions concerning causality
2	Legitimization of values for institutionalized sectors	Specification of norms according to institutional sectors	Generalized performance capacity	Codification of knowledge
3	Legitimization of rewards	Specification of norms according to types of roles and organizations	Trained capacity	Technology, or specification of knowledge in situational terms
4	Legitimization of individual commitment	Specification of requirements for individual observation of norms	Transition to adult-role assumption	Procurement of wealth, power, or prestige to activate Level 3
5	Legitimization of competing values	Specification of norms of competing institutional sectors	Allocation to sector of society	Allocation of effective technology to sector of society
6	Legitimization of values for realizing organizational roles	Specification of rules of cooperation and coordination within organization	Allocation to specific roles or organizations	Allocation of effective technology to roles or organization
7	Legitimization of values for expenditure of effort	Specification of schedules and programs to regulate activity	Allocation to roles and tasks within organization	Allocation of facilities within organization to attain concrete goals

(left margin: More specific ↓)

More specific →

in social life. The analysis is often conducted through historical and cultural comparisons of relatively large-scale systems, the construction of ideal types, and the Verstehen approach noted by Rossides (p. 208). As Rossides indicates in regard to Weber, there is often a concern with the ironic aspects of social life or, in other terms, the latent functions, the ways the actual patterns deviate from the ideal and the conditions promoting such. A number of the more empirically oriented researchers in this tradition have been particularly active in using survey research to assess collective orientations in a social system such as the nature and distribution of attitudes, values, beliefs, etc.

As for the value position that has tended to characterize this approach, while there has been a general recognition of the way that values shape the selection of problems, there has also been an emphasis on the possibility and desirability of value neutrality and scientific rationality. Of course, this could be regarded as a form of a liberal ideological stance in itself. Certainly a number of theorists in this tradition seem to be essentially liberals— manifesting a relatively benign and pluralistic view of society, concerned to see society evolve to a "better" material and spiritual existence for individuals and groups with increased equality of opportunity and freedom of individual choice, emphasizing a gradual evolution, and neither being very critical of contemporary society nor seeing the future ideal society (insofar as that is even discussed) as that radically different from modern industrial society.

I do not see these values as inherent in this perspective. Because an approach uses notions such as system or equilibrium as major conceptual tools does not necessarily imply that the approach favors the persistence or equilibrium of the system in question or that it is necessarily opposed to its radical alteration any more than because Marx used capitalism as a major reference point did he favor capitalist society. Further, one must distinguish between analytical and empirical propositions. For example, the symbolists might be quite correct in their analytical propositions, for example, that norms are a major source of integration in society, while they may be incorrect about their empirical proposition that American society is actually or happily integrated. I would agree with the critics however that important concepts and propositions have not been well developed or well integrated within the symbolist perspective given its apparent value position and I look forward to the increasing liberation of this perspective.

PLAN OF THE BOOK

The body of the work consists of six overview essays and four sets of critiques and rejoinders. The overview essays present symbolic interactionism, exchange theory, contemporary Marxism, the Weberian approach, Lipset's comparative sociology, and a piece linking exchange theory, structural functionalism, and the new political economy. Authors were invited to discuss the principal concepts and propositions of each of these perspectives, evaluate their major strengths and weaknesses, review many of the major findings and studies, and suggest where the perspectives might fruitfully be developed. The critiques provide a representative of another perspective with a chance to evaluate the paradigm under consideration and the rejoinders give the initial authors an opportunity to defend their paradigms and themselves.

Let us develop this preview somewhat further. In addition to providing a particularly cogent and well-integrated review of symbolic interactionism's basic assumptions and concepts, Hall presents one of the boldest and most original extensions of the theory to more macro-level political phenomena—touching on such notions as symbolic mobilization of support, political impression management, control of information flow, and society as negotiated order. He is also concerned to explore some of the theory's potential for radical critical analysis as opposed to many of the more liberal uses to which it has been put. For example, he points up a number of less than democratic aspects of American politics. Kanter, while acknowledging a number of Hall's contributions, draws out some of the limitations generally associated with symbolic interactionism and points to ways a systemic approach might deal with them. She goes on to emphasize the need for integration of both perspectives and to indicate some of the ways in which they can complement each other. She also suggests that some of the limitations of the theory such as its treatment of "power," relate to its "liberal" biases—an imputation to which Hall takes strong exception in his rejoinder, at least on behalf of himself and the "new" symbolic interactionism.

The debate between Waldman and Easton continues the micro-macro controversy in the context of exchange theory. Some interesting implicit contrasts between symbolic interactionism and exchange theory in their treatments of political structure and process are also available. In both his original essay and rejoinder, Waldman presents the concepts and propositions of exchange theory (particularly as represented in the works of Homans and Blau) with applications to such phenomena as legitimacy, political structure, government centralization, and the dynamics of interest groups. Easton focuses on two of the major alternatives to systems theory—functionalism and exchange theory (the latter being one of the major "rational choice" models)—and presents a sketch of the systems approach. His critique can be seen as pointing up the importance not only of macro-level structural or emergent properties of political and social systems that exchange theory seems to neglect or to have difficulty conceptualizing, but also touches on substantive factors particularly in the interactional and ideal sectors other than those emphasized by exchange theory.

Next, Werlin distills the basic assumptions and conceptions of the Marxist perspective, particularly bringing out some of the important notions concerning the nature of human beings. Werlin also deals with a number of traditional liberal-pluralist criticisms of Marxism, suggests some applications to contemporary American politics and society, and critically reviews some of the major strands of contemporary Marxist political analysis—especially as represented by C. Wright Mills, Paul Sweezy, Herbert Marcuse, and Jurgen Habermas.

Max Weber's political sociology is analyzed in a highly original essay by Rossides. He seeks to revise traditional North American views of Weber's work and emphasizes Weber's critical stance and profound ambivalence about the modern state, bureaucracy, rationalism, and the like. One gets the sense of a near "Greek tragic vision" of the fundamental dilemmas in the political order that seems to underlie Weber's thinking. Rossides concludes with a number of critical applications to contemporary American life that Weber might have made.

The final two sets of essays can be seen particularly as explorations in synthesis. The focal authors, Lipset and Clark, have been quite eclectic in drawing on elements of the above paradigms.

Seymour Martin Lipset is clearly one of the major figures in contemporary political sociology. It was felt useful to include a discussion of his work since he seems generally regarded as one of the most prominent comparative analysts and someone who has developed a distinctive blend of middle-range structural functionalism with aspects of Parsonian, Weberian, and Marxist theory. Romalis evaluates Lipset's contribution to comparative political sociology and tries to document his increasing conservatism and conversion into an apologist for America through an analysis of the apparent biases and omissions of his empirical studies. His critique also deals with some of the issues in Marxism that space limitations forced Werlin to omit, particularly concerning economic imperialism in international relations and colonialist consciousness. Romalis also provides an example of a quasi-Marxist sociology of knowledge in suggesting how Lipset's professional mobility might have influenced his ideology which in turn affected his scientific analysis. By implication, Romalis also suggests his own critical analysis of American society and foreign policy. Lipset then responds to Romalis "(and other critics)," seeking to correct interpretations of his work and arguing that he has maintained his commitment to the democratic left. He seeks to clarify and justify a number of his assumptions as well as to represent his distinctive synthesis which is then further critiqued by Romalis.

Clark focuses on an analysis of institutionalized and non-institutionalized political phenomena and of factors in coalition formation. He develops some propositions concerning institutionalized payoff coefficients and coalition formation that could prove useful in bridging structural functionalism, exchange theory, and the new political economy which he sees as incomplete by themselves. Parsons critiques Clark's analysis, particularly of institutionalized behavior. Along the way, Parsons provides some interesting observations on the sense in which he could be regarded as an exchange theorist, the utility of biological theory, the distinction between values and norms, and he touches briefly on some of his own recent work on evolution. The exchange concludes with a brief rejoinder by Clark.

LOOKING FORWARD

It should be obvious to the reader that I have hardly scratched the surface of important and fundamental questions that could be raised in regard to this material. Certainly the answers I have suggested are incomplete, tentative, and impressionistic. Much of the essay has been built on the work of Thomas Kuhn. We have suggested that one of the most important ways to approach any field such as political sociology is to understand and compare its principal paradigms. We have also tried to identify assumptions and major thrusts of some of the principal paradigms presently employed and potentially of much use. We have projected an image of science as an evolving enterprise in which theory may be seen as increasingly differentiating out of and being liberated from its broader philosophical and ideological foundations. We have sketched an impressionistic comparison in terms of a modified version of Kuhn's framework for considering any paradigm and suggested a number of points where the "essence" of paradigms could be distinguished from how they have been used thus far by particular theorists.

In these closing paragraphs, let us suggest some directions that these paradigms are likely to take, and perhaps should take, in their development. First and perhaps most obviously, I think we shall see considerably greater effort to explore the complementarities and potential points of linkage among the various paradigms. A number of the authors included in this work—Hall, Clark, Kanter—seem to recognize the value of building bridges among the paradigms as one major way of dealing with the limitations of each of their perspectives. For example, Hall sees Marxist theory as a way of complementing some of symbolic interactionism's neglect of conflict and of structural constraints. Kanter points up a number of the complementarities between macro-level systems theory and micro-level symbolic interactionism and the way that, taken together, they could offer a more adequate grasp on the whole of social phenomena. This is not to suggest that a sociological era of good feeling is about to arise. It is more probable that the proposed mergers among theories will be more like attempted takeovers than well-integrated syntheses.

At the same time, we shall probably see an effort to develop paradigms in themselves even further. This is likely to involve attempts to forge more systematic linkages among hypotheses, to refine or create new concepts, to solve crucial anomalies, to qualify and test major propositions, to operationalize important dimensions, to develop more precision in predictions (perhaps by building mathematical models) and the like.

In very general terms, we are likely to see the micro-level theorists make an even more conscientious effort to take into account macro-level conditions, and vice versa for the macro-level theorists. No doubt, they are bound to pass each other somewhere in the middle range. For the micro-level theorist this is likely to imply a greater concern with cultural and subcultural variations as well as with historical and comparative studies to bring out the ways individuals adapt to and are shaped by a concrete network of contextual factors. The macro-level theorists' efforts to become the reigning paradigm may well take the form of attempts to articulate the cultural level components more clearly with social structural factors, and these in turn with more individual and role level performances. This will probably call for an intensive search for articulating mechanisms among these various levels and development of the concept of political culture. In general, we are likely to see many more intensive studies of concrete processes of interaction over time both as a way for micro-level theorists to pin down more carefully the phenomena they generally work with and as a way for the macro-level theorists to identify their bridging mechanisms.

Another set of substantive concerns that is likely to receive considerably more attention as the relatively liberal tradition of North American political sociology becomes more radicalized will be various processes of conflict within society, various linkages among powerful groups and individuals, and the subtly coercive and oppressive aspects of modern society. We can also expect that, as the political interdependence among nation-states increases, the international level or organization will receive more attention and treatment as a system or entity in itself.

We may speculate on what focal anomalies will receive greatest attention in the foreseeable future. Marxists will probably increasingly turn their attention to analyzing ways of making revolutions in bourgeois societies and identifying new potentials for class conflict as society evolves; the symbolists and Parsonians to the sources of change in symbol systems; symbolic interactionists to why negotiation is successful at all, and so on.

It is of course difficult to prophesy what new paradigms or grand theorists might emerge, what major social problems will become faddish, what new calamities will befall us, and the like—all of which could significantly shape the future of the field. For the time being, the crisis stage is likely to continue accompanied by its frantic search for solutions, open conflict among paradigms and challenges to traditional assumptions, etc. Perhaps the principal general thrust of the near future can be seen as an increasingly applied political sociology. I would foresee it becoming more applied in at least three senses of the term. First in the sense indicated above of empirical work being increasingly the result of paradigm specification. Thus we can look forward to research that will be more theoretically grounded and be more explicitly oriented to making theoretical contributions. Second, we can look forward to work that will be applied in the sense that it will be involved in developing positive programs and policies to improve the functioning of present institutions. Finally, and perhaps most interestingly, I suspect there will be a dramatic increase of political sociology as praxis. This would involve a closer interrelationship and even fusion of theory, research, and action that would serve both to inform or refine the paradigm as well as to reconstruct society. The work of Freire (1970) is perhaps most exemplary here in which theory is built and refined by working closely with "the people" to the extent that the theory comes to reflect their worldviews and their perspectives in turn are deeply influenced by it as it evolves.

All this conflict, search for theoretical complementarities, development of paradigms' distinctive strengths, increasing interchange among perspectives and everyday concerns, etc., I would see as desirable and important parts of the evolution and perhaps liberation of our knowledge of political life. Complete liberation may be impossible—perhaps even undesirable. Paradigms may be inherently (as opposed to merely historically) "doomed" to be fused with broader value concerns, ideological positions, etc.—and may even draw much of their richness and strength from them. Hence, the one true and glorious paradigm—if such exists—may be impossible to create or will never emerge. However, that does not mean that we should not attempt to improve, in our own limited mortal way, the paradigms with which we must work.

REFERENCES

Bendix, Reinhard, and S. M. Lipset
1966   "The field of political sociology." In Lewis Coser (ed.), Political Sociology. New York: Harper and Row.

Bidwell, C. E.
in press   "Schooling and socialization." Interchange 3 (December).

Blumer, Herbert
1969   Symbolic Interactionism: Perspective and Method. Englewood Cliffs, N.J.: Prentice-Hall.

Coser, Lewis (ed.)
1966   Political Sociology. New York: Harper and Row.

Dreeben, Robert
1968   On What Is Learned in Schools. Reading, Mass.: Addison-Wesley.

Easton, David
1965   A Systems Analysis of Political Life. New York: Wiley.

Eisenstadt, S. N. (ed.)
1971   Political Sociology. New York: Basic Books.

Freire, Paulo
1970   Pedagogy of the Oppressed. New York: Herder and Herder.

Gouldner, A. W.
1970   The Coming Crisis of Western Sociology. New York: Basic Books.

Hanson, N. R.
1958   Patterns of Discovery. London: Cambridge University Press.

Homans, G. C.
1964   "Bringing men back in." American Sociological Review 29 (December): 809–818.

Janowitz, Morris
1968 "Political sociology." Pp. 298–307 in D. L. Sills (ed.), International En-
    cyclopedia of the Social Sciences. New York: Macmillan.
1970 Political Conflict. Chicago: Quandrangle.

Kuhn, Thomas
1970 The Structure of Scientific Revolutions. Chicago: University of Chicago Press.

Kuklick, Henrika
in press "A 'scientific revolution': sociological theory in the United States, 1930–
    1945." Sociological Inquiry 43.

Lasswell, Harold
1930 Psychopathology and Politics. Chicago: University of Chicago Press.

Levy, M. J., Jr.
1952 The Structure of Society. Princeton: Princeton University Press.

Lipset, S. M. (ed.)
1969 Politics and the Social Sciences. New York: Oxford University Press.

Marx, Karl
1959 "The eighteenth brumaire of Louis Bonaparte." In L. S. Feuer (ed.), Marx and
    Engels. New York: Doubleday.

Molotch, Harvey
1970 "Oil in Santa Barbara and power in America." Sociological Inquiry 40:
    131–144.

Parsons, Talcott
1961 "Some considerations on the theory of social change." Rural Sociology 26:
    219–239.
1963 "On the concept of political power." Proceedings of the American Philosophical
    Society 107 (June): 232–262.
1964 "Evolutionary universals." American Sociological Review 29 (June): 339–357.
1968 Societies. Englewood Cliffs, N.J.: Prentice-Hall.

Parsons, Talcott and Neil Smelser
1956 Economy and Society. New York: The Free Press.

Parsons, Talcott, E. A. Shils, Kaspar Naegele, Jesse Pitts (eds.)
1961 Theories of Society. New York: The Free Press.

Smelser, Neil
1959 Social Change in the Industrial Revolution. Chicago: University of Chicago
    Press.

1962 Theory of Collective Behavior. New York: The Free Press.

Toulmin, Stephen
1957 "Crucial experiments: Priestley and Lavoisier." Pp. 481–496 in P. P. Wiener
    and A. Noland, (eds.), Roots of Scientific Thought. New York: Basic Books.

A Symbolic Interactionist Analysis of Politics

PETER M. HALL
University of Missouri, Columbia

The purpose of this article will be to outline a symbolic interactionist approach to the study of politics in the United States. In the course of this presentation, the basic assumptions and concepts of the interactionist perspective will be presented, culminating in a model of society as a negotiated order. This model in conjunction with definitions of power and politics will provide the basis for analyzing the processes of power. The article will focus on and emphasize two mechanisms of power, information flow control and symbolic mobilization of support, which have previously been unrecognized and unanalyzed. In the conclusion, the strengths and weaknesses of the approach will be discussed.

PART I: SYMBOLIC INTERACTION AND A POLITICAL MODEL OF SOCIETY

a) The Symbolic Interactionist Perspective

Symbolic interactionists have been primarily defined as social psychologists and are expected to deal with the relationships between society and personality, between the group and the individual, or with interaction within small groups. Courses in sociological social psychology, basically, are expected to examine two major processes: (a) the socialization process—the internalization of the culture, such as values, norms, and meanings, and (b) the development of the self—the creation of a way of perceiving one's self via internalizing the views of significant others. Strauss, for example, stresses the fact that the selections from G. H. Mead which were incorporated by functionalist theorists like Parsons, Merton, and Davis dealt with this internalization of culture in terms of self-control as a reflection of social control (Strauss, 1964:xii). As a consequence symbolic interaction is perceived as dealing with only the interpersonal level of human behavior and incapable of handling societal issues and structures. It is not viewed as possessing a model of a society or a distinctive concept of social structure.

It is of course quite obvious that symbolic interactionists have dealt with matters far beyond the "micro" level as reflected in the work of Shibutani

I wish to acknowledge my personal and intellectual debt to Tamotsu Shibutani and Gregory Stone for transmitting the excitement of symbolic interaction and for demonstrating, in their teaching and writing, the many applications and insights of this perspective. I am also extremely grateful to René and Clara Millon for their encouragement to proceed with this work.

35

(1965, 1966) on rumor and race, Turner and Killian (1957) on collective behavior, the Langs (1968) on mass communications, Hughes (1952, 1958) on work and race, Strauss (1964) and Dalton (1959) on complex organizations, Becker (1963) and Scheff (1966) on deviance, Cressey (1970) on crime and Klapp (1962, 1969) on social types and cults. The commonality of their approach, however, is reflected in the utilization of the subjective perspective in dealing with societies, institutions, and groups and in viewing social reality, be it culture, structure, groups, role, power, value, norm, or consensus, as problematic and constructed rather than given and static.

Herbert Blumer and Anselm Strauss have both stated that the nature of social organization is implicit in the thought of G. H. Mead and they both, in their own works, have sought to make it explicit (Blumer, 1969:1; Strauss, 1964:xiv). In actuality, symbolic interaction does contain within it a distinctive view of man, interaction, and society. In order to develop this point it is useful to explicate the perspective in terms of its assumptions and concepts.

Perhaps the most basic assumption is that of *emergence* which characterizes man as being distinct and unique from all other forms of life because he has the capacity of speech, language, and therefore thought, communication, and coordination. While this uniqueness rests upon anatomical and physiological characteristics, man has developed in such a way as to free him from some of the constraints of other animals and to create a world of his own and apart from the exigencies of nature. The assumption of emergence leads symbolic interactionists to focus their study of man on his distinctive qualities and to emphasize the characteristics and consequences of the use of language. Interactionists resist and oppose efforts to explain the behavior of man on reductionist grounds or on sociologistic grounds that deny man's basic qualities (Rose, 1962; Stryker, 1959).

The second assumption, that of *process,* derives from the philosophical school of pragmatism and the writings of James, Dewey, and Mead (Rose, 1962). This assumption characterizes all aspects of human behavior including consciousness, thought, selfhood, activity, interaction, and society as being dynamic and continuously in flux. It assumes these objects not to be static, at rest, or in equilibrium but always to be in process. The emphasis is not on structure but on action. Activity is the assumed normal course of events for man so that instead of asking how do we motivate man to activity, the interactionist becomes perplexed at lack of activity or interested in changes in activity. The assumption of process is extremely difficult to convey because of the subject-verb-object structure of our language, concomitant scientific cause-effect models, and popular conceptions of human nature as lazy.

A third assumption, that of *voluntarism,* views the individual as the basic acting social unit and defines man as an actor rather than a reactor, as active rather than passive. The image of man, as represented by Blumer, Goffman, and Stone is that of a creator of his own world. Not only is he capable of learning cultural elements, but he also discovers, invents, innovates, and initiates new forms. Within this framework, man is not seen simply as a responder to or vehicle for biological impulses and/or social demands but rather as the possessor of selfhood who creates objects, designates meanings, charts courses of action, interprets situations, and controls his field. This assumption stressing independence and autonomy is supported by Ralph Turner's account of role-making, Erving Goffman's concept of role-distance, and Nelson Foote's classic work on motivation as a consequence of self-generated identities (Blumer, 1969; Stone and Farberman, 1970; Turner, 1962; Goffman, 1961; Foote, 1951).

One of the questions symbolic interaction has sought to answer is how men are able to act together. Answers to this question involve the assumptions that man lives in a symbolic environment as well as a physical environment and that because man can learn and use symbols he is able to interact with other men. "A symbol is defined as a stimulus that has a learned meaning and value for people and man's response to a symbol is in terms of its meaning and value rather than in terms of its physical stimulation of his sense organs" (Rose, 1962a:5). Thus the culture or sets of shared symbols mediate between the physical environment and man and provide him with ways of dealing with that environment which he shares with other men. It also involves the fact that while symbolic interaction eschews the society versus individual controversy, society with its culture precedes any existing individual. Thus the newborn infant is seen as asocial with active impulses which become channeled as he learns the culture from other more mature members of the culture. The consequence of learning the culture, the process which we call socialization, allows men to be able to understand one another, to have behavioral expectations for one another, and consequently to orient their own behavior to that of others. Symbols are the means by which people orient themselves to the world, to others, and to themselves. They facilitate the process of social integration because they serve to define the world, channel thought processes, motivate actions, justify interests, and coordinate activities.

In order to clarify the previous sentences it is necessary to discuss the following concepts: meaning, the self, action, and interaction. This will provide us with the means to view society as symbolic interaction. Meaning is the key to understanding the interactionist perspective because its establishment and consequences are the lifeblood of human activity. There are three basic aspects of meaning—namely, meaning is extrinsic; it is behavioral, and it arises out of communication and social interaction. The meaning of an object is not inherent to that object or defined by its physical characteristics but is conferred from the outside on the basis of its intended use. Meaning is also not fixed for all time but will vary with time, culture, situation, and the people acting toward it. The latter phase represents the second aspect of meaning which is that it is a way of acting toward or treating an object. Thus a chair is an object to be sat upon or, in a particular setting, to be stood upon when seeking to command attention or as a weapon in the typical western barroom brawl. A bank is a different object to student radicals, its managers, its employees, loan-seekers, or hold-up men. Each has a different way of acting toward the bank and therefore to each it is a different object and has a different meaning. Such meanings arise and are transformed in the context of communication with others as one learns from others the meaning of objects as they see them and as one takes part in offering his own meaningful view. Whether one is confronted by the absence of meaning in an ambiguous situation or is being indoctrinated into a business organization or political group, the establishment of meaning occurs through the exchange of social interaction. The establishment of meaning through this process is essential because individual action or collective coordination requires symbolization or objectification for mobilization of action. Without meaning, people lack the ability to know how to act toward a "thing." In fact, it is the transformation of the "thing" into an object that makes for action. To name it is not only to know it but to be able to deal with it. Symbolizations therefore represent knowledge, communication, and action.

One category of objects in the social world is the self-conceptions of individuals. As the self is an object, it has meaning for the individual like any other object. As such, the self consists of ways the individual has of acting toward himself or treating himself. The self, like other objects, emerges in a process of interaction as the individual responds to and internalizes aspects of definitions of him by others. Cooley codifies this process by labelling it "the looking-glass self." Out of this process and functioning in every situation, sets of meanings are established for the self which guide the individual in his actions on the basis of the kind of object he is to himself. An individual who comes to view himself as good, as competent, as a writer will act on that basis.

Because of language and communication the individual is able not only to be a subject or actor but is also able to be an object to himself and to see himself as others see him. The capacity to be both subject and object constitutes a vital distinction for man. He is able to interact with himself. Thought and consciousness are in fact, internal conversations between self as subject and self as object as the individual assesses his circumstances and charts courses of action. The existence of the self means that rather than simply responding to external stimuli, the individual's behavioral response to the outside world is mediated by an interpretive process. Action occurs only after the individual has made indications to himself about his situation by noting objects in his field and evaluating them in terms of their relationship to his intended action (Blumer, 1969:12–14).

The last phrase is most significant in terms of symbolic interaction because of the implications of such terms as intention and volition. Human action is based upon voluntarism. Individual action is not "caused" as in natural science thinking or released as tension from a spring but rather is built-up and constructed by the individual as he confronts an environment which he objectifies on the basis of what he takes into account. What is taken into account varies from person to person according to their goals and their assessment. But the action that occurs is a result of the individual acting upon the environment and, in fact, making of the total possible environment a more compact personal environment in which to act. This latter environment is defined on the basis of relevance to the situational interests of the individual. People act, according to this perspective, not from such things as need dispositions or conformity to role-expectations but *toward situations*. The clear implication is that action emerges from the meaning given to the situation by the individual as a result of the interpretive process which occurs continuously and constantly as the individual moves from situation to situation.

So far we have discussed symbolic interaction and human behavior as if the individual did not have to deal with other individuals doing the same things in regard to action. To leave this impression would clearly distort the actual situation and make unintelligible, for example, the processes of socialization and selfhood. As people act toward situations, they have to take account of the presence, intentions, actions, and expressions of other people. Much of what we do is dependent on interpreting the gestures of others which we symbolize and then acting on the basis of our objectification. Symbolic interaction then is defined as *activity in which human beings interpret each other's gestures and act on the basis of the meaning yielded by that interpretation* (Blumer, 1969: 65–66).

But the situation is clearly complicated by the fact that the other person is doing the same thing. The ability of people to interact effectively is dependent on their ability to take the role of the other. Role-taking is the establishment for ego of the meaning of the other, i.e., the discovery of the line of action that gives the specific acts of the other a direction, coherence, and significance. Thus, we attempt to judge others in terms of their significance for us and their implications for our plans of action. We do not know how to deal with the other person until we have established his meaning for us and our meaning for him. We do this by attributing an identity to him and interpreting the actions as flowing from this identity. Once we have discovered what we assume to be his identity and role, we alter our own course of action on the basis of what we judge to be his implications for our manifest and latent plans (McCall & Simmons, 1966: 130–136). Thus, interaction proceeds back and forth as actors emit and respond to their judgments of each other's intentions and actions. That is, in interaction the participants project identities for themselves and for each other. Not only do they present a particular image of self but they also cast the alter in the position that they would like him to assume. People will try to devise their own lines of action to make the best use of alter's lines of action. What usually transpires in interaction is that persons are seldom allowed to perform exactly the roles they would like nor do they comply exactly with the role projected upon them by alter. Continuation of interaction and relationships appears to be dependent on the ability of the participants to accept or to accommodate to the projected and interpreted identities and roles. We use accept or accommodate rather than agree or consensually validated because the latter imply a much closer fit than frequently exists. What develops is a working agreement that allows them to get on with the business at hand and is characterized not by agreement but the absence of large degrees of disagreement (McCall & Simmons, 1966: 137–146).

b) Society as Symbolic Interaction

Two points remain to be developed in this section for our symbolic interactionist perspective on social organization, namely to explicate a view of collective action and of society. In regard to the former, we are interested in what Blumer calls "joint action" which is the fitting together, the merging, the alignment of separate lines of action of members of a group. Society comes to be viewed as a complex network of joint actions involving acting individuals. Blumer's extrapolation of joint action to society is as follows:

> The picture is composed in terms of action. A society is seen as people meeting the varieties of situations that are thrust on them by their conditions of life. These situations are met by working out joint actions in which participants have to align their acts to one another. Each participant does so by interpreting the acts of others and, in turn, by making indications to others as to how they should act. By virtue of this process of interpretation and definition joint actions are built up; they have careers. Usually, the course of a joint action is outlined in advance by the fact that the participants make a common identification of it; this makes for regularity, stability, and repetitiveness in the joint action. However, there are many joint actions that encounter obstructions, that have no pre-established pathways, and that have to be constructed along new lines. Mead saw human society in this way—as a diversified social process in which people were engaged in forming joint actions to deal with situations confronting them. (Blumer, 1969:72)

To call attention to action, living, and ongoing activity is to orient away from the standard sociological notions of society as structure, as the mechanical or automatic exchange between positions, and to focus on the level of what people actually do. At the same time there is an awareness of the continuous and dynamic processes of social life which calls attention to its vitality, openness, and problematic character and the seriousness of inter-action. The emphasis on action and living gives rise to a consciousness of energy and effort. The basis for joint action is the establishment through interpretive interaction of common definitions of the situation. Even though much of joint action is in the form of repetitive patterned responses to common situations, each instance of it has to be recreated, reconstituted, and reenacted. But over and above these situations, there are numerous contingencies, ambiguities, constraints, problems, and conflicts which require new or changing definitions. Thus the quality of social life is characterized by greater degrees of uncertainty and requires stronger conscious effort than normally described. Joint action is all of these because it is like a chemical compound rather than a mixture. It is more than the aggregate of its parts; it is a synthesis that results from inter-subjectivity, feedback, consensus, and co-ordination. It is a merging, an alignment of actions that develops in the course of assessing the situations, determining what has to be done, assigning tasks, and carrying them out. It is clearly a complicated process. It arises in the context of "problems" and the outcome is problematic. Blumer indicates that joint action outcomes are subject to uncertainty because they may not be initiated; once initiated they may be interrupted, abandoned, or transformed, or participants may not reach common definitions; or new situations may lead to breakdown, confusion, and exploration (Blumer, 1969: 71–72).

In order to both extend and intensify the discussion of Blumer's approach, it is useful to turn to a formerly residual field of sociology which has long been identified with symbolic interaction. Collective behavior has been considered residual because it dealt with such unorganized or disorganized forms of behavior as disaster, panics, crowds, riots, and fashions. One point to note is that the line between institutional behavior or collective behavior is much narrower and less clear. It is harder to distinguish between the two because much of everyday behavior seems like collective behavior in the sense of meeting problematic or ambiguous situations that have to be confronted, defined, and acted toward. We note that Turner characterizes his view of collective behavior in terms of emergent norms—namely, that in situations where norms are lacking, inapplicable, or contradictory, people will collectively interact to specify the situation, i.e., to define, structure, and *normalize* it (Turner, 1964). Collective behavior can then occur regularly in the family, in the peer group, in the corporation as well as during disasters, political elections, or revolutions. Symbolic interaction then becomes commonplace. Similarly Shibutani has indicated that collective behavior occurs in situations of low institutionalization which allows for high degrees of personal intervention (Shibutani, 1966: 124). In these situations people are free from cultural constraints and role expectations and free to create new courses of actions and new sets of meanings. This concept of personal intervention in collective behavior reinforces the ideas of voluntarism.

In concluding this section we are left with four questions for further resolution. First, Blumer and others have long talked about situations and the definition of situations but have not specified, mainly due to the complexity and variety of social life, the general category of things that are taken into account in defining situations. There needs to be more systematic examination of the concept of situations and its definition. Secondly, Blumer speaks of man in a generic sense and thus in describing the general situation treats men as if they were all alike and fails, at least in this latest work, to take into account the effects of differentiation. This point is related to the third which is that Blumer with his emphasis, following Mead, on joint action seems to imply that cooperation is the desired outcome—that men when confronted with problematic situations will collectively define them and align their actions or at least that they want to. In accounting for the failure of joint action Blumer alludes to the continuation of separate courses of action or the reliance on other considerations than common definitions. Nevertheless, one is left with overwhelming emphasis on the democratic and cooperative nature of social life. But most basic to the entire discussion is the fact that although joint action is taken as the basic social fact, we are left without a clear understanding of that process. It must be stated that these questions are not intended as damning criticisms, but simply as problems for more complete resolution.

c) *Society as Negotiated Order*

It is useful at this point to turn to the conception of the *negotiated order*. While Strauss et al. present this as a model of complex organization, and specifically of a hospital, they believe that its utility extends to societies as well.

> "Pushing our logic to its extreme, we might even argue that the very idea of 'nation' or 'society' is only a fiction and that, if the sociologist subscribes to this common-sense fiction, rather than viewing a nation or society as an exceedingly complex arena (with attendant exceedingly complex negotiation), he may fall into the deadly trap of merely studying the fiction as if it were a fact. We do not claim that our own perspective is the only useful one for study of these various types of human associations or even that it should dominate studies of hospital. But we do argue for its investigatory power." (Strauss, et al., 1964:377)

This model, as we will see, is indeed quite useful in describing the nature of social relations in society as well as providing major insights into the political realm. In this section the utility of the negotiated order model will be analyzed on two levels. In both instances, it provides answers to questions that were raised about Blumer's view of society. The first is that Strauss and his co-authors provide specifications of the character of those things that require interpretation and definition in society. Secondly, the negotiated order model provides analysis of the nature of the process of joint action. We now become aware: (1) of what social objects are likely to be problematic, ambiguous, conflict-full, and tension-producing, and (2) the most common way people go about accommodating these problems, ambiguities, conflicts and tensions—namely through a process of bargaining and negotiation.

Strauss, et al. take a basic Meadian problem as central to their concerns: how can there be order under conditions of change and how can change be made orderly? The basic position stressed by the authors is that students of formal organization tend to underplay the processes of internal change and overestimate the stable features of organizations such as their rules and authority hierarchies. Order or structure is not something that automatically occurs but rather must be worked at and must occur, to the extent that it does, out of the repeated, reaffirmed, reconstituted acts of participants. This led Strauss and his co-workers to the position that what, in fact, characterizes organizational life—that which is repeated, reaffirmed, and reconstituted are shared agreements, tacit understandings and contracts, which develop out of processes of give and take, diplomacy, and bargaining. Hence the notion of the negotiated order (Strauss, et al., 1963: 147–169).

Within the hospital situation, the following elements are conducive to negotiation situations since they cannot simply be taken for granted nor assumed to be acceptable to all participants. As an organization, the hospital has a goal—in this case, "to return the patients to the outside world in better shape." This goal, and we take this to be an example of the general category of values, is vague and ambiguous. Metaphorically speaking, it is the symbolic cement, in fact the only singly shared element, which holds the hospital together. It is never questioned, always assumed because it does constitute the generalized mandate for the organization. But such an abstract distant concept masks a considerable amount of disagreement and discrepant purpose. Problems occur regarding the concord because while everyone superficially concurs, they are often moved by other considerations including individual and sub-group goals. In addition, implementation of the goal(s) is a matter of interpretation and definition requiring much activity. The questions arising from how to get patients collectively or specifically better invites a number of alternative courses. Also, if we expand the hospital model to a university, for example, which is a multi-purpose organization, then we quickly become cognizant of the constraints, ambiguities, conflicts, and negotiations which arise from trying to fulfill all the goals with equity.

We must therefore see as flowing out from the nature of values and goals in society the following three things. Societal values about which there is presumed to be consensus are: (1) vague, abstract, and distant from the everyday life of the citizenry so that the definitions, such as they are, are not clearly meaningful or directly applicable; (2) since they are so abstract and far removed from everyday life, they are not organized into an internally consistent belief system and frequently contradict each other (e.g. law and order vs. justice, human rights vs. property rights, free enterprise vs. public welfare); and (3) implementation of plural goals leads to "political" behavior as priorities are set, decisions made, budgets created and actions charted.

We should also add, as Strauss indicates and other students of complex organizations have demonstrated, that where there is a highly differentiated and specialized organizational structure the specialized groups and individuals within them begin to develop their own goals and interests apart from those defined by "the organization," i.e., those who have power to define goals in the organization. These sub-groups then frequently cloak their own interests in terms which are to represent the assumed collective goals.

In addition to the division of labor and its effects, it should be noted that the hospital is a locale for ongoing complex transactions among differentiated types of actors—characterized by profession, connection to the institution, ideologies, stage of career, training, commitment to institution, length of employment, reference groups, and communication networks. All of these factors predispose the participants to different values, interests, perspectives, and actions which must somehow be pieced together as order in the hospital. Thus we should anticipate different expectations on the part of individuals in the same role and certainly between occupants of roles given these differentiating factors. The problem is, of course, compounded by turnover and new personnel. Therefore as in society, we should expect problems of consensus, communication, and coordination.

The solution to such problems aside from establishing goals and socializing members has often been felt to be *rules* (the specifications of the *norms,* the means to the goals). The authors' discussion of this element is particularly revealing. We know that values and goals tend to be abstract and transcendent but rules are supposed to be the height of clarity and coverage. The fact is that rules are not extensive, clearly stated, or clearly binding. They too require interpretation and definition as they apply to specific situations. In addition there will always be situations that have not been anticipated and contingencies that cannot be met simply by applying a rule— consequently a problematic case. Furthermore, no one knows all the rules or what those on the books meant when they were enacted. Turnover creates problems of continuity. In addition, rules are used and misused according to the interests of the participants and even "authority" may find it to its advantage to ignore certain rules.

The solution to the problems of values and goals, abstractness, division of labor, differentiated participants, and rule-application, the authors see as day-to-day agreements which are negotiated by participants to meet the situations that they confront both as a consequence of external and internal change and unexpected contingencies. As an undercurrent to this situation, and as the norm of norms, Strauss indicates that existence of negotiations as a way of life is like a self-fulfilling prophecy, that it breeds further negotiations.

Have we depicted a scene of sheer chaos? Strauss makes two points here to show the existence of order: (1) "there is a patterned variability of negotiation in the hospital pertaining to who contracts with whom, about what, as well as when these agreements are made. Influencing this variability are hierarchical position and ideological commitments" (Strauss et al., 1963: 162). (2) "It is especially worth emphasizing that negotiation—whether characterized as 'agreement,' 'understanding,' 'contract,' or by some other term—has a temporal aspect" (Strauss et al., 1963: 163). Those agreements run for specific to nonspecific terms and are subject to later review and alteration. Hence, "the hospital can be visualized as a place where numerous agreements are continually being terminated or forgotten but also as continually being established, reviewed, revoked, revised. Hence at any moment those that are in effect are considerably different from those that were or will be" (Strauss et al., 1963: 164).

We have advanced our position in that we now can see the kinds of things that are problematic—values, goals, rules, roles, collective vs. group vs. individual interests, new situations, resource constraints, and courses of action. In addition, joint action is now seen as a complex process involving all the manifestations of bargaining and negotiating—strategy, tact, intelligence, maneuvering, persuasion, inducement, constraint, threat, and exchange. The model of society that derives from the negotiated order is one characterized by a complex network of competing groups and individuals acting to control, maintain, or improve their social conditions as defined by their *self*-interests. The realization of these interests, material and ideal, are the outcomes of negotiated situations, encounters, and relationships.

A similar societal view is implicit in the thought of Max Weber, according to Reinhard Bendix. "Each society is a composite of positively or negatively privileged status groups that are engaged in efforts to preserve or enhance their present 'style of life' by means of social distance and exclusiveness and by the monopolization of economic opportunities" (Bendix, 1960: 267). In this competition between status groups, some are more successful than others. Their success allows them to impose structural limitations on the ability of the other groups to compete or negotiate. The successful groups organize the institutions of the society for their own purposes and values so that the less powerful groups are consistently screened off from access, skills, and resources. The situation perpetuates itself because the elites of those institutions have great power to reward and penalize. The tendencies are to reward your own and penalize those who are different. The current analysis of institutional racism clearly demonstrates this (Knowles & Prewitt, 1969). As a consequence of the emerging domination, Weber also recognized that justifications for the domination came to be present in the culture of the total society. People who are on top feel they belong there by right and it is right that they belong there. They therefore indoctrinate the rest of the society with the values that they claim brought them to the top.

The consequence of these points for our model is to demonstrate that the existence of negotiation, its content, the ability of a given person or group to enter into negotiation, the likely effectiveness of one's negotiative efforts and the means used to bring about an outcome are limited both structurally and culturally. This is the point that Strauss et al. had in mind when they said that hierarchical position and ideological commitment influence the patterned variability of negotiation. A related point is that while symbolic interaction as a perspective cannot account for what people bring to situations in terms of differentiation or stratification, it can analyze the processes of interaction that result from those social conditions and is therefore able to explain the maintenance or change in those dimensions.

This leads us to conclude this section by noting that Weber, like Mead, believed that while every social situation constrained individuals to some degree and some more than others, he also believed there were numerous opportunities for action due to the instability of social structures (Bendix, 1960: 269). Negotiated interactions remain essential albeit constrained as men find themselves in new, problematic, undefined, or flexible situations.

d) Power, Politics, and the Negotiated Order

The problem of explaining participation in and effectiveness of bargaining is a significant one. We need to be able to explain how a given bargain is made; why a particular group is successful; how a given definition of the situation is developed; why a particular norm emerges; and why some groups are self-conscious and assertive. Introduction of the concept *power* provides us with a vehicle for understanding the outcomes of negotiated interactions and for analyzing the processes by which those outcomes were determined.

The concept power, however, is noticeably absent in the writings of the interactionists. Arnold Rose, for example, in criticizing symbolic interaction pointed to its neglect of power relations while in his own work on political power, he explicitly neglected the perspective (Rose, 1962: x; Rose, 1967). Scheff indicated, but did not discuss, that power was a factor to be considered in the establishment of consensus and coordination (Scheff, 1967). The absence of the concept may, in part, be due to its typical definition in non-symbolic terms. However, a recent definition of power by Walter

Buckley allows us to merge symbolic interaction and the negotiated order with power.

Power, however, is typically linked to and therefore must be distinguished from authority because they have often been defined in terms of each other (e.g. authority as legitimate power, authority as the institutional matrix for power) and because both are forms of control. The difference however is crucial: they emerge or exist in qualitatively different kinds of social situations and involve qualitatively different kinds of behaviors. In passing, we should note that the response of many sociologists has been to overestimate the extent of authority in American society because it mistook obedience or acquiescence to mean consent (Mann, 1970). In so doing, the discipline has, on the whole, failed to discover the pervasiveness of power behavior. This is clearly a relative matter and, perhaps, a result of definition but the consequences of these definitions are to call attention to modes of control that are too often ignored.

Walter Buckley in an insightful discussion differentiates between the two concepts as follows:

> . . . power as control or influence over the actions of others to promote one's goals without their consent, against their will or without their knowledge or understanding (for example by control of the physical, psychological, or sociocultural environment within which others must act). The mechanisms involved may range from naked force, through manipulation of symbols, information, and other environmental conditions, to the dispensing of conditional rewards. The emphasis here is on the lack of ascertainable 'consent,' considered as something socially and psychologically deeper than mere acquiescence or overt compliance. A closely related characteristic is the emphasis on private goal orientation rather than on collectivity goal orientation.

> Authority is the direction or control over the behavior of others for the promotion of collective goals, based on some ascertainable form of their knowledgeable consent. Authority thus implies informed voluntary compliance which is a definite psychological state and a coordination or identity of the goal orientations of controller and controlled. (Buckley, 1967:186)

Authority occurs in situations characterized by collective goals, consensus, and cooperation. It requires a definite commitment by the members of the collectivity to the actions and "commands" of those in office. On the other hand, power occurs in situations characterized by private goals, dissensus, and competition when people comply either through fear, inducement, persuasion, or ignorance. While it may be argued by some that Buckley confuses or mixes control, influence, manipulation, force and power and that his definition involves certain tautological aspects, he is to be commended for making some differences very explicit and significant. We have all too often confused acquiescence and compliance with authority and taken the absence of conflict as a measure of stability and legitimacy of rule. Events of the past few years in the U.S. have rudely brought that home.

Secondly, our attention is now turned to the manner in which individuals and groups maintain or achieve control through power mechanisms and resources. To make this more explicit, Buckley's statement of the social conditions of power—private goals, dissensus, competition—reinforce the conception of the negotiated order and link power to it. In addition, given the nature of contemporary society, the emphasis placed on force and the use of negative sanctions in usual definitions of power is moderated because other mechanisms are recognized as significant. Other means of achieving one's ends such as inducements, secrecy, and persuasion are widely and frequently used and noted. There is also the recognition that compliance may occur without force or threat because of ignorance or a sense of powerlessness.

Finally, Buckley's recognition of the multiple mechanisms of power directs our attention to the manifold resources or *bases* of power. The participants are clearly likely to use the resources that are most likely to be effective and they will quite often be different as they reflect different positions and perspectives. According to Dahl, the base of an actor's power constitutes all the resources that he can muster to control the behavior of the other (Dahl, 1957). Gamson, in discussing resources in some detail, points out, however, that the amount of resources is not equivalent to the amount of power because participants will not commit all or be able to effectively mobilize all their resources for any one or a series of encounters (Gamson, 1968; cf. Bachrach & Baratz, 1970; McCall & Simmons, 1966; Blau, 1964). These factors reinforce our position that the outcomes of interactions are problematic because of ranges of commitment and importance to the participants and the problems of predicting the orientation of the other. Consequently, establishment of *self*-interest and ability to take the role of the other are factors in the outcomes of these interactions as they affect the use of power.

To this point, our discussion has dealt with interaction and society in general. Our specific concern here, however, is with politics and government. If one equates, as has been done, power with politics, then one can say that all social life involves politics from the dyad, the family, the peer group, to the club, the church, and the community. We choose, however, to limit the remaining discussion to the politics of political institutions in the society— those that have the function of considering, making, implementing, and evaluating laws, rules, and norms that are binding on the entire society. No other institution has the ability to effect authoritative societal decisions. According to one definition, government has two functions—to maintain the established code and to readjust this order to new conditions and emergent needs. (MacIver, 1947: 65). Mannheim's view of government sees the former as administration, namely the handling of already rationalized and routinized matters, and the latter as politics, which reflects the unorganized and unrationalized new issues (Mannheim, 1936). Thus, politics represents the areas of social concern which reflect the undefined and unresolved issues which are deemed by participants to necessitate the creation and application of a norm. The implication of this orientation is that at every stage or phase in the political process, the outcome is problematic because it involves negotiated interactions. Even the supposed more stable area of government, like politics, shows evidence of ambiguity, process, conflict, and emergence and is characterized by bargaining behavior. The aphorism "Politics is the art of compromise" marks as a virtue the underlying process of the negotiated order. Such negotiations are central in the emergence and identification of issues, the charting and defining of alternatives, the debating and deciding of resolutions, the allocation of resources and personnel, the execution of actions, and the evaluation and adjudication of "problems"—all of which constitute the essential elements of the political process.

We turn now to an explication of some of the processes of power (e.g., manipulation of symbols, control of the flow of information, and dispensing conditional rewards). Because of space limitations, we will emphasize the first two processes because they have been underemphasized elsewhere. Our primary purpose, rather than a complete analysis, is to indicate the directions such an approach would take.

PART II: THE PROCESSES OF POWER

Little attention has been paid in the social scientific study of government and politics to power in action. Existing work has focused primarily on the structural consequences of power or theoretical and mechanistic discussions of its existence. The intention here is to focus on the processes of power. We will not be concerned with situations characterized by authority or those power situations where naked force is its primary representation but rather the concern will be with situations characterized by differentiated or potentially differentiated interests. The situations have been dichotomized into those which involve the exchange of tangible and material benefits and those which primarily involve symbolic exchanges.

a) Bargaining over Material Resources

We shall first discuss the dispensation of conditional rewards and inducements through the negotiation process. While we recognize the major significance of this activity, this discussion is consciously severely limited because of its detailed analysis elsewhere. These resource exchanges, as Edelman has pointed out, tend to occur among the organized groups and with government as they reach agreements affecting their relationships (Edelman,

1964: 22–43). We are quite familiar with the contexts in which these occur, e.g., collective bargaining, diplomatic negotiations, lobbying, the establishment of coalition governments, and conference committees. These are among the more open accepted ones while the political deal, the payoff, the smoke-filled room, and in general, the corruption of authority represent the shadier side of this activity.

While bargaining and negotiating do involve the gaming stance—the exchange of manipulated overt gestures and sometimes threats, and public performances to set the stage for such interactions—they are basically private as opposed to public activities, private in the sense that only the participants are present and no audience witnesses the arrangement. Examination of the bargaining process in general can be found in Schelling (1967). Invoking Goffmanesque vocabulary, bargaining generally occurs *backstage* where the actors are free to vary from their public role or the explicit demands of their constituencies. To arrive at a working consensus will require flexibility that audience awareness, involvement, or reaction would inhibit because the parties need to feel one another out, make offers and counter-offers, and be friendly when perhaps they are supposed to be hostile. While many of these arrangements are eventually to be made public, and require ratification, many also are to remain private as they involve illegal acts, role conflicts, or contingent activities.

As politics is defined by the process of compromise, so the caucus is defined as its basic aggregate or essential institution.

> Its use here implies a meeting having a definable character, usually private, certainly informal, and often marked by that somewhat stylized bonhomie typical of relations between men who, even if not friends, know that they need each other and must respect each other as independently situated. A caucus of American politicians, in other words, is—as within the American system it must be—a personal meeting but one between men who come together to discover if among their several needs their may be personal advantages. (Roelofs, 1967: 252–253)

The caucus is ubiquitous and continuously occurring at all levels of government and politics. It crosses partisan and organizational lines and can take place in every nook and cranny of life from the cloakroom, the office, the restaurant, the home and via the telephone. Even where conferences, meetings, and sessions have formal encounters where staged presentations are made, the work and the agreements take place in the private and informal settings (e.g., Paris Peace talks). Murray Edelman, supporting the position presented here on the pervasiveness of bargaining and the caucus, astutely notes that the language style used in this activity is clearly different from hortatory, legal, and administrative political languages. It has its own style because it is used in private and because its aim is "a deal, not an appeal" (Edelman, 1964: 146). Its style is specific, deliberate, calculated, and secret.

b) Political Talk, Impression Management, and Definition of the Situation

In addition to the private arena of politics, the public arena is also of considerable importance. The relationships among the organized groups and official role players constitute only a part of the action. Insofar as the activities of government and politics are concerned, the bulk of the population are spectators and members of the audience. The results of voting and the development of public opinion are a function of how many members of the audience are mobilized and in what direction—recognizing, of course, that they exist initially in different states of readiness. On the whole, little attention has been paid to the *means* by which the spectators become involved. Their relationship to the political arena is often determined by what they hear, see, and read and their interpretations of those things.

The basic element of politics is, quite simply, talk. On the one hand, politics constitutes the transformation of physical confrontations into verbal ones, and on the other, the resolution or accommodation of these confrontations involves the use of political rhetoric, i.e., "the use of public discourse to persuade." We must be therefore interested in understanding the processes of political talk in determining how the audience is activated (or perhaps deactivated or deflected). The maintenance and activation of power come from being able to convince others of the correctness of your position, of being able to appeal to those symbols which strike a resonance, of presenting one's self in the appropriate and desired style. The sociology of political talk encompasses briefings, speeches, debates, press conferences, rallies, protests, diplomatic notes, and revolutionary ideology. It represents the analysis of *political impression management.*

The basic assumption of impression management is that control over the conduct of others for one's own interests is achieved by influencing the definition of the situation in which all are involved. This is accomplished by acting in such a way that creates an image of the actor that leads others to voluntarily act as he wishes them to act (Goffman, 1959: 3–4).

Power, the control of others, is accomplished by getting others to accept your view and perspective. This is achieved by controlling, influencing, and sustaining *your* definition of the situation since, if you can get others to share your reality, you can get them to act in the manner you prescribe. The original formulation of W. I. Thomas on the definition of the situation included the sentence, "If men define situations as real, they are real in their consequences" (Thomas and Thomas, 1928: 572). That is, if consensual meaning is achieved, people will act on that basis. If you accept my premises, then you accept my conclusions.

Further insight into controlling the definition of the situation can be attained by introducing the dramatistic pentad of Kennth Burke (1962: xvii–xxv). His five key terms of dramatism are act, scene, agent, agency, and pur-

pose. The explanation of any event must take into account: *the act*—what
was done, what took place in thought or deed; *the scene*—the background of
the act, the situation in which it occurred, when or where it was done; *the
agent*—who did it, what person or kind of person performed it; *the agency*—
how it was done, the means or instruments used; and *the purpose*—why it
was done. Burke's pentad serves an important organizing function since political definitions of situations and definitions of political situations often
come to be constructs or, as Burke notes, they are "necessary forms of *talk
about* experience" rather than "necessary forms of experience" (Burke,
1962: 317). The organizing function occurs because, according to Burke,
as a principle of drama, for example, the nature of the acts and agents must
be consistent with the scene. From the general principle of dramatic consistency, Burke deduces ratios between all elements to measure their consistency, e.g., scene-act and scene-agent ratios. With reference to the interrelationships Burke states:

> There is, of course, a circular possibility in the terms. If an agent acts in
> keeping with his nature as an agent (act-agent ratio), he may change the na-
> ture of the scene accordingly (scene-act ratio), and thereby establish a state
> of unity between himself and his world (scene-agent ratio). Or the scene may
> call for a certain kind of act, which makes for a corresponding kind of agent,
> thereby likening agent to scene. Or our act may change us and our scene,
> producing a mutual conformity. Such would be the Edenic paradigm appli-
> cable if we were capable of total acts that produce total transformations. In
> reality, we are capable of but partial acts, acts that but partially represent us
> and that produce but partial transformations. Indeed, if all the ratios were
> adjusted to one another with perfect Edenic symmetry, they would be immu-
> table in one unending moment. (Burke, 1962:19)

The definition of situation, encompassing all of these elements, is important because of the compelling quality of their interdependencies. It is
vital to be able to set the stage, identify the actors, determine the action,
specify the means, and avow the purpose to control the show. Being able to
assert one of these elements is a decided advantage in calling out others.
Accepting it means accepting a number of interlocking dynamic elements
which delimit alternative courses of action. In fact, much of political rhetoric
boils down to trying to piece together the connections between purpose, act,
agency, agent, and scene.

The Edenic symmetry fails to exist partially because new situations often
occur, old ones are re-enacted, and ambivalence often exists about the purpose and the agents. It also often fails to occur because in partisan politics
the parties constantly contest the dramatistic elements at some place and on
some level. Because of the pervasive effects of politics and the fuzzy line between politics and government, efforts to define the situation in such a way
as to mobilize your supporters while disarming or attacking your opponents
are an on-going process. It is for this reason that the manipulation of sym-

bols becomes so important in a "democracy" where discussion and rationality are supposed to be the means to the ends.

In politics, the failure of Edenic symmetry or problems with impression management occur because "contradictions" are institutionalized. The existence of the two major political parties means that on some level and for most issues, there are contending definitions of the situation which compete for the attention and acceptance of the populace. Such contending definitions also serve to create the impression that there are real differences between parties, that the political process is open and that members of the society do have meaningful choices. Representatives of each party therefore strive to create impressions, images, and symbols supportive of their position. The verbal battle between those who are in office and those out of office is an on-going affair. In American society there is unlikely to be a single definition of the situation. The concern of the politicians, however, is to be able to assert the dominant one, recognizing full well that tomorrow may bring a new dominance. The struggle is ongoing therefore as administrations manipulate symbols in order to mobilize support and deactivate or insulate dissent while the opposition seeks to expand its support by capitalizing on the alleged failures of the administration and the new issues of the day. At the same time, growing out of the nature of the two-party system, the proposed definitions often are not too dissimilar as they both seek to control the center of the political spectrum.

This manipulation of symbols takes place in the context of existing sets of symbols or a political culture. Political symbol-users draw upon their knowledge of this culture in attempting to choose the appropriate symbol for the occasion. To invoke the notion of political culture is not to imply a cohesive, coherent, integrated, consensual belief system because that is not the reality of the situation. Rather what exists are numerous values and beliefs which are only partially integrated, partially conscious, and often in contradiction with one another. These partial awarenesses, integrations, and conflicts provide the background circumstance for a basic ambivalence in the political arena between government vs. politics, authority vs. power, statesman vs. politician, collective vs. individual, and clean vs. dirty. To say that someone is a politician is to color him dirty while to refer to statesman-like actions is to evoke the highest form of integrity.

Political activity is a fragile and problematic enterprise because at the same time one is being applauded for self-sacrifice, he is being criticized as self-serving. The past of the society is replete with the crumbling of idols and the revelation of incompetence and corruption as well as the creation of heroes, myths, and history. This is to call attention to (or suspect the existence of) the fact that some people know of the bargaining and the manipulation behind the scenes—but that is often reserved for the party of the others. Nevertheless in the back of one's mind, and increasingly so, is the feeling that no party is exempt from the practices. In these circumstances impression management requires increasing care and expense. Exposés, bad reviews, and the unexpected always threaten political performances.

As government comes to politicize more of everyday life and international commitments make the world a smaller and more dangerous place in which to live, we find that anxiety and uncertainty are increased. Edelman argues that the unorganized and essentially powerless, i.e. the mass of the audience, look for the alleviation of this anxiety through symbolic reassurance (Edelman, 1964: 189). He argues that the bulk of political talk serves this function of reassuring the mass that they are in good hands and all goes as well as can be expected. While this may not be the complete truth, we should recognize that definitions of the situation often are facile, superficial, short-lived, and designed for purposes of impression management.

c) Control of Information Flow

Political impression management can be divided into two basic forms: controlling the flow of information and symbolic mobilization of support. The former refers primarily to backstage behaviors involving insulation, concealment, secrecy, structuring and planning, while the latter involves public performances of persuasion. This dichotomy is clearly for analytical purposes as the two in reality are part of the same process.

"Knowledge is power" is an increasingly accepted belief which has been dramatized by the cybernetic revolution where information is equivalent to control. Since our guiding interest is in how people control situations, and accepting the premise that those who are able to define situations are able to control them, we shall examine some of the ramifications of the relationship between power and controlling the flow of information. Using Goffman as a starting point:

> One over-all objective of any team is to sustain the definition of the situation that its performance fosters. This will involve the over-communication of some facts and the under-communication of others. Given the fragility and the required expressive coherence of the reality that is dramatized by the performance, there are usually facts which, if attention is drawn to them during the performance, would discredit, disrupt, or make useless the impression that the performance fosters. These facts may be said to provide 'destructive information.' A basic problem for many performances, then, is that of information control; the audience must not acquire destructive information about the situation that is being defined for them. In other words, a team must be able to keep its secrets and have its secrets kept. (Goffman, 1959:141)

Because of the multiple performers, the situations involve more than concealment of destructive information but also the creation and gathering of intelligence about the other performers and the audience, the planning, structuring, and rehearsing of the performance, and the creation and flow of knowledge within the team. Attention then becomes focused on the networks of communication as well as the content. Basic to the entire issue is that actors need to limit the outflow of information to positive supporting information and to maximize the in-flow of accurate information about the nature of the world in which they are performing. These kinds of activities take place in the back region where the performers want insulation and limitation of access to the small group of people who will function together as a team. The backstage is the area where performances are prepared and performers can relax from formal role demands.

One of the interesting aspects of contemporary democratic society is that the line between front and back region is becoming increasingly thin, partly as a result of intrusions by media and partly through the conscious acts of political performers. Politicians can often make gains by politicizing their personal life. The public has shown an interest in the family and social activities of political leaders. On the other hand, political figures often draw back or feel intruded upon when such public attention to their private lives does not suit their intentions. Another aspect of this ambiguity lies with the use of the media by public officials, and political actors often energetically work to shut out media intrusions because what is defined as "news," that which is really exciting, is revelation of secret actions. It is somewhat paradoxical but the more information we have, the more educated, and democratic we become, the greater are the pressures exerted by people in power to make more of their activities secret.

In order to know how to act in a problematic situation, the actor has to assess the situation. He has to gather data about all those objects which he defines as relevant. The calculation of appropriate action on his part depends on knowing the expectations and intentions of others in the situation. If his aim is control over a competitive or potentially competitive situation in which some participants are to be up-staged and others to be persuaded, then he must have information to predict their actions and information to reveal to him the extent of his resources and support from his teammates and the audience. In a problematic situation, all other things being equal, clearly greater control will go to the party that has the most accurate information. For just such reasons, increasing efforts in politics and government are being spent on research, information-gathering, and intelligence.

As in poker, the maintenance of secrecy about one's strengths and weaknesses and his knowledge of the opposition is crucial. Secrecy is vital so that one does not indicate his likely future intentions. In the current situation, the national administration has means of increasing its power through manipulation of the intelligence function. It does this by its ability to classify public documents as restricted, confidential, or secret and through the censorship of legislative hearings. The opposition is either denied access or prevented from the privilege of using the information under the guise of national security.

All too often, in common-sense fashion, people believe that facts speak for themselves, that information-gathering is a highly rational activity; and that the authorities or purchasers of information get what they want. The context of intelligence is of exceeding importance since raw data must be put into "intelligible" form and recipients of intelligence often receive information from several sources whose facts and interpretations may be contradictory. Harold Wilensky (1967) has severely criticized the ability of complex organizations to effectively organize intelligence activities because they tend to produce unreliable, incomplete, biased reports. Much of this is due to the hierarchical, centralized, specialized nature of a complex organization as well as the "information explosion" producing more data than can be adequately handled. As an example, information on the My Lai massacre indicates that as reports went up the military hierarchy, the number of civilians reported killed went down. We are also aware that in the partisan political battle of words, Democrats and Republicans looking at the same economic situation choose different sets of facts with which to discuss the situation (e.g. inflation).

Political actors use their intelligence activities to assess the audience, for example, by using public opinion polls, examining letters to the editor and to government personnel, or by informal discussions with community representatives. At the same time, they try to keep track of their political opponents through reviewing the media, coopting defectors, attending public meetings of the opponents, having informal discussions with media people who have access to the opposition, and perhaps even by infiltration. Knowing what the public wants (this is an oversimplification of the public) and what opponents will do allows one to anticipate and respond ahead of time to maintain the advantage.

Controlling the flow of information and limiting access to the backstage allows the planning, structuring, and rehearsing of the performances. Political acts, despite the attention paid to solo performances, are most often joint efforts whether they involve election campaigns, policy decisions, or legislative voting contests. They are also prepared ahead of time, in private, and require coordination of diverse interests and persons to effect a united front. Thus, the team members evaluate the "intelligence" of the outside, spell out their own interests and goals, define ways to achieve them, anticipate actions and reactions of others, and determine how they will respond to (or ignore) them. These kinds of activities often entail attitudes of cynicism, selfishness, manipulation, uncertainty, informality, and immoderation which cannot be revealed in public. Such planning will give rise to internal dissent which must be kept within the team so as not to destroy the public image of unity. Reviews of the campaigns of 1960 and 1968 will point up the private care taken for public performances.

An extension of the preparation of public performances is the concern with structuring and scheduling the emission, volume, and rate of communication flow. The backstage planning will deal not only with content but also, in dramaturgical terms, with the setting of the stage. Being able to determine the place and the props has a strong influence on the content that will occur. Several examples of this are the "Daniel in the lions' den" gambit of Teddy Kennedy debating Eddie McCormack in South Boston and the general presidential use of television and press conferences (cf. Levin, 1966). The attempt to change protest into discussion is an attempt to move the communication into the manageable constraints of the conference room or the informal chat. The control of timing is also important in political campaigns which attempt to build the tempo to reach a crescendo just before election day, not before and certainly not after. A further corollary of this general point is the power that derives from the ability to schedule meetings and formulate agendas. This means that persons in charge can control when controversial items occur. Outsiders who want to communicate must wait their turn, time, and place, and, as often happens, the outsiders' time comes when many people are tired or have left. Power can come from controlling the format and consequently the content (Stinchcombe, 1968:243–5). While the scenes may appear spontaneous and normal, their staging has often been predetermined offstage.

Efforts also must be taken to see that little or no discrediting or disconfirming information is released. Using Goffman, we note the kinds of things that must be concealed. We have referred already to the suppression of internal dissent so as not to give aid and comfort to the enemy by giving the impression to the audience that the team is incompetent. Other matters for concealment are those which are inconsistent with the standards associated with the position or activity. Goffman refers to inappropriate pleasures and economies which in politics and government could refer to such items as bribes, overseas junkets, or high life; errors and mistakes such as the failure of the M-16 rifle or youthful indiscretions; the viewing of the product in process such as the interim report or memo intended for internal consumption (e.g., Moynihan's "benign neglect" statement) or the confusion and disorder of a meeting; conflicting purposes such as the serving of special interest groups, or rapid alteration of position for personal power, or revelation of less than ideal motives for acquiring the positions such as having made "deals" when it is incumbent to say "I make no deals" (Goffman, 1959:43–45).

The line between the front and back stage and between the performers is like a semi-permeable membrane. Some material may pass in and may not pass out again, but not all necessary material will pass in. Some internally created information passes out in different form than intended. Recent events in the U.S. have indicated that mistakes occur or misconceptions develop because important information is not received or accepted. Certain groups in the society are unable to communicate with the centers of power or the gatekeepers and consequently actions are taken which further polarize the society. The relationship between students or blacks and the present administration illustrates this problem. Articles in newspapers following the Kent State-Cambodia situation were written which indicated that the President was isolated not only from these groups but from members of his own government who should be gatekeepers for incoming information. The "Pentagon Papers" further underscore this situation.

To conclude this section, both in a positive and negative sense, the possession of information and control over its use allows insulation, independence, and flexibility on the part of the possessor. Possession gives rise to control either because others are kept in the dark about the dangerous disconfirming, discrepant information because they have limited access to the communication channels or because the actions of others can be anticipated and therefore controlled. Too little attention has been paid to these phenomena in political sociology and here as well but they clearly deserve extensive study.

d) Symbolic Mobilization of Support

Symbolic mobilization of support calls attention to front-stage performances where symbols, verbal and non-verbal, are used to strengthen or maintain the position of the political actor(s). As examples of this process, the function of ideology in social movements, the creation of political character, the definition of issues, and the management of discontent will be discussed. All of the examples involve the use of symbols for creating audience acceptance of the identity, intentions, and actions of the actor(s).

Analysis of this general process necessitates a consideration of the nature of the audience. Any given political situation or the total possible audience will be composed of (a) strong and partial supporters, (b) undecideds, neutrals, and know-nothings, and (c) partial and strong opponents. The kinds of symbols used to mobilize support from these segments will clearly differ and the symbols intended for one segment of the audience if heard by another would probably not have the same effect and might, in fact, be damaging. An actor will be more partisan, hortatory, and specific before strong supporters while he will tend to be more community-oriented, general, and reassuring before a mixed audience. Were the mixed audience to hear the partisan talk, they would probably be offended or unimpressed by the "extreme" symbols. Supporters hearing a talk before a mixed audience often feel let down and they often need backstage re-charging. The development of television with its large, heterogeneous audience has meant a de-partisanization and de-specification of much of political communication. It clearly follows that knowledge of the nature of the audience and perceptions of the audience are necessary for sociological analysis of symbolic mobilization of support.

In general, given a fairly even balance in audience disposition, the aim of the performers is to revitalize their supporters, persuade the partials and in-betweens, neutralize and undermine the remainder of the in-betweens and partial opponents and attack the strong opponents. Counter to the general image of rational and open civic discussion, the political actor does not attempt to persuade his opposition to change their position.

The chances of that are slim and since his resources and energy are most often limited, activity occurs where it is likely to provide pay-offs. Only if the actor is either in an extremely strong position or an extremely weak position is he likely to concern himself with persuading the opposition and then primarily with his partial opposition. Generally, the primary concern with the opposition is to neutralize or isolate it and to use it as a strategic weapon. The mobilization of support has two sides to its currency which involve creating positive images of your side and negative images of the opposition. Thus, while a political performer may be stressing the qualities of his leadership, the benefits of his program and his commitment to community, he may explicitly or implicitly be labelling the opposition and imputing unfavorable motives to them. Analysis of this process must therefore include examination of announcement and placements of identity, avowal and imputation of motives, explicit and implicit referents, and emphasis on mobilization through self-presentation and/or negation of the opposition. The ratios of these usages are empirical questions and depend upon varying situations which have not been explored in much depth.

The type of desired behavior is a variable in this process since the continuum ranges from mere acquiescence and acceptance of a statement, to voting or signing a petition, to joining a civic or political organization, to self-immersion in a radical group. In general, the farther along the continuum, the more encompassing is the behavior and therefore the stronger, the more extensive and intensive, the more complete and integrated will be the symbols necessary to mobilize the desired response. The kinds of symbols needed for total commitment are radically different from those simply encouraging a person to vote for a candidate.

The form of symbolic belief system called an *ideology* should be viewed as an action system because its function is to turn listeners into believers and believers into actors. The acceptance of an ideology constitutes a commitment to a new social cosmology and the rejection of current standards of reality. Acceptance also means the creation of persons with a single identity and the formation of a "community" out of a "society" because all will share "a unified and internally consistent interpretation of the meaning of the world" (Bittner, 1963:932). Bittner says that this radicalism, which we take here as ideology, is morally binding and must (theoretically) be applied in all occasions of actual conduct. Internalization of an ideology means a continuing self-consciousness so that the ideology is constantly in the forefront of the adherent's mind and therefore serves as permanent motivator of actions. In this context, both Coser and Selznick have demonstrated the relationship between ideology, conflict, and action mobilization (Coser, 1956 & Selznick, 1952). Ideology is differentiated from common sense notions of reality which are segmentalized, transitory, situational, superficial, and thoughtless. Common sense deals with things that can be taken for granted while ideology deals with matters that must not be taken for granted but must be changed. Since they must be changed, adherents must be activists and combatants.

To bring this about, an ideology will include the following elements: (1) definition of the current situation as being dismal and requiring immediate alteration; (2) destruction of any rationale for reforming or adjusting the existing social order; (3) development of a utopian vision with contrasting values and norms to existing practices; (4) invocation of ideal human values and/or those of the ideal existing society; (5) categorization of heroes, villains, and (maybe) fools; (6) a programmatic statement of a hierarchy of ends and tactics by which they will be achieved and (7) definition of the appropriate audience and appropriate leaders.

The use of the term ideology often obscures the analysis of the situation since observers assume its existence in complete and static form over time. In fact, ideologies are most often incomplete or in process and as such always involve definition, ambiguity, and interpretation. They parallel the social movement form of social organization and collective behavior. Social movements are themselves in flux and emergent; they represent coalitions of groups, quasi-groups, and individuals at different levels of commitment; they respond to internal dynamics as well as external pressures. Each leader and each group therefore puts forth their own variant of truth and seek to have their interpretation of the scripture accepted as prophecy. Ideologies cannot be divorced from but should serve as rhetorical indicators of the conditions in which they are created, the intentions of the people who fashion and use them, and the consequences on the audiences for whom they are intended as well as those who respond against them.

In general, however, the American political system is not characterized by ideologies or even political parties but rather by personalities and issues. National political parties lack organization and impact and the average American shows a remarkably low correlation among beliefs on political issues (Sorauf, 1968, and Campbell, et al., 1964). Political candidates, rather than relying on the parties, tend to create their own personal political organizations. The lack of ideological orientation means that political performances point to candidate position on separate issues and stress the image of the person. This emphasis on the individual political entrepreneur means that the *creation of political character* or the political presentation of self is crucial for the career of the politician and for an understanding of electoral politics.

The politician is potentially always on stage. Every aspect of his behavior can become part of a public performance which must be managed and controlled to mobilize support. Many of his activities will be essentially symbolic, i.e. for the purpose of creating the desired identity in order to draw the audience into *his* drama. It is also true that he may not be able to control the situation because he cannot be assured of audience support or even awareness, because other performers will be competing with him and offering negative impressions of his performance, and because he may have to respond to situations not of his making. The creation of political character is a problematic event because like all social encounters it requires a negotiation of identities of the interactors. The actor may find his projected identity rejected, ignored, or modified and he must respond to the response and try to shift it to his advantage. Klapp has a detailed discussion of the dialectic and problems of establishing an identity (Klapp, 1964: 34–35). The situation, however, is different from the negotiations that occur in two-party or face-to-face interactions. The political drama has numerous performers acting partially opposite each other and partially in the absence of each other. They are in front of sometimes similar, but not identical, and sometimes different audiences. While the actor may be performing in reference to another actor, his eye will be on the audience as well. While he may be projecting an image of himself to the audience, one of the other actors may be casting him quite differently.

Before pursuing some aspects of the negotiation process, it is important to include certain problematic aspects of character control. The advent of television has made us more conscious of the effects of non-verbal forms of communication. To be able to see as well as hear the performer lays open the responses not only to the content but to the appearance and intonation of the performer. While with radio, people were probably attuned to tonal qualities, these become emphasized with television. Thus a performer, as with the principle of dramatic consistency, must also be concerned with the congruence between these three channels of communication—content, tone, and appearance. He must be communicating the same message on all three at the same time or else the contradictions or ambiguities result in unanswerable questions or rejections. Clearly, many cannot control these aspects, even with rehearsal, but the concern with this aspect of image is quite real. Their effects can be noted in the preparations for and the consequences of the first 1960 debate, the supportive response of moderate Republicans as well as left-wing Democrats to Eugene McCarthy because of the cool, calm image, and the apparent contradictory support for Robert Kennedy of blacks and northern working-class Wallace-supporting whites.

From the point of view of the actor, the creation of political character involves the overlapping processes of identification-differentiation and ego casting and altercasting. With reference to the first, not all office-holders or aspirants to office can command the attention of the audience. Some by virtue of their position, their resources, and their "charisma" are more likely to be in the spotlight. The American polity is also not known for its overwhelming interest in politics nor for its attention to detail. In a world which suffers from a surfeit of stimuli, the political performer finds it a highly competitive and difficult situation in which to put on *his* show and to create *his* character. He must try to create an identity that is somewhat unique. He must dramatize himself in such a way that he sets himself off from the typical political performer. By creating his own identity, he differentiates himself from others. He may, of course, do this in a number of ways —by associating himself with a new and viable issue, by adopting a particular style, or by being David fighting Goliath or Daniel in the lions' den. Visibility requires differentiation. To say who one is, is also to say who one is not. Perhaps the key to the surprising, although limited, success of Eugene McCarthy may be attributed to the fact that he was the personification of the non-politician. Nothing he did seemed to be what campaigners usually do and this refreshing situation seemed to represent honesty, integrity, and intellectuality. Identification is also revealed by connecting the self to those constituencies, values, heroes, myths, shrines, causes, and styles which are popular and sacred in the society. The building of political character requires connections of the self with the past, present, and future and with expansive entities and beliefs so that the political self is seen as representative of and as an extension of transcendent and awe-inspiring symbols.

At the same time that one is projecting an identity of himself, he is directly competing with others for support, particularly during campaigns. The actors are generally interested in the middle of the audience, the partials and uncommitteds, who tend to be mobilized on the basis of personality and style. Consequently, not only do they cast ego but they also try to create an identity for their opponent in the eyes of the audience. This process of altercasting is, as Weinstein and Deutschberger indicate, a basic technique of interpersonal control since it limits alter's freedom and effectiveness and forces him to deal with images not of his making (Weinstein & Deutschberger, 1963:454). This is significant because people support a candidate not only in terms of what they like about him but also in terms of what they dislike about his opponent (Levin, 1966:81). Candidates try explicitly or implicitly to emphasize the negatives of their opponent. For example, Ronald Reagan successfully cast Pat Brown, the former governor of California, as a professional politician while creating his own image as a citizen-politician. Richard Nixon, himself a victim of altercasting in the form of "would you buy a used car from this man?" hung Hubert Humphrey by constantly linking him with LBJ in referring to the Johnson-Humphrey administration so that Humphrey could not easily disassociate himself from previous policies. Some candidates implicitly create an ineffective image of their opponents by never mentioning them. The ability to carry this off by not having to respond to charges demonstrates that one is in dramaturgical charge and control of the situation. This is a position front-runners attempt to maintain. They begin to lose if they have to play the other man's game. On the other hand, if one is out of power and running behind, he must be more explicit in his altercasting and many are able to capitalize, not on their own strengths, but rather on what the audience dislikes about the incumbent opponent who by virtue of incumbency has become the target of discontent.

One of the tasks of those in public life is to be able to be a legitimate exhibitionist. They must find ways in which to show the effects of their work. These symbolic acts mean that in some sense public officials are always campaigning since it is necessary to dramatize their work (Goffman, 1959: 30). Dramatic realization occurs in many forms: a newsletter to constituents; coming to the home district to speak to local groups; maintaining office(s) which emphasizes constituent concerns; ceremonially inaugurating public and civic projects; having photographs taken with notables; leading or being part of legislative investigations; appearing on television or radio talk-shows; and speaking out on current problems. The point is to be seen and known through activities which represent accomplishment, experience, knowledge, and energy. By way of contrast, the number two man, such as the vice-president or lieutenant governor, have significant difficulty in dramatic realization since their work is often residual, ceremonial, or by assignment. It is therefore harder to become known and to have the freedom to carve out their character since they do not have the freedom of the legislator, the responsibility of the executive or the access to the media.

Candidates, in or out of office, often must not be seen as campaigning. To announce too early means they become a target and have to respond to queries and attacks before resources are organized and also because they may be seen as too eager and excessively power-oriented due to the already discussed ambivalence about politics. The candidate must present an image of a controlled and reasonable drive for office. His declarations of candidacy, when they finally come, are couched in terms, not of individual ambition or sub-group interest, but rather of public service, societal values, the current critical situation, and community pressure to run. The candidacy is most often presented in terms of long and arduous deliberations after being urged to run by numerous responsible members of the community. This can be seen as an example of idealization in which the performance conveys the impressions of representing the officially accredited values and ideal motivations and qualifications for aspiring to the position (Goffman, 1959:46).

Given the creation of political character desired by the performer, which is problematic, it is imperative that he stay in character in order to assure support. This also assumes that the scene is sufficiently stable to demand or infer the same character over time. Nevertheless, politicians often stumble on stage or fail to rise to the occasion and elections are very often lost rather than won. Because the media or one's opponents are always looking for contradictions or failures in character, danger is always there because of American emphasis on the *kind* of man one is. The reactions to the sporadic activity and alleged irritability of McCarthy, the "admission" of brainwashing by Romney, and the Chappaquidick incident reveal the problems of failing to stay in character. One of the basic images of political leadership, and consequently of political character, is the assumption of responsibility. The leader or aspirant is expected to act as if he is in control of or is capable of controlling the situation (Edelman, 1964:73–94). He is expected to be able to specify the cause, issue the resolution, and take the actions and consequences. John Kennedy's response to the Bay of Pigs disaster was to still the situation by saying "I am responsible" and then to take action. Richard Nixon, with reference to Indo-China, emphasizes the role of commander-in-chief and points to responsibility by saying "The buck stops here." Staying in character means to give the impression of control by being cool, calm, and collected and acting with decisiveness rather than hesitancy.

The admission or evidence of indecision, weakness, fear, guilt, or loss of control, is often disastrous to the career of the aspiring leader because it throws doubt on his ability to cope with the serious responsibilities of leadership. However, errors, failings, and ambivalent qualities can often be negated and turned into positives by humor, humanization, and down-to-earth images. Goffman (1959:67) discusses mystification as means of impression-management by maintaining social distance and evoking awe and respect. The leader must convey the impression that in order to lead he is above the people. However, a tension has always existed in American politics between Hamiltonian and Jacksonian images of government. The candidate, the aspirant, and the leader must demonstrate also that they are human beings and "of the people." American democracy still possesses the myth of the common man so that the baby-kissing, back-slapping, smiling, waving, hand-shaking, hot-dog-eating politician is still on the scene. Superseriousness and distance make for too strong a sense of separation and the successful politician can be one who can laugh at himself, err gracefully, and then admit it with a "Boy, I goofed" image. Satisfactory presentation of self must be good but not perfect because if it is felt to be too good a performance, suspicion will develop that it is a performance and not real.

In addition to the styles of and attitudes toward leadership, there is a core of politics which involves content, namely issues and problems and the ability of those in or out of office to offer and enact solutions. Mobilization of support can come through the *definition of the issue,* the establishment of alternatives, enactment and implementation of the solution. Issues, social problems, controversies, accidents, unexpected events, failures, and gaps, can be seen as breakdowns or interruptions in an otherwise orderly and meaningful system. Commonsense assumes that interactions, institutional relationships and societal functioning will continue to operate on a predictable, knowable, satisfactory, and sensible course. Breakdowns, failures or other problematic events are extra-ordinary, abnormal, deviant, and unsettling and therefore must be explained. But insofar as they involve power, responsibility, and persuasion, such situations are not defined in a vacuum or merely described.While facts may be important, in and of themselves, to indicate the act, the creation of context, the nexus of scene, purpose, actor and agency, is part and parcel of the definition of socio-political issues. More symbolic effort tends to be spent on defining the context rather than the act(s) themselves.

For example, one of the basic myths of American politics is that issues and problems are separate, unconnected, and isolated events which sporadically occur, are resolved, and then new ones emerge. The view taken by radicals that these are interrelated, part of and a consequence of a structure, and never solved but displaced is generally rejected. Tension, however, develops when social movements begin to link issues and begin to integrate them into an ideology. The ability to maintain the separation of issues reinforces the legitimacy and effectiveness of the government and the society.

The legitimate opposition, being out of power, often attempts to create the context by listing but not linking issues. Solutions, they suggest, come from changing the actors rather than the theatre. Their goal will be to try to create a scene implying crisis, urgency, "these are times that try men's souls" and a demand for action on the part of these actors. They will talk about gaps, shortgages, deficits, rising rates, shrinking assets, conflict and cleavage, incompetence, inefficiency, and short-sightedness. The style of actor suggested from this stage setting will be active, dynamic, crusading, and "hot." They will manifest anger and moral outrage albeit rational and controlled. The point of all this is to demonstrate that the definitions of issues have their antagonists and protagonists who actively strive to dramatize. Those in office, for example, are likely to respond to opponent's crisis staging by remaining cool, deriding prophets of doom and gloom, appointing commissions and consultants, acting dramatically if necessary, and going before the people to solemnly explain the situation. But they will not say "it is *not* my fault" or "I cannot do anything" because that would be an abdication of responsibility and an admission of failure and would allow another actor to step in and seize the scene.

The emergence of an issue, the development of a controversy or the revelation of failure are all problematic. They may fail to occur because of
ignorance, concealment, or complacency. They often require a dramatic
event, staged or otherwise, to draw public attention; access to the media for
prolonged discussion; and the support of established political leaders for
legitimation and nationalization of the issue. Civil rights as an issue in the
early 1960s depended on sit-ins, beatings, murders, vicious dogs, and an
assassination for its culmination. Gun control only became a potent issue,
although not overly successful, after several major assassinations. Vietnam
had its greatest impact and led to the Kennedy campaign only after the Tet
offensive. While many had, in small groups and in out-of-the-way journals,
bemoaned what man was doing to his environment it took events like the
Santa Barbara oil spill to bring the matter home and to focus attention on
ecology and aggregate the people concerned with different kinds of pollution
into one collectivity. No issue really develops without some staging around
a dramatic event.

Another significant symbolic aspect of the emergence of issues is that
people tend to personify the issue. Issues somehow have to be associated
with individual spokesmen for concreteness and reference. One of the problems with pollution is that it remains too abstract and unconnected to an
individual frame of reference. The issue of personification is double-edged.
In the first place, media people, in looking for a spokesman, may create a
leader. Movements based upon participatory democracy like FSM and
SNCC found that the outside society could not deal with them unless they
created a "leader." Bob Moses left the field because of this and observers of
FSM have for some years privately discussed what John Searle wrote in the
New York Times, namely that Mario Savio was one of many but was created
as the leader by the media (Searle, 1968:14). The other edge of personification is that respectable people, particularly politicians, are necessary to
legitimate a concern. They, in fact, provide the forum for national discussion. They reach out to an issue and make it "theirs" since they need issues
to keep them alive. As a result they politicize, legitimize, and nationalize the
issue. This can be seen in regard to pollution, consumer protection, the
plight of the Indians and the Grape pickers, the war, and student dissent.
First King and Spock and then Fulbright and Kennedy were necessary to
take the war issue out of arena of extremism and make it quasi-respectable.

The definition of an issue requires moving from the specific act(s) to the
scene or setting in which the drama is played. The creation of the scene is a
powerful tool because it surrounds the acts with justification, reality, and
force. Descriptions of life in the ghetto provide the social conditions which
explain rioting. Ghetto life becomes intelligible in the context of white
racism. The establishment of social conditions and individual states of mind
lays the foundation for and calls forth the acts. Examination of the settings

and symbols used to justify the war in Vietnam find the utilization of all the ratios of Burke's pentad. The symbolism of purpose—freedom, peace, justice, commitment, defense against aggression cast the drama in a noble and courageous setting while the symbolism of acts and agency make the enemy despicable. And so it is with all issues that performers seek to surround the action with appropriate screens. Political slogans such as "the Politics of Happiness," "We can do better," "We shall overcome," and "Off the Pigs," quickly define the situation and imply further consequences. To counter such effects, one seeks to destroy the legitimacy of the setting by violating the implications of the setting. The confrontations that have occurred on campuses and in some courtrooms are demonstrations of outrageous behavior designed to shock and destroy by conscious inappropriateness.

The agency-purpose ratio lays bare a significant connection in the definition of issues. The relationship between means and ends often presents a tension as to whether the means are appropriate—either effective or legitimate—to achieve the ends. Current concern with violence and definitions of violence involve both defenses and rejections as either fitting or not fitting the ends or being appropriate or inappropriate to the scene. Conflict situations often find symbolic attempts to keep the process within normative bounds while continued conflict supposes that the means move to non-legitimate and illegitimate means. Radical or revolutionary purpose will find it fitting to use "any means necessary" but since normal people will not perceive the situation similarly such rhetoric is extreme and criminal. In fact what becomes obvious about arguments over means is that the other elements of the situation are also at variance.

This leads up to the final concern in defining issue, namely the identity and intentions of the actor. While this would include the star performers, emphasis has already been directed toward them in the discussion of political character. I am concerned here with what might be called *political deviance,* namely the labelling of the deviants and the attribution of motives to their actions. Issues tend to be asserted and come to be identified with groups of protagonists or practitioners. One way of explaining the issue or the actions is by giving the actors an identity or a motive so that protestors are hippies or "out for kicks." Of significance is the fact that to impute a motive is to place an identity and vice versa so that one fills out the person, puts him in a category, and then can respond to him. Thus, the understanding of public reactions to political protest and collective behavior is an extension of interactionist analyses of both deviance and interaction breakdown. Understanding public reaction and perception is quite significant because of the general assumption of individual responsibility which forces explanation of unusual events. Mills, in his original formulation on motives (1940) used them in the context of facilitating and expediting interaction. While this is true they also are imputed for the purpose of preventing and terminating interaction.

They become tools of maintaining social distance and justifying one's position. The basic similarity of motives is that they provide meaning to deviant behavior so that social cohesion is maintained, deviants are isolated and identified, and appropriate courses of action are, at least, symbolically provided for them. The ability to label actors as deviant means that the issue they represent is destroyed or deflected. Public opinion polls after the Chicago police riot and the Kent State massacre clearly lay responsibility and blame on the demonstrators and not on the police or National Guard. Ralph Turner (1969) shows how easily this can be done in the perception of public protest. Star performers in the political arena often take an active role in the definition of political deviants by linking identity and motive to actions. The speeches of Vice-President Agnew have been challenged for precisely this fact.

Anyone in office must be concerned with controlling dissent and *managing discontent* because they are deemed responsible for its causes and control. Those out of office often seek to capitalize on the discontent and hope to turn it into political capital. Officials first attempt to control this dissent symbolically in order not to change their positions or use other resources. They often seek to insulate and isolate the dissenters by presenting justifications which will be acceptable to the general audience or to cool out the discontented by altering the nature of the conflict and/or appearing to accept the concern of the dissenters. Those in office tend to have greater access to the media than the dissenters and are able to make more effective communication. The accounts of political figures tend to be justifications rather than excuses as defined by Scott and Lyman (1968) because of the presumption of responsibility. In confronting the responses to issues and breakdowns, i.e. discontent, the administrations attempt to cloak themselves within the purposes and values of the community, to place negative labels and motives on their opponents, to identify themselves with the audience in such a way as to mobilize non-involved members of the audience, e.g. appeals to the Silent Majority. Their purpose in engaging in this activity is to undermine the position of the opposition; saying in positive terms that they are acting correctly in pursuit of high purposes and in negative terms to negate the opposition by showing their bad qualities, intentions, and actions. And as Scott and Lyman (1968:59) emphasize, *"Every account is a manifestation of the underlying negotiation of identities."*

One form of account which is often exceedingly powerful is a system of beliefs which may be called the administrative ideology. It has its roots in current common sense notions of reality, organizational philosophy, and political practice. This line of persuasion goes as follows: The existence of any problem, particularly if seen as a failure of administration, is due to a breakdown in communication resulting in misunderstandings or ignorance. Problems, conflicts, or controversies are not the result of basic conflicts of interests, values, or goals but arise because those who perceive the problem do not know what or why the leaders have been or are doing. The solution to these problems therefore lies in establishing communication by having discussion and dialogue so that those who are discontented will discover they are misinformed and will alter their position. Or perhaps a compromise can be reached between reasonable and sensible men since they share the same ultimate goals.

The assumptions of the administrative ideology which are often made explicit are that we are all members of a single community with a consensual value system and that we therefore have collective interests and goals. Our leaders, as part of this community and chosen by us to represent us, are completely and totally system-representatives pursuing our collective goals. They do not have any other aims such as individual or sub-group goals in mind. Since this is the case, any conflict or disagreement cannot be basic but may be a disagreement about means or simply due to misunderstanding. Rational discussion will bring about an awareness of the sincerity of the participants and their commonality so that an agreement can be reached.

At the same time, the leader invoking the administrative ideology will probably mention the following points. In the first place, he will point to the consequences of internal dissent which gives aid and comfort to the enemy. He will emphasize his own activities in the collective behalf in the arena with the opposition or the enemy. And he will finally say, while revealing some previously "secret" or unknown information, that there remains some information that he knows that completely justifies his position but which for "security" reasons cannot be revealed at this time. The leader thus seduces the audience by taking it into partial confidence and then mystifies it by invoking security and responsibility (Hall & Hewitt, 1970). In general, people who have degrees of control or influence attempt to create circumstances of consensus, community, and cooperation. They seek to have situations defined so that they impressionistically transform power into authority.

PART III: EVALUATION OF THE PARADIGM

I will depart from the usual impersonal detached academic style in this section dealing with the strengths and weaknesses of the paradigm because it is unreservedly a reflection and expression of my own self. When I first began teaching political sociology I had no formal training in it but as I had grown up with politics, it was a strong personal interest. The sociological material on politics available at that time, epitomized by Lipset's *Political Man,* which I used in my course flew in the face of my personal and sociological background. However, at that time I felt that students should know the dominant disciplinary orientation in preparation for graduate school. I even agreed to write a text on political sociology using this material.

Teaching this material soon began to grate on me because I was not being myself, i.e., presenting the material using the perspective with which I identified myself, namely, symbolic interaction. However, no interactionist at that time had dealt with the political system. Consequently I began to lose interest in political sociology and my classes seemed to lose their involved quality. It was then, by accident, that I discovered *The Symbolic Uses of Politics* by Murray Edelman. The excitement generated by reading and re-reading the book was immense. The work was full of significant insights and imaginatively applied symbolic interaction to some segments of politics. It provided a strong beginning upon which to build this paradigm. My intellectual debt to Edelman is profound.

Since then I have continued to add elements that broaden the scope, intensify the depth, and extend the systematization of this analysis. What you have read here, however, remains rudimentary and can only be seen as sensitizing and orienting. In writing it, I was frustrated at many points because I could not elaborate my discussion or develop areas that I have not yet seriously considered. There is a great deal of work that remains to be done in specification, refinement, extension, and application.

The ability to come as far as I have is due, as well, to changes or new emphases in symbolic interaction. Its initial formulation was strongly influenced by biases in favor of democracy, consensus, progress, cooperation, intelligence, social reform, and responsible individualism. And as Mills indicated (1966), social psychology of this type was ideally suited to liberals. To some extent such a flavor still exists. On the other hand, the work of Turner (1962), Goffman (1959), Strauss (1963), and Blumer (1962) has emphasized sources of coordination other than consensus. Such changes were being made concurrently with some functionalist introspection (Gouldner, 1959; Blau, 1964; Goode, 1960). Thus sociology in general and interactionism specifically were "toughened up" and better suited to the realities of the world. At the same time there was much concern with social change and conflict and the emergent, voluntaristic, problematic, progress side of Mead began to be emphasized in interactionist writings. The paradigm, once harnessed to a concern with stratification and power, is ideally suited to handling the inevitable sources, manifestations, processes, and consequences of conflict and change. It seems designed to deal with the vitality and reality of a social life which has a political system that never stops or runs down but faces new contingencies, issues, groups, conditions, and decisions as well as the reinterpretation of formerly rationalized matters.

The potential contributions of this approach have been ignored because sociology incorporated what was congruent and ignored contradiction and because critics superficially wrote off the perspective as being unresearchable, micro-level, overly subjective, indeterministic, lacking content and unsystematized (Denzin, 1970; Kuhn, 1964; Kantor, 1971; Meltzer, 1964).

In preparing to write this section, I spoke to many of my colleagues with particular reference to critiques of interactionism and their own personal criticisms. On the whole, they repeated the above criticisms but indicated they were not well informed of the perspective or responses to it. My colleagues, I should add, are all in different areas of sociology and received their graduate training at different universities. Suffice it to say, that a great deal of research has been conducted using this perspective: macro-concerns have been analyzed; subjectivistic elements have been objectified; determinism has been utilized; and systematization is developing. None of the alleged criticisms negate the perspective nor are inherent to it.

This paradigm was designed, in part, to correct weaknesses that I perceived in American political sociology. It assumed the existence of consensus, a dominant collective orientation, authority, and stability of American society and its political system (and therefore its effectiveness and success). Its dominant concern has been with feeding inputs from the society into the political system and assuming that these objects—public opinion, voting behavior, and pluralistic interests—automatically develop and are substantially acted upon in their original form. As a result political sociologists have failed to examine the internal processes of the political system, the effects of political outputs on the society, or the creation of opinion by the "agents of the political system." Closely related to this is the image created of the politician which is that of a passive reactor or mediator rather than an active initiator. Flowing from the same general approach is the misplaced emphasis on studying community power at a time when national power is obviously more significant and pervasive. In general, the results of political sociology convey an impression of American society and politics that omits essential issues and areas and also commits serious errors of distortion (cf. Bottomore, 1970). The interactionist, negotiated order, impression management model at least begins to deal with these matters and when fully developed would provide a more balanced view.

In order to fully develop the model, I am aware that there would need to be more attention paid to *all* phases of the political process from the nascent issue up to law enforcement. The area of political culture as background expectancy to political action requires infinitely greater explication. I have focused on elites in this work and more specifically those in office. Further work should deal, as well, with those out of power, the public, and the development of community organization, collective opinion, and social action. More attention deserves to be given to inter-organizational activity, the exchange of resources, and the use of inducements and, conjointly, to the bargaining process. The coercive aspects of power as well as authority deserve more emphasis than they have received here.

Criticisms will no doubt be made of the impression management orientation toward politics. As one fellow sociologist recently told me, "You may know something about symbolic interaction but you don't know anything about power politics." My Marxist friends have criticized me for ignoring imperialism, capitalism, and class. Their position is that the substance of this paper deals with politically trivial matters like electoral politics and public opinion and not with what forms or misinforms this process. My Parsonian friends criticize me for being cynical, for denying the importance of values, and for failing to see how political leaders strive for collective ends. They continually point out to me the cultural constraints upon conflict and negotiation.

In response, the position taken here that both the material and ideal elements come to be reflected in and expressed through the interpretive processes of the self-conceptions of the actors. To say as I do, that men act out of *self*-interest is to emphasize the self and the interests, ideal or material, with which it actively identifies. Sociology of all kinds typically answers the "what" question by indicating relationships between variables but infrequently demonstrates the processes which, in fact, connect those variables, the answers to the "how" question. This paradigm should be able to determine the balance between Marxian and Parsonian positions. If the nature of the negotiated order is as tight as some Marxists allege, then this perspective should be able to demonstrate its existence and sources and processes of maintenance. If the solidarity of the social order is a reflection of common values, then this should be reflected in the interactions of men.

To summarize the essential view of man and society expressed here and in order to point toward future theoretical alignments, I would like to close by quoting from Alvin Gouldner's review of *History and Class Consciousness* by Georg Lukács. The similarity between Lukács and Blumer is readily apparent. Such a convergence offers a powerful and fruitful line of inquiry.

> . . . The social 'totality' is composed of an interaction of social elements that, unlike interacting billiard balls, do not remain the same; they change not only their positions but also their character. The social system must be seen as a historical product, as a thing made and fashioned by men as active 'subjects,' as continually remade and daily enacted by the ongoing doings of men, and hence as capable of being undone or redone by their future actions.

> The system, in short, depends upon men. The social system is not something given in history, but is a social object that is selectively interpreted and is actively conceptualized by men in the here and now; it is seen as the product of the interaction of 'subject' and 'object.' Lukács understood that men establish their social worlds by constituting them conceptually, as well as by their practical enactments. (Gouldner, 1971:4)

REFERENCES

Bachrach, Peter, and Morton Baratz.
1970 Power and Poverty. New York: Oxford.

Becker, H. S.
1963 Outsiders. Glencoe: Free Press.

Bendix, Reinhard
1960 Max Weber: An Intellectual Portrait. Garden City: Doubleday.

Bittner, Egon
1963 "Radicalism and the organization of radical movements." American Sociological Review 28 (December): 928–940.

Blau, Peter
1964 Exchange and Power in Social Life. New York: Wiley.

Blumer, Herbert
1969 Symbolic Interactionism: Perspective and Method. Englewood Cliffs, N.J.: Prentice-Hall.

Bottomore, T. B.
1970 "Conservative man." New York Review of Books 15 (October 8): 20–24.

Buckley, Walter
1967 Sociology and Modern Systems Theory. Englewood Cliffs, N.J.: Prentice-Hall.

Burke, Kenneth
1962 A Grammar of Motives and A Rhetoric of Motives. Cleveland: World.

Campbell, Angus, Philip Converse, Warren Miller, and Donald Stokes
1964 The American Voter—An Abridgement. New York: Wiley.

Coser, Lewis A.
1956 The Functions of Social Conflict. Glencoe: Free Press.

Dahl, Robert
1957 "The concept of power." Behavioral Science 2 (July): 201–218.
Dalton, Melville
1959 Men Who Manage. New York: Wiley.

Denzin, N. K.
1970 "Symbolic interactionism and ethnomethodology." Pp. 261–284 in Jack D. Douglas (ed.), Understanding Everyday Life. Chicago: Aldine.

Edelman, Murray
1964 The Symbolic Uses of Politics. Urbana: University of Illinois Press.

Foote, Nelson
1951 "Identification as the basis for a theory of motivation." American Sociological Review 16 (February): 14–21.

Gamson, William A.
1968 Power and Discontent. Homewood, Ill.: Dorsey.

Goffman, Erving
1959 The Presentation of Self in Everyday Life. Garden City: Doubleday.
1961 Encounters. Indianapolis: Bobbs-Merrill.

Goode, William
1960 "A theory of role strain." American Sociological Review 25 (August) 483–496.

Gouldner, Alvin
1959 "Reciprocity and autonomy in functional theory." Pp. 241–270 in L. Gross (ed.), Symposium on Sociological Theory. White Plains: Row, Peterson.

1971   Book review: History and Class Consciousness by George Lukács. New York Times, 18 July, pp. 4–5, 14–15.

Hall, Peter, and John Hewitt
1970   "The quasi-theory of communication and the management of dissent." Social Problems 18 (Summer): 17–27.

Hughes, Everett
1958   Men and Their Work. Glencoe: Free Press.
Hughes, Everett, and Helen Hughes
1952   Where Peoples Meet: Racial and Ethnic Frontiers. Glencoe: Free Press.

Kanter, Rosabeth
1971   Book review: Symbolic Interactionism by Herbert Blumer. American Sociological Review 36 (April): 333–334.

Klapp, O. E.
1962   Heroes, Villains, and Fools. Englewood Cliffs, N.J.: Prentice-Hall.
1964   Symbolic Leaders. Chicago: Aldine.
1969   Collective Search for Identity. New York: Holt, Rinehart and Winston.

Knowles, Louis, and Kenneth Prewitt
1969   Institutional Racism in America. Englewood Cliffs, N.J.: Prentice-Hall.

Kuhn, Manford
1964   "Major trends in symbolic interaction in the past twenty-five years." Sociological Quarterly 5 (Winter): 61–84.

Lang, Kurt, and Gladys E. Lang
1968   Politics and Television. Chicago: Quadrangle.

Levin, Murray B.
1966   Kennedy Campaigning. Boston: Beacon.

MacIver, Robert M.
1947   The Web of Government. Glencoe: Free Press.

McCall, George, and J. L. Simmons
1966   Identities and Interactions. New York: Free Press.

Mann, Michael
1970   "The social cohesion of liberal democracy." American Sociological Review 35 (June): 423–439.

Mannheim, Karl
1936   Ideology and Utopia. New York: Harcourt, Brace.

Meltzer, Bernard
1967   "Mead's social psychology." Pp. 5–24 in Jerome Manis and Bernard Meltzer (eds.), Symbolic Interaction: A Reader in Social Psychology. Boston: Allyn and Bacon.

Mills, C. Wright
1940   "Situated actions and vocabularies of motive." American Sociological Review 5 (December): 904–913.
1966   Sociology and Pragmatism. I. L. Horowitz, ed. New York: Oxford.

Roelofs, H. Mark
1967   The Language of Modern Politics. Homewood, Ill.: Dorsey Press.

Rose, Arnold
1962   Human Behavior and Social Processes. Boston: Houghton Mifflin.
1962a   "A systematic summary of symbolic interaction theory." Pp. 3–19 in A. Rose (ed.), Human Behavior and Social Processes. Boston: Houghton Mifflin.
1967   The Power Structure. New York: Oxford.

Scheff, Thomas J.
1966 Being Mentally Ill. Chicago: Aldine.
1967 "Toward a sociological model of consensus." American Sociological Review 32 (February): 32–46.

Schelling, Thomas C.
1963 The Strategy of Conflict. New York: Oxford.

Scott, Marvin, and Stanford Lyman
1968 "Accounts." American Sociological Review 33 (February): 46–62.

Searle, John
1968 "A foolproof scenairo for student revolts." New York Times Magazine 29 December, pp. 4–5.

Selznick, Philip
1952 The Organizational Weapon. Glencoe: Free Press.

Shibutani, Tamotsu
1966 Improvised News. Indianapolis: Bobbs-Merrill.

Shibutani, Tamotsu, and K. M. Kwan
1965 Ethnic Stratification. New York: Macmillan.

Sorauf, Frank
1968 Party Politics in America. Boston: Little, Brown.

Stinchcombe, Arthur L.
1968 Constructing Social Theories. New York: Harcourt, Brace and World.

Stone, Gregory, and Harvey Farberman
1970 Social Psychology Through Symbolic Interaction. Waltham: Ginn-Blaisdell.

Strauss, Anselm, editor
1956 The Social Psychology of George Herbert Mead. Chicago: University of Chicago Press.
1964 George Herbert Mead on Social Psychology. Chicago: University of Chicago Press.

Strauss, Anselm et al.
1963 "The hospital and its negotiated order." Pp. 147–169 in Eliot Friedson (ed.), The Hospital in Modern Society. New York: The Free Press.
1964 Psychiatric Ideologies and Institutions. New York: Free Press.

Sutherland, Edwin H., and Donald R. Cressey
1970 Criminology. 8th ed. Philadelphia: Lippincott.

Thomas, W. I., and Dorothy S. Thomas
1928 The Child in America. New York: Knopf.

Turner, Ralph
1962 "Role-Taking: process versus conformity." Pp. 20–40 in Arnold Rose (ed.), Human Behavior and Social Processes. Boston: Houghton Mifflin.
1964 "Collective behavior." Pp. 382–425 in Robert L. Faris (ed.), Handbook of Modern Sociology. Chicago: Rand McNally.
1969 "The public perception of protest." American Sociological Review, 34 (December): 815–831.

Turner, Ralph, and L. M. Killian
1957 Collective Behavior. Englewood Cliffs, N.J.: Prentice-Hall.

Weinstein, Eugene, and Paul Deutschberger
1963 "Some dimensions of altercasting." Sociometry, 26 (December): 454–466.

Wilensky, Harold L.
1967 Organizational Intelligence. New York: Basic Books.

Symbolic Interactionism and Politics in Systemic Perspective

Rosabeth Moss Kanter
Brandeis University

If we begin with certainties, we shall end in doubts; but if we begin with doubts, and are patient in them, we shall end in certainties.

—Francis Bacon

Seek simplicity, and distrust it.

—A. N. Whitehead

Symbolic interactionism is a useful and appealing perspective on social life. It offers a humanistic viewpoint in which people are seen as utilizing their reasoning and symbolizing capacities and flexibly interpreting and adapting to circumstances depending on how they themselves come to define the situation. It acknowledges and permits conscious thought before action occurs, expressed resistance to programmed behavior, the lack of perfect fit between person and role, and unexpressed ambivalence toward called-for or expected behaviors. It indicates the impact that people have on one another and, in fact, on shaping each other's humanness. It points out the great role of culture, symbols, and meaning systems in eliciting and changing behavior. And it provides graphic and often colorful pictures of the numerous human dramas that occur in society.

Now Peter Hall has taken symbolic interactionism out of the realm of everyday life in which people work out their relationships through mutual interpretations and adjustments in face-to-face encounters, and has applied it to the larger realms of societal politics and government. In so doing, he has both stretched the perspective further than many people would have thought possible and has demonstrated that much of what is true in microcosm of everyday life can also account for events and processes of major consequence for all members of the society.

Hall's paper represents an important contribution in several respects. First, like Murray Edelman (1971), Hall reminds us how much of political life occurs through symbolic manipulation and exchange. Perceptions and hence behavior of great political consequence stem from changes in meaning systems; people are both socialized into traditional patterns of behavior and

---

Much of the thought that went into this paper was first stimulated by William A. Gamson. Barry A. Stein, George Ross, and Marilyn Halter provided helpful comments and discussion.

77

mobilized for new action on the basis of available symbols for interpreting and responding to the world. In fact, symbolic interactionism is potentially the most useful perspective for analyzing political socialization and re-socialization and the mobilization of changes in opinions, behaviors, expectations, and demands. In addition, Hall's emphasis on the most problematic and negotiable areas of politics also helps focus attention away from the more fixed, formal, public, and official institutions and toward the backstage areas which often shape issues before they even enter the public arena; Hall proposes fruitful lines of inquiry directed toward caucuses, coalitions, and lobbying. Finally, the focus on process helps correct dominant sociological concern with structure.

Hall makes the positive case for symbolic interactionism very well; he indicates that it has previously unrecognized utility for approaching and analyzing certain aspects of political life. He uses symbolic interaction theory in an impressive and creative way and adds new concepts, such as his usage of power, where the paradigm has not been adequate. In this paper I do not challenge his reading or his usage of symbolic interactionism; rather, I attempt to indicate some of the limits of the paradigm by looking at some of the issues which it does not address very well.

TWO TRADITIONS OF POLITICAL ANALYSIS

Two traditions in political sociology can be identified: the behavioral and the systemic. The behavioral approach considers the interactions and exchanges among political actors as they struggle for power and influence. It deals with the intended effects of actors on the decisions of other actors. The systemic approach, on the other hand, considers the system as a whole, the relation of system parts to one another, and how the overall system maintains itself or disintegrates over time and regulates conflict. It deals with the conditions for social order and disorder as well as the relationship that parties in conflict have to one another. It considers the collective purposes of politics as well as the private interests in contention. Symbolic interactionism is part of the behavioral tradition; in many ways, it improves upon other lines of inquiry and analysis in this tradition.

The behavioral and systemic traditions are analogous in some respects to what William Gamson (1968) has called the "influence" and "social control" perspectives on politics. The behavioral or influence perspective, as represented in Hall's article on the symbolic interactionist paradigm, takes the point of view of actors in the system and considers how they act so as to have their wants and demands met. Its perspective is subjective, and its methodology, as Herbert Blumer (1969) has pointed out, is most appropriately participant-observation. In contrast the systemic approach (similar to, but not identical with the social control perspective), attempts a view from outside or above the system on the behaviors and interactions of system members. The behavioral approach is concerned with the strategy of conflict rather than its regulation. According to Gamson, it deals with how groups try to get what they want and the conditions under which they succeed, rather than the consequences of activity for the stabilization or integration of the system. The behavioral approach deals with social structure only insofar as it constrains or limits the behavior of actors; the systemic approach considers social structure and social organization to be important independent and dependent variables—the "state" of the system at various points in time. The behavioral approach tends to deal with relatively short time-spans and to consider subtle changes or small variations in short periods; the systemic often encompasses long time-spans and the "sweep of history," considering regularities over long periods, rather than small differences within one period. The behavioral approach, particularly as represented by symbolic interactionism, tends to examine single cases or processes within a single system; systemic analysis is more often comparative. Behavioral analysis is most useful for understanding the impact and outcomes of direct interactions; systemic theories, on the other hand, can also account for the impact on one another of changes in parts of the system that are not in direct interaction. Finally, as Gamson indicates, each approach has its own biases. Behavioral analyses tend to overemphasize the influence process and see decisions as much too free; systemic analyses, in contrast, tend to overemphasize the impact of structural limits on behavior and see decisions as much too constrained. There are also areas of agreement between theorists undertaking each approach and times at which the same analyst will move between perspectives, as did classical theorists such as Simmel and Weber. But it is useful to understand each viewpoint, its advantages and its limitations. Both question and explain different aspects of social reality.

The contrast between the behavioral and systemic approaches in political sociology parallels similar debates in other disciplines. Almarin Phillips, for example, attempts to adopt a systemic perspective in economics and contrasts it with traditional economic theory in which all actors are seen as operating to maximize their own self-interest. He argues:

> A game [an economic exchange] is not an unorganized coming together of several individuals for 'no-holds-barred' combat. It is instead a well-defined set of rules which limits the freedom of the players in their selections of strategies and moves. Different results occur if different games are played not because the players are motivated by different objectives but rather because varying constraints are imposed on their behavior. Nothing in the mathematics of game theory, however, goes to the problem of how the game is chosen, who establishes the rules and how they are enforced. The game is apparently set by an anonymous outside authority. From an organizational point of view, this outside authority is in the real world the vast, complex, institutional-

organizational framework of society, including near the apex of its hierarchical structure the several layers of formal government. . . . (Phillips, 1962: 43–44)

Phillips speaks for the integration of behavioral economics into a systemic framework.

Given the virtues of both behavioral and systemic analysis, symbolic interactionism is not enough by itself. Just as Gamson argues that both the influence and social control perspectives are needed to provide an adequate paradigm for political analysis, this paper also argues that there is a need to integrate the behavioral and the systemic perspectives and to find linking concepts between behavior and system. Even among the most die-hard system theorists, there are those who recognize the value of a behavioral analysis such as that Hall advances, and hold that both systemic and behavioral perspectives are needed for a complete paradigm. David Easton's *A Systems Analysis of Political Life* makes this point:

> . . . A theory of political allocation would differ from that undertaken through systems analysis. Support does seem to turn on the way in which members may mobilize others in the pursuit of objectives and thereby it does seem to influence the way in which the valued things in a society are authoritatively divided and distributed . . . Alternatively . . . insofar as political analysis and research have been attempting to explain and understand allocative functions within a system, the system within which the allocations take place has been consistently overlooked. Yet, without the existence of the system of behavior, we would be unable to discover those allocative processes, the variations in which require explanation. . . . (1965:476)

SYMBOLIC INTERACTIONISM IN SYSTEMIC PERSPECTIVE

The limits of symbolic interaction theory (and, indeed, all behavioral theories) as a paradigm for political analysis can be understood, then, in contrast to a systems perspective. First, the level of analysis of symbolic interaction theory is micro-sociological. By calling it a micro-theory, I am not thereby relegating it only to the study of small groups and face-to-face interaction; Hall's article admirably demonstrates its applicability to behavior in large systems, to inter-group interaction, and to non-face-to-face exchanges. Rather, the theory is micro-sociological because it deals with the behavior and interactions of *elements* of a system rather than considering the system as a whole. Attention to the ways in which actors attempt to influence each other and to mobilize support for their own particular interests or interest groups involves a simultaneous neglect of the joint context of interaction, the system in which these actors operate. Both actors and spheres of activity bear a structured relation to each other than can be seen not from the perspective of any one element but only from viewing the system as a whole. The actions of elements of the system have impact on one another not only because they change the distribution of valued goods but also because they may change the nature of the system as a whole and the system's relative degree of cohesion or lack of cohesion, of stability and endurance, or instability and breakdown. Certainly the relative positions of actors and system elements are negotiated and changeable, as the interactionist perspective points out. Yet, some systems persist relatively unchanged in outline over time while others change rapidly. These differences cannot be understood merely from the perspective of each actor or interest group but only from considering the overall system within which they operate. Looking at "who wins" in bargaining or conflict or interactive situations, or analyzing whether and how the interests of each party to the interaction are advanced does not answer questions of whether or not the system in which they come to interact will continue, change, or dissolve.

The lack of a notion of system is related to a second limit of symbolic interaction theory: by focusing on the interests of the parties in interaction, it lacks a coherent concept of *collective* interests. As Hall indicates:

> The model of society that derives from the negotiated order is one characterized by a complex network of competing groups and individuals acting to control, maintain, or improve their social conditions as defined by their *self-interests.*

But the self-interests of actors alone is inadequate as a basis for and a description of the social order. In addition to the goals, perspectives, and interests of the actors in a system there are also systemic interests. While actors within the system are negotiating with one another for goods, resources, and influence over authoritative decisions and generally see only that limited view of their activities, the system as a whole is mobilized to produce results for that system with respect to its environment. To varying extents, depending on the relative equity or inequity of distribution, all elements in the system may have a stake in the production of such goods. That there often are shared values and collective goals above and beyond the particular interests of particular actors should be taken into account. It is as limited a perspective to emphasize the conspiratorial nature of decisions (that the interest of some group over some other group is advanced by every authoritative decision) as to emphasize the altruism of authorities as system agents (that the greater good of the whole is advanced by authoritative decisions). It is important to keep in mind the Parsonian view that power may have collective as well as distributive aspects. Power represents not only the ability of one set of actors to get what they want from another set of actors but also the ability of a society to mobilize and generate resources to attain collective goals. Non-recognition of collective interests from a systemic perspective means that legitimation is never more than "a contrivance by those who succeed in monopolizing power in any given society," and collective goals are "always a sham imposed by the power-holder without genuine independent convictions of the ruled" (Eisenstadt, 1971:15). Eisenstadt argues, rather, that collective goals have an important independent meaning derived from the needs for and advantages of social order:

> The exercise of political power—that is, of the 'necessity' for a political order —was derived . . . from two systemic or prerequisite needs of any social system in general and of a total society in particular. These are the maintenance of order and the regulation of force on the one hand, and, on the other, the implementation of some common goals perceived as representing the collectivity. (1971:14)

The symbolic interactionist concept of society only as an order negotiated out of individual interests and not also as an overarching vehicle for the attainment of shared goals does not lend itself to analysis of the existence and relative importance of *collective* interests. The viewpoint Hall advances takes into account only the interests of actors who can agree to agree (and thus formulate shared goals in any particular interaction situation) or agree to disagree (and thus wage conflict). A systems perspective, on the other hand, would hold that there is some minimum degree of joint interest merely by participation in the same system, whether or not actors from their limited vantage point choose to agree with the decisions of authorities. Collective interests are more than the sum of individual interests or the areas of agreement between individuals. They are the conditions for the care and feeding of the shared social order, for the regulation of the vehicle through which individual needs are met. Systems theory and the social control perspective may overdo the existence of collective interests, but behavioral theories go too far in ignoring their existence.

Hall's rendering of symbolic interaction theory, furthermore, tends to reject the one aspect of the perspective that did leave room for the possibility of a concept of collective interests: the old tradition in symbolic interaction that saw actors as attempting to ensure cooperative, harmonious, smoothly-running relationships and as striving to achieve and maintain a consensus. Instead, he adopts the more modern stance proposing limited cooperation only for the purpose of maintaining a definition of the situation long enough for actors to attempt to maximize their own interests over that of others. There thus appears to be no concept of degrees between Cooley-type utopianism and Goffmanian cynicism. If those following in the Cooley tradition see humankind as "over-socialized," Goffman's concept of the presented self may err in the direction of seeing humankind as "under-socialized" and overly calculating. The latter view posits essentially one human need: maximize your gain over others' in the social game of life; there are no other motives. But both the cooperative, collectively-oriented, utopian perspective and the cynical, "war of all against all" conflict perspective might be true under different system conditions. Then we again need systemic theories which propose the conditions under which cooperation or conflict, conspiracy or altruism, and identity or non-identity of interests prevail. Symbolic interaction theory does not offer a basis for differentiating between the two conditions or fully explaining the commitment that provides cohesion for many a political system.

Symbolic interactionism understands commitment in one of two ways: it is either cultural or behavioral. In the cultural sense, people in power employ symbolic manipulation to create meaning systems for others which cause them to act as the power-holders wish; that is, the power-holders control the definition of the situation. (Here symbolic interactionism does seem particularly useful for the analysis of political socialization and re-socialization.) In the behavioral sense of commitment, a person's own previous behavior may serve to lock him into future courses of action because other people perceive him differently or he "burns his bridges behind him" or because he stakes other resources on favorable future outcomes of a line of behavior. This is Howard Becker's (1960) concept of commitment as the making of "side bets."

Both understandings of commitment are useful for some kinds of situations, but neither contain a concept of collective interests. A person is socialized or locked into a social order, but social orders themselves are not differentiated or seen as securing commitment because they enable the fulfillment of individual interests. Concepts of commitment are needed which involve a notion of collective as well as individual interests and which can characterize and differentiate between social systems and political situations on these dimensions. One such definition would see commitment and alienation as end points on a continuum, with commitment the identity of individual and collective interests and alienation the non-identity of these two sets of goals. That is, the commitment condition holds when a person or group considers that taking his or their place in the social order and agreeing to regulation by the agents of that system enables the attainment of what they want and need for themselves. Alienation is the opposite: participation and obedience prevent the person or group from fulfilling their interests. We then ask politically relevant questions: what are the conditions under which collective and individual interests are integrated or differentiated? What are the conditions under which larger system regulation and sub-group or individual interest attainment are in conflict? Rather than assuming, then, that there is always conflict and differentiation of interests, we look for their variation under different circumstances. Protest and conflict between individuals and sub-groups or groups and system agents then, may be not only a function of "symbolic arousal" (see Edelman, 1971) but also of very real breakdowns in the cohesion and integration of the social system. Political analysis deals not only with the interplay between interest groups but also with the bases for integration or disintegration of the social order. Here Smelser's (1963) analysis of collective behavior is useful. Mobilization, often through the use of symbols, is certainly an important step, in the creation of social movements and interest groups, but this is more likely to occur under structurally conducive conditions. Certain kinds of outbursts occur only at some times and in some places and not others, even when the mobilizing symbols are more universally available. Why, for example, in American history have feminist, black, and communal movements occurred with particular fervor in the 1840s and 1850s and the 1960s and 1970s?

Next, as Hall indicates, symbolic interaction theory has been accused of having no content, as dealing only with process. On one level this is a naive criticism, for to the extent that the perspective deals with meaning and symbolization, it is almost inherently a theory of content. It proposes that people are mobilized around symbols that have meaning for them; it thus offers to link culture and behavior. However, it is again at the level of system organization that symbolic interactionism lacks content. Hall discusses a number of important political processes, including bargaining and symbolic mobilization of support, whereby actors or groups gain influence over one another. But who are the actors? How did they become the actors in the political drama? What is the nature of the drama itself? At this point, symbolic interaction theory again needs to be supplemented with systemic theories and concepts. Contrasting "allocative theories" (or behavioral and interactionist theories) with systems theories, David Easton writes:

> Theories of party politics, interest groups, legislative behavior, political leadership, administrative organization, coalitions, voting behavior, and the like seek to understand varying parts of the allocative processes. They deal with those structures or practices through which the outputs are influenced, formulated, and implemented and that thereby determine the way in which the valued things of society are allocated . . . [In contrast] a systems approach draws us away from a discussion of the way in which the political pie is cut up and how it happens to get cut up in one way rather than another . . . To escape this bias, we need a theoretical framework that helps us understand how the very pie itself comes into existence and changes in its basic content or structure. (1965:474–475)

In short, we also need a theory to explain the existence of differential interests, the kind of pie they are negotiating over, and the consequences for the future of the pie of the outcomes of the negotiations. We need to explain who will have a better chance to win the biggest slices and who will exclude themselves or be excluded from the eating. We need to know what is negotiable and what is not at any given time. We need to understand the regulatory processes by which the pie is kept from being totally consumed and thus disappearing, if indeed the regulation is successful. With respect to these issues, there has been in the history of social theory an almost unbridgable gap between the process view of symbolic interactionism and comparative systems analysis that describes, for example, the political organization of industrialized and non-industrialized nations or that contrasts democratic and authoritarian or mass and pluralistic societies.

Symbolic interaction theory does not ignore the structural context of interaction. Hall agrees that meaning varies with a person's position in the social structure and that each situation has its own definition and imposes its own constraints. He makes use of macro-sociological concepts such as the Weberian notion of status groups to explain who the parties in conflict might be. But for the most part, the symbolic interactionist perspective relegates to the status of an "environmental constraint" on interaction what are some of the most important concepts for dealing with large scale changes in societies and other social systems over time. Areas with great political ramifications include technological innovations, changes in population size and system complexity, the distribution of decision-making functions, and characterizations of total societies as industrialized or non-industrialized, capitalistic or non-capitalistic. Such phenomena not only shape the content of issues for decision-making but they also help define who will make decisions, who will influence decisions, and what interest groups exist with what stake in which decisions. Hall's analysis, as an example, begins at the point at which actors have already entered the political arena. But the symbolic interactionist perspective cannot very conveniently address itself to issues of the type of arena and who has access to it. Some groups are systematically excluded, and not only because of a conspiracy by power-holders to maintain their own power, but also because of wider system characteristics. Hall's emphasis on the negotiated character of society and politics as interaction and exchange is misleading without taking a structural and systemic overview of society. The working class, for example, is among those potential interest groups so important to Marxist analyses but which tends not to be party to some negotiations for societal resources and which tends to be excluded or exclude itself from many of the political dramas Hall mentions.

In addition, the emphasis on relatively short-term interactions without investigating or conceptualizing the "state of the system" may offer a misleading view of social change. The view that the social order is negotiated and always in the process of construction, taken together with Hall's emphasis on electoral politics, coalitions, and lobbying, leads one to believe that change is always taking place. Yet some changes and some decisions, as radicals and cynics often point out, may not really be changing anything basic about the system. They may just be shifting around the same goods among the same set of players, providing the illusion of change while more general conditions remain the same (and in the process, the illusion of change itself may serve social control functions). (*Plus ça change, plus c'est la même chose.*) This criticism has certainly been made of electoral politics;

the personnel change, and this change is important to them from the perspective of their own interest maximization, but the overall course of American society and even many internal conditions may remain the same. Furthermore, for people inside the bargaining arena, it can be important whether X or Y wins a negotiation or whether A or B is decided. For people outside the arena, such changes are irrelevant and trivial; the basic structure of society remains the same for them. The difference can be seen in contrasting those analysts of social stratification who write from a middle class perspective and recognize infinite gradations, shifting alignments, and changes in resource allocation in society (because they are inside the arena), and those who write from the perspective of the outsiders, recognizing only two categories: haves and have-nots.

The need for a systemic view to complement symbolic interactionism is underscored in another way. Systems theories provide a perspective for looking at the total system such that functional areas of activities, networks of actors, and interest groups are identified not only in isolation but in relation to one another. They can deal with degrees of integration or differentiation with overlap (cross-cutting ties) or cleavage with links between actors and between system levels. These systemic distinctions have proven to have great utility in accounting for political behavior. Lipset (1960) has pointed out, for example, that while voting studies were designed as studies of conflict, voting in the United States has in fact been a key mechanism of consensus. But this in turn is a function of the number of cross-cutting loyalties and secondary organizations characteristic of American society, which do not permit strong cleavages to develop.

Finally, Hall himself points out the neglect in the symbolic interaction tradition of the concept of power and introduces a notion of power compatible with the perspective. But as used in the article (and as he states at the end), power is generally equated with "impression management" and is the result of the manipulation of symbols and information. This is not all there is to power politics, nor does it explain the differential access to power of various groups in the society. A more structural and systemic perspective can add to the understanding both of power bases and their distribution.

Symbolic manipulation is a relatively mild political weapon compared to some. Power politics also involves the use of force, the bringing to bear of great financial resources, the withholding of resources and decisions, or the invoking of legitimized authority to control others. Negotiating, bargaining and impression management give way quickly to guns, bombs, and huge sums of money. A Howard Hughes or a Rothschild does not gain or lose influence by the kind of impression he makes or the symbols he invokes. If a policeman points a gun at a Black Panther, that weapon is more than a symbol and certainly takes precedence over any other "definition of the situation." Bureaucrats can control and sanction welfare mothers not by symbolically manipulating them or bargaining with them but by invoking the "rules" to prevent them from obtaining their payments; sanitation inspectors, similarly, can close communes, merely by utilizing their legitimate authority and without any negotiation.

Symbolic interactionism's limited view of power as well as many of the other limits mentioned can be understood if the perspective is put in its own historical and societal context. The identification of symbolic interactionism with American liberalism is not an idle exercise in the sociology of knowledge but can reveal the ideological roots of some of symbolic interactionism's blind spots. For one thing, the perspective is one of the few indigenous American social theories. The following elements of the perspective can be fruitfully viewed in connection with middle-class liberalism and the American historical experience:

1. All of social life is negotiable. Decisions are more free than constrained.
2. The social order is an externally imposed artifact with no reality of its own.
3. People are autonomous and self-determining, able to define and act on their self-interests. Most action is voluntary.
4. Social life consists of continual encounters with new situations of uncertainty and ambiguity onto which people impose their own definitions.
5. Politics consists of bargaining and negotiation. *Talk* or non-verbal symbols are the primary means by which power is exercised. (T-groups and consciousness-raising groups are overwhelmingly middle-class.)
6. Everyone's opportunity to engage in political action is pretty much equal, so that people who make the best impression and know how to influence others in interaction tend to win in political situations. If some people don't have power, it is their own fault; they don't bother to compete for it.
7. There are many interest groups all competing for power and hence offering the possibility for real change in society.
8. Anything is possible. The social order is constructed and emergent rather than fixed and static.
9. Social change takes place through meeting the new demands of old interest groups and mobilizing new ones, rather than through structural reorganization.
10. People are out for themselves, to get what they can for themselves. But it's all a game. People pretty much agree to play the game like gentlemen and ladies. People cooperate in order to compete.

From this admittedly exaggerated characterization, it is possible to see the conditions under which the symbolic interactionist paradigm might be most appropriately used: under conditions of relatively low institutionalization and relatively equal power when the outcome of negotiations are to be explained. Under other circumstances and when other issues are addressed, its utility is limited and its insight may even be biased.

A DISTRIBUTIVE VIEW OF POWER

I am suggesting that Hall's use of symbolic interactionism for political analysis is limited in its utility without simultaneously employing concepts that link behavioral to systemic notions. Gamson's *Power and Discontent* (1968) is one excellent attempt to relate the two traditions of political analysis; he indicates the importance of considering the sets of interest groups in a society and the consequences of their interrelationships for the stability of the system. Other linking concepts are also needed. The remainder of this paper will sketch the outlines of one viewpoint that can perhaps help relate symbolic interactionism to systems theory and link the micro- and macro-levels. The perspective to be proposed builds on some systemic notions that are already implicit in the symbolic interactionist perspective; it attempts to add those systemic viewpoints that fill the gaps outlined earlier in symbolic interactionism.

The perspective is a distributive view of power. Power is seen as a distribution characterizing the system as a whole. It is not a property of persons of groups or elements; it is, rather, a property of parts of the system only insofar as they bear a structured relationship to one another. This perspective, like Gamson's, builds explicitly on both social psychological and sociological theories.

Many typologies and definitions of power and bases of power have been proposed; my treatment here builds on French and Raven's (1959) typology of power bases.

We may see four major kinds of distributions in the system: the distribution of *resources* (the basis of reward or punishment power); the distribution of *functions* (the basis of legitimate power); the distribution of *information* (the basis of expert power); and the distribution of *attractiveness* (the basis of referent power). Thus, to the extent that the power-holder is the one who makes decisions and sets policy in certain areas, as in Bavels's concept of leadership as function, then power is based on an asymmetrical distribution of functions. To the extent the powerholder has the most personal appeal (as in Weber's notion of charisma), then power is based on the asymmetrical distribution of attractiveness. To the extent that the influencer in the one who sets the initial or further definition of the situation in interaction as in symbolic interaction theory, then power is based on the distribution of information. To the extent that the influencer is the one who has something to exchange in return for compliance (as in Homans's exchange view of social life), influence would be based on the asymmetrical distribution of resources. By considering power a distribution characteristic of a *system* of relationships, we are able to take cognizance not only of major conceptualizations and typologies of power and authority but also of major formulations of the nature of social control in interaction. This perspective also stresses the *relational* nature of influence; a person influences another primarily because he has more of something than the other does.

Such a viewpoint has several advantages. First, it provides a systems perspective in which the relative equity or inequity in distributions of power bases can be identified. Social class (a concept to which Blumer, 1962, has attributed no reality since only groups, not classes, act) thus becomes a matter of inequities in the distributions; whether or not people with the same relative power position ever identify their common interests and act together is problematic. But the class can be identified on the basis of system distributions. We can identify oppressed classes that are low on the distribution not only of resources but also legitimate decision-making functions and information. Similarly, we can identify "power elites" that are high on all distributions. The overlap or lack of overlap between the power bases of power holders is also a variable. The power-holders themselves, in a systemic view, are constrained by the system and by their relations with those over whom they have power.

The whole system can be characterized, further, the interactional context identified, and the types of power struggles or their absence can be accounted for by this perspective. The whole system view can also take into account collective goals, for the distribution that exists in any given system is in part a function of the entire system organizing so as to adapt to its environment and attain shared ends. It is also possible to integrate political (or allocative) analysis with institutional analyses of society, since functions are distributed among elements of the system as well as resources, attractiveness, and information. How differentiated these are and how differentially distributed also provides a picture of the structural conditions of the society. Whether amounts of and kinds of power are distributed so as to create overlapping or differentiated interest groups is another politically important structural characteristic that could potentially be examined with such a distributive view of power. This view, finally, picks up on the symbolic interactionist notion of the importance of symbolization, but sees it as only one from among a number of bases of power and sees it, too, as distributed among people or system units.

This kind of systemic analysis is not an answer to any political questions. What I hope that it, or related perspectives, provide are the raw material: the content, the structural or systemic variables to complement an interactionist perspective and overcome some of its limitations. This is only one possible kind of linking concept between behavioral and systems political analysis, but hopefully it will underscore the need for others.

I should add that not all structural or systemic theories are structural-functionalist in the sense of following dry Parsonian dogma. Systemic theories include Marxism as well. Second, systemic theories have a bad name in part because of their use, not their merit. No paradigm is inherently conservative or radical—saying what is doesn't mean I like it that way; it may be the first step toward changing it. The resurgence of interest in symbolic interaction today (Goffman as front-page hero) *is* congruent with a prime contemporary radical strategy: "consciousness-raising," including a growing awareness of the "politics of everything"—that politics occurs not only in the realm of government and public life (from which realms Hall draws his examples) but also in private life. Power distributions and inequities occur in every sphere of life. Here is symbolic interactionism's radical potential: in women's liberation groups; in Paulo Freire's "pedagogy of the oppressed;" in R. D. Laing's "politics of experience." Consciousness-raising strategies often do involve the kind of exploration of face-to-face interactions and influence and channelling processes that symbolic interactionists write about powerfully and well. And the processes of coming together in such groups, of developing collective identification and new definitions of the situation in order to protest the existing order, are also well explained and documented in the interactionist collective behavior literature.

But significant change (as opposed to the expressive outlets that every society permits its discontented) involves structural critiques and structural changes in social systems. Those same consciousness-raising groups whose *process* can be explained as symbolic interaction often rely for their *content* on systemic theories to understand their current position and what must be changed. Here even structural-functionalism has its radical uses. The 1972 Massachusetts Sociology meetings, for example, explored how monopoly capitalism has functioned to perpetuate sexism, the exclusion of minorities, and the war in Vietnam, because certain forms of social organization have been functional for others. And many radical feminists believe that merely replacing a few powerful men with a few women through bargaining, negotiation, and influence processes (akin to the changing of the names of the players that is involved in the electoral politics and corporate lobbying in Washington of which Hall writes) is no change at all without changing the basic distributions of power and the structural and organizational constraints of the system. In fact, we could argue, insiders (elites) behave differently from outsiders regardless of sex, but real changes occur from shifting system boundaries, distributions, and activities. Which corporation's lobby gets the government's contract is one interesting phenomenon for socio-political analysis; another is the joint existence of corporations, lobbies, and government contracts.

In the struggle for a humanistic sociology that puts the person and his or her thoughts, feelings, and construction of existence back into society, I hope we will not lose the other question of trying to understand how and why many people's joint or independent activities fit together in the way they do, or clash and lay the groundwork for change. In large, very complex systems—the American nation, the spaceship Earth—not all of the elements are in direct contact, nor are they always aware of how their independently constructed behavior or outputs may impact on far distant parts of the system. To assume otherwise is to see vast conspiracies where there instead may be many people and groups, some powerful and some not, all equally restricted and bound by system constraints.

We have coined such terms as "institutional racism" and "institutional sexism" to explain the fact that a variety of structural circumstances above and beyond individual prejudices have together reinforced the exclusion of minorities—not necessarily conscious decisions or self-interest maximization on the part of people who willfully constructed their world around discrimination. We have also learned that changing the attitudes of key people toward women and blacks may not in itself be enough, without changing the structural arrangements of the society. Some employers, for example, may prefer women, wish to hire more, but the organization and demands of other parts of society, e.g., the training available in schools, the possibilities for family life, may reinforce an unplanned and unwilled exclusion. Symbolic interaction—the conscious, interpretive reaction of one person or group to another—is not the only component necessary to understand, or to change, social life. We also need theories that not only take into account situational constraints (because symbolic interactionism does, I agree, take them into account) but also systematically understand them in their own right.

The important question is not which paradigm is best under all circumstances, since all of them capture some elements of "the truth" at some times, but rather, how to find concepts and models which relate one paradigm to another. Symbolic interactionism does many things well that systemic theories may ignore. Its emphasis on the importance of symbols and humanity's symbolizing capacities, its emphasis on process and emergence and the creation of new forms of action through people's negotiations with and adjustments to one another—all of these should be built on and linked to systemic concepts. The task for the future is to confront perspectives with one another and from this confrontation develop ever more sensitive tools for understanding social and political life. William Cowper, an eighteenth-century British poet, wrote:

> And differing judgments serve but to declare
> The truth lies somewhere, if we knew but where.

REFERENCES

Becker, Howard S.
1960 "Notes on the concept of commitment." American Journal of Sociology 66 (July) 32–40.

Blumer, Herbert
1962 "Society as symbolic interaction." Pp. 179–192 in Arnold M. Rose (ed.), Human Behavior and Social Process. Boston: Houghton Mifflin.
1969 Symbolic Interactionism: Perspective and Method. Englewood Cliffs, New Jersey: Prentice-Hall.

Easton, David
1965 A Systems Analysis of Political Life. New York: Wiley.

Edelman, Murray
1971 Politics as Symbolic Action: Mass Arousal and Quiescence. Chicago: Markham.

Eisenstadt, S. N.
1971 Political Sociology. New York: Basic Books.

French, John R. P. Jr., and Bertram H. Raven
1959 "The bases of social power." Pp. 150–167 in Dorwin Cartwright (ed.), Studies in Social Power. Ann Arbor: University of Michigan, Institute for Social Research.

Gamson, William A.
1968 Power and Discontent. Homewood, Illinois: Dorsey Press.

Kanter, Rosabeth Moss
1972 Commitment and Community: Communes and Utopias in Sociological Perspective. Cambridge, Mass.: Harvard University Press.

Lipset, Seymour Martin
1960 Political Man: The Social Bases of Politics. New York: Doubleday.

Phillips, Almarin
1962 Market Structure, Organization and Performance. Cambridge, Mass.: Harvard University Press.

Smelser, Neil J.
1963 Theory of Collective Behavior. Glencoe, Illinois: Free Press.

The Negotiation of Identities: Ego Rejects Alter-casting or Who Is a Liberal?

PETER M. HALL

As I began reading Professor Kanter's commentary on my paper, my first response was to simply accept it because it was what I expected and because I had no time to develop a systematic rejoinder. But as I got to the end of her paper, I exploded in disbelief at her charge that the perspective I presented could be subsumed under American liberalism. If there is anything that I am not, it is an American liberal, and if there was anything I was criticizing in American sociology, political sociology, and symbolic interaction, it was its consensual, pluralistic, liberal bias. I can only conclude that Professor Kanter misunderstands or has misread my paper. Paradoxically, I feel it is the perspective that she offers as an alternative, functional systems analysis, which possesses the liberal bias. Consequently, I had to find time to reply because there are some things no self-respecting political sociologist can tolerate: being a behaviorist, yes, but a liberal, no.

A review of the section on the evaluation of the paradigm will show the kinds of criticisms made of pluralist political sociology. I also stated in that section that Mills (1966) was accurate in his view that Meadian social psychology as developed in the past was an outgrowth of liberal thinking but I noted that recent changes in symbolic interaction and neo-functionalism had de-emphasized consensus as the basis of coordination. The effect of these changes now makes symbolic interaction better suited to the realities of the world. It is ironic that Professor Kanter complains that I avoid the early Cooley cooperative harmonious approach which was so outrageously liberal and then attacks my current stance on one page as being cynical and on another as being liberal. Trying to put me in the liberal bag strikes me as bizarre. To paraphrase Phil Ochs, I'm not a liberal till I die. The recognition of stratification and power in my model and the awareness of institutional racism and the administrative ideology do not sensibly give rise to her "admittedly exaggerated characterization." The limits on the negotiation process as to exclusion-inclusion, definition of content, and success at

I want to acknowledge the strong support, useful criticism, and stimulating conversations with Yars Lozowchuk that helped me make this response. Professor Kanter, likewise, should be thanked for her positive comments about my paper and as well for raising significant issues about the applicability of the perspective.

93

bargaining are clearly stated and recognized in the paper. It is, from my perspective, precisely those "systems theorists" that Professor Kanter cites, Easton, Parsons, Eisenstadt, Lipset, and Gamson, who have argued the equity and liberalism of the American political system.

It is perhaps quite significant that Professor Kanter misses the import of my last paragraph where I point toward a future theoretical alignment between Lukács and Blumer, i.e., between Marxism and Symbolic Interaction. I did not say in the paper that symbolic interaction was sufficient by itself. In fact, I stated that currently symbolic interaction could not account for the state of the stratification system but it could deal with the processes that lead to the maintenance and change of that system. To paraphrase a current "agent of the social system," let me be perfectly clear about my position on systems analysis. I do not eschew systems per se but I cannot accept mechanistic or organismic systems models that are so obviously irrelevant to reality and which have been so completely exposed by Buckley (1967), Gouldner (1970), and Murphy (1971) among others. The choice of a systems model that makes more sense to me, and why I quoted from Gouldner's (1971) review on Lukács, is a Marxian one albeit one that takes into account the activity and humanity of men. It is my intent in a future work to propose an integration of symbolic interaction with conflict theory, a merger of Mead and Marx, to present a view of society that recognizes what Buckley (1967) calls morphogenic *and* morphostatic properties.

I do not deny the need to see the totality of the society, its interdependencies, feedbacks, and impacts, i.e., society as a system. I recognize the failure of sociology and the rest of the social sciences to do this. But I also strongly believe that current dominant systemic theories have failed to do this because their models have false assumptions or partial concerns. Professor Kanter makes claims for that perspective which so far have not been fulfilled and given the positions of its leading theorists are not likely to be fulfilled. I would argue that such theories or the results of studies or analyses using those models have not, on the whole, been totalistic, historical or comparative. They have not been capable of realistically dealing with social change. They have not been very much interested in or able to explain the development of social movements. They have shown limited capacities to understand the bases of exclusion from the American political system, what is negotiable in it, or "the kind of pie" that is being negotiated over. They have been singularly imprecise in dealing with the power of the policemen, Howard Hughes, or the welfare bureaucrat.

To exemplify this, one question Professor Kanter raises in her pitch for a systemic perspective is why in American history have certain movements arisen in the 1840s and 1850s and 1960s and 1970s? She cites Smelser's (1963) analysis of collective behavior as being useful because he can account for structurally conducive conditions for such movements. Having taught collective behavior for some years, I have found Smelser's analysis to simply provide labels and a proposed sequential ordering of conditions and to fail miserably when called upon to describe and analyze the process itself, or what he calls mobilization. It does not answer why movements arise at certain times. On the other hand, those who have read the interactionist works on those subjects (Blumer, 1951; Turner and Killian, 1957; Lang and Lang, 1961; Shibutani, 1966) are aware that both social conditions and historical contexts are given major emphasis. Interactionists have long noted that collective behavior occurred under certain social conditions and the particular forms of it also varied with conditions. It would be unfair to say that such analyses do not deal with the causes, characteristics, and consequences of collective behavior in a systematic fashion. I would argue therefore in favor of systems models that are premised on change and conflict and which seem closer to the real world of behavior.

It would be nice if old theories, like old soldiers, just faded away but they do not because their proponents actively seek to define the sociological situation for us all. However, rather than continue this particular discourse I will only cite Father Berrigan's recent response on "Meet the Press" when asked if he were a revolutionary or was he trying to overthrow the government? His response, more or less accurately, was that the government was doing a good job of overthrowing itself and that he did not have to overthrow it. Rather he would assist in picking up the pieces to build a better society. From my perspective, there is some justice in seeing government and systems theory as analogous.

Moving on, I find in reviewing Professor Kanter's criticism that I am charged with ignoring things that I explicitly said I would not discuss or that I mentioned in Part III needed additional and significant attention. To wit, I am not saying that there is always conflict and differentiation of interests or that the formulation of shared goals is restricted to a particular interaction situation. These issues together with the establishment of conditions for cooperation and conflict are dealt with in the section that differentiates power from authority. And insofar as power is concerned, I am not dealing at all with situations characterized by low institutionalization or relatively equal power nor do I equate power with impression management or symbolic manipulation. Finally, my analysis does not begin at the point of which actors have already entered the political arena. Whether "out" or "in" is an empirical question and should be clear from discussions of the negotiation process, the stages of the political process, the definition of issues, and the control of discontent.

I conclude that Professor Kanter has misinterpreted my aim in writing this paper or that I have not made myself clear. To set the record straight, this paper had a special focus and set limits as to its goals and coverage. It was not intended to be a complete analysis of politics nor a complete analysis of American politics. What I set out to do was a rudimentary analysis of contemporary American politics using symbolic interaction supplemented by the concept of power. Among the aims of the first part of the paper was the questioning of the myth of consensus as a basis for behavior and to seriously examine the existence of shared collective values as the foundation for the operation of the American political system. I concluded that the notion of shared collective values is a fiction or of limited significance because the United States is a complex, heterogeneous, pluralistic, differentiated, changing society. This fact means that subsociety interests and values predominate, that competition exceeds cooperation, and that dissensus is greater than assumed. In other words, that the social conditions of American society *at the societal level* give rise not to authority but to power. Shared values exist or can exist at the group or community level and in social movements where common identifications and cooperation are engendered. Therefore to understand the state and development of the American political system attention must be focused upon the distribution, bases, resources, operation, and *processes* of power as it relates to groups within the society. Such groups and their members are presumed to operate upon *self*-interest, i.e., those goals, values, conceptions, interests with which they identify as group members as well as individuals, and which they may share with others. *Self*-interest is not purely individualistic, materialistic, or necessarily rational. Individuals are clearly group members and affected by those relationships. My model of society sees these groups as acting to control their social environment given their own interests and resources. As they compete with one another, they attempt to set conditions which limit others and liberate themselves. In so doing, politics becomes involved because the state possesses the authoritative decision-making power over all groups within the society.

The structure and operation of the state in the U.S. have been characterized by many eminent sociologists as a stable democracy which is both legitimate and successful. The leaders of that democracy are presented as agents of the social system who are striving to achieve collective goals. Characterizations of the democratic political process see issues emanating from outside the state, being processed through the state and presented successfully as outputs which resolve the issues. In addition to this view, the functionalist perspective has sought to demonstrate the systemic properties that maintain the system, such as the existence of trust, the consensual aspect of voting and the assumption of shared values. My own view of American democracy is quite different as the section on power and authority should have implied. I chose therefore to examine the most basic relationship in a democracy, that of government to the mass, and to show that there were significant forms of power limiting the operation of democracy or, at least, which cast its alleged authoritative operation in a new light. I consciously chose to ignore force and coercion as forms of power, not because they do not exist, but because they are used far less in relation to the mass than other forms in American society. A full-scale analysis of politics, power, and American society would without question necessitate such a concern. I chose to limit the discussion of the exchange of tangible benefits not because I downgrade their significance or their pervasiveness but because others have discussed this and space was a problem. I chose to emphasize forms of power that I felt had been previously ignored or under-analyzed and which were extremely relevant to the operation of government and its relation to the public. I do not maintain that political impression management explains all such relationships and behavior but no understanding is possible, for example, of the use of force and violence by the United States at home and abroad without an awareness of the development of a legitimating climate through the utilization of information flow control and the symbolic mobilization of support. Dramatization or symbolic manipulation is not a relatively mild political weapon, at least, in its consequences.

It seems appropriate here to underscore the choice of the Goffmanesque perspective which Professor Kanter characterizes as under-socialized and overly calculating. While I believe there is much to recommend Gouldner's (1970) analysis of Goffman, my own interpretation of the dramaturgical model is that it is most appropriate when applied to formal organizations, secondary relationships, and status differences where instrumentality, competition, and control are dominant. The political arena meets the criteria of instrumentality, competition, and control and is therefore a setting in which the impression management model provides a singularly informative analysis. Except when confronted by external conflict and internal crisis, and not even always then, are there system conditions which lead to a "cooperative, collectively-oriented, utopian perspective." More often than not, we find a struggle between groups attempting to persuade sizable sectors of the audience to take their side or to conceal from others their selfish activities. Using the Goffmanesque model says nothing as far as I am concerned about all social relationships or those that are characterized as intimate or egalitarian and which may occur in primary groups. In fact, on the whole, in such situations it probably does not apply. In any case, it is a matter of degree and in the political arena, impression management makes good sense.

I would like to conclude this rejoinder by briefly discussing inadequacies to be associated with the concept of collective interest and with the view of those in office as agents of the total social system. It is my view that continual emphasis on the social control perspective of Parsons (1960) and Gamson (1968) grossly distorts analysis of American society qua society. First, I would call to Professor Kanter's attention a confusion she makes by failing to separate shared values and collective interests from systemic interests. What people believe collectively is not necessarily what maintains the system. Both Ellis (1971) and Mann (1970) have indicated the dysfunctions of consensual values. In addition, the common beliefs or values that conflict is bad and everyone is equal are quite the opposite from functional theories of the institutionalization of conflict and the theory of stratification. Should the response come back that there are shared beliefs of the opposite kind in reference to conflict and stratification, I would agree. I would also point out that this indicates the problems with the concept of collective interests. The problems are (1) that the meaning of such abstract diffuse terms is impossible to establish except as they apply to particular situations which will involve interpretation and negotiation; (2) that collective interests are not internally consistent and often contradict one another; and (3) that there exist multiple collective goals which when implemented require political behavior for implementation. Mann's (1970) article demonstrates the wide degree of dissensus in the society and strongly calls into question an earlier Parsonian (1959) statement that the collective goals of American society are to be found in the Preamble to the Constitution. Mann also indicates that it is those who share in power who need to develop consistent societal values. Their need to justify themselves is to be found in their use of those values. This was demonstrated by Hewitt and myself (1970) in relation to the President's activity during the Kent State-Cambodia situation.

The view that leads to that kind of analysis questions whether it is accurate to view officials as agents of the social system. Gamson's conclusion to his prize-winning volume laments his emphasis there on control and failure to discuss leadership in search of collective interests and shared values. He cites, in support of this, the active push of federal officials for "maximum participation of the poor" in the poverty program. My information, reading, and small scale participation with OEO told me that there was no such active push. The war on poverty was never fought except in terms of impression management. Gamson's agents of the social system are always partisans. While the President is president of all the people, he is also a Republican, a conservative, business-oriented, white and many more. Every action, whether in foreign policy or for what might be deemed a collective goal, is clearly coated with special interests, at least, in regard to elections or public opinion. And as labor has discovered in reference to the wage-price freeze, every attempt to achieve a collective goal means implementation that has differential affect on some groups and those groups negatively affected always are those out of power or low in resources.

Finally, even those officials who are deemed to be nonpartisan and objective like judges and civil servants have been found consistently to operate on the basis of subgroup values and interests. Those values and interests can change through socialization, insulation, security, and changing constituencies but they rarely can be explained in terms of a commitment to achieve collective goals. Those who clamor about collective interests and agents of the social system keep us in the dark. Hopefully, sociology and society will eventually come out of the cave and recognize the real world for what it is and change it to what it could be.

REFERENCES

Blumer, Herbert
1951   "Collective behavior." Pp. 176-220 in Alfred M. Lee (ed.), Principles of Sociology. New York: Barnes and Noble.

Ellis, Desmond
1971   "The Hobbesian problem of order: a critical appraisal of the normative solution." American Sociological Review 36 (August): 692–703.

Gouldner, Alvin
1970   The Coming Crisis in Western Society. New York: Basic Books.

Murphy, Robert
1971   The Dialectics of Social Life. New York: Basic Books.

Parsons, Talcott
1959   "Voting and the equilibrium of the American political system." Pp. 80–120, in Burdick and Brodbeck (eds.), American Voting Behavior. Glencoe: Free Press.
1960   Structure and Process in Modern Societies. Glencoe: Free Press.

Exchange Theory and Political Analysis

SIDNEY R. WALDMAN
Haverford College

In the last twenty years two major conceptual frameworks have played dominant roles in political science: structural-functionalism and systems analysis. The former has been primarily developed within the discipline by Gabriel Almond (1956) and his colleagues (Almond and Coleman, 1960; Almond and Powell, 1966). The latter has had as its most important advocate David Easton (1953, 1965a, 1965b). These authors have utilized the theoretical work of other disciplines, especially sociology (Parsons, 1949, 1951, 1954, 1961; Merton, 1957; Levy, 1952; Radcliffe-Brown, 1952), though they have adapted this work in trying to develop a conceptual framework suitable for the study of politics. The theoretical tradition on which Almond and Easton drew has come in for a variety of criticisms (Dahrendorf, 1958; Gouldner, 1959; Harsanyi, 1969; Hempel, 1959; Homans, 1964). These criticisms have prompted political scientists and their colleagues in the other social sciences to search for more adequate frameworks and theories.

It is the author's view that exchange theory, as originally formulated by George Homans (1961,1967) and refined by Peter Blau (1964), can with some refinements (Waldman, 1972) provide political science with the fundaments of the general theory for which it has been searching. Before introducing this theory to the reader, however, we want to briefly discuss some of the major problems with extant conceptual frameworks in order to suggest how alternative theoretical formulations can avoid these problems.

Both structural-functionalism and Easton's systems analysis have been centrally concerned with the problem of the maintenance and persistence of political systems and the processes and structures which enable systems to persist. Functional theorists, for example, have focused on the ways in which structures, institutions, roles, and norms contribute to the maintenance of the political system *as a whole*. System theorists have also been concerned with "the basic processes through which the political system, regardless of its generic or specific type, is able to persist in a world of either stability or change" (Easton, 1965a). This focus on what allows for and is functional for system maintenance has created substantial difficulties for those employing this orientation. As Harsanyi (1969) has pointed out, the analyst faces great problems of definition and empirical identification as he

101

tries to identify what is meant by the maintenance or persistence of the political system as a whole. He must make rather arbitrary distinctions between those characteristics of a political system that are and are not essential for maintaining its identity as "the same system." For example, how large are the changes that could be made in the political or economic institutions of American society without turning it into a "different political system" and without making us say that "the system has not persisted." If no changes can be imagined in the American political system that would enable us to say it no longer persists, one wonders about the utility of an analysis whose purpose is to account for persistence, a variable that does not vary. Even if we could agree on the bases of these distinctions, we frequently do not know enough about the empirical laws governing the operation of political and social systems to be able to state whether a given institution does or does not make any significant contribution to maintaining the essential characteristics of that system (Harsanyi, 1969). Furthermore, we are rarely in a position to be able to establish this one way or the other through empirical research. Even if we could solve this problem, showing that a social institution makes a significant contribution to the maintenance of the political system as a whole *does not explain the existence of that institution.* That explanation cannot occur until the causal mechanisms by which the survival needs of the society are translated into individual behavior are specified (Harsanyi, 1969). As George Homans (1964b) has argued, functional and system theorists have had more interest in establishing *what* the relationships of institutions are than in *why* they are as they are, more interest in the consequences of an institution for the system as a whole than in its causes. These theorists have not asked why particular roles or norms should exist at all and why particular institutions exist. They have not attempted to *explain* the functional relationships and interdependencies that their orientation has revealed because they have failed to provide the causal mechanisms which would account for or explain these interdependencies.

These difficulties and lacks have made a number of social scientists search for alternative theoretical orientations that might avoid some of these problems. One such orientation is based upon concepts and propositions that describe and explain individual behavior. A theory based on propositions about individual behavior has a variety of advantages. For example, individuals are more readily identified than systems. We are more likely to know what we are talking about in describing the interactions and exchanges between individuals than in speaking about the exchanges across "boundaries" separating "the political system" from "other systems" or "the political system" from its "environment." While it is difficult *to establish* the contributions given institutions, roles, and norms make toward maintaining a particular political system, it is much less difficult to establish the ways in which these institutions, roles, and norms benefit or harm given individuals, as they perceive things, and the ways in which these structures have affected individual men in the past. By focusing on the consequences of structures, roles, and norms *for individual men,* one can probably explain the structure and operation of given institutions in greater detail than one could by looking at the contributions these institutions make to the maintenance of a given system (Harsanyi, 1969). This is because it is easier to identify the specific ways in which given individuals and groups benefit from particular forms and procedures than it is to identify how specific forms and procedures are functional for maintaining the political system as a whole. Most important, by using the benefits that people obtain or expect to obtain as our basic explanatory variables, we do not have to worry about how these variables get translated into individual behavior because the proposition that men act to increase benefits and reduce costs is a sufficient explanation of their behavior. While we do not know the empirical laws that relate the existence of given structures to system maintenance, we do know the laws that largely describe and explain human choice and action. These are the laws of learning psychology, and we shall argue that they provide the basis of a paradigm capable of explaining political and social behavior.

THE BASIC PROPOSITIONS

The basic laws or propositions that explain human behavior are straightforward. As presented by Homans (1967), they are:

1. If in the past the occurrence of a particular stimulus or set of stimuli has been the occasion on which a man's activity has been rewarded, then the more similar the present stimulus situation is to the past one, the more likely he is to perform the activity, or some similar activity, now.[1]
2. The more often within a given period of time a person's activity is rewarded, the more likely he is to perform the activity.[2]
3. The more valuable the reward of an activity is to a person, the more likely he is to perform that activity.
4. The more often in the recent past a person has received a particular reward, the less valuable any further unit of that reward becomes to him.[3]

---

[1] "Similarity" of context, as it affects behavior, is that perceived by actors in making choices and behaving. The perception of similarities and dissimilarities, like all behavior, is rewarded or not rewarded, which affects whether the perception will continue.

[2] The pattern or schedule of reward of an activity, as well as its frequency, also affects the likelihood of that activity's occurrence. See Waldman (1972).

[3] The possibility of satiation suggested by this proposition may mask proposition two's impact on behavior, though it does not undermine the latter's validity. Proposi-

5. When a person's activity does not receive the reward he expects, or receives punishment he does not expect, he is more likely to be angry and, in anger, the results of aggressive behavior are rewarding.[4]

These propositions describe the ways in which behavior is conditioned by rewards, whether the latter result from the activities of other men or from the physical environment. Many of the most valued rewards that men receive, and they may be material or spiritual, selfishly or altruistically motivated, come from the activities of other men. For example, love, affection, esteem, a feeling of belonging, approval, wealth, power, food, shelter, sex, and safety can all be gained as a result of the activity of other men. Even knowledge can result from the activities of others. The activities of others, as all activity, depend on rewards. If we focus on the activity of men as the source of reinforcement for the activity of other men, as Homans (1961) originally did, we can also express certain of our basic propositions in an alternative form.

2. The more often within a given period of time a man's activity rewards the activity of another, the more often the other will perform the activity.
3. The more valuable to a man a unit of activity another gives him, the more often he will perform activity rewarded by that activity of the other.
4. The more often in the recent past a man has received a rewarding activity from another, the less valuable any further unit of that activity becomes to him.

It should be clear that the above versions of propositions three to five are particular cases of those same propositions as originally presented, the only difference being that in the latter formulation it is a man's activity that reinforces the activity of another whose behavior we seek to explain. We present both of these versions to suggest the connection between the latter one (Homans, 1961) and the more general formulation (Homans, 1967). Furthermore, once we recognize that men's activity is based on the experience of reinforcement and that men can reinforce each other and thus mutually affect each other's behavior, we recognize the possibility of the exchanging of rewards or, for that matter, of punishments as men try to gain the rewards they want by affecting each other.

---

tion two, like the other propositions, should be prefaced with the phrase, "other things being equal." The "other things" that must be equal are the other variables in the five propositions. In other words, all of these propositions operate together in affecting a man's behavior.

[4] For purposes of brevity and convenience we are presenting this proposition in this form, as Homans (1967) does. Homans (1961) and Waldman (1972) present it in a somewhat altered version which can be related to this formulation. The other formulation introduces the concept of distributive justice, a man's conception of his just due, and states that when a man does not receive what he considers to be his just due, he becomes angry, and in anger the results of aggressive behavior are rewarding.

The above propositions are hypotheses about behavior that have received a great deal of empirical support from the careful and painstaking research of psychologists (Skinner, 1938, 1953, 1959; White, 1958; Verplanck, 1955; Kimble, 1961; Berkowitz, 1962). They do not share the axiomatic nature of fundamental postulates about behavior in economics, despite the fact that they serve as the fundament on which we construct our theory.

Before we deal with the definitional, conceptual, and operational questions which these propositions present, we want to note the importance of one of their aspects, *viz.,* their great generality. The rewards, activities, and contexts described in these laws might be any rewards, any activities, and any contexts. Thus, the actions of parties, voters, leaders, businessmen, etc.; the contexts of guerilla war, totalitarian control, politics as usual, a legislative committee, etc.; and the rewards motivated by highly altruistic as well as narrowly selfish concerns can be accommodated by the theory. Consequently, it is possible that a great variety of phenomena can be explained in terms of this single set of propositions. The generality of the propositions is important for another reason. Any theory that attempts to explain social and aggregate phenomena in terms of propositions about individual behavior faces particular criticisms. One frequent criticism suggests that men do not act in groups as they act outside of groups, and that they do not act in particular roles as they would in other roles or in situations in which no role prescriptions exist. It is of course true that what men do depends on the (social) context in which they do it. Nevertheless, this criticism is not overwhelming because the propositions are as true when it is other men who are reinforcing behavior as when it is the physical environment. While activity, reward, and context may vary according to the social situation, e.g., whether men are or are not members of groups, the basic laws of behavior which relate activity to context and reward remain unchanged and operating. In fact, those very laws lead us to expect differences in human behavior, depending on the social context, because what is rewarded and reinforced depends on that context (Waldman, 1972). Thus, these propositions can handle a variety of contexts precisely because of their very generality.

It is time to deal with the definitional, conceptual, and operational questions raised by our basic propositions. Clearly, the concept of reward is critical to the theory. To understand it we must first introduce the construct "value" as "value satisfaction" in our view is the basis of reward. The degree to which something is valuable to a person depends on (1) the degree to which it is valued (by him, not the observer) and (2) whether or not he has gotten some, much, or little of it recently (Homans, 1967: 43–44). Thus, value has two components, each of which must be measurable for the theory to be testable.

Once we allow for reward, we must also allow for punishment. If reward depends on getting what one wants or needs, punishment is either being deprived of these or getting what one does not want or needs to avoid. Punishment may be conceptualized as a direct cost, the avoidance of which is rewarding.[5]

There are a variety of ways to establish how rewarding a given activity is to a person. One may ask him or subject him to psychological tests aimed at revealing this. These methods are not free of ambiguity and difficulty, but are useful and capable to some extent of reliable indication. One may also use the fact that people with similar backgrounds (experience) are more likely to have similar values (Homans, 1961: 45–46); at a minimum, this sensitizes us to the relationship between experience and values and allows a starting point for investigation. A third more exact approach is to observe behavior over given periods and in given contexts and infer what values (wants, needs) motivated that behavior. (Each of these approaches involves difficulties and limitations; see Waldman [1972: chap. 2] for a more extensive discussion of these.) With these various methods one can develop a profile of a man's values, which may be presented as a preference order.[6] With that preference order based on measurements or inferences made at a given time and within a given context, one can make predictions *at a later time* about which behaviors will be more valued than others. Clearly, this approach requires some constancy in men's values over time and contexts. This requirement is not overwhelming, despite the fact that men sometimes do change their values over time and contexts. Within limited time spans most men usually exhibit a certain constancy of values; in addition, we can infer value changes in the same way that we infer values.

Perhaps the most important proposition that can be derived from our basic propositions is that *men seek "profit" in acting*. To understand this term we must first define the concept, "cost." We conceptualize cost as a negative value, the opposite of reward, which is a positive value. Cost consists of the value of the activities foregone by a person when he performs a particular activity (in other words, the economic notion of opportunity cost). Cost may also be a directly experienced stimulus of negative valence or value.[7] Since cost is a negative value, by proposition three we may say that *the more cost a person incurs in performing an activity, the less often*

---

[5] Punishment should be distinguished from "negative reinforcement," as that is conceptualized by psychologists. Negative reinforcement describes the way in which the avoidance of punishment can be rewarding and reinforce behavior. Any behavior that is motivated by the avoidance of aversive stimuli has been negatively reinforced.

[6] Developing instruments capable of inferring preference orders is difficult though there is no reason to consider the task insuperable. Once such instruments are seen to be critical to theoretical development, the achievement of this task will be accelerated.

[7] These two ways of conceiving cost are related as the cost of a negatively valued stimulus or experience may be conceptualized as the avoidance of it which has been foregone.

he will perform it. "Profit" is the reward of an activity minus its cost (Homans, 1961:62).[8] The exchange of activities is more likely to occur if each of the parties to the exchange is gaining a profit. This is true in that each party to the exchange is giving the other behavior that is more valuable (in what it elicits) than costly and getting from the other behavior that is more valuable to other (in what it elicits) than costly. (Chester Barnard [1938: 253–255] originally formulated this principle of exchange.) We want to emphasize that two people may engage in exchange without one person's reward having to be greater than or equal to the other's, or his cost having to be less than or equal to the other's. All that is required is that each person's reward from the activity be greater than his cost. This is important in that it means that we do not have to face the problem of interpersonal comparisons of utility, an extremely difficult and perhaps impossible measurement problem. Since we are comparing the positively valued outcomes of a person with his negatively valued ones, we need only worry about his value scale without having to compare it to those of others.

The need for profit, i.e., the choosing of the more preferred alternative over the less preferred one, follows from our basic propositions. As proposition three suggests, *ceteris paribus,* the more valuable the reward of an activity is to a person, the more likely he is to perform that activity. Thus, if a person has two alternatives before him (as he sees things), he is more likely to choose the alternative which has the greater reward. In choosing that and foregoing the less rewarding alternative, he is seeking profit. It is also clear that action is affected not only by the value of a reward that some activity *might* bring, but by the probability that the activity will bring a reward, as that probability is judged by the actor. Men act as if they make estimates of the probable value of given activities. The taking into account of the probable rewards of action is described by proposition two. If two alternatives are open to a man, he is more likely, *ceteris paribus,* to choose that alternative that has been more frequently rewarded in the past, because that affects his expectation of being rewarded for that action again. It is also clear that a man's evaluation of the probable rewards of two alternatives is contextually determined (proposition one). In addition, the evaluation of given alternatives is conditioned by the degree to which a man has been deprived in the recent past of the particular rewards available from these alternatives (proposition four). Thus, our four basic propositions are intimately related to the

---

8 Even if satisfactions can be quantified, and in principle this is possible, they are not necessarily additive in some simple way. A given amount of satisfaction is not necessarily simply cancelled by an equal amount of dissatisfaction. In fact, the state in which roughly equal amounts of satisfaction and dissatisfaction derive from the same behavior may cause anxiety and itself be aversive (Homans, 1967). Thus, one must keep an open mind about whether rewards and costs may be simply summed. This is a matter for further empirical inquiry.

need for profit and together determine what is seen as profitable. In making these connections we are tying together some of the fundamental axiomatics of economic theory to empirically verified propositions of learning theory.

Now that the reader has been introduced to the concepts of reward, cost, and profit, we can show how they can be used in analyzing interactions between people (Homans, 1961:57–68). Let us assume that a person wants help from another and is willing to give him approval in return. We assume that the other is interested in the first's approval, for if that were not the case, the first would soon learn that approval would not get him the help he wants and would have to search for another commodity that the other values. By propositions two and three we can see that the rate of exchange of approval for help should tend to equal the proportion that profit per unit approval bears to profit per unit help (Homans, 1961:55). This "rate of exchange" is defined as the number of units of activity one person performs within a limited period in return for a specific number of units of another activity performed by the other. This construct is analogous to the notion of price in economics for price specifies the number of units of a commodity that may be exchanged for a given number of units of another commodity.

Given this definition of the rate of exchange characterizing the interaction between two people, we can identify some of the specific factors that affect this rate. As we suggested, profit is a function of two variables, reward and cost. Reward in turn depends on two components, the degree to which a person has been recently deprived of some valued thing and the degree to which that thing is valued. If the value a person seeks is highly scarce, given his demand and the demand of others for it, he is more likely to have been recently deprived of it. Thus, the supply of and the demand for particular values affect how profitable some given exchange will be. Further, given decreasing marginal utility (proposition four), as a person continues to exchange approval for help, each man's marginal profit decreases until the exchange terminates. It terminates when either man finds a more profitable way to employ his activity. Thus, the theory can explain and predict whether a given activity will continue to be performed or whether some alternative (including the alternative of doing nothing) will occur. In this way the theory can explain *changes* in activities over time.

What happens when we introduce some third person or persons into the analysis of the interaction of two people? We were doing that implicitly when we used the concept of cost since the activities foregone by a person include the interaction he could have had with some other(s). A person is interested in profitable interaction and will go where there are greater profits to be had if he knows of them. Thus, third persons cannot be ignored in the analysis of exchange. What is interesting about human interaction is that sometimes there are no alternative sources of the rewards that a person wants. This is why intrinsic attachments are important (Blau, 1964:35–38).

Insofar as a person enjoys interacting with another, not because he gets value satisfactions from that interaction that could be gotten somewhere else, but because the value he enjoys depends on its being from that other, he has no alternative source of that reward. Love can exemplify such a relationship.

We have suggested that men choose the more preferred over the less preferred alternative in seeking profitable action. Given this criterion of choice as a basis of action, we might ask whether this constitutes maximizing behavior. The concept of behavior that tries to maximize rewards is a multifaceted one, and we will not go into all of the facets here. (For a more complete discussion see Waldman, 1972: chap. 2.) One of the most important aspects of a maximizing strategy, in our view, is that a person *deliberately* decides how much of his resources he will devote to searching for alternatives better than those of which he is currently aware. We believe that few men regularly do this; rather, we believe that they "satisfice" (Simon, 1957: 247–254), *viz.,* that they develop minimally satisfying outcomes and cease searching for additional alternatives when they have achieved one of these outcomes. What is minimally satisfying to a man in a given context depends on his past experience in gaining satisficing outcomes in that context. If he has gained satisficing outcomes without great effort, his satisficing level will increase; if he has had great difficulty in gaining minimally satisfying outcomes, his satisficing level will decrease. In addition, the degree to which he is willing to search for additional alternatives in response to his failure to achieve satisficing outcomes, like everything else, is conditioned by his past successes and failures in such search behavior. The fact that men frequently limit their searching for additional alternatives means that the analyst must be aware of the limited number of alternatives which the actor perceives if he is to predict which of those alternatives will be adopted in a situation. Since one alternative every actor faces in every situation is that of searching for additional alternatives, the analyst must also have an idea of what constitutes minimally satisfying outcomes for an actor; otherwise, he will not be able to predict whether the actor will choose one of the alternatives that he already perceives rather than searching for additional alternatives.

We have devoted some attention to our first four propositions; now it is time to examine our fifth and last. That proposition states in part that when a person's activity does not receive the reward he expects or receives punishment he does not expect, he is likely to be angry. This immediately raises the question, what do men expect in the way of reward for their activities and what determines this? Our other major propositions are useful here. What a man expects is defined by proposition one (Homans, 1967:39). If in a given context in the past a particular activity of a person was followed by certain rewards, then that person will expect the same or similar rewards when he again performs that activity in that context. If those rewards are not forthcoming, he is likely to be angry. In fact, he is likely to be more angry the more often he was successful in that context in the past (proposition two) and the more valuable the reward he gained in that context in the past (proposition three).

We can clarify these bases of expectation by looking at some examples. If men have learned in the past that those who give more to others get more from them (and such men do get more because they can), they will believe that someone who is capable of providing a substantial reward to them should receive more from them. Similarly, if those who have received more from others in the past have been people who contributed more, men will expect that those who receive much from them must give much. If in their experience men have seen that those who present particular stimuli, for example, substantial age, nobility, or great skill, have contributed more and received more, then they will expect that those who have these characteristics will contribute more and receive more than those who do not have them. If these various expectations are not met and men do not receive what they expect, especially if *they* are short-changed, they will be angry. In a word, human conceptions of what is to be expected and what ought to be are largely affected by the experience of what has been in the past; what men think ought to be is, usually, largely what has been.[9]

Men learn to expect certain things in interacting with others. For example, they learn that those who have certain kinds of skill and training can, if they are properly rewarded, provide scarce and valued rewards (proposition one). They may also learn that those who exhibit certain ascribed characteristics, for example, being an aristocrat, if they are properly rewarded, can provide scarce and valued activities to them. Thus, men come to believe that people who exhibit certain characteristics, whether achieved or ascribed, can provide substantial contributions to them in return for substantial reward. They come to believe that giving much to these people in return for their substantial contributions is to be expected, that it ought to be, and that it is just. Similarly, men learn that if they exhibit certain characteristics which have allowed them to contribute much to others in return for much, they will be similarly rewarded by others for similar contributions. Thus, men come to see particular outcomes of certain exchanges as just and if they do not receive their just return, *viz.*, what they expect, they will be angry and may engage in aggressive behavior. Thus, proposition five as originally stated has as one of its special cases the following derivative:

_____

[9] One of the most interesting and important questions that political science can deal with is why some men, a minority, seem to be less affected by their experience of what has been in imagining and conceiving of what ought to be and taking their dreams seriously. The study of this can help us understand more completely than we now do how and why change occurs.

5. The more to a man's disadvantage the rule of distributive justice fails of realization, the more likely he is to be angry, and in anger, the results of aggressive behavior are rewarding (Homans, 1961).

Justice is a matter of expectation as to what rewards a man should receive for his contributions. The "rule of distributive justice" mentioned in the above formulation simply states that the more a man gives, the more he should get; the more he gets, the more he should give; and that those with certain characteristics, whether ascribed or achieved, are expected to make greater contributions and receive a greater return for them.[10] All of these expectations about the distribution of rewards depend on proposition one. This is because in the past the occurrence of particular stimuli (men exhibiting certain characteristics) was the occasion on which a particular activity (giving someone highly scarce and valuable activity) was rewarded (by a substantial reward). Thus, men come to expect that in similar contexts in the present the activity which was rewarded in the past will be similarly rewarded again; if those expectations are frustrated, they become angry. (See Waldman, 1972: chap. 2, for a more complete analysis of distributive justice.)

Every person in an exchange asks himself whether he is getting as much as other men, who make similar contributions and bear similar costs, get in circumstances like his. Every man asks whether the other is giving him as much as other men, in similar circumstances, would give. In any interaction men exchange not only primary benefits, such as help for esteem, but secondary ones, i.e., justice for approval. If a person believes that another has not given him his just due, he will be angry and is likely to disapprove of the other; he may even discontinue his exchanges with the other (depending on his alternatives), which may be costly for that other.

We have argued that what men expect as their just due is most frequently affected by their experience, that is, by what has been and what is. Often, however, what is changes and this and the anticipation or imagining of such changes cause differing expectations among people and disagreements about what is just (Homans, 1967:67). This is one fertile source of revolt and of social and political change.

Proposition five states that when expectations are frustrated, anger is likely to occur and, in anger, aggressive behavior is rewarding. This does not mean that aggression always results from anger. Aggression may be displaced or sublimated, especially if its expression in the past in particular contexts has resulted in punishment. We also note that aggressive behavior

---

[10] This is why men expect and need status congruence, and why status congruence affects the ease of interaction, the solidarity, and the productivity of men. See Lenski (1954) and Adams (1953). We also note in passing that the principle of distributive justice was originally proposed by Aristotle in his *Nichomachean Ethics,* Book V, chaps. 3 and 4.

in response to anger may not always be overt; it can occur in thoughts and fantasies as well as in more or less direct forms. Nevertheless, it is generally true that there is a strong tendency to attack directly the perceived frustrating agent and that the strongest aggressive response evoked by frustration is directed against the perceived source of the frustration (Dollard, *et al.,* 1939:39). Nevertheless, there are a variety of other responses to frustration that one can observe, for example, goal change, change in instrumental activity, fixation, anxiety, goal regression, and instrumental-act regression, to mention some of the most important ones.[11]

In concluding our discussion of distributive justice and our fifth proposition we simply note that men are not necessarily conscious of adhering to and demanding adherence to the principle of distributive justice. The requirement of consciousness applies to none of these basic propositions, though it is clear that some men have been conscious of some of them at various times. Rather, we are arguing that men behave *as if* they were conscious of these laws of behavior, both in their face-to-face interactions and as members of larger collectivities where such direct interaction does not occur between all members.

We have laid out the fundamentals of the exchange paradigm. It might be useful here to point out the processual or dynamic aspects of exchange analysis. It should be clear that exchanges between two or more people at time one affect their exchanges and the possibilities thereof at a later time. A person's being satisfied and being dealt justly with by another at an earlier period affects the probability that he will do business with that other at a subsequent period. The confidence built up over time as a result of trusts that have been kept and benefits that have been mutually enjoyed allows not only for more exchanges, but for more extensive exchanges over time. There are other aspects of the theory that explain change over time. The phenomenon of satiation can account for the termination of certain exchanges and the initiation of others, either with the same or different persons. Changes in interactional patterns and structures can also result from changes in values, changes in resources, and changes in conditions (which cause changes in what is instrumentally valuable). Thus, the theory can accommodate and explain interactional (structural) change as well as stability. We note these sources of change to emphasize the dynamic possibilities of the theory.

We also want to note one other aspect of the theory, its ability to accommodate conflict as well as stability and consensus. Unlike functional and systems theory, exchange theory does not have as its central task explaining the survival and maintenance of political systems, though this is something with

---

[11] We will not discuss the factors that affect which of these responses are likely to result from the experience of frustration. A more complete analysis of this may be found in Waldman, 1972: chap. 2.

which it surely must be concerned. Consequently, it has no need to overstate and only focus on the degree of consensus and social integration found in political systems. By examining the needs and wants of different individuals in a system, the theory must take into account the fact that different individuals and groups frequently have competing needs and that, to some extent, the satisfaction of the needs of some may preclude or limit the satisfaction of others. A theory of politics that turns on the ways in which men try to increase their net benefits, of necessity, is concerned with the possibilities of conflict that can result from human values. Exchange theory can as readily analyze social conflict as social cooperation and even "those uneasy mixtures of the two that characterize most empirical social situations" (Harsanyi, 1969:515). To the extent that men are rewarded by cooperation based on the exchange of benefits, the theory can handle cooperation. To the extent that men are frequently in greater or lesser conflict as they try to gain rewards and as they interact to determine the terms of trade of their interaction, the theory can handle conflict. Exchange may be of benefits or deprivations, rewards or frustrations. The gains from exchange may be constant sum, which is conducive to conflict, or variable sum, which is conducive to cooperation. Thus, exchange theory itself is not biased in looking for social integration and stability and overlooking disintegration and change.

APPLICATIONS

We have introduced the major concepts, propositions, and theoretical orientations of exchange theory. Now we wish to suggest how they may be used to explain certain phenomena in which political science is most interested. These illustrations of the applications of the theory are taken from Waldman (1972) and are meant to exemplify the great variety of problems to which the theory can address itself. They in no way exhaust either the important questions in which political science is interested nor do they exhaust the possible applications of the theory. They are merely suggestions of how exchange theory might be applied in political analysis.

One of the most central questions facing political science is why certain governments and regimes are accorded legitimacy by their citizens and others not. Exchange theory suggests that men want certain values satisfied (usually material ones, but often nonmaterial ones such as dignity, basic rights, etc.) and enter into exchanges with the state in order to be so satisfied. They also expect that what they get from the polity will be a just return, given their contributions to it. If these expectations of value satisfaction and a just return are not met, citizens become angry. Since they are neither receiving minimally satisfying value satisfaction nor justice from the state (as they perceive matters), they are less likely to accord it legitimacy. As we have stated earlier, what a citizen expects from his government is a function of his past experience; thus, two citizens in two different political systems may be objectively gaining the same return in exchanges with their respective governments with one extremely frustrated and the other not at all so. This is why one cannot only look at the objective payoffs a citizen receives to determine whether he will accord legitimacy to his government; rather, one must judge this in terms of what he expects, which depends upon his past experience.

This explanation of legitimacy (for a much more complete explication see Waldman, 1972: chap. 4) is not inconsistent with other explanations that have been offered; in fact, it refines and explicates some of them, such as that of Max Weber (1947). Exchange theory suggests that tradition-based legitimacy is accorded because a regime (or government) is viewed as having produced value satisfactions in accord with expectations; this leads to an intrinsic valuing of the former. If a regime is associated over a moderately long period of time with repeated rewards for an individual, then that regime itself and the traditional way it does things will come to be valued; this occurs through the process of secondary reinforcement. The traditional way of doing things will be perceived as conditions (stimuli) within which certain available activities regularly bring valued rewards. After a period these conditions will themselves come to be viewed as valuable and rewarding. This, of course, is characteristic of the process of secondary reinforcement. As with traditional authority, charismatic authority is also based on the provision of extrinsic benefits in ways that meet expectations. The charismatic leader is perceived as having powers over the environment which allow him to satisfy the needs of his followers. If he is unable to satisfy these needs over an extended period, he will lose his charismatic authority. Similarly, authority based on rational-legal methods must also satisfy the wants and needs of the citizenry if it is to be maintained. Our own recent failures that have led to the questioning of reason and law should have sensitized us to this fact.

As Homans (1967) and Blau (1964) have shown, power depends on the ability to unilaterally provide valued rewards that are scarce. (For a more complete discussion of why this is so and how it follows from our basic propositions, see Waldman, 1972: chap. 3.) Governmental officials and other political leaders are sometimes in a position which allows them unilaterally to provide scarce and valued services to the citizens of some system. In return for that provision, they gain power over that citizenry. If, however, they demand more power than the citizenry believes they should have, given their contribution, that power will not be considered legitimate. Once one recognizes that the according of legitimacy to government depends on what a citizen gains in his exchanges with government, one also becomes sensitive to the factors that affect a citizen's expectations, for example, the alternatives he perceives as open to him. This sensitizes the analyst to the importance of the political market structure in which the citizen finds himself and in which he engages in exchanges. For example, if a citizen is faced with a government that completely monopolizes the supply of values that he wishes, he will be in a less strong exchange position than if he were in a more competitive situation in which many would-be leaders competed in offering those values in return for power and legitimation.

Our analysis of the according of legitimacy can be indirectly tested by looking at those individuals who do not accord legitimacy to culturally given goals and means, those whom Robert Merton (1957) calls the anomic. These individuals, and they may be found in most societies, are generally unable to achieve culturally approved goals through culturally approved means. Their failure to achieve success in "legitimate ways," as specified by social norms, means that those ways promise no reward; consequently these means come to be perceived as having little value. If the according of legitimacy to given institutions and procedures did not depend on those institutions and procedures producing rewards, then the withholding of legitimacy by the anomic would not occur as it does. Frequently, the anomic adopt deviant methods of achieving culturally approved goals and consider these alternative means legitimate, precisely because they are instrumental in producing desired ends. The reasons for this response by the anomic can be understood if we remember that all activities must be rewarded if they are to be maintained. People can be expected to act in socially approved ("legitimate") ways only if they are adequately rewarded for that action.

Another major concern of political science is political culture, in particular whether a given polity's culture will be parochial, subject, or participant (Almond and Verba, 1963:3-42). Once again exchange theory focuses on the reward bases of action in predicting the kinds of attitudes and behaviors given citizens will exhibit with respect to their political system. If a person finds that activity in a given setting, for example, the public sector, is not productive of rewards, he is likely not to engage in activity in that setting (proposition one). Equally important, he is less likely to be aware of the setting, recognize it with some cognitive clarity, and worry about it. The awareness of context, as any activity, is a function of reinforcement experience. A person's awareness of some context is more likely if that awareness has been the occasion on which some activity of his has produced rewards. If an awareness of the political context has not been instrumental in allowing a person to be rewarded, he has little incentive to maintain and develop that awareness. In contrast, if a man's parochial activities, *viz.,* those in the private sector, have been frequently reinforced with valued outcomes, those activities and that context are most likely to concern him and command his effort (propositions one, two, and three). If the rewards for political action are negligible and the rewards for more private actions, such as planting and harvesting, are more frequent and more valuable, then the opportunity costs of political activity are high, and men, seeking profit, will focus their energies on their private rather than public concerns. (These same factors that affect a parochial's behavior are not absent in the experience of more participant and politicized individuals and frequently affect the latter's degree of politicization by limiting it.) The more difficult the attaining of rewarding political outcomes is perceived to be, the more likely a man is to see the great relative costs of such action; in such an instance, the citizen is likely to choose more rewarding contexts and activities and focus his cognitive and evaluative powers on nonpolitical contexts.

If a citizen finds that his activity in the political sector is rewarded and that these rewards are greater than the opportunity costs of that action, he is likely to engage in political action. In this case the question arises, will he primarily be a "subject competent," that is, one who focuses on the output processes of politics (for example, decision-making at the bureaucratic and rule-applying level) or a "citizen competent," one who focuses on the input processes of the system (the rule-making process, for example). (These terms come from Almond and Verba, 1963:19–21.) A citizen's orientation and activity, according to exchange theory, will depend on his reinforcement experience. If in the past his attempts to improve his outcomes by dealing with the rule appliers and rule adjudicators have been successful, he is likely to maintain that activity (propositions one, two, and three). If, on the other hand, that activity was less frequently successful and produced less valuable rewards than his attempts to influence the lawmakers, he will be input rather than output oriented. Obviously, success in both contexts will lead him to employ both strategies in his attempts to satisfy his wants and needs. The citizen learns which stimulus situations, given certain activities, produce or allow rewards (proposition one) and thus repeats those activities. If the rewards available from the bureaucracy differ from those available from lawmakers, then satiation with one kind of reward may cause a change of focus in attempts to get the other kind.

Basically the same analysis can be used to suggest why certain groups within a given political system are more likely to turn to politics than other groups. For example, those Americans who find their activities in the private sector not rewarded, for example, many black Americans, face lower opportunity costs for action in the public sector and so turn to that sector to gain value satisfactions. The degree to which they will maintain this politicized orientation will, of course, depend on the degree to which their activities are rewarded, that is, on the degree to which the public sector is responsive to their needs and demands, and on the degree to which their activities in the private sector are rewarded. The same approach can also explain why those with particular interests, who have much to gain or lose from given policies, can be expected to engage in vigorous political activity in trying to affect those policies (compared with those marginally affected by such policies, for example, the general public), especially if they have succeeded in the past in such activity. This of course is why special interests in many systems frequently exert more influence over policy than their numbers might make one expect. It also explains why "issue publics" in America are narrow, fragmented, diverse, and more powerful than their numbers warrant. Obviously, there are a variety of other aspects of political culture that one can explain with exchange theory (see Waldman, 1972: chap. 5), but our purpose is only to illustrate possible applications in this area rather than to present a more complete analysis.

Another major concern in political science involves explaining and predicting the degree of governmental power, control and responsiveness in various political systems. For example, why is power highly centralized in particular systems with the autonomy of political parties, interest groups, courts, and the like sharply limited, whereas in other systems no such centralization and restrictions occur. Once again, we look for the incentive basis of action. Thus, we argue that certain elites learn that if they do not preclude or highly limit the decentralization of power, substantial demands will be made of them, which they cannot satisfy without sacrificing more prior goals. Thus, the centralizing of power allows them the rewards they wish and, given their alternatives, is profitable. We can illustrate our argument with an example. In a country that wishes to capitalize rapidly, the surplus generated by the economy is in scarce supply and cannot be distributed to the people in the form of consumer goods if it is to be used for capitalization. The leadership of such a country is therefore unable to legitimate its rule or motivate the behavior it desires by providing sufficient material benefits to its people in the form of a higher standard of living. Consequently, such an elite either tries to develop other bases of legitimacy and motivation or protects its rule and attains its purposes through coercion and the limitation of free choice by its citizenry. The substitute benefits such a regime tries to give its citizens include medals, feelings of righteousness, and a collective consciousness because these "rewards" are not scarce and not costly. In addition, it attempts to raise the value of the protection it gives its citizens by raising the image of a grave threat of danger from external sources. Since men's expectations of the exchanges they engage in with their government depend on their experience, this kind of regime tries to control the experience its citizens have. It does this by limiting their contact with the outside world, by rewriting history, and by limiting the degree to which men can freely imagine and talk about alternative ways of living. All of these attempts arise because of the basic exchange relationship between the leadership of particular kinds of regimes and the citizens of those regimes, a relationship that requires the governments involved to somehow motivate the behavior of its citizens in desired ways. Because these regimes cannot achieve this motivation by material incentives because of a scarcity of resources, they must develop substitute resources or utilize coercion. In this exchange relationship, as it develops over time, both government and citizens reinforce each other's behavior by acting in the desired ways or failing to do so.

Once the leaders of this type of political system have been able to use system resources to achieve capitalization, their resource problem becomes less difficult. Consequently, they develop the capacity to satisfy some of the material wants of their citizens and use these satisfactions to motivate the latter and gain some legitimation. Thus, these regimes gradually become more legitimate and responsive as they develop.

The above analysis suggests why most political systems, as they develop economically, become more responsive. Those who rule generally learn fairly quickly that their citizens will be more productive and contribute more to the economy if they are not frustrated in their expectations and if they receive their satisficing share of benefits. The granting of economic, social, and political benefits, *ceteris paribus,* strengthens the legitimacy of the political and socioeconomic order and motivates the performance of system members in their various tasks. Thus, when resources are sufficiently plentiful, the provision of these benefits is compatible with the growing strength of the political system and with the goals of the established powers. Thus, it is no accident that mass suffrage, political freedom, and greater consumer benefits have been a by-product of and then a contributing force to industrialization, both in western and in communist political systems. It is, of course, true that the forces producing pressures toward greater freedom may be limited by the constraints of the established powers, who fear for their positions in a period of growing democratization and heightened expectations. Nevertheless, these pressures are real and can be explained by the goals, resources, and exchange requirements of the governments and citizens of political systems.

The exchange paradigm can be used not only to explain the degree of governmental power and responsiveness in the allocation of values, but also to explain the nature of the particular policy areas in which governments are most likely to intervene. We will illustrate how the theory can do this by examining the factors producing governmental intervention in the production of collective goods. (We are indebted to Olson, 1968, for much of this argument.) If one examines governmental action, one realizes that frequently it produces what the economists refer to as "public goods" (also called "collective goods"), *viz.,* goods that all, or practically all, members of the collectivity benefit from, *regardless of their contribution to the collective effort* that produced these goods. For example, the American victory in World War II benefited almost every American, regardless of his contribution to the war effort. A successful medical effort to cure cancer will benefit many, regardless of their contribution to that effort. In cases such as these the individual has little incentive to keep up his end of the costs, since he can increase his profit by not contributing. If, however, all members of the collective tried to increase their profit by not contributing and being "free riders," the collective effort would fail and the benefit from the collective good would not occur. Because few desire the latter outcome, the citizenry supports the intervention of government, which makes contributing to the production of the public good compulsory. The citizens support this because they recognize that certain benefits can only occur in this way. This analysis of why governmental intervention frequently occurs in the production of "collective goods" makes sense in exchange terms. The problem of collective action occurs because men, in seeking to increase profit for themselves, have an incentive not to contribute to the production of collective goods, thereby precluding that production from which they all would benefit. Because they can profit from the production of these goods, even if they contribute to that production (as long as others also contribute), they support governmental compulsion of such contributions. Thus, the problem of collective action and its solution can be explained and made sense of by exchange theory. (For further analyses of different kinds of governmental interventions in various policy areas see Waldman, 1972: chap. 6.)

The exchange paradigm, as we have tried to suggest, can account for properties of the political system, for example, whether government and regime will be perceived as legitimate, what certain aspects of the political culture will look like, and to what extent government will have power and be responsive. It can also help us understand the dynamics of *substructures* within the system, for example, political parties. All cooperative systems, of which parties are one type, have to secure the cooperation of their members (Barnard, 1938). For this to occur, individual members must derive profitable satisfaction from participation and membership. In addition, any who would organize cooperative systems must have some incentive to do so. Thus, one can see the political party as involving the efforts of political entrepreneurs to secure the services of party members and supporters and simultaneously maintain conditions of exchange satisfactory to both the latter and to themselves. The value satisfactions that are exchanged and are the bases of our major parties are readily apparent. Parties cut the voter's information costs, give him some basis of decision about candidates and policies, suggest what the important issues are, provide him with an opposition and ways of criticizing the in-party, organize the effort to run for office, etc. Parties and their leaders provide these services in return for the rewards of office, status, power, money, social solidarity, ideology, etc. (Many writers have explicitly or implicitly concerned themselves with the kinds of exchanges that occur between political parties and their clientele; for example, see Downs, 1957; Eldersveld, 1964; Michels, 1959; Barber, 1965; Schlesinger, 1965.) Since the party as an institution is based on the exchange of rewards, its fate depends on its ability to satisfy the wants and needs of its supporters. One sees this in examining what happened to the urban political machines that were so powerful earlier in this century in America. When the needs of immigrants for personalized welfare and job help, which urban machines distributed, were no longer so pressing, one of the bases of urban machines was undermined. Similarly, when these machines no longer provided the best channels for upward mobility for these immigrants and when the creation of a civil service based on merit reduced the number of jobs that machines could provide, the latter's ability to satisfy certain needs was reduced and its power reduced.

Once one recognizes that parties are based on systems of exchange that allow certain value satisfactions to political entrepreneurs and their followers, one also sees that those individuals within parties who are unilaterally able to provide highly scarce resources, whether money, victory, organization, ideas, or whatever, will be relatively powerful. One also sees that the degree and nature of cooperation between local, county, state, and national party organizations depends on the degree to which mutually profitable outcomes can be facilitated by such cooperation (Joseph Schlesinger, 1965).[12] For example, whether the constituencies of two candidates are congruent, enclaved, or disjointed affects the mutual profitability of these candidates' cooperating, and consequently the likelihood of their cooperation. One can identify the kinds of exchanges that can go on between party organizations; for example, in this country local Democratic or Republican organizations provide workers for the candidates of state and national parties in return for money and the support of well-known national candidates. Insofar as the national organizations cannot withhold resources from local organizations, and they sometimes cannot withhold money or the party name, they will be in a relatively unfavorable bargaining position vis à vis the local organization; this of course leads to a decentralization of power within "national parties." When the national party has such a popular national candidate (for example, Eisenhower) that it does not need local workers to help gain victory, it will be in a stronger exchange position vis à vis local parties. If the national party lacks such a candidate and critically depends on the help of local and state workers in highly populated and competitive states, then it will have to grant favorable terms of trade to the local and state party organizations within those states in coming to terms with them. If, however, it can mobilize nonparty regulars to work for its candidate, as Eugene

---

[12] Schlesinger (1965) has shown to what extent party organization can be explained by using exchange theory, though he does not *explicitly* utilize the theory in his analysis.

McCarthy was able to do, its position vis à vis state and local organizations improves. When a state's electoral votes are assured beforehand, do not amount to much (this depends on how close the presidential election is expected to be), or are impossible to get, the state organization has little to give to the national organization and consequently little bargaining power. Thus, by examining the kinds of exchanges that occur between national, state, and local organizations, one can begin to specify the conditions that will favor one or another of these organizations as they cooperate with each other; in addition, one can begin to specify the conditions which will preclude or limit their cooperation. These various analyses, of course, can be used to explain and predict the strength of given parties in given contexts.

One can use exchange theory not only to analyze the nature and degree of cooperation between different party organizations in different contexts, but also to analyze the nature of leadership within parties in various settings. For example, the paradigm can help one understand whether the iron law of oligarchy, as originally formulated by Robert Michels (1959), will describe the relationship between party leaders and party members in American parties. We have already suggested that the unilateral provision of scarce and valued resources is the basis of power. Consequently, an examination of the degree to which this unilateral provision occurs in any party will tell us whether some member(s) of that party will be in a dominant position. Insofar as the leaders of the major American parties need people to enter their structures at the top and bottom of those structures, viz., attractive candidates and party supporters and workers, and insofar as these people are not totally dependent on these parties for their livelihood and other highly valued rewards, party leaders will not be in an overwhelmingly strong bargaining position vis à vis these contributors and potential contributors (Eldersveld, 1964). Since party organizers and leaders are often dependent on their clientele, they cannot totally ignore the wants and needs of the latter. Obviously, political parties that are not so dependent on gaining the support of attractive candidates and party supporters will be more powerful vis à vis their clientele. Thus, the exchange paradigm suggests the conditions under which Michels' description of party rule can be expected to hold and the conditions under which it will not hold. The same analysis can be used to predict the conditions under which moneyed interests will be powerful within parties and the conditions in which they will be less powerful (see Waldman, 1972: chap. 7).

The exchange paradigm can also be used to shed light on the dynamics of interest groups. As Robert Salisbury (1969) has shown, the origins, growth, lobbying activity, and demise of interest groups may be better explained if one regards these groups as based on exchange relationships between entrepreneurial organizers, who invest capital in a set of benefits, and prospective members to whom these organizers offer benefits at a price, that of membership. Perhaps the most interesting result of this theoretical analysis is that it accounts for the weakness of interest groups in bad economic times and their strength in good times. Given the exchange bases of interest groups, organizational entrepreneurs must provide profitable benefits to their members and must themselves derive profit from their activity if they are to sustain it. In bad economic times these entrepreneurs frequently have great difficulty providing the (usually material) benefits necessary to mobilize and sustain a membership. Their potential clientele also has difficulty providing the resources and material support required for a sustained organizational effort. In good times the necessary material rewards are more readily attainable by both members and organizers. This analysis, of course, is not surprising, given our understanding of the requisites of successful material exchange. What is surprising is that it leads to an expectation *antithetical to that predicted by the major theorists of interest group behavior,* for example, David Truman (1951). Truman's homeostatic theory of group organization argues that potential group members are activated when times are bad. The homeostatic equilibrium in group structure, which Truman predicts, does not describe what occurred in the initial decades of agrarian interest organization in this country nor, for that matter, does it describe the actual rise and fall of union strength in America (Salisbury, 1969:9). If Truman were right, group membership would rise in conditions of adversity, and decline or stabilize when adversity was overcome; this has not occurred historically. Thus, exchange theory not only leads to a prediction antithetical to that dominant in writing about interest groups, but to a prediction confirmed by empirical research (Salisbury, 1969). The theory also suggests why another theory of interest group formation, the so-called "proliferation hypothesis," also fails to account for the rise and fall of interest groups in American history. The proliferation hypothesis suggests that as social differentiation occurs, differentiated sets of values or interests result with the consequent appearance of more and more diverse specialized groups in the political arena. This hypothesis, however, does not take into account the resource requirements necessary for the exchanges that are the basis of interest group formation. Consequently, it cannot explain the declines of interest groups in the last hundred years, notwithstanding the growing structural differentiation of American society in that period.

Once one recognizes the exchange requirements that must be met for interest groups to form and be maintained, one becomes sensitive to the social capital necessary for these organizations to exist, whether that capital is in the form of material, solidary, purposive, or expressive benefits (Clark and Wilson, 1961). With the exchange orientation one becomes sensitive to the need for ways of predicting what kinds of social capital exist in given situations and in what supply they exist. One also can make judgments about the substitutability of one kind of social capital for another, for example, of solidary benefits for material ones (Salisbury, 1969: 18). One can estimate how valuable particular benefits will be to some potential group by asking if there are any alternative sources of such benefits; for example, in the post-Civil War farming frontier there were no associations that offered solidary rewards, which made the formation of agrarian interest groups, which offered them, more likely and more viable (Salisbury, 1969: 18). One can even assess the different propensities to form different kinds of groups in different conditions. For example, it requires relatively little capital for an entrepreneur to establish an expressive or purposive group. The capital that one does need, of course, is the belief on the part of potential members that working on behalf of the cause is not a useless enterprise (this capital can be depleted). While it is true that it takes little to form an expressive group, it is also true that for the same reason it takes little to factionalize such a group, in fact, much less than it takes to form a new group based on material benefits. This is why groups based on material benefits have leadership tenure that is fairly secure, while expressively based groups are frequently characterized by insecure tenure, bitter schisms, and fragility. In sum, the exchange paradigm gives one the theoretical orientation that permits such insights and allows an understanding of the origins, growth, and breakdown of political interest groups.

There are a variety of other phenomena one might attempt to explain with the exchange paradigm. In our book (1972) we not only focus on the subjects already mentioned (in much greater depth), but also devote substantial attention to explaining the conditions under which conflict will be peacefully adjusted. We do this by examining the requirements for those exchanges that allow the peaceful resolution of conflict. (See Coleman, 1964, for a similar analysis that implicitly utilizes exchange theory.) We also account for certain characteristics associated with modernization and political development; for example, we utilize the exchange paradigm to account for the structural differentiation and cultural secularization that accompany economic and political development. We also show how the same theoretical orientation can explain the institutional decay that frequently accompanies modernization (Huntington, 1965). In dealing with these topics and those we have previously discussed, our purpose has not been to exhaust any of these subjects. Rather, we have tried to suggest that the exchange paradigm can account for a variety of important aspects of different phenomena. We could have focused on other phenomena and on other aspects of those we examined. Our purpose, however, has been to illustrate the potential of the theory in explaining a great variety of phenomena. We hope our effort will stimulate further refinements of the theory and its utilization and testing in empirical research.

AN AGENDA FOR FUTURE WORK

We have introduced the basic concepts, propositions, and orientations of exchange theory and illustrated some of their possible uses. We want to conclude by discussing some of the analytic and empirical problems that confront the theory and that necessitate further work. For example, it is not clear how propositions two and three of the theory work together in affecting behavior. As currently formulated, these propositions are of the form, "the more x, the more y." Obviously, we would prefer a more precise relation to be specified in our basic propositions (ideally taking the form of a mathematical function). We would also like to know how powerful frequency of reward is in determining activity compared with value of reward. In other words, we would like a model that more precisely compares the forces described in these two propositions. We would also like to have a better understanding of the processes of stimulus and response generalization (and discrimination) as they operate *in natural settings,* since these affect the specific ways in which proposition one conditions behavior. While these are theoretical questions, they may be solvable only through careful empirical research. The same might be said about the question, do men really satisfice rather than maximize? It would be desirable to be able to establish whether men follow the satisficing procedures we describe. In our work we simply posit that men satisfice, and while there are a variety of reasons to believe that this is the case, additional evidence is needed.

Given that men do satisfice, the development of instruments capable of revealing the satisficing levels of a man in a given context would be of great use. These instruments should be capable of generating such measures before a man acts so that they can be used to predict his action. Exchange theorists could also benefit from methods which would permit inferences as to what outcomes a man expected from actions in a given context. It would also be desirable to know the factors that determine the degree to which individual men consider what might be and what ought to be in developing expectations and notions of what satisfices. If the exchange paradigm has the promise we believe it to have, men's values are critical in determining what they do. If this is true, research on the factors that affect these values takes on a new relevance. Work in this area may be as important as any task facing social science.

We suggested in our opening remarks that policies, procedures, and institutions come to be and are maintained because they allow profit to men. Rarely, however, does a given structure or policy allow profit to every man, let alone allowing equal profit to everyone. Some men benefit more from given structures and policies than others, and the existence of particular structures and policies frequently reveals differences in the power of individuals in given systems. In doing an exchange analysis of particular structures, we frequently must be able to identify *before the fact* the more powerful members of a system, since it is the consequences of structures for these individuals that determine whether they will be maintained. Insofar as exchange theory explains the bases of power, it gives the analyst clues as to who will be more powerful in given contexts, but further work is required to develop ready means of predicting differences in power in given settings.

Exchange theory posits that men satisfice. As we have suggested, a variety of alternatives usually satisfice a given man in a particular context. This creates a problem for the analyst who would like to make *unique* predictions about which alternative will be chosen in a given context. Ideally, exchange theory might be refined so that we could reduce the number of satisficing outcomes for a man in a given context, and thereby attain more unique predictions of behavior. If this cannot be done, at least work might be initiated which examines the processes by which a man chooses among the various alternatives that are satisficing. Is a man's selection of one from among the set of satisficing alternatives random or are there systematic factors that affect his choice?

Exchange theory presents the political scientist with some additional operational tasks. Further work is required in developing instruments capable of allowing the observer to infer what a man values and what his preference order is in a given context. These instruments must measure values before a man acts, so that the values generated by the instruments can be used to predict his action. While a variety of psychologists have discovered the difficulties involved in developing such instruments (Robinson and Shaver, 1969: 405–504), we believe that the theoretical developments that led to exchange theory will stimulate work in this area. Finally, empirical work is required to test the exchange analyses that have already been attempted (for example, Waldman, 1972).

Work on these theoretical, operational, and empirical tasks is worth doing, in our view, because of the promise of the exchange paradigm and because of its various strengths in comparison with competing frameworks and orientations (see our opening remarks). Whether the exchange paradigm, as tested and refined, can provide political science (and, for that matter, social science) with the general theory for which it has been searching, only time will tell. In the meanwhile, the work is exciting and challenging as it attempts to bridge the micro-macro gap and the various disciplines into which we have divided the study of men.

126

PERSPECTIVES IN POLITICAL SOCIOLOGY

REFERENCES

Adams, S. N.
1953 "Status congruency as a variable in small group performance." Social Forces 32: 16–22.

Almond, G. A.
1956 "Comparative political systems." Journal of Politics 18 (August): 391–409.

Almond, G. A., and Coleman, J. S. (eds.)
1960 The Politics of Developing Areas. Princeton: Princeton University Press.

Almond, G. A., and Powell, G. B.
1966 Comparative Politics. Boston: Little, Brown.

Almond, G. A., and Verba, Sidney
1963 The Civic Culture. Princeton: Princeton University Press.

Aristotle
Nichomachean Ethics

Barnard, C. A.
1938 The Functions of the Executive. Cambridge: Harvard University Press.

Barber, J. D.
1965 The Lawmakers. New Haven: Yale University Press.

Berkowitz, Leonard
1962 Aggression: A Social Psychological Analysis. New York: McGraw-Hill.

Blau, Peter M.
1964 Exchange and Power in Social Life. New York: Wiley.

Clark, Peter, and Wilson, James
1961 "Incentive systems: a theory of organization." Administrative Science Quarterly 6 (June): 129–166.

Coleman, J. S.
1964 "Collective decisions." Sociological Inquiry 34 (Spring):166–181.
1966 "Foundations for a theory of collective decisions." American Journal of Sociology 81 (May): 616–627.

Dahrendorf, Ralf
1959 Class and Class Conflict in Industrial Society. Stanford: Stanford University Press.

Dollard, John, et al.
1939 Frustration and Aggression. New Haven: Yale University Press.

Downs, Anthony
1957 An Economic Theory of Democracy. New York: Harper, Row.

Easton, David
1953 The Political System. New York: Knopf.
1965a A Framework for Political Analysis. Englewood Cliffs, N.J.: Prentice-Hall.
1965b. A Systems Analysis of Political Life. New York: Wiley.

Eldersveld, Samuel
1964 Political Parties: A Behavioral Analysis. Chicago: Rand McNally.

Gouldner, Alvin W.
1956 "Some observations on systematic theory." Pp. 1945–1955 in Hans Zetterberg (ed.), Sociology in the United States. Paris: UNESCO.
1959 "Reciprocity and autonomy in functional theory" in Llewellyn Gross (ed.), Symposium on Sociological Theory. New York: Harper, Row.

Harsanyi, John
1969   "Rational-choice models of political behavior vs. functionalist and conformist
        theories." World Politics 21 (July): 513–538.
Hempel, Carl
1959   "The logic of functional analysis" in Llewellyn Gross (ed.), Symposium on
        Sociological Theory. New York: Harper, Row.
Homans, George C.
1961   Social Behavior: Its Elementary Forms. New York: Harcourt, Brace.
1964a   "Contemporary theory in sociology," in Robert E. L. Faris (ed.), Handbook of
        Modern Sociology. Chicago: Rand McNally.
1964b   "Bringing men back in." American Sociological Review 29 (December): 809–
        818.
1967   "Fundamental social processes" in Neil Smelser (ed.), Sociology. New York:
        Wiley.
Huntington, Samuel P.
1965   "Political development and political decay." World Politics 17: 386–430.
1968   Political Order in Changing Societies. New Haven: Yale University Press.
Kimble, Gregory A.
1961   Hilgard and Marquis' Conditioning and Learning. New York: Appleton-Crofts.
Lenski, Gerhard
1954   "Status crystallization." American Sociological Review 19: 405–413.
Levy, Marion J.
1952   The Structure of Society. Princeton: Princeton University Press
Merton, Robert K.
1957   Social Theory and Social Structure. Glencoe: The Free Press.
Michels, Robert
1959   Political Parties. New York: Dover.
Olson, Mancur Jr.
1968   The Logic of Collective Action. New York: Schocken.
Parsons, Talcott
1949   The Structure of Social Action. Glencoe: Free Press.
1951   The Social System. Glencoe: Free Press.
1954   Essays in Sociological Theory. Glencoe: Free Press.
1961   Structure and Process in Modern Societies. Glencoe: Free Press.
Radcliffe-Brown, A. R.
1952   Structure and Function in Primitive Society. Glencoe: Free Press.
Salisbury, Robert
1969   "An exchange theory of interest groups." Midwest Journal of Political Science
        13 (February): 1–32.
Schlesinger, Joseph
1965   "Political party organization." Pp. 764–801 in James March (ed.), Handbook
        of Organizations. Chicago: Rand McNally.
Skinner, B. F.
1938   The Behavior of Organisms. New York: Appleton.
1953   Science and Human Behavior. New York: Macmillan.
1957   Verbal Behavior. New York: Appleton.
1959   Cumulative Record. New York: Appleton.
Truman, David B.
1951   The Governmental Process. New York: Knopf.
Verplanck, W. S.
1955   "The control of the content of conversation: reinforcement of statements of
        opinion." Journal of Abnormal and Social Psychology 51: 668–676.

Waldman, Sidney
1972   Foundations of Political Action: An Exchange Theory of Politics. Boston: Lit-
       tle, Brown.
Weber, Max
1947   The Theory of Social and Economic Organization, trans. Talcott Parsons.
       New York: The Free Press.
White, S. H.
1958   "Generalization of an instrumental response with variations in two attributes of
       the CS'." Journal of Experimental Psychology 56: 339–343.

Some Limits of Exchange Theory in Politics

DAVID EASTON
University of Chicago

The editor has asked me to comment on some alternatives to systems analysis for the formulation of theoretical approaches to political phenomena at the most general level, with special attention to exchange theory as presented by Sidney R. Waldman in this issue. Unfortunately it is difficult to locate well-developed alternatives. There have been a number of promises, as in decisional and group points of view. But these have appeared only in a loose and informal way with no rigorously developed formulation. Only one other general theoretical orientation has hitherto attracted the attention of a significant number of political scientists, namely, functional analysis. At one time there was some indication that this point of view might receive sufficiently serious attention to offer a fully elaborated alternative. Unfortunately functionalism in political science has never taken shape as anything more than a posture toward research.

FUNCTIONALISM IN POLITICAL ANALYSIS

As an orientation toward research, political functionalism has held that variable structures and processes can be shown to meet functions that are constant across systems. For political science, the utility of this rule of thumb, borrowed intact from sociology and anthropology, is not to be underestimated. In its day it sensitized comparativists to the need to look behind the formal similarities and differences in political institutions for a more insightful understanding of the relevance of these institutions for the systems of which they were a part.

Perhaps one of the reasons that functional analysis did not generate an independent body of concepts and orientations is that its major expositor, Gabriel Almond, never did commit himself to this point of view exclusively, or for long. Instead, initially he folded into it parts of Parsonian action theory[1] and subsequently[2] adopted many of the major categories of systems

---

[1] G. A. Almond, "Comparative Political Systems," 18 *Journal of Politics* (1956) 391–401.

[2] G. A. Almond, "Introduction: A Functional Approach to Comparative Politics," in *The Politics of Developing Areas,* eds. G. A. Almond and J. S. Coleman (Princeton: Princeton University Press, 1960) pp. 3–64; G. A. Almond and G. B. Powell, *Comparative Politics: A Developmental Approach* (Boston: Little, Brown, 1966).

analysis. In the end functionalism became subordinate to a truncated form of systems analysis that has tended to dominate in Almond's writings. Indeed it is these very kinds of additions to the functional orientation that have provided the major foci of interest in Almond's theoretical writings. Each year, however, brings about modification in Almond's theoretical presuppositions so that it is not easy to pin them down to a stable point of view.

It is no accident of personality that functionalism has not remained intact and has not been elaborated into a body of coherent, systematic concepts. The fact is that if one confines oneself exclusively and strictly to a functionalist approach, there is little theoretical content available. The central feature of functionalism is found in the general hypothesis that the maintenance of a social system is dependent upon the fulfilment of specifiable processes (functions) at some minimal (although empirically undesignated) level of adequacy. Hence the search has been for the identification and agreement on the minimal requisites for the maintenance of social systems, either in general or by types.

The theoretical limitations of this approach have been dealt with exhaustively in the literature. Functionalism directs attention to system maintenance rather than system change although, under attack, efforts have been made in recent years to overcome this predisposition for the status quo. But the shift to a more comprehensive mode of analysis that includes both stability and change has produced increasing complexity and inelegancies in functionalism. The outcome is that to the degree to which functionalism seeks to include change, it becomes less appealing as a theoretical approach.[3]

Furthermore, insofar as there have been systematic efforts in political science to search out the prerequisites for special system types, such as democracies, or political systems in general, we have been led into an unremitting numbers game. How many minimal requisite functions are there for the maintenance of political systems? It proves impossible to achieve consensus on either the numbers or types. This in itself need not be a permanently damaging kind of handicap; in time, we might assume, some kind of consensus might emerge in the scholarly community. In fact, however, no one has come up with a logical way of finalizing any list. It is impossible to demonstrate logically that a given function is either necessary or sufficient for system maintenance (or for change, for that matter).

These and numerous other kinds of shortcomings are now familiar complaints in the literature. But far more important for understanding the limits of functionalism is the recognition that the specification of requisites represents about all the theoretical content that functionalism, in itself, contains. Most of the other rules of comparison, set forth by Merton in his well-

---

[3] See G. A. Almond and G. B. Powell, *op. cit.*

known piece on structural-functional analysis, are really little more than guidelines, important for all research, whether or not it calls itself functionalism. Insofar as the writings of a functionalist, such as Parsons, contain richer theoretical implications they follow from his introduction of action theory and, recently, of some elements of systems analysis rather than from any logical expansion of functionalism itself.

Theoretically, functionalism is rather sparse. Beyond the rules of interpretation formulated by Merton and the enumeration of various functional requisites, this approach has proved itself unable to give birth to second and third generation categories of analysis. Having made certain assertions about the minimal prerequisites of a system and about the variability of structures for meeting these, the research worker is left to his own devices in analyzing structures, their components, compatibility, determinants, and consequences. At the very point where we might have expected a conceptual framework to have been of some use, functionalism in political science leaves off. And even if it did not stop there, any additional conceptualization would probably have no intrinsic connection to the functional base of the analysis. By itself functionalism leads to a dead end.

To assess functionalism in political research in this way does not imply that it has left no beneficial residue. Whatever its shortcomings it has contributed significantly to the tendency in contemporary political science to move beyond individual reductionism and to recognize the advantages of interpreting political life as an interconnected system of behavior. In effect it has lent support to what systems analysis has argued more directly and vigorously: that a political system is other than the "summation" of the way in which individuals or groups act. Adequate interpretation of political processes requires us to view political life as an interrelated pattern of behavior, an organized complexity. It is not enough to demonstrate the consequences of what happens in a political system for the individual members as such, although this is a necessary part of all analysis. We also need to be able to relate political processes and structures, constituted by individual and group behavior, to the operation of the system as a whole. The point of reference for understanding the significance of the parts of a system is their relationship to the system as a whole. Functionalism has helped to signalize the importance of this part-whole connection, however inadequately it was able to follow through on this insight.

EXCHANGE THEORY AND ECONOMIC MODELLING

In recent years one other potential alternative to systems analysis has appeared. It has taken the form of economic modelling, or more generally, a rational choice approach. As the name suggests, this is not a descriptive way of looking at political data but rather a formal model based upon assumptions of rationality and availability of information, patterned after thinking in economics. Few have argued that it is possible to formulate a general theory for politics along these lines. Most attention has been restricted to fairly well defined subfields of political research. Forays in the direction of rational choice modelling have led into party behavior[4], coalitions[5], conflict, voting, and other miscellaneous topics in which the subject matter has seemed to lend itself to the application of this mode of analysis[6]. An occasional scholar has sought to cast the rational choice model more broadly so as to include large parts if not all of the discipline[7]. Here I shall confine my remarks to only one such comprehensive approach, that of exchange theory, as represented in the article of that name by Waldman in this issue. Furthermore, I shall treat Waldman's application of this approach to politics independently of exchange theory as formulated by its inventor, George Homans. In this way we can avoid attributing to either analyst the particular or fortuitous formulation of the other.

At the outset, it is important to bear in mind that few seriously elaborated theoretical approaches can ever be said to be wrong or totally useless. Every approach opens its own window on the empirical world and permits the analyst to focus on somewhat different aspects of the same general landscape. For this reason, especially in the early stages of theory development in a discipline, it may be wise, indeed, necessary, to accept and use more than one approach depending upon the specific problem to which one wishes to address himself. Only as theories appear that are increasingly inclusive in character will it be possible to opt in favor of a single theoretical approach. Certainly we have a long way to go before reaching this stage in any of the social sciences. What this means is that we have a twofold test for theoretical adequacy: how useful is the approach for understanding and explaining political reality; how much of that reality is the approach successful in helping us to explain.

It has been my contention that systems analysis stands fairly high on both these measures. It can help us to understand the real world; it concerns are comprehensive, leaving out little that has been of central importance to political science in the past and opening up numerous new areas of interest. Nonetheless I have always maintained that at this early stage in the development of political theory we can expect that other approaches may have some

---

[4] Anthony Downs, *An Economic Theory of Democracy* (New York: Harper, Row, 1957).

[5] William H. Riker, *The Theory of Political Coalitions* (New Haven: Yale University Press, 1962).

[6] See *Public Choice* for characteristic areas of application.

[7] J. M. & W. C. Mitchell, *Political Analysis and Public Policy* (Chicago: Rand McNally, 1969); L. L. Wade and R. L. Curry, *A Theory of Political Exchange* (Englewood Cliffs, N.J.: Prentice-Hall, 1969).

special significance which, by the nature of the theory, is not readily associated with systems analysis or some other orientation.[8]

Economic modelling, for example, has the peculiar merit of constructing ideal rules for making rational choices. If we seek to act rationally, this model guides us in calculating how we ought to behave, given the specific goals and other constraints of varying types of situations. Models of this sort usually do not pretend to describe the real world or to predict how people will in fact behave. On occasion, where the conditions permit, claims have been made that behavior does follow the model.[9] But most advocates of rational choice theory would argue that it has different purposes. First, it provides a normative model against which actual behavior can be compared. Deviations from behavior expected according to rational criteria will suggest modifications in the model to bring it into closer accord with reality. In this way, in due course, the model may become genuinely explanatory of behavior. Second, however, if economics itself is used as an illustration, even on the basis of rationalistic assumptions we may be able to make certain predictions about the real world. The unreality of the assumptions can be ignored as long as the theory does in fact permit useful predictions. The proof of the theoretical pudding is in the eating. The adequacy of the theory lies not in its formal validity or correspondence to the real world but in its usefulness for predictive purposes.

However acceptable these criteria may be in economic modelling, the rational choice approach in political science has not yet been cultivated to the point where it permits of any significant degree of application, especially of the kind required for prediction. Hence we do not as yet know whether the measure of success in economics (which is itself subject to serious challenge) will be achieved in political science as well.

Exchange theory, however, is not economic theory even though, as developed briefly in the paper by Waldman, it certainly stands as a subset of a rational choice approach (see his p. 107). Waldman seems to differentiate his theory from that of economics on the grounds that his five basic axioms are not identical with those underlying economic theory (see his pp. 103–104). More important, he argues that they are grounded in experience and have been verified through testing in the area of learning theory. In the end, however, in their general tenor, the axioms do not diverge markedly from those of economic theory. Although Waldman is correct in asserting that economics does not subscribe explicitly to the five axioms, exchange and economic theory do converge on one underlying assumption. Both consider it essential to postulate that men seek to maximize (or in more modest for-

---

[8] David Easton, *A Framework for Political Analysis* (Englewood Cliffs, N.J.: Prentice-Hall, 1965) p. 23.

[9] See Riker, *op. cit.* This claim is of course not undisputed.

mulation, in Simon's term, to satisfice[10]) their utilities—they choose "the more preferred alternative over the less preferred one" (see Waldman's p. 107); and that men act *as if* they were making a rational calculus of outcomes—they "act *as if* they make estimates of the probable value of given activities" (his p. 107, my italics), so as "to increase benefits and reduce costs" (his p. 103). Both exchange and economic theory are variants of a rational choice model for which the cost-benefit or profit-loss calculus is central.

THE EMPIRICAL STATUS OF EXCHANGE THEORY

The adoption of the economic calculus as its basis creates the first major difficulty for exchange theory as proposed by Waldman. He seems to want the best of two theoretically opposing worlds. At times he explicitly states that learning theory has demonstrated the acceptability of his axioms as a description of actual behavior. At other times, however, he waxes less enthusiastic and ventures only so far as to say that people act "as if" they did calculate costs and benefits. If the latter is what Waldman really intends to argue, then in the end we have no more than we have in economics, a rational model that acts as a criterion to assess behavior, not as a description of actual behavior.

The ambiguity about the factual status of the behavior model leaves the reader in something of a quandary. If Waldman were to stick with economics in postulating a *homo economicus* and just interpret the objective behavior of individuals *as if* they did engage in a rational calculus, we would not have to be concerned about the validity of the assumptions. Economists protect themselves cleverly from the need to become psychologists. They have argued that they can be indifferent to the validity of the rational choice model. All they need to worry about is whether by adopting it, they are able to predict economic outcomes. As long as their theories permit testable predictions about states of the economy, they argue, the correspondence of the rational model with the empirical world is irrelevant. But Waldman does not seem content with an interpretation such as this. He implies it only as a secondary and less dependable line of defense. He seems to want to take his stand on the validity of the hypothesis that in every enduring social relationship there must be some kind of exchange of activities or sentiments assessed by the participants to be mutually rewarding.

The five axioms of exchange theory, based as they are on operant condi-

---

[10] It is arguable, of course, that a strategy of "satisficing" is in fact a maximizing one. Under special conditions, such as uncertainty, an actor can maximize his utilities only by choosing the most satisfactory course (satisficing) without waiting for the additional information that at a later time might dictate a different path of behavior. To maximize one's utilities it makes sense at times to satisfice.

tioning psychology, are clearly not free from serious question as statements about actual behavior. Yet, to put Waldman's position on its strongest grounds, I shall assume for this discussion that they are beyond dispute. The benefit of the apparent cost of this concession will be that if under these generous circumstances Waldman's exchange theory does not measure up to its claims, it would be much less likely to do so if its postulates themselves were demonstrated to be questionable.

THE SIGNIFICANT THEORETICAL CONTENT OF EXCHANGE THEORY

In addition to the doubt that Waldman leaves about the truth status of his exchange theory, a second point is clear.[11] If exchange theory did provide us with a valid description of individual behavior, it would be of genuine assistance to political analysis, but not for the reasons offered by Waldman. He is seeking to develop a general theory of politics, one that will presumably cast its net as broadly as possible so as to include the whole range of important political problems to which students of politics have characteristically addressed themselves. In fact, at most, he appears to offer us a theory, not about all major aspects of politics, but only about political learning. And even this more restricted intention may not be entirely fulfilled. Waldman is probably only developing what appears to be a special theory about the motivations for various modes of political participation and involvement.

Contrary to his own apparent beliefs, even assuming the validity of exchange theory, it can only be construed as a partial theory of politics. It deals with the cost-benefit conditions under which members of a system will be likely to support various political institutions and practices. It represents, therefore, a psychologically based theory about the input of support, not a broader theory about how the learning of political attitudes, beliefs, and practices occur and certainly not a general theory capable of coping with the whole range of major political problems.

---

[11] Space prevents me from dealing with a number of erroneous statements that Waldman makes about systems analysis in politics. For example, [p. 101,] Waldman states that Harsanyi criticizes the *persistence* concept of systems analysis as well as the system *maintenance* premises of functionalism. Yet nowhere does Harsanyi mention the concept of persistence or show any awareness of systems analysis as a theoretical approach in politics. The fact is that Waldman has himself extended Harsanyi's critique of functionalism to systems analysis without informing the reader. Further, Waldman commits the easy error of associating persistence with system maintenance. A normally careful reading of my *A Systems Analysis of Political Life* should quickly dispel this confusion. But if not, I would refer him to the special Epilogue of the recent French edition of the same book where I emphasize, once again, the difference and to "Systems Analysis in Politics and Its Critics" in H. J. Johnson (ed.), *Political Theory* (Holland: Reidel, 1972), forthcoming.

Thus Waldman's exchange theory in politics seems to be at its best when it explores the grounds upon which individuals continue to support given structures, institutions, and practices, or reject them for new ones. As Waldman puts it, ". . . policies, procedures, and institutions come to be and are maintained because they allow profit to men" (p. 124). In systems analytic terms, exchange theory helps us to understand variance in the area of the input of support (especially specific as against diffuse support[12]) for the regime, the authorities (government), and structural subunits in a system such as parties and interest groups.

This limited scope of the theory reveals itself in any review of the examples given in the section on applications in Waldman's paper. These illustrations deal largely with the way in which material and psychic benefits are exchanged for the support of members for government, organizations, or leadership. The discussion of legitimacy, for example, deals largely with the support for the regime. Political participation, in another illustration, is interpreted as an indicator of support for the system. Similarly support is the focus of the section dealing with the centralization of power and the responsiveness of government. These phenomena are viewed as being based on "an exchange relationship between the leadership of particular kinds of regimes and the citizens of those regimes" (p. 117). Waldman is here analyzing the conditions under which subjects-citizens will have sufficient incentive to support their leaders. Similarly in another application of the theory, the members of a political system are seen as supporting their government in the production of "collective goods" because of the net benefits they can expect and do experience.

In brief, then, as it is presented in Waldman's paper, exchange theory does not deliver on the promise of breadth that we might expect from a general theory of politics. The exchange produces something that looks more like a partial or special theory of politics adapted to understanding the bases of support for various political objects, as broad as the regime and government and as narrow as specific organizations like parties or interest groups.

If exchange theory were acceptable as a valid explanation of political motivation, this partial theory would be no mean achievement in itself. The input of support for various political objects is a crucial aspect of all political systems, and a partial theory around this theme would carry us well beyond our present knowledge. However, unfortunately, any possible application to political matters of even this limited theory would first have to overcome the numerous hurdles put in the way by the prevalent criticism of its underlying operant conditioning psychology borrowed from B. F. Skinner.

---

[12] See my *A Systems Analysis of Political Life* (New York: Wiley, 1965), Part III.

THE REDUCTIONIST TENDENCY OF EXCHANGE ANALYSIS

In addition to offering us, at most, a partial theory of the motivational basis of political support rather than a comprehensive general theory, exchange theory presents us with a third major hurdle. It is founded on an individualistic psychological approach to political analysis. This leaves the theory in an awkward position for dealing with structural phenomena. If this is true and if, for the sake of argument, we do not challenge the theory's psychological validity, the benefits it gives us in dealing with motivational problems are undercut by the losses we suffer in being unable to deal systematically with structured interaction.

Exchange theory runs into difficulty if it seeks to demonstrate either the way in which political structures arise and change, or the constraints these structures place on behavior, or the consequences they have for the operation of political systems. Fundamentally the weakness of exchange theory derives from its implicit attempt to substitute psychological explanation of individual behavior for social understanding. It assumes we can explain the numerous aspects of political relationships by reference exclusively to the subjective sentiments and cost-benefit assessments by the individual participants in the aggregate. In the final analysis, it represents a form of psychological or individualistic reductionism.

The explanation and understanding of political phenomena require us to ask how individuals feel about institutions and practices and why they respond in the way in which they do. A rational calculus of costs and benefits may help us to shed some light on these problems. But in addition we need to be able to understand a number of other kinds of phenomena which are more recalcitrant to explanation on purely individualistic grounds. Regardless of any desire to maximize or satisfice our utilities, at any moment in time only certain options are available. Our social environment imposes certain constraints on our behavior. Any effort to understand the sources, nature, and consequences of these constraints drives us well beyond a calculation of motives, to what Durkheim had characterized as social facts explainable only by other social facts and not by an appeal to individual behavior.

One problem obscured by an individualistic emphasis is the difference between the mere presence of certain sentiments in a political system and their organized manifestation for action. Political systems are not just aggregates of human beings. They are complex entities organized for getting things done: for permitting the expression of the needs and wants of all or some of the members of the systems (depending on the type of system), for establishing goals in the name of the whole entity, for mobilizing members and resources in the implementation of these goals, and the like. Knowledge about the distribution of sentiments among the members of the system gives us little insight into how the organized entity called the political system does or will in fact operate.

For example, in a dictatorial system based on terror, a cost-benefit analysis might reveal why individual members chose not to act in open opposition to the regime or the authorities. Presumably the individual costs would be too high. One of the key questions that this kind of analysis would not help us to understand, however, is the nature of the conditions under which action against the dictatorship might occur. In terms of exchange theory, we could sum the costs and benefits for each member of the system. If we found that the regime and authorities no longer had the support of most of the members in the aggregate, this would be a significant piece of information. Nonetheless we would still have little knowledge about the probability of the survival or collapse of the dictatorship even if general support had disappeared.

The maintenance or change of a regime is not determined by the distribution of incentives alone. On an individual basis dissatisfaction may be widespread; many persons may consider the costs of conforming to be far too high. Yet change may not occur. The system may be organized in such a way as to throw predominant power in the hands of a minority which may be extremely difficult to dislodge, even if individuals are prepared to pay the ultimate cost by exposing themselves to violent death. The discontent of even an overwhelming majority may not find expression in a viable political movement that can mobilize the necessary material and organizational resources to drive a minority out of power and establish an acceptable substitute regime.

Change in sentiments or in their distribution in a population only paves the way for possible institutional change; it does not give any promise of being able to predict or anticipate such change even if the members of the system are prepared to bear the costs of open opposition. The upset of the regime may turn not only on a cost-benefit calculus by participants but on the recruitment of skilled personnel and on the availability of material and other resources to oppositional groups. Correspondingly, the in-elite may be able to retain political power, even in the face of active opposition, not only because it has more to gain by doing so (an important motivational consideration of course) but because it has the organizational effectiveness to ward off any challenge to its power.

The hazards of reducing analysis to a study of the distribution of individual incentives (with groups viewed as individual-like units) is easily revealed by one of Waldman's own illustrations. He seeks to explain how it comes about that in developing systems an initial centralization of power yields in time to a relaxation of control (pp. 117). In incentive terms he attributes this to an exchange relationship between rulers and ruled determined by the availability or scarcity of material resources for distribution between both groups. The analysis is suggestive as far as it goes and reveals one of the important dimensions in the concentration of power. With limited material benefits to offer and under the pressure of potential discontent, political authorities may rely on psychic rewards to keep a population in check. As material resources increase, these may be shared to some extent with the members of the system. As a secondary consequence, Waldman suggests, the authorities will fear their subjects less and will be prepared to allow them to share in the exercise of political power.

Yet this calculus of exchange relationships is scarcely able to explain why, in systems in which material goods are indeed available, the authorities may decide against meeting the demands of its members, as in late eighteenth-century France prior to the Revolution or in various authoritarian systems in industrialized societies today. Even in face of generalized discontent, the organized power of those in control may be such as to permit them to remain unresponsive to or even to destroy an organized opposition. Thus under certain conditions, contrary to Waldman's interpretation of the operation of the rational calculus, it may not be true that "most systems, as they develop economically, become more responsive" (p. 118). The relaxation of control by authorities will often depend on the credible threat presented by an organized or threatening opposition.

Incentive or motivation is only one aspect of political relationships. Its expression (or failure to express itself) in organized form may be no less significant for the history of a political system. Waldman's political intuitions warn him against neglecting the importance of structure. "It is, of course, true that the forces producing pressures toward greater freedom may be limited by the constraints of the established powers, who fear for their positions in a period of growing democratization and heightened expectations" (p. 118). But he quickly veers away from the necessary additional analysis of the kind just indicated.

The point here is that however important an understanding of the motivational basis for the input of support may be, it is not the only problem of significance for a general theory of politics. We cannot answer all central questions by assessing the state of the sentiments of the individual members of the system. A political system is more than just an aggregate of members. It provides a context in which actors may organize themselves for influencing political outputs as well as the overall political structures within which political conflict and cooperation occur.

Waldman's version of exchange theory does not hold out great promise for doing what it proposes to do, in its own terms. Exchange theory has argued that we ought to explain the rise, maintenance, and change of institutions by the costs and rewards that individuals experience and the exchanges of benefits in which they are prepared to participate. We have seen that to confine the analysis to these dimensions is to neglect the impact of organization and resources as limits on the capacity to keep what one has in a political system or to change things.

THE NEGLECT OF STRUCTURAL CONSTRAINTS

In addition to obscuring the organizational element in political change, the individualistic reductionism of exchange theory diverts attention from a further type of structural variable in the operation of political systems. The existing structures in a political system constrain the options available for behavior. Members of a system are not free to act in any way they choose. Each system acts as a set of limits which can of course be changed, given both the incentive and means, as we have just seen. But until these limits *are* changed they cannot be ignored either by the actor or by the student of political behavior. In this neglect of structure we have a fourth central deficiency in exchange theory. It is not very successful in helping us to understand the way in which existing patterns of political relationships may constrain behavior over and above the limits imposed by the feelings of the participants.

In some ultimate sense, of course, it is arguable that existing structures can be related to the degree of individual satisfaction and that changes may occur as members of a system become increasingly dissatisfied with existing arrangements. But the possibility of change cannot distract us from recognizing that at any moment in a given system, persons are limited in the action choices they can make. For example, they may be able to choose only among two political parties rather than among many to express their demands or support, they may have the option of joining interest groups or remaining part of an unorganized public, and the like. The structural arrangements coincident with the participation of the member in politics restrict the options available at the time. The range of these options may generate discontent or satisfaction, and these effects may have long range consequences for the maintenance or change of the pattern of relationships. But at a given moment of time, as the political system is functioning to process demands and support into policies and actions, what happens is a product not only of incentives or sentiments among the members but of the limits on action inherent within the existing pattern of political relationships.

To put the matter directly, the kinds of decisions made in a system and the actions taken cannot be explained exclusively by some calculus of costs and benefits. Even within the context of such a cost-benefit analysis, the alternatives available for action within and through the system are clearly restricted by the existing structure of the system. To argue otherwise would be to say that it does not ever matter, for problems of major political signifi-cance, whether we have, for example, a single or multiple member constitu-ency, a democratic or authoritarian structure of authority, a centralized or federal division of powers, or a single or competitive party system.[13] It is the consequences of structural arrangements such as these which individual-istic reductionism has difficulty in handling. This is an old problem in the social sciences but exchange theory raises it once again.

The claims of exchange theory force us to make certain statements that are deceptive in their simplicity and transparency. But the simple and ob-vious, when lost from sight, at times accounts for major distortions in analy-sis. We all recognize that a political system is not a mere sum of individual behaviors or actions. It consists of interactions patterned in certain ways. In addition, it is an *organized* set of interactions through which authoritative decisions are taken and implemented. Through organization, whether well-defined or not, political systems are able to take account of needs and wants, discuss and assign goals, change these as desired, mobilize members of the system in pursuit of these objectives, provide and utilize existing com-munication nets for information relevant to action, and the like.

No amount of knowledge about the costs and benefits to individual or group members will answer certain central questions for us about the limits that any particular mode of organization imposes on behavioral options in a system. First, an exchange approach helps us little in appreciating the con-sequences that different kinds of structural arrangements may have for the outputs (policies) of political systems. Exchange theory has little room for explaining variations in outputs that may be associated with varying types of political systems, or even, at a lower level, with varying kinds of party arrangements (see footnote 13), or legislative and executive organization (presidential as against parliamentary systems), and electoral systems (single as against multi-member constituencies). At most, exchange theory is ap-propriate for seeking to shed light on the possible bases of support and op-position to any particular arrangement of political relationships.

Second, not all structural arrangements are consistent and compatible with each other. A democratic structure of authority within the factory is un-likely to sit well with authoritarianism in the political arena. How are we to understand the limits of structural compatibility through the rational cal-culus of benefits by participating individuals and groups?

Third, structures do not remain constant over time. Democracies have

---

[13] See the extensive literature on the relationship of the structure of the state party systems on the outputs of the authorities in the fifty American states. The structure of the party system seems to make little difference. But aside from the dispute over the validity of these findings, one cannot automatically extend them to national political systems where the relationship is probably different.

become one-party systems; dictatorships have been transformed into democracies. Systems evolve from type to type. Although exchange theory may have something important to say about the reasons for the growth of dissatisfaction with existing institutions, it does not help us to understand why, among alternative regimes, one form emerges dominant over another at a given time in the evolution of a system. It is true, through a torturous process of explanation, every choice can be reduced to costs and benefits, in much the same spirit that Bentham could calculate all behavior in terms of pleasure and pain. It would seem, however, that more economic and elegant explanations can be found by reference to the cultural options already available in a changing society, the distribution of power among the members, the nature of preceding decisions, and the like. Although exchanges based on costs and benefits may be a significant variable in the evolution of political institutions, the availability of these benefits only prepares the ground for change. They do not narrow the range of choice sufficiently for us to be able to understand why one or another among a number of equally plausible options might have been chosen.

Thus exchange theory does not prepare us to deal systematically with questions about structural consequences, structural compatability and articulation, or structural origins and change. Nor does it give us any assistance in understanding the basis of variations in structural types of systems.

Can we fault exchange theory for not providing us with adequate tools for handling these matters? Not if it had advertised itself solely as a theory seeking to explain the input of support or the motives underlying political behavior. But given its pretensions as a general theory of politics, it leaves much to be desired in its comprehensiveness, even assuming, as we have, the adequacy of its psychological underpinnings.

Waldman at one point offers a strange, almost quixotic reason for avoiding these central structural problems with which most political science has dealt from time immemorial. An individualistic, non-structural approach appeals to him because "we do know the laws that largely describe and explain human choice and action" whereas "we do not know the empirical laws that relate the existence of given structures to system maintenance" (p. 103). This excuse smacks very much of Abraham Kaplan's law of the drunkard's search. The drunkard knows he has lost his keys in a dark alley but searches for them under a nearby street lamp because there is more light there. The criterion for testing the utility of an approach is surely theoretical, not merely the availability of knowledge. Even if it were true that we knew the laws of individual human choice, the critical question for the social scientist is not whether we have this knowledge, but whether, having it, we need additional kinds of knowledge to understand the kinds of questions it is important to ask.

THE WHOLE *VS* THE AGGREGATE

Over and above the difficulties exchange theory encounters in dealing with the structural constraints on behavior, its reductionism leads to a final major deficiency. This reductionism helps to obscure the special problems involved in understanding the kind of organized complexities[14] constituted by political systems. An organized social entity normally displays properties that are different from the properties of its constituent parts and from a mere aggregation of those parts. Hence knowledge about the behavior of individual members of a political system does not necessarily enable us to understand the properties of the behavior of all those members organized into the complex whole that we call a political system.

The familiar way of phrasing this thought is to say that the whole is greater than the sum of its parts. The mere summation of our knowledge about the parts does not permit us to understand the operations of the whole. Classical analytic science, in physics, for example, had left the impression that we could understand the nature of the atom if we started at the bottom and built upwards. By decomposing the atom into smaller and smaller particles and studying the behavior of these particles, the knowledge so gained could be summed and thereby we would understand the behavior of the whole atom. From the principles governing the elementary particles we would deduce the operation of the whole atom.

Biology and other sciences, and finally modern physics itself, has found this assumption unsatisfactory. No amount of knowledge about the elementary parts of the human organism, for example, seems to be able to permit the observer to deduce the way in which the whole human system interacts to sustain a preferred state called life. Regulatory (homeostatic) processes of the human organism are properties of the way the system is organized and they are not directly deducible from properties of the parts or component subsystems.

Dissatisfaction with traditional analytic science has led to the strategy now associated with a systems approach. Through this strategy the objective is to begin with the whole, search out its characteristic properties, break it up into its component parts or subsystems, decompose these parts in turn into smaller subsystems at a second order of analysis, and so on in a descending order until we come to the lowest "particle" of behavior. Some day it may be possible to move from the properties of the individual to the very different properties of collections of individuals organized in complex relations for the pursuit of goals. But until that time is reached, we can take into the account the impact of organization on behavior by beginning at

---

[14] A phrase invented by Weaver, "Science and Complexity" 36 *American Scientist* (1948) 536–44.

the most inclusive level for the subject under consideration. In the case of politics this means that we begin with the political system. This is the overall meaning behind what I would call methodological holism,[15] the notion that it is useful to interpret the whole as being greater than the sum of the parts.

Although this way of putting the matter often has metaphysical over-tones—we ought to say only that the whole is *other than,* not more than, the sum of its parts—it does contain certain fundamental empirical truths. Neglect of these can easily lead to premature and arid individualistic re-ductionism. In the first place, to say that the whole is greater than the sum of the parts can often serve as an elliptical way, in social science, for re-ferring to the fact that the behavior of a person has different consequences depending upon the context in which that person acts. If he acts in relative isolation, he may have few effects on others. If his actions are visible to others while he stands in no fixed relationship to them—as a person mixing anonymously in a crowd—the consequences will be of one sort. But if his actions occur within an organized structure of relationships, the actions may have discernible and predictable consequences for the outcomes of the whole organization.

For example, the expression of discontent by the charismatic leader of an organization may have far graver consequences for political stability and change than a similar degree of discontent expressed severally by a consider-able percentage of the followers. The high status and power of the indi-vidual concerned, that is, location in the political structure, may account for more of the variance in the behavior of the members of the political system than the benefits and costs calculated by individuals with lower status and less power. To understand what happens in politics we need to know more than the incentives of those involved. We need to have some idea about how they relate to each other and how variations in these relationships influence the results of their respective actions.

Theoretically, if we had the detailed knowledge necessary, we might be able to deduce from individual behavior all of the collective consequences. This is why social scientists can and need to remain reductionists in some ultimate sense. But in practice, because of the enormous complexity of or-ganized relationships, we cannot begin with individuals and trace through the consequences of their behavior for the collective results made possible through the fact of their organization. It is simpler and more profitable to begin with the organized form of behavior and decompose it into manage-

---

[15] *Methodological holism* may be contrasted with what I would call *philosophical holism* (or organicism). Methodological holism stands between pure individualistic re-ductionism and philosophical holism. That is to say, while asserting the need to reduce behavior to observable individual interactions, at the same time methodological holism recognizes the need to take account of the special properties found when individuals interact as an organized group.

able parts. For reasons linked to the nature of our general understanding of complexity, we are able to understand an organized whole better by looking at its components in descending order of detail.[16]

The ambiguous phrase that the whole is greater than the sum of the parts contains a second empirical truth. It is that an organized set of relationships displays properties that are different from the properties of aggregate individual behavior and that are not easily derived from the study of the individual. These characteristics are not, of course, supra-individual in the sense that we can describe group behavior without referring to the actions of the persons involved. All the properties of groups must be reducible to observable individual behavior. To suggest otherwise would be to fall victim to the older metaphysics of organicism in which the group had a will, purposes, and personality independent of its constituent members (and usually represented by a select ruling few). But the individualism of the sort intended here need not deny that groups do display properties that are very different from those of mere aggregates of individuals. Such individualism in research is, therefore, not only consistent with methodological holism but is implied by it.

By way of illustration I shall apply this perspective to politics. In that event we have to begin with the obvious premise that a political system is a complex and organized entity. It is complex in the sense that all political systems are composed of many parts and their relationships are difficult to sort out. It is organized in the sense that the parts are not haphazardly related. They stand in some determinate order so that from these relationships characteristic consequences result that are not otherwise attainable. These consequences I have designated as authoritative allocations of values, the form in which decisions about political goals appear. Organization, involving as it does some kind of focused division of labor, implies and makes possible goal choice and implementation for a group. These properties are clearly different from those associated with mere aggregates.

The task of research is to identify and understand the nature of these system characteristics in politics. At the initial level of analysis, certain system properties can be distinguished by looking at the major subsystem components associated with the activities typically found in all political systems. These components may be identified as input, conversion, output, and feedback subsystems of behavior.

Because of the typical way political systems are organized, for example, they are able to consider the demands of all or a few members, to combine, reduce or otherwise relate overlapping and competing demands, to transform them into issues, and ultimately to convert them into outputs. Through the output subsystem, the goals so selected in the name of the whole political

---

[16] See H. A. Simon, *The Sciences of the Artificial* (Cambridge, Mass.: The M.I.T. Press, 1969), chap. 4.

system can be implemented with the authority of the system behind them (even if in fact these goals represent only the effective choice of a few, such as a ruling class or a dictator or a bureaucracy). The outputs of a system are very different usually from the individual choices of the members, if such a summation were feasible.

The conversion of demands into outputs and the implementation of outputs, to take only two of the significant subsystems at the highest (most inclusive) level of a political system, cannot be deduced in any simple way directly from the behavior of individual members. Not that we can understand the complex nature of political systems unless we do document our explanations by reference to interactions among individuals. But we need to see the individuals in context, as participants in interactions through which demands are converted into outputs and we need to appreciate the way this conversion process is related to the overall organization of a political system.

In short, we can initiate our understanding of the properties of a political system by first reducing it to manageable subsystem components. The properties of the whole system (of members in organized interaction) are different from the properties of its individual actors (of members viewed in relative isolation, as in exchange theory). Because we cannot derive these system properties from our knowledge of the constituent individuals, at least in organized complexities such as political systems, a simpler strategy calls on us to begin with an attempt to understand the relationship of the component subsystems to the whole organized entity.

Somewhere in the distant future we might be able to raise the issue of how we go about deducing the behavior (properties) of the system as a whole from knowledge about its elementary particles, the individual actors. Today the connection between the discrete actions of the individual and the overall consequences of the organized interactions we call a political system are far too involved to hope to be able to sort them out. We are not able to move directly from the individual to the organized, goal-directed properties visible in the operations of political systems. Insofar as exchange theory seems to be seeking, through its individualistic laws of rational choice, to provide an understanding of complex behavior, it would appear to be overly ambitious and premature.

CONCLUSION

In conclusion, then, as I have suggested, it is not a matter of exchange theory being right or wrong in any ultimate sense. I am concerned rather with the limits of its utility. At the very least it does help us to construct a model of rational behavior, based on a limited number of motives, however, and on a certain type of learning theory. Yet there is sufficient doubt about the validity of this learning theory so that by viewing exchange theory only as an "as if" scheme, we can put it on a much firmer footing. Exchange theory could then be interpreted as recommending that we assume that people behave as if they sought to maximize or satisfice their rewards even though in reality they do not behave in this way at all. From this purely heuristic premise, it could be anticipated, we would be able to predict the relationships to which individuals are likely to commit themselves. Yet, at best, even if this approach worked, it could help us to predict only certain kinds of aggregate support behavior, as I suggested earlier.

On the other hand, if exchange theory failed to offer us predictive power even for those limited kinds of behavior, it need not lose its interest for us. It might still be used to provide a model against which we could compare actual behavior. By refining such a model in the light of experience, we would be able to improve its correspondence to the real world to the point where it could give us relatively reliable predictions within the limits of motivational explanation.

If, however, we retained strong doubts about its utility as a rational model that could offer us a first approximation to real behavior, we would not be compelled, even then, to reject exchange theory entirely. It might still have some residual value of a meaningful kind. At the very least it could tell us how a person ought to behave to maximize his utilities, under specifiable circumstances. It could stand as an interesting normative or prescriptive model. Analysis of the criteria underlying rational behavior has a long history in the social sciences. Exchange theory, interpreted in this light, would be another contribution by political science. Unfortunately this is a far cry from an explanation of actual behavior, the original intention behind the theory. But it is not inharmonious with the nature of most rational (or economic) modelling in political science.

In pointing up the deficiencies of exchange theory for the study of politics, therefore, its possible merits for limited purposes, such as those just described, need not be denied. Undoubtedly the book to which Waldman refers—and of which his paper is presumably an excessively lean summary—will flesh out these useful parts. But even so, as presented in his paper, the theory leaves much to be desired. As formulated by Waldman, exchange theory casts doubt on its own truth value. Even if considered only as a theory of the motivations underlying political support, its reductionist basis handicaps it for grappling with both the organizational and the general structural context of political behavior. In the outcome, the exchange approach offers a rather shaky foundation on which to build a general political theory, especially one that is called upon to identify and understand the kinds of organized behavior typically found in political systems.

And yet, as suggested earlier, every theory worth the effort throws some light on a new area, and exchange theory, when applied to politics, need not disappoint us. Whatever its theoretical status, it does succeed in enhancing our sensitivity to the motivational basis of political support. Challenging experimentation such as this can help us to forge ahead in the development of general theory in political science.

Response to Easton's "Some Limits of Exchange Theory in Politics"

SIDNEY R. WALDMAN

The editor has given me the opportunity to respond briefly to David Easton's critical review of my paper on exchange theory. I appreciate the opportunity, since I find Easton's comments thoughtful, but basically misleading, and in my view mistaken. I will deal with his criticisms in the order in which they appear in his article.

Easton begins by suggesting that I am not clear as to the nature of the five propositions that form the core of exchange theory. He suggests that on the one hand I argue for the empirical validity of the propositions, as tested and verified by learning psychologists, and on the other that I treat these propositions as constituting a model which can allow us to predict behavior, whether the parts of the model are or are not empirically valid. I do believe that these propositions are more than axioms, that they have been developed, tested, and verified by empirical work in psychology. It is also true that I sometimes argue that men "act *as if* they make estimates of the probable value of given activities." A careful reading of my article, particularly starting with the last paragraph on p. 107, reveals that I try to derive the need for profit and the fact that men act as if they made probability estimates of the outcomes of their actions from my basic propositions. Thus I tie together some of the fundamental axiomatics of economic theory to the empirically verified propositions of learning theory. The reason that I utilize the "as if" language is that the propositions of exchange theory, to be valid, do not require that men be conscious of them and the way they operate. Exchange theory does not imply that men consciously calculate costs or benefits, that they consciously try to satisfice, or that they consciously calculate the probable outcomes of the various actions they see open to them. As a result, when we try to understand the actions of men, we say that men act *as if* they engage in such a rational calculus. Insofar as the need for profit follows from the basic propositions, and I have shown it does, then the motivation for profit does indeed affect behavior, whether men are conscious of that motivation or not. Occasionally in the text I do speak as if men were conscious of some of the things I include in my theory. I do this because men frequently are conscious of some of these things, and because it is convenient to talk as if they were, but consciousness of the propositions and what they imply, for example, the need for profit, is not

149

required for the validity of the theory.[1] Even if it were the case that the need for profit was not based on these basic propositions but rather was part of a theoretical model, as is the case with most economic theory, that would not mean, as Easton suggests, that we would have nothing more than a criterion to assess behavior; rather, we would have a theoretical model of behavior whose intent was to explain behavior, not merely or even necessarily to normatively assess it.

Easton's next major criticism is that the basic propositions of exchange theory, because they are based on operant conditioning psychology, are "clearly not free from serious question as statements about actual behavior" (p. 134–35). While it is true that a variety of criticisms have been addressed to the validity of these statements, I do not find that questioning convincing. If Easton does not introduce his specific questions or doubts, which he does not do, I cannot respond to them. At a minimum the reader should recognize that exchange theory creates a strong link between political science, a theoretically and methodologically powerful tradition within the field of psychology, and economics. Continued work on exchange theory will strengthen and develop these ties.

Easton argues that exchange theory, despite its claims, is only a special theory which attempts to explain variation in support for political institutions and practices. A reading of the basic propositions, however, should readily convince the reader that the theory is intended to explain all behavior, not merely behavior that involves support—or its lack—for regime, government, political party, or other institutions. To use Easton's own distinctions, the five propositions can as readily be applied to explaining variance in the nature and frequency of demands as variance in support. For example, if the making of specific demands in particular contexts has proven rewarding in the past, these demands are more likely to be made again in the same or similar contexts. If they have not been reinforced, they are more likely to be extinguished. If certain demands have been met leading to the satiation of particular needs, then new demands involving other needs are more likely to occur. The five propositions can be used to account for more than variance in support and demands; they can also be used to account for apathy. With a little imagination the reader can anticipate how the five propositions might be used to explain this phenomenon. In my paper I actually do utilize the basic propositions to account for certain demands. For example, I attempt to explain whether a given individual will engage in political activity and, if so, where he will focus his efforts (pp. 116–17). This analysis can

---

[1] The fact that I suggest that men may be conscious of certain of these propositions should immediately suggest to the reader that I am not a strict Skinnerian and that the attacks on Skinner's philosophy of science do not necessarily apply to exchange theory as it has been developed.

readily be generalized to explain what kinds of demands a man is likely to make under given conditions and to whom he will address those demands.

Exchange theory, to continue with Easton's language for the moment, can account for the outputs of a political system as well as inputs into it. A set of propositions that can explain the actions and decisions of governmental actors cannot be said to focus only on the input side of things. For example, in trying to explain why governments choose to centralize or decentralize power (p. 117), why governments grant mass suffrage, political freedom, and consumer benefits (p. 118), and why governments are likely to intervene in particular policy areas under certain conditions, I am attempting to account for outputs. If in doing these analyses I simultaneously focus on the support for certain governmental actions, I do so because all governments, even non-democratic ones, need some support for their decisions, whatever the motivational bases of that support. In describing what parties and interest groups have to do to persist and be viable, I am focusing on their decisions as producers of outputs as well as inputs. In Waldman (1972, chap. 8) I also utilize exchange theory to account for the probability that given conflicts within a political system will be resolved, which concerns the capacity of a given system to make certain kinds of decisions. In view of the text of my article and the nature of the basic propositions it is difficult to understand how Easton can conclude that exchange theory only applies to explaining variance in the input of supports for a given system or institution.

Easton argues that exchange theory is incapable of dealing with structural phenomena, with *organized* social behavior, and with the constraints that limit what men can do. While the theory does focus on the cost and benefit possibilities inherent in the situations facing men and sometimes on their subjective assessments and sentiments, it certainly does not ignore the ways in which the objective situation affects the incentives and constraints that men confront in acting. If anything, it sensitizes us to the need for examining these constraints in detail. Insofar as certain constraints limit what actions an actor may try, and consequently what actions may be reinforced, they are, as Easton suggests, important. They do merit attention and cannot be completely explained in terms of the motives of those they constrain. On the other hand, the source, nature, and persistence of these constraints to a substantial extent can be explained in terms of our basic propositions since they frequently are the result of human action. In addition, many of the important consequences of these constraints can be powerfully understood by seeing the ways in which they affect the incentive structures in which individuals find themselves.

One can try to explain social facts with other social facts, but insofar as both sets of "social facts" can be accounted for in terms of the motivational bases of behavior, we ought to try to do so to gain more complete understanding. There are occasions when it is simply too difficult and not worth the effort, given our particular purposes, to account for every social fact in terms of its exchange basis. This does not mean that in principle that cannot be done, but in given situations we may choose not to try to do it. In such instances one takes *as given* certain constraints or conditions, which are then used along with our basic propositions to explain individual actions. These conditions affect which activities will be rewarded and which will not, and the means (resources) that determine which actions can be tried and consequently which actions can be reinforced. In addition, they constitute the stimulus context that is a key variable in the operation of proposition 1 as it affects human behavior. Our basic propositions do not operate in a vacuum; in substantively affecting behavior they depend very much on the conditions in which actors find themselves, something that I apparently failed to make clear to Easton in my paper. The fact that in our explanations we take certain things as given conditions need not bother us. The explanation of a finding is the process of showing that the finding follows as a logical conclusion, as a deduction, from one or more general propositions *under specified given conditions.*[2]

The fact that political systems are not just aggregates of individuals, but are complex entities organized for getting things done does not invalidate the wide applicability of exchange theory or its validity. In fact, exchange theory is useful in explaining how certain organizational and structural forms come to exist, persist, and change (see Waldman, 1972, chap. 3, and Blau, 1964, chaps. 5, 8, 9), how certain established goals persist or fail to do so; and how and in what ways the mobilization of people and resources in the implementation of these goals can occur. A knowledge not of the sentiments of members of a political system (Easton's interpretation of exchange theory notwithstanding) but of the incentive structures in which these members find themselves will give us insight into how a political system does in fact operate.

There are certain things exchange theory and, for that matter, learning theory upon which it is based cannot explain. It cannot explain in a completely satisfactory way how and why a particular action is first tried (the concepts of stimulus and response generalization, while helpful, do not completely solve this problem), but it can explain whether a given action is likely to be repeated, which is crucial for understanding an *ongoing* social or political system. Perhaps an example will help. While it is true, as Easton suggests, that exchange theory by itself may not be able to specify the *particular* action against a dictatorship that will occur in particular conditions, it can

---

[2] For a more complete analysis and discussion of the nature of explanation see George Homans (1967). Homans's view of explanation is that of R. B. Braithwaite (1953) and C. H. Hempel (1965).

help us understand why certain actions are most unlikely. Further, once a given action does occur (presumably one of the set of possible actions that the theory predicts as likely options), our framework can help us understand whether that action is likely to persist and what the response to that action is likely to be, especially over time. An examination of the incentive situations of the various actors in the dictatorial situation will help a great deal in doing the analysis.

If given opponents of a regime are unable to muster the necessary material resources required to overcome that regime, Easton is correct in asserting that we cannot predict their success, however great their motivation to overthrow the regime and however great the costs they are willing to pay. Why that is a problem for exchange theory I fail to see. There is nothing in the theory that necessitates its being blind to the material conditions that affect what is and is not possible. Exchange theory is not insensitive to the ways in which men may be coerced or materially constrained in their actions. If men are coerced into acting in particular ways, then the theory will focus on this rather than on the motivational bases of their voluntary action. (For an example of the way in which we are sensitive to coerced action and constraint in applying our theory see p. 117–18). In most of the analysis in our paper and in our larger work we focus on the uncoerced actions of men as dependent variables, largely because these require more effort to explain than do the coerced actions of men. In the latter case what is interesting as a problem for analysis is explaining the actions of the men doing the coercing rather than the actions of the coerced. In any case, exchange theory need not be blind to the non-motivational limits on action though these limits, as independent variables, are not its primary focus.

Insofar as exchange theory is sensitive to the costs of an action, it is sensitive to many of the important constraints operating on an individual, both structural and otherwise. Insofar as the theory can explain the pattern of social relationships that constrain behavior, whether by operating on incentives or means, it can do more than note these constraints; it can account for them. Of course, to account for these constraints it needs to be sensitive to them. There is nothing in the theory that would preclude such sensitivity.

Exchange theory, Easton notwithstanding, can help us appreciate the consequences of different structural arrangements for the outputs (policies) of political systems by sensitizing us to the ways in which these structural arrangements affect the incentives that men face in acting with regard to policy options and policy initiation.[3] An analysis of the work that has been

---

[3] Space prevents me from dealing in detail with Easton's criticism of my analysis of why centralized governments in particular conditions tend to become more responsive over time. Because I have utilized exchange theory to analyze a particular scenario describing the greater responsiveness of centralized governments over time and have tried to give the exchange bases of that scenario does not mean that exchange theory

done (for example, Downs, 1957) in showing the connections between party arrangements and policy output, for example, will reveal that most of the critical propositions relating these two variables implicitly or explicitly involve propositions of the sort described by exchange theory. The theory can also help us understand why and how particular tensions may emerge within a social system because of coexisting but varying structures of relationships. To be specific, our theoretical orientation can help us understand why a democratic structure of authority within the factory, for example, is unlikely to sit well with other existing structural arrangements, such as authoritarianism in the political arena. Our focus on the ways in which learning based on experience in one area may be generalized to other areas sensitizes us to the difficulties that may be caused for individuals and for a social system by such different, but coexisting structures of authority. If the reader desires further evidence that exchange theory can be used to analyze and explain structural origins, structural change, structural consequences, and structural articulation and compatibility, we recommend chapters 3, 8, and 9 of Waldman (1972). While these chapters represent preliminary analyses, they give the reader an indication of the way to proceed in doing what Easton claims exchange theory cannot do.

Easton emphasizes the fact that organized social entities normally display properties that are different from the properties of their constituent parts and from an aggregation of those parts (which is not a "mere aggregation," as is clear to anyone who has tried to do this). The real issue, of course, is not that system properties differ from the properties of individuals, but whether the former can be derived from or explained in terms of the latter. In my view they can, and I try to suggest by argument and example how one might go about showing this. If it is the case that one can find regulatory processes governing social and political systems, as Easton suggests, it is my view that the sources and nature of these processes may be explained in terms of basic propositions governing the behavior of men. In this regard exchange theory poses a challenge and a promise, a challenge to political and other social scientists to find the connections and a promise that, if found, we would have a new, more powerful understanding of the human situation than any we have had heretofore.

---

automatically and necessarily predicts such a scenario in all conditions. As incentives and resources change, the predicted scenario changes. It is not difficult to imagine how our five propositions could be used to explain the willingness of authorities who have been reinforced in being oppressive to continue being so, even when politically they could do otherwise. Because our basic framework can handle this set of developments as well as those I originally described in my paper, careful work must be done in searching for the variations in incentives, past conditioning, and resources that lead to these differences in elite behavior.

Easton seems to believe that exchange theory is unaware of and unable to cope with the basic fact that the behavior of a person has different consequences depending on the context in which the person acts and on his attributes (status, power). Insofar as the context of a man's actions and his attributes affect how a man reinforces others and is reinforced by them, exchange theory is sensitive to the importance of those variables. Our granting of the fact that context is important does not necessarily mean that "the whole is different from the sum of its parts," which may or may not be the case. Rather, it does mean that the "parts" that are somehow combined to explain the whole depend for their very nature on the context in which they occur. Exchange theory, neither in the way it is conceptualized nor in the way it is applied, denies this. The issue is not whether the whole is different from an aggregation of its parts, but what "aggregating" means and what it is that one should be aggregating.

Our general argument should not be misunderstood. An exchange framework does not require the analyst to start with analysis at the individual level. He may choose to start with system or subsystem properties and try to explain them by means of statements about the behavior and choices of individuals rather than building from the ground up, so to speak. The point is not where one starts, but where one finishes. Our goal is finally to utilize propositions of the theory in explaining phenomena, however one gets to that point. In doing this, it should be clear that nothing in the theory requires us to analyze the behavior of men in isolation or free from context, nor does it require us, as Easton suggests, to consider only a limited set of motives. Further, utilizing the theory in explaining phenomena need not blind us to the fact that systems of behavior are just that, systems in which the behavior of men is interconnected, organized, and patterned. In fact, the very nature of exchange and the fact that men reinforce each other in systematic ways leads us to expect patterned effects. Finally, utilizing the exchange framework need not blind us to the fact that political processes and structures relate to the operation of the system as a whole. That needs to be understood and recognized to the extent that it is true, but its *explanation* finally must be in terms of the actions and behavior of men, understood in terms of general propositions that can account for their actions and behavior over time. In our view the propositions we need and that we can use as fundaments are those of exchange theory.

By now it should be clear to the reader that one cannot know at this point whether Easton's doubts and skepticism or my claims are justified. Empirical work is needed to test the possibilities of exchange theory. To say this is not to argue that work is not also required to test the possibilities of competing frameworks, for example, that of Easton, but it is to argue that only if such work is attempted can one resolve the argument that Easton and I are having. It may be that in the course of this work, my formulation and/or his will be modified, but without that work, no satisfactory assessment of his position or mine is possible.

REFERENCES

Braithwaite, R. B.
1953   Scientific Explanation. Cambridge University Press

Downs, Anthony
1957   An Economic Theory of Democracy. New York: Harper, Row.

Hempel, C. H.
1965   Aspects of Scientific Explanation. New York: The Free Press.

Homans, George
1967   The Nature of Social Science. New York: Harcourt, Brace.

Waldman, S. R.
1972   Foundations of Political Action. Boston: Little, Brown.

Marxist Political Analysis

ROBERT J. WERLIN
Cowell College
University of California at Santa Cruz

I

Marxism is not only a perspective through which we can analyze societies and their histories; it is itself a part of history, its ideas shaping societal action. And given the nature of these ideas it is not surprising that in the past decade, a decade of intensified social conflict and upheaval, there has been a renewed interest in Marx's thought as a way of understanding the contemporary world. This activity has given rise to a variety of neo-Marxisms, some seemingly more "neo-" than Marxist but still claiming kinship to Marx's own work. This variety complicates my task of analyzing "the Marxist paradigm." In order to develop a coherent perspective it is necessary to go back to the work of Marx himself, to isolate its basic features and the tensions and ambiguities they involve, and then to assess the work of contemporary Marxists in the light of this heritage. While the central task of this essay is a critical review of the Marxist contribution to political analysis, such a focus must be located within the scope of Marx's theory as a whole, rather than separated out and isolated as one dimension of the theory. Marx's theory deals with the totality of society and the significance of any single element within the whole, in this case politics, can only be understood in terms of its relationship to the whole. Further, the realm of the political is not confined for Marx within a single institutional sphere; rather, it is a pervasive dimension influencing all areas of social relationships. For these reasons I will begin with a general review of Marx's social theory and then explore his analysis of the political realm in the light of the societal problems defined by the theory as a whole.

THE DIMENSIONS OF MARXIST SOCIAL THEORY

There are three major dimensions in Marxist theory: the philosophical, social structural, and historical. The philosophical dimension, and its implications for the other two, has been a primary cause of the gulf between Marxism and other sociological perspectives, particularly in the United States. In the context of the positivistic and empiricist assumptions which govern most sociological approaches in this country, the nature and importance of Marx's social philosophy has either been misunderstood or ignored altogether. Yet both the substantive problems of Marx's sociology and the methods used to understand these problems are intimately linked to the social philosophical assumptions with which he starts. Therefore a proper understanding of Marx's relevance to political analysis must start with this dimension.

Marx begins with a definition of man as self-creative and as creative of the world through his labor. Man struggles with nature for control of his environment; he uses and appropriates nature to satisfy his needs.

> The way in which men produce their means of subsistence depends first of all on the nature of the actual means they find in existence and have to reproduce. This mode of production must not be considered simply as being the reproduction of the physical existence of the individuals. Rather it is a definite form of activity of these individuals, a definite form of expressing their life, a definite *mode of life* on their part. As individuals express their life, so they are. What they are, therefore, coincides with their production, both with *what* they produce and with *how* they produce. The nature of individuals thus depends on the material conditions determining their production. (Marx and Engels, 1947: 7)

But an individual cannot conquer nature alone. Men must labor together in order to satisfy their needs. Production is therefore a social activity and out of this activity different forms of society develop.

> The production of life, both of one's own in labour and of fresh life in pro-creation, now appears as a double relationship: on the one hand as a natural, on the other as a social relationship. By social we understand the co-operation of several individuals, no matter under what conditions, in what manner and to what end. It follows from this that a certain mode of production, or industrial stage, is always combined with a certain mode of co-operation, or social stage, and this mode of co-operation is itself a "productive force." (Marx and Engels, 1947: 18)

These two components which define man for Marx, his productive nature and his social nature, imply an *ideal* of human existence in society: a realm of freedom in which men may relate to nature and to each other so that the fulfillment of their human needs is possible; a self-fulfillment through social cooperation which rationally masters the world in terms of true human needs. But this ideal has not been realized in any society up to now. Instead, society is characterized by the opposite condition, the alienation of men from themselves, the labor process, the products of their labor, and from other men (Marx, 1964: 122). Alienation is the negation of the ideal embodied in Marx's definition of man, a process in which "man's own deed becomes an alien power opposed to him, which enslaves him instead of being controlled by him. . . . The consolidation of what we ourselves produce into an objective power above us, growing out of control, thwarting our expectations, bringing to naught our calculations." (Marx and Engels, 1947: 22f.)

The philosophical anthropology developed by Marx in his early writings is multi-faceted and complex (cf. Lobkowicz, 1967; Avinieri, 1968; Tucker, 1961; Berger and Pullberg, 1966). Whatever elements of these early writings Marx may later abandon, and this itself remains a matter of controversy among Marxists, the central thrust generated by these works remains central to Marx throughout his life. Given his definition of man, and the negation of man's potentials through alienation, Marxism becomes not only an analysis of society but also a critique of society and a prescription for its cure.

In the early Marx the tension between man's creative potential, the alienation which negates that potential, and the struggle to overcome this condition are pitched on a universal level. The central tendency of all history, the struggle to overcome alienation, is embodied in Marx's very definition of man (cf. Meyer, 1954: chap. 1–4). The struggle appears as a universally inevitable one rather than the product of particular social and political conditions that can be empirically studied. But even in these early works, the *Economic and Philosophic Manuscripts* of 1844 and *The German Ideology,* written with Engels a year later, Marx is beginning to ground his social philosophy in the specifics of social life, within particular historical societies. This is implicit, for example, in his attack on the Young Hegelian philosophers who, while using "alienation" as a critical concept, are attacked by Marx for placing their critique purely in the realm of ideas.

> Since the Young Hegelians consider conceptions, thoughts, ideas, in fact all the products of consciousness, to which they attribute an independent existence, as the real chains of men . . . it is evident that the Young Hegelians have to fight only against these illusions of consciousness. . . . They forget, however, that to these phrases they themselves are only opposing other phrases, and that they are in no way combating the real existing world when they are merely combating the phrases of this world. (Marx and Engels, 1947: 5f.)

Marx attacked the critique of the Young Hegelians as ideological for two reasons: first, as the above quote states, because their view of reality is a mistaken, distorted one. And further, given their focus on the realm of ideas, "it has not occurred to any one of these philosophers to inquire into the connection of German philosophy with German reality, the relation of their criticism to their own material surroundings" (Marx and Engels, 1947: 6). Their critique cannot be an effective agent of change given its placement in the realm of ideas and ideals, and so in the guise of an attack on society their work is really a support of German society in its present form; a politically and socially conservative force.

In contrast to the Hegelians who deal purely in abstractions, for Marx,

> The premises from which we begin are not arbitrary ones, not dogmas, but real premises from which abstraction can only be made in the imagination.

They are the real individuals, their activity and the material conditions under which they live, both those they find already existing and those produced by their activity. These premises can thus be verified in a purely empirical way. (Marx and Engels, 1947: 6f.)

Fourteen years later in the preface to *A Contribution to the Critique of Political Economy* Marx speaks of "the economic conditions of production, which can be determined with the precision of natural science," and speaks of the *German Ideology* as the essay in which "(we) settle our accounts with our former philosophic conscience." These statements, and similar ones which can be found throughout Marx's writings, clearly establish the scientific, empirical intentions of Marxist social theory. Unfortunately the matter is not that simple. In spite of these statements of intention, the evaluative and prescriptive elements remain an integral part of his social theory and his strategies for understanding society remain tied to these elements. To put it briefly in terms of the area on which I will shortly focus, Marxism is both a mode of political analysis and itself a political tool. And as we will see as we now turn to a review of the social structural and historical dimensions of Marx's work, his empiricism is not only a scientific investigation of social reality, but also a search for a particular kind of social reality, one in which the fulfillment of the ideals discussed above is possible.

The central distinction which characterizes the structure of society for Marx is the distinction between the substructure and the superstructure, and the proposition that the former, the economic basis of society, determines the latter, which is comprised of the other societal institutions and their culture. Within the substructure the mode of production contains both technological and social elements. The former, usually referred to by Marx as the forces of production include natural resources, tools, machines, and other technological instruments used in production, the skills of science and engineering, and the power of human labor itself. The ways in which this technology is put to use is organized by the relations of production, the actual social relationships which organize the processes of production.

These social relations of production are synonymous with the class structure of society. The two other key terms which define the relations of production are the division of labor and property relations, the latter being the distinction between the owners and non-owners of the means of production. Property relations create the economic necessities which define a man's place in the division of labor and this in turn defines his place in the class structure. For example, under the capitalist mode of production the majority of men are forced to work as wage laborers in the service of the bourgeois capitalist class, for the latter own the means of production and without access to these means, the wage laborers cannot produce. By virtue of their ownership of the means of production this class is able to appropriate the laborers' surplus product as their own private property; thus the relationship between these classes is basically exploitive and antagonistic.

This antagonism is what necessitates and determines the superstructure of society. The idea that the substructure determines the superstructure primarily implies for Marx a functional relationship: given the antagonism and potential for conflict found in the class structure, the superstructure functions to legitimate the class structure, minimize class conflict that would threaten the mode of production, and when necessary, through the use of institutional power, to repress such conflict in the interests of the ruling class. The state is obviously a key superstructural institution in this respect. In various writings Marx refers to the state as "nothing more than the form of organization which the bourgeois necessarily adopt both for internal and external purposes, for the mutual guarantee of their property and interest"; he comments that "legislation, whether political or civil, never does more than proclaim, express in words, the will of economic relations" and that "the executive of the modern state is but a committee for managing the common affairs of the whole bourgeoisie" (Miliband, 1965; 282f.). And Engels in "Socialism: Utopian and Scientific" amplifies these scattered statements, explicitly defining the state in functional terms as the maintainer of order in the light of the inherent class conflict found in the substructure.

> Society thus far, based upon class antagonisms, has had need of the state. That is, of an organization of the particular class which was *pro tempore* the exploiting class, an organization for the purpose of preventing any interference from without with the existing conditions of production, and, therefore, especially for the purpose of forcibly keeping the exploited classes in the condition of oppression corresponding with the given mode of production (slavery, serfdom, wage labor). . . . As soon as there is no longer any social class to be held in subjection, as soon as class rule and the individual struggle for existence based upon our present anarchy of production, with the collisions and excesses arising from these, are removed, nothing more remains to be repressed, and a special repressive force, a state, is no longer necessary. (Marx and Engels, 1959: 106)

This analysis can also be applied to other institutional and cultural areas of society.

This exposition of Marx's model of the structure of society brings us to the heart of his political analysis. Political power arises out of the social relations of production and is therefore centered in the class structure rather than in the state and its politics. As Marx puts it in his final work, the third volume of *Capital,*

> It is always the immediate relation of the owners of the conditions of production to the immediate producers—a relation whose specific pattern of course always corresponds to a certain stage in the development of labor and its social force of production—in which we find the final secret, the hidden basis of the whole construction of society, including the political patterns of

sovereignty and dependence, in short, of a given specific form of government. (Dahrendorf, 1959: 13)

I noted above that Marx's empiricism is one in search of a particular type of social reality. Given this, his model of society is not an attempt at full description; rather he isolates those elements considered essential for the existence of the social reality he is searching for. And what is essential for Marx are the forces developing within society that will bring about revolutionary change. This brings us to the final dimension of Marx's theory, the historical dimension. History develops for Marx through social revolutions, and given that societies are concerned with the maintenance of order it is necessary, in order to understand the potential for revolution, to penetrate its "hidden basis," to find the contradictions inherent in society that can only be resolved by a revolutionary change in its social structure. The essential propositions involved in this task are set out in the preface to *A Contribution to the Critique of Political Economy*.

> At a certain stage of their development the material forces of production come in conflict with the existing relations of production, or—what is but a legal expression for the same thing—with the property relations within which they had been at work before. From forms of development of the forces of production these relations turn into their fetters. Then comes the period of social revolution. With the change of the economic foundation the entire immense superstructure is more or less rapidly transformed. (Marx and Engels, 1959: 43f.)

To briefly elaborate with respect to capitalist society, the historical form of primary interest for Marx, the class relations between capitalist and wage laborer or proletariat serve the needs of the productive forces in its early stages. Wage labor is necessary for the creation of surplus value, the profit needed for capitalist expansion. But as the capitalist productive forces continue to develop, the class structure originally supportive of these forces becomes increasingly incompatible with such development.[1]

These contradictions provide the necessary objective conditions for revolution, but, Marx's own rhetoric aside, such conditions do not in themselves establish the inevitability of such a revolution. It remains for the exploited

---

[1] Marx's analysis of this contradiction is a many-faceted one, too complex and detailed for presentation here. Paul Sweezy's *Theory of Capitalist Development* (1942) provides the best exposition of Marx's analysis of contradictions in the capitalist mode of production. More recently, Martin Nicolaus's reading of Marx's *Grundrisse* (Nicolaus, 1969) demonstrates how Marx saw technological development under capitalism eventually providing a new basis for the creation of surplus value, thus rendering wage labor obsolete as a source of capitalist profit. When this happens the forces of production no longer support the capitalist class structure which necessitates wage labor, and the continued existence of this class structure becomes a fetter on the further development of productive forces.

class, the proletariat, to become conscious of these developments, to recognize their own class interests and how they can be served by a social revolution which will put an end to a class structure rendered obsolete by changes in the forces of production. Robert Tucker has summed up this process as follows: "The revolt of the productive powers against the existing social relations of production finds its manifestation in class warfare in the economic arena, culminating in the political act of revolutionary overthrow of the state. If revolutions are the locomotives of history, class struggles are the locomotives of revolution" (Tucker, 1969: 17).

Marx's theory of the revolutionary transition from capitalism to socialism contains an objective component, the transformation of capitalist productive forces to the point where their further development is incompatible with the existing class structure, and a subjective component, the development of proletarian consciousness to guide their actions as a revolutionary class. In *Capital* Marx details the objective side of the process, demonstrating the contradictions which develop within the capitalist mode of production. There is the implication in this work that the economic crises continually generated by the capitalist mode of production help educate the working class, define the necessity of revolutionary social change. But the subjective problem, the problem of class consciousness is not dealt with by Marx in a systematic manner. From various writings of Marx it is possible to find references to this problem. The factors specified as leading to the development of such class consciousness have been identified by Bendix and Lipset (1966:8) as:

1. Conflicts over the distribution of economic rewards between the classes;
2. Easy communication between the individuals in the same class-position so that ideas and action-programs are readily disseminated;
3. Growth of class-consciousness in the sense that the members of the class have a feeling of solidarity and understanding of their historic role;
4. Profound dissatisfaction of the lower class over its inability to control the economic structure of which it feels itself to be the exploited victim;
5. Establishment of a political organization resulting from the economic structure, the historical situation, and maturation of class-consciousness.

Obviously this list begs as many questions as it answers. It is evident from statements in the third volume of *Capital* that Marx planned to treat the problem of class consciousness, but he died before this key problem in his theory of revolution could be elaborated systematically.

II

What are the main problems confronted in contemporary Marxist political analysis and how do they relate to the elements of Marx's own work reviewed above? While the Marxian model of class structure and class conflict may be usefully applied to a variety of historical societies, his theory of revolution, derived from this model, was most fully elaborated by Marx with respect to capitalist industrial societies. Therefore I will focus on these societies, particularly the United States which provides its most advanced form (as England did in the time of Marx), in assessing the usefulness of contemporary Marxian analysis.

The social and political development of capitalist-industrial societies since the death of Marx has produced changes which provide challenges both to Marx's model of this form of society and his theories about its social and political evolution. The fact which most haunts Marxist analysis is the failure of social and political revolution to develop in advanced industrial societies. While the prediction of such a revolution was the culmination, the climactic moment of Marx's theory of the development of capitalist-industrial society, its failure to come about does not in itself render Marxism useless as a tool for political analysis. What must be asked is whether Marxism can provide an understanding of the transformations that have taken place in contradiction to the revolutionary developments anticipated by Marx. Given Marx's central equation of political power and social class, the transformations in class structure since Marx's time are of crucial importance. The two central developments which pose the greatest challenge to Marxian theory are first, differentiation within the bourgeois capitalist and working classes, and second, the failure of capitalist-industrial society to polarize along the lines of these two classes.

These developments, which are obviously interrelated, are often cited by liberal-pluralist critics of Marxism (cf. Dahrendorf, 1959: chap. 2) as social facts which effectively refute Marxian theory. However, these facts in themselves do not constitute an adequate social analysis; they remain to be interpreted. The test of the Marxian model and theory in terms of these facts rests on the adequacy of a Marxian explanation of them and the revisions in Marxism necessitated by this explanation. In this respect, most contemporary Marxist social science is invariably engaged in debate with the liberal-pluralist interpretation of contemporary society. Further, the debate is not merely confined to problems of conceptualization and interpretation; the dispute about the nature of this society takes place on an empirical level as well.

We can begin to see the outlines of this debate when we consider the first development mentioned above: differentiation within the bourgeois and proletarian classes. Such a development challenges Marx's prediction that the two classes would each become more homogeneous, thus exacerbating the basic antagonisms between them and pushing capitalist society closer to revolution. Within this area, the greatest source of controversy has been the differentiation within the capitalist class and I shall begin with this problem.

The basic contention underlying pluralist discussions of differentiation of the capitalist class is that within the giant corporation which is the dominant economic unit in advanced capitalist-industrial society there has developed a significant separation between those who own the corporations (as stockholders) and those who manage the corporations. This thesis was originally set forth almost forty years ago by Berle and Means (1932) and since that time there has been a continuing debate about its validity. Marxists such as Paul Sweezy (1953a and b) and Victor Perlo (1957) have argued that the empirical evidence produced since the publication of the Berle-Means study does not support their main contention. A more recent summation of evidence may be found in Domhoff's *Who Rules America?* (1967: 50) where a similar conclusion is reached.

> The biggest shareholders in large corporations are actively involved in determining the general policies and selecting the managers of these companies. If . . . they do not bother with day-to-day operations, they still have the power to change management when they are not satisfied with the companies' performance. This fact has been demonstrated time and time again throughout the past 30 years.

The *extent* of the separation between ownership and management in the giant corporations continues to be the subject of empirical dispute. Unfortunately, empirical arguments over who owns what percentage of stock in General Motors and what constitutes corporate control in terms of such percentages tends to isolate the problem from the larger socio-historical context which a Marxist perspective should encompass. The larger implication of this dispute is the question of whether there is a ruling class within American society and whether corporate capitalism provides the basis for its power. Pluralist theory which sees competing interest groups at the center of American politics, rather than a ruling class, views the rise of the corporate managers as a crucial differentiation which renders Marx's notion of a ruling class obsolete for this society. Dahrendorf argues, for example, that the owner-manager separation "produces two sets of roles the incumbents of which increasingly move apart in their outlook on and attitudes toward society in general and toward the enterprise in particular. Their reference groups differ, and different reference groups make for different values" (Dahrendorf, 1959: 46).

While this differentiation may exist on middle levels of management, the evidence with respect to higher corporate executives does not support Dahrendorf's argument. Domhoff's studies have demonstrated that "on the one hand, it is clear that many members of the upper class continue to acquire the expertise necessary to function in the complex world of modern corporations and law firms. On the other hand it is clear that rising executives are assimilated into the social institutions of the upper class" (Domhoff, 1968: 269). Domhoff provides evidence that points to both the social and economic (through stock ownership) assimilation of higher executives into the upper class. C. Wright Mills in *The Power Elite* also concluded that there was no disparity between the higher corporate managers and the older upper class families in America; both groups are part of a single unit he labels the corporate rich. He characterizes this development as

> the reorganization of the propertied class, along with those of higher salary, into a new corporate world of privilege and prerogative. What is significant about this managerial reorganization of the propertied class is that by means of it the narrow industrial and profit interests of specific firms and industries and families have been translated into the broader economic and political interests of a more genuinely class type. Now the corporate seats of the rich contain all the powers and privileges inherent in the institutions of private property. . . . The old-fashioned rich were simply the propertied classes, organized on a family basis and seated in a locality, usually a big city. The corporate rich, in addition to such people, include those whose high 'incomes' include the privileges and prerogatives that have come to be features of high executive position. (Mills, 1956: 147f.)

Finally, in the most recent assessment of this issue, Gabriel Kolko reaches a similar conclusion.

> Recent literature on the nature and exercise of power stresses the functional unity of major political and business leaders, especially in the form of an "Establishment" of elites who went to the same schools, married into the same families, belonged to the same clubs, and shared the same values. The existence of such a group or, better yet, key family-interest dynasties is a fact that one can document easily from any number of valid sources. (Kolko, 1971: 233)

There is one other dispute that has developed out of the problems discussed above: the extent to which the so-called managerial revolution has changed the goals of the modern corporation itself. In their now classic study, Berle and Means first stated the case for a qualitatively new form of corporate responsibility.

> It is conceivable—indeed it seems almost inevitable if the corporate system is to survive—that the "control" of the great corporations should develop into a purely neutral technocracy, balancing a variety of claims by various groups in the community and assigning to each a portion of the income stream on the basis of public policy rather than private cupidity. (Quoted in Baran and Sweezy and Baran, 1966: 21f.)

Over twenty years later, Carl Kaysen spoke in a paper before the American Economic Association as if the development put forth by Berle and Means was now an accomplished fact.

No longer the agent of proprietorship seeking to maximize return on invest-
ment, management sees itself as responsible to stockholders, employees,
customers, the general public, and, perhaps most important, the firm itself
as an institution. . . . From one point of view, this behavior can be termed
responsible: there is no display of greed or graspingness; there is no attempt
to push off onto workers or the community at large part of the social costs of
the enterprise. The modern corporation is a soulful corporation. (Quoted in
Sweezy and Baran, 1966: 21f.)

Liberal analysts of the modern corporation such as Galbraith (1967: chap.
15) continue to accept the thesis that the separation of ownership and management has produced a significant shift in corporate goals. This contention
has important implications for the Marxist analysis of capitalism and its ruling class. Since the objective basis of class antagonism for Marx was the ex-
traction of surplus value from the laborer as the source of capitalist profit,
the Berle-Means thesis implies that exploitation and class antagonism have
been mitigated by the decline of the profit motive in the corporation and the
substitution of a wider social responsibility among its goals.

   This thesis has remained unchallenged empirically until very recently.
Robert J. Larner (1970) has discussed the problems of economic analysis
involved and has reviewed the state of the argument up to the present. He
then tests the hypothesis that profit rates of management-controlled corporations are smaller than those of owner-controlled corporations through a study
of 128 firms in the former category and 59 in the latter, all drawn from the
top 500 corporations and concludes that both types are approximately
equally profit-oriented. He further found in a study of 93 chief executives
"that the corporation's dollar profit and rate of return on equity are the
major variables determining the level of executive compensation . . . it would
appear that the nature of financial incentives and rewards in management-
controlled corporations is such that executive compensation and income have
been effectively harnessed to the diligence with which managers pursue the
interest of stockholders." (Larner, 1970: 262)

   With respect to the problem of power in American society, Marxist theory
therefore continues to insist on the existence of a ruling class whose basis is
the ownership and control of the capitalist means of production. However,
given the nature of Marxian theory, the empirical defense of this proposition
introduces an element of distortion through its emphasis on the subjective
behavior of those who make up this class: the interpersonal ties which link
them to each other and the values and motives which guide their behavior.
From a Marxian point of view such evidence may serve a demystifying
function, penetrating the façade of democratic ideology under which ruling
class power is veiled. It still remains, however, to stress the *objective* basis
on Marx's theory of the ruling class, as Paul Sweezy attempts to do in
several essays in his volume, *The Present as History*.

Sweezy's essays make several relevant points. First, while it is clear that there are more than two classes in American society, the nature of capitalism as a system of property relations still defines the capitalists and wage laborers as the decisive classes for this society. Second, social mobility and fluidity between classes does not destroy the existence of such classes as objective entities. A class is not defined by the personal characteristics of the individuals who make it up at a particular moment, and class actions are not determined by personal whim either; rather they are an expression of the objective position of the class in the structure of economic relations. The motivations of individual capitalists are therefore a false issue.

> The objective of expanding capital is thus not one which capitalists are free to take or leave as they choose; they *must* pursue it on pain of elimination from the ruling class. This holds equally for actual owners of capital and for those who, though not themselves substantial owners, come into the "management" of capital. Neither is in any sense a free agent. The ruling class under capitalism is made up of the *functionaries of capital,* those whose motives and objectives are prescribed for them by the specific historical form of their control over the means of production. (Sweezy, 1953a: 60)

Finally, this objective position provides long-run unity within the ruling class in spite of apparent differences and conflicts between its members.

> Capitalists can and do fight among themselves to further individual or group interests, and they differ over the best way of coping with the problems which arise from the class position; but overshadowing all these divisions is their common interest in preserving and strengthening a system which guarantees their wealth and privileges. (Sweezy, 1953b: 137)

In his essays, Sweezy also deals briefly with the question of how the ruling class rules, the relationship of the ruling class to the state. Here, somewhat inconsistently in the light of his analysis of the objective nature of social classes, he reverts to the more descriptive level of interpersonal connections and motivations, stressing that members of the ruling class either fill high governmental positions themselves or provide the chief financial support for the political parties which fill these positions. The main implication of this analysis is to deny any autonomy to the realm of the state.

This relationship of the ruling class to the state was challenged fifteen years ago by C. Wright Mills in *The Power Elite*. Mills called himself a "plain Marxist," in that his approach stressed the large-scale structural interrelations within society from a broad historical perspective. However the model of power in American society which he developed through this approach has not met with acceptance from other Marxian analysts. Since a recent volume (Domhoff and Ballard, 1968) has been devoted to a discussion of Mills's work and the arguments raised against it by Marxists among others, only a brief review is necessary here.

Basically, Mills sees a "power elite" controlling American society instead of what Marxists designate as the ruling class. In a long footnote Mills outlined his departure from the Marxist conception.

> 'Ruling class' is a badly loaded phrase. 'Class' is an economic term; 'rule' a political one. The phrase, 'ruling class,' thus contains the theory that an economic class rules politically. . . . Specifically, the phrase 'ruling class,' in its common political connotations, does not allow enough autonomy to the political order and its agents, and it says nothing about the military as such. It should be clear to the reader by now that we do not accept as adequate the simple view that high economic men unilaterally make all decisions of national consequence. We hold that such a simple view of 'economic determinism' must be elaborated by 'political determinism' and 'military determinism'; that the higher agents of each of these three domains now often have a noticeable degree of autonomy; and that only in the often intricate ways of coalition do they make up and carry through the most important decisions. Those are the major reasons we prefer 'power elite' to 'ruling class' as a characterizing phrase for the higher circles when we consider them in terms of power. (1956: 277)

In place of an economically based ruling class Mills sees a tri-partite elite composed of the top political, military, and corporate leaders. It is their institutional position, as heads of giant bureaucracies, rather than property ownership, which accounts for their power, and the primary interest which guides their exercise of power is the maintenance of these institutional structures. The institutional interconnections between the upper levels of the corporate, military and political realms, along with similarities in life style establish lines of unity between these three elite groups. It is obvious that Mills draws heavily on the work of Max Weber in constructing his analysis. Indeed, his major contribution to the study of power in American society develops out of Weber. What Mills defines so brilliantly is the consequences of the bureaucratic legitimation of power which has developed in this country since the New Deal. In doing this he also achieves a more convincing refutation of "managerialism," the liberal-pluralist interpretation of the bureaucratization of power, than is found in the work of more orthodox Marxists.

There are a number of confusions in Marx's own reflections on the bureaucratic state (cf. Papaioannou, 1969) and, because of this, Marxist critics of Mills have failed to confront directly this central aspect of his work. Instead they see the degree of autonomy which Mills grants to the political realm as the central issue and confront this challenge merely by restating the classic Marxist proposition that the state is the executive arm of the ruling class. At best they reluctantly modify this proposition in the face of Mills's analysis with qualifying phrases such as "in the long run" (Domhoff, 1968: 262f.). This procedure characterizes Ralph Miliband's *The State in Capitalist Society;* as the fullest treatment of the subject to appear by a Marxist since Mills's study, it is a disappointment. While the study is an empirical one, Miliband does not test Marx's proposition but rather accepts it at the start as a given, and then proceeds to demonstrate that the social origins of members of the economic and political elites are similar and that they are linked by ties of status and class. The problem is that this is the same evidence used by Mills to demonstrate the power elite thesis, and instead of any analytic progress we are merely left with a clash between different interpretations of the same data.

Nicol Poulantzas in a critical review of Miliband's study makes an advance over this impasse by stressing the objective basis of Marx's view of the state.

> The *direct* participation of members of the capitalist class in the State apparatus and in the government, even where it exists, is not the important side of the matter. The relation between the bourgeois class and the State is an *objective relation*. This means that if the *function* of the State in a determinate social formation and the *interests* of the dominant class in this formation *coincide,* it is by reason of the system itself: the direct participation of members of the ruling class in the State apparatus is not the *cause* but the *effect,* and moreover a chance and contingent one, of this objective coincidence. (1969: 73)

While not mentioning Mills directly, he does deal with the problem of bureaucratization by suggesting that the relative autonomy of the state in relation to the ruling class is necessitated by its function of uniting diverse factions within the ruling class. "This State can only truly serve the ruling class in so far as it is relatively autonomous from the diverse fractions [sic] of this class, precisely in order to be able to organize the hegemony of the whole of this class" (Poulantzas, 1969: 74). The bureaucratization of the state means that individuals from diverse social origins can participate in the service of this function. Poulantzas's analysis also allows for an incorporation into Marxist theory of more flexible, autonomous behavior on the part of the modern state. In fact, this interpretation is truer to the dialectical spirit of Marxism which sees a reciprocal interpenetration between state and economy than the more rigid assertions of a one-way economic determinism.

I have spent a rather large portion of this essay on the problem of the ruling class because in the on-going debate between Marxists and pluralists, this problem has received the most attention. It should be clear by now that Marxists reject the hypothesis that differentiation within the capitalist class has fractured its unity to a degree where the idea of a ruling class based on the control of the means of production loses its validity. For Marxist theory, the objective structure of advanced capitalist-industrial society, particularly in the United States, continues to support a ruling class.

The situation is quite different with respect to the decomposition of the working class. Marxists have been unable to challenge the validity of a number of social developments that have effectively worked to prevent the homogenization and unity of the working class predicted by Marx. Bottomore has summed up these developments as follows:

> The modern working class remains highly differentiated in respect of levels of skill, even though differences in earnings have tended to diminish; that increasing specialization of occupations has created a far more complex status system, as well as a multiplicity of sectional interests; that the expansion of the middle classes has reduced the proportion of industrial workers in the total population and thereby diminished their social influence; that greater social mobility has undermined the solidarity of the working class; and that the general improvement in levels of living has led to the *embourgeoisement* of the working class as a whole, which is now adopting middle class standards and patterns of life. (1966: 29f.)

This final development, the absorption of the working class into middle class life styles is commonly taken as a sociological truism, but studies by Goldthorpe and Lockwood in England and Serge Mallet in France challenge its validity. Briefly, the research of Goldthorpe and Lockwood suggests first, that the economic progress of the working class in relation to the middle class has been exaggerated, and second, that a wide gap still exists between these classes in terms of social relationships and life styles (Bottomore, 1966: 31). Mallet's research distinguishes between the spheres of consumption and production, arguing that in the former sphere the worker does share aspirations and standards of life style with the middle class. In the sphere of production however, "the fundamental characteristics which distinguish the working class from other social strata seem to have remain unchanged" (Bottomore, 1966: 32). In terms of the broader historical thrust of Marxist theory, these studies attempt to keep alive the possibility of the development of a revolutionary working class consciousness in the face of other social realities which appear to undermine such a potential. I will return to this problem later in the essay.

Obviously the failure of a unified working class to develop is related to Marx's prediction that the class structure would simplify and polarize into an absolute confrontation between capitalists and proletarians. The most important social development which contradicts Marx on this critical point of his theory of revolution is the rise of a broad and diversified middle class. Until recently, Marxist theory faced an impasse in terms of its ability to account for this development. However, in one of the most important pieces of Marxian social analysis to appear in recent years, Martin Nicolaus (1967) has convincingly demonstrated, using major manuscripts of Marx which are only now beginning to appear in English, that Marx's mature work on the nature of capitalist society contains a coherent theory of the rise of the middle class. This theory supersedes Marx's earlier prediction, such as in *The Communist Manifesto,* that capitalist society would polarize into two classes.[2] In his later theories, following his own study of capitalist economics, Marx demonstrated that the tendency of the *volume* of capitalist surplus to rise (a fact which is not incompatible with Marx's notion that the *rate* of profit would tend to decline) necessitates the rise of a surplus class, a middle class of non-producers for two reasons:

> First, as productivity rises, the number of unproductive laborers required to service and maintain the growing capital establishment also rises. The number of the traditional unproductive workers increases, e.g. clerks, bookkeepers. More significantly, entirely new branches of unproductive work are called into being, of which the banking system, the credit system, insurance empires and advertising are the most obvious examples, but the growth of the scientific and technological establishments, as well as an increase in public education generally, are also in this category. Marx himself pointed to the growth of this requirement for nonproductive services.
>
> The second reason why there must be an increase of nonproductive workers is that an increase in the surplus product requires an increase in the number of people who can afford to consume it. Surplus production requires surplus consumption. The capitalist system is based on the extraction from the laboring class of more commodities than that class is permitted to consume; the system would collapse if there were not also a class which consumed more than it produced. (Nicolaus, 1967: 39f.)

Nicolaus's conclusion that "it must be considered one of Marx's great scientific achievements . . . to have not only predicted that such a new middle class would arise, but also to have laid down the fundamental economic and sociological principles which explain its rise and its role in the larger class structure" (1967: 46) seems appropriate. But as I will emphasize below it still remains for Marxists to fit this social development into a political analysis which preserves the revolutionary thrust so important for Marx.

By placing the changes in class structure discussed above in the more comprehensive framework of the total society, the central challenge for Marxist political analysis posed by these changes can be seen. The relationship of this class structure to the productive forces which form its basis continues to embody the contradictions which Marx saw as the central catalyst of class conflict. On the one hand, the productive capacity of advanced

---

[2] Nicolaus demonstrates that the two class theory was abandoned once Marx had developed the concept of surplus value, which allowed him to construct his mature theory of the economics of capitalism. Before his full scale study of economics, Marx had to depend on what Nicolaus calls "Hegelian choreography," in order to chart the development of capitalist society. This Hegelian movement was "the inevitable process by which contradictions unfold, affirm, negate and gracefully vanish from the scene with a dazzling *Aufhebung*. . . . It was Marx's captivation with this choreography . . . which led him to the prediction that capitalist society must inevitably become polarized into two directly antagonistic classes . . ." (Nicolaus, 1967: 23).

capitalist-industrial society continues to grow; on the other hand, the society because of its class structure is unable to use this capacity to meet its social needs. Wealth remains concentrated in the top levels of the class structure (cf. Lampman, 1962; Kolko, 1962; Miller, 1964) while poverty, urban deterioration, and a variety of other all too familiar social problems remain unsolved.

Yet in spite of the continued existence of these contradictions, the intensity and location of class conflict today is problematic, and this in turn renders Marxist political analysis problematic. The Marxist search for the agency of change, the social class which would provide the link between theory and practice, actualizing the ideal embodied in Marx's social philosophy becomes more difficult. Some of the reasons for this are obvious. As a large segment of the working class no longer exists on a level of material misery the need for revolution loses its natural, material base (Gorz, 1967: 3). But, as Norman Birnbaum has pointed out, Marxist sociology has been deficient in its attempts to redefine class conflict in the light of these obvious facts.

> The obscurity and at times latency of class conflict have combined with its fragmentation to blind Marxists and non-Marxists alike to newer forms of class conflict. . . . Both bourgeois and Marxists sociologies of the working class, in sum, have been curiously defective; the one has welcomed evidence of integration [of the working class into the larger society] the other has deplored it, but both have failed to depict the fate of the working class as a component of the larger development of the social structure. A renewed appreciation of the potential social role of this class may indeed signify a consolidation of historical insight in Marxist sociology; at the moment, insight and analysis both remain fragmentary. (1968: 356–359)

The potential for class conflict in the new middle class also must be analyzed. While Nicolaus has demonstrated that the Marxian model can account for the development of this class, its revolutionary potential in the light of its role in the total social structure remains to be explored. The beginnings of such an analysis have been made; McDermott, for example, has noted the contradiction between the training such a class must receive, "while at the same time the advance of technical rationality in work organization means that those skills will be less and less fully used" (McDermott, 1969: 34). Since Marxists such as Mallet have argued against the *embourgeoisement* of the working class, a fuller analysis of the new middle class perhaps will focus on the possibility of its proletarianization.

The above suggests one major path which Marxist political analysis is taking today: developments within the class structure which will reveal new potentials for class conflict in terms of the continued contradictions between the forces and relations of production. The other major path is the study of the role of the institutional superstructure in containing class conflict in the face of such social crises.

This latter analytic focus has led to the conclusion that the integrating powers of these institutions has rendered Marx's distinction between substructure and superstructure obsolete. O'Connor, for example, has analyzed the fusion of the state with the economic base, contending that because of this fusion the class struggle has shifted from the sphere of direct production to the sphere of state administration (O'Connor, 1970a and b).

The apparent success of the superstructure in containing class conflict is a major theme in the work of Herbert Marcuse. While a full discussion of Marcuse's richly complex and wide-ranging thought is not possible here, it is important to see how he revises Marx's political analysis in terms of the attenuation of class conflict. Marcuse, along with Adorno, Horkheimer, and the younger Jurgen Habermas, is one of the major figures of the Frankfurt school; over the past fifty years this school has developed the concept of critical theory. Critical theory takes us back to the starting point of this essay: the philosophical basis of Marxism. Whereas positivistic social science treats social facts as objective entities, thus reifying human activity into a thing-like form,

> A critical theory . . . transcends its facts, rendering them meaningful, but at the same time placing them in the context of the tension between the given and the possible. . . . By first expressing what a social totality holds itself to be, and then confronting it with what it is, a critical theory is able to break down the rigidity of the object. (Schroyer, 1971: 132)

Critical theory thus sees the evaluative dimension embodied in Marx's social philosophy as central. For Marx the tension between the given and the possible was located, unified in the proletariat; this class embodied both the exploitive negativity of capitalist society and the potential for overcoming that exploitation, the potential for a qualitatively different society. Marcuse contends that the objective conditions cited by Marx as necessary for revolution have been realized but the final step has not been taken because the subjective factor, the proletariat, has not developed revolutionary consciousness. Marcuse has been ambivalent about the present status of the proletariat but his tendency is to discount this class now as a possible revolutionary force.

This containment of revolutionary potential is the central fact to which Marcuse's theories respond. The pacification of the working class becomes in his theories a model for the pacification of the total society. Whereas for Marx technology was a progressive force helping to create the objective conditions for revolution, for Marcuse technology today has become the force which is responsible for this total domination.

> The subordination of man to the instruments of his labour, to the total, overwhelming apparatus of production and destruction, has reached the point of an all but incontrollable power: objectified, *verdinglicht* behind the technological veil, and behind the mobilized national interest, this power seems to

be self-propelling, and to carry the indoctrinated and integrated people along. (Marcuse, 1969b: 34)

Given a level of total domination unforeseen by Marx, much of Marcuse's work is an explanation of its power. In this analysis Marcuse develops the idea of a one-dimensional society (cf. Marcuse, 1964). Primarily an interpretation of advanced industrial culture, he sees culture itself as part of the mode of production helping to contain its contradictions.

> Another factor which promotes the unification and integration of the society is a highly effective scientific management of needs, demand and satisfaction. This scientific management, which operates most forcefully in the publicity and entertainment industry, has long since ceased to be merely a part of the superstructure; it has become part of the basic productive process and of the necessary costs of production. (Marcuse, 1967: 410)

In analyzing the benign, pleasant totalitarianism which characterizes power in advanced industrial society, Marcuse extends political analysis into areas such as language and modes of sexuality (cf. Marcuse, 1955; 1964: chap. 3). He argues that the earlier stages of industrialism necessitated the repression of individual needs in the service of societal needs, so that a contradiction between the individual and society provided a basis for the development of a radical consciousness which could define the need for a qualitatively different mode of social existence. Today however, a technologically advanced society can allow for the satisfaction of these individual needs, but in a perverted form, so that their satisfaction does not challenge the basic premises of the society. The liberation of such needs is really their confinement (Cohen, 1969: 39). Social needs and individual needs merge inside the individual on a biological level and the perception of contradiction necessary for radical consciousness is no longer a possibility.

> Once a specific morality is firmly established as a norm of social behavior, it is not only introjected—it also operates as a norm of "organic" behavior: the organism receives and reacts to certain stimuli and "ignores" and repels others in accord with the introjected morality, which is thus promoting or impeding the function of the organism as a living cell in the respective society. In this way, a society constantly recreates, this side of consciousness and ideology, patterns of behavior and aspiration as part of the "nature" of its people. . . . (Marcuse, 1969a: 11)

Marcuse's neo-Freudian biologism has been subjected to a great deal of criticism (cf. MacIntyre, 1970: 100). What is important from our point of view is the problem it creates for political analysis. Earlier I concluded my review of Marx's work by noting that he never systematically worked out the problem of class consciousness; rather he concentrated on demonstrating how capitalism created the objective conditions which would bring about social crisis and revolution. Marcuse and other members of

the Frankfurt school create through their use of Freud a social psychology
to analyze the problem of consciousness neglected by Marx. But rather
than using this approach to demonstrate the possibilities for social crisis and
revolution, they use it to explain the *absence* of these conditions. "Marcuse's
whole social analysis is premised upon the assumption of a stable relation
between the needs of the controlling agents of the system and the needs
of those subordinate to those agents" (Walton, 1970: 650). The idea of
objective contradictions becomes subordinate in his work and the thrust
of Marx's materialistic dialectic is broken. If, as Marcuse believes, society
is truly one-dimensional, then no class with a revolutionary potential can
exist within it. Marcuse has struggled against this implication in his work,
searching for new revolutionary forces. At various times he sees students,
impoverished blacks, and third world liberation fronts as possible revolutionary classes. But he cannot link these forces to his societal analysis in a
dialectical way and therefore his hopes remain unconvincing.

As a result of this pessimistic analysis, objective contradictions give way
to metaphysical contradictions (Walton, 1970: 650). Critical theory itself
becomes the only remaining embodiment of radical protest. For Marx, the
truth of his theory was to be realized in the revolutionary activity of the
proletariat; such activity would achieve the unity of theory with practice.
In Marcuse's work, theory cannot find its counterpart in practice and therefore, divorced from a societal base it tends to become its own practice,
moving toward Hegelian idealism.

This idealist tendency, while present in Marcuse's work remains latent
for the most part, given his continuing search for a revolutionary class. In
the work of Jurgen Habermas, the younger member of the Frankfurt school,
the idealist tendency becomes dominant. While Habermas opens up new
ranges of insight into advanced capitalist-industrial society, his insights
move him out of the Marxian system on which he builds.

Briefly, Habermas begins by seeing the nature of domination in this
society in much the same terms as Marcuse, stressing the power of science
and technology both as a dominant force of production and as a legitimating ideology.

> In the advanced industrial countries, technology and science have not only
> become the primary productive force, laying the basis for a peaceful and
> satisfying existence, but also a new form of ideology, legitimizing an admin-
> istrative coercion cut off from the masses. (Quoted in Therborn, 1971: 80)

He labels the ideology of positivistic science "scientism." Under such a
system,

> Scientism increasingly becomes the prescriptive decision-matrix for ever new
> spheres of society. Insofar as more spheres of decision making are con-
> strued as "technical problems" requiring information and instrumental

strategies produced by technical experts, they are progressively removed from political debate. (Schroyer, 1971: 134)

Thus coercion is benign, conflict is attenuated, and society becomes one-dimensional for Habermas as it does for Marcuse.

Given this condition Habermas sees his task as the penetration of the ideological façade of scientism, demonstrating that instead of the neutral approach to knowledge which it pictures itself as, it is rather a system of social action which serves the interests of domination and technical control. Up to this point Habermas seems to be operating on the level of a classic Marxist critique of ideology. But he then introduces an almost total revision of the Marxian model of society, arguing that with the development of scientific knowledge itself, "the knowledge industry," as the main force of production, Marx's terms become obsolete. A new model is necessary in order to generate an adequate critique of scientism. For example, he replaces the mode of production with "systems of purposive rational action," and Marx's superstructure with "systems of symbolic interaction." While a full exposition of Habermas's revisions of Marx and the assumptions behind them are not germane to this essay (see Therborn, 1971 for a critical exposition) what is important to note here is that as a result of these revisions, Habermas's focus becomes almost purely epistemological. Language and other modes of symbolic expression are no longer linked to a material mode of production but become instead an autonomous sphere. Classes as agencies of social change disappear from his analysis.

Because of this, once Habermas demonstrates the link between positivistic or "strict" science and the interests of manipulation and control, the opposition to this interest is not a class or other collective political entity, but rather another system of ideas, "critical science." This latter system is based on man's capacity for self-reflection which allows him to penetrate the seemingly natural forces of nature and history so that the interests of domination these forces serve can be revealed and overcome.

> All critical science attempts to restore missing parts of the self-formation process to men and in this way to force a process of self-reflection which will enable them to reinterpret the legitimacy of existing control systems. Insofar as these reconstructions are able to link repressed dimensions of historical structures to both individual and collective self-forming processes, and can be accepted as fitting all available facts, we can be liberated. That is, insofar as men become aware of the structuring of their self-formation they can distinguish between historically necessary modes of control and those that are but unnecessary patterns connected to distorted communicative systems. In this self-reflective recognition of a pseudo-"necessity" the conditions needed to perpetuate unnecessary behavioral orientations are removed and men can enter into a realm of self-discovery. (Schroyer, 1971: 144)

Liberation in this extremely abstract analysis is not a question of collective political struggle but of individual insight that appears to take place

purely in the realm of the mind. That such idealism will be able to cope
with the material forces of repression in this society seems at best a problematic proposition, at worst an absurd one. Therborn's judgment that with
Habermas we leave the world of Marx and enter the world of Hegel and
Talcott Parsons is an accurate one (Therborn, 1971: 78). But his work
also dramatizes the Marxist dilemma of where one is to locate the sphere
of radical consciousness today given the society's apparent ability to obscure its contradictions and contain its conflicts. Given this impasse it is
clear that new directions must be taken if a Marxian analysis of consciousness is to remain viable. The bulk of the work of Lukacs and Gramsci is
now appearing for the first time in English translation and will hopefully
stimulate American social scientists to develop new formulations.

With respect to this problem one final body of material must be noted:
the writings of New Left activists which have emerged in the wake of the
social and political conflicts of the past several years. These conflicts in
themselves appear to provide an effective refutation of the theory of one-
dimensional society. And, given the activist commitments of New Left analysts of society, new conceptualizations of the unity of theory and practice
are likely to develop in their work.[3] While the diversity and fragmentary
character of the political analysis contained in these writings precludes any
systematic discussion of their relationships to the Marxist tradition at this
time, one significant direction may be noted. Many participants in the
rebellions of the late 1960s have returned to the early Marx as a means of
understanding and responding to their experiences. Not only is the early
Marxist concept of alienation seen as central to the causes of these rebellions, but also his early notion of revolutionary praxis, the idea that revolutionary consciousness will develop in the process of revolutionary action
itself has come to the fore again in these analyses.

In one of the most articulate statements to emerge from the New Left,
Cohn-Bendit's first hand account of the French student-worker rebellion
of 1968, he writes,

> What had emerged at last, and had hitherto been no more than the pious
> hope of some of the extreme-left groups, was the explicit demand for re-
> sponsibility and control over production, and it sprang from the sense of
> brotherhood that had developed in the struggle itself, and pointed towards a
> new and better society. It was this that made our movement so truly revolu-
> tionary, it is because of this that we can be sure it will spring up again. (Cohn-
> Bendit, 1968: 93)

> The workers need no teachers; they will learn the correct tactics from the class
> struggle. And the class struggle is not an abstract conflict of ideas, it is people
> fighting in the street. (Cohn-Bendit, 1968: 104)

---

[3] For an informative sampling of the best of these writings see Oglesby, 1969.

Given the vast scope of Marxism, a scope that in the course of the history of the past 100 years has become a sprawl, a neat summation and conclusion is impossible. I am painfully aware that for every point discussed in this essay, another point had to be eliminated. (The problem of imperialism is perhaps the most glaring omission.) In the course of my discussion I have suggested some of the problems future Marxist political analysis must confront. In more general terms, the social and political conflicts of the past several years will demand a consciousness among Marxist social scientists of the relation between their own theories and practices which may lead to major revisions in the Marxist tradition. Recent essays, such as those by John Horton (1971) and David Colfax (1971) not only offer incisive radical critiques of establishment social science but also suggest the necessity of the unity of theory and practice for radical social scientists and sketch out what such a unity would involve both for political activity and political research.

Finally both the eclectic nature of the best of the writings on the New Left and the rapidly changing nature of society itself will mean that Marxism in its confrontation with other varieties of radical analysis and with changing social realities will undergo extensive modifications. With respect to this possibility it seems appropriate to borrow Norman Birnbaum's conclusion to his excellent analysis of "The Crisis in Marxist Sociology." (1968: 380)

> It may be, however, that those sociologists most aware of their debt to the Marxist tradition will have to transform and transcend it; if so, the crisis in Marxist sociology may mark the beginning of the end of Marxism. Those Marxists who fear this eventuality would do well to re-read the original texts: a revolution in Praxis which cannot begin with its own theoretic presuppositions is in fact not a revolution at all.

REFERENCES

Avineri, Shlomo
1968   The Social and Political Thought of Karl Marx. Cambridge: Cambridge University Press.

Baran, Paul, and Paul Sweezy
1966   Monopoly Capital. New York: Monthly Review Press.

Bendix, Reinhard, and Seymour Martin Lipset
1966   "Karl Marx's theory of social classes." Pp. 6–12 in Bendix and Lipset (eds.), Class, Status, and Power. (Second Edition) New York: Free Press.

Berger, Peter, and Stanley Pullberg
1966   "Reification and the sociological critique of consciousness." New Left Review (January-February): 56–71.

Berle, Adolf, and Gardiner Means
1932   The Modern Corporation and Private Property. New York: Macmillan.

Birnbaum, Norman
1968   "The crisis in Marxist sociology." Social Research 35 (Summer): 348–380.
Bottomore, T. B.
1966   Classes in Modern Society. New York: Vintage Books.
Cohen, Jerry
1969   "Critical theory: the philosophy of Marcuse." New Left Review (September-
       October): 35–51.
Cohn-Bendit, Daniel, and Gabriel
1968   Obsolete Communism: The Left-Wing Alternative. New York: McGraw-Hill.
Colfax, J. David
1971   "Varieties and prospects of 'radical scholarship' in sociology." Pp. 81–92 in
       Colfax and Roach (eds.), Radical Sociology. New York: Basic Books.
Dahrendorf, Ralf
1959   Class and Class Conflict in Industrial Society. Stanford: Stanford University
       Press.
Domhoff, G. William
1967   Who Rules America? Englewood Cliffs: Prentice-Hall.
1968   "The power elite and its critics" in Domhoff and Ballard (eds.), C. Wright
       Mills and the Power Elite. Boston: Beacon Press.
Domhoff, G. William, and Hoyt B. Ballard (eds.)
1968   C. Wright Mills and the Power Elite. Boston: Beacon Press.
Galbraith, J. K.
1967   The New Industrial State. Boston: Houghton Mifflin.
Gorz, Andre
1967   Strategy for Labor. Boston: Beacon Press.
Horton, John
1971   "The fetishism of sociology." Pp. 171–193 in Colfax and Roach (eds.), Radical
       Sociology. New York: Basic Books.
Kolko, Gabriel
1962   Wealth and Power in America. New York: Praeger.
1971   "Power and capitalism in twentieth-century America." Pp. 217–229 in Colfax
       and Roach (eds.), Radical Sociology. New York: Basic Books.
Lampman, Robert
1962   The Share of Top Wealth-Holders in National Wealth, 1922–1956. Princeton:
       Princeton University Press.
Larner, Robert J.
1970   "The effect of management-control on the profits of large corporations." Pp.
       251–264 in Maurice Zeitlin (ed.), American Society, Inc. Chicago: Markham.
Lobkowicz, Nicholas
1967   Theory and Practice: History of a Concept from Aristotle to Marx. Notre
       Dame: Notre Dame University Press.
MacIntyre, Alasdair
1970   Herbert Marcuse. New York: Viking Press.
McDermott, John
1969   "Technology: the opiate of the intellectuals." New York Review of Books 13
       (July 31): 25–35.
Marcuse, Herbert
1955   Eros and Civilization. Boston: Beacon Press.
1964   One-Dimensional Man. Boston: Beacon Press.
1967   "The obsolescence of Marxism." Pp. 409–417 in Nicholas Lobkowicz (ed.),
       Marx and the Western World. Notre Dame: University of Notre Dame Press.

1969a An Essay on Liberation. Boston: Beacon Press.
1969b "Re-examination of the concept of revolution." New Left Review (July-August): 27–34.

Marx, Karl
1964 Early Writings. New York: McGraw-Hill.

Marx, Karl, and Frederick Engels
1947 The German Ideology. New York: International Publishers.
1959 Basic Writings on Politics and Philosophy. New York: Anchor Books.

Miliband, Ralph
1965 "Marx and the state." Pp. 278–296 in Miliband and Saville (eds.), Socialist Register 1965. New York: Monthly Review Press.
1969 The State in Capitalist Society. London: Weidenfeld and Nicolson.

Miller, Herman
1964 Rich Man, Poor Man. New York: Signet Books.

Mills, C. Wright
1956 The Power Elite. New York: Oxford.

Nicolaus, Martin
1967 "Proletariat and middle class in Marx: Hegelian choreography and the capitalist dialectic." Studies on the Left 7 (January-February): 22–49.
1969 "The unknown Marx." Pp. 84–110 in Carl Oglesby (ed.), The New Left Reader. New York: Grove Press.

O'Connor, James
1970a "The fiscal crisis of the state: part I." Socialist Revolution 1 (January-February): 12–54.
1970b "The fiscal crisis of the state: part II." Socialist Revolution 1 (March-April): 34–94.

Oglesby, Carl (ed.)
1969 The New Left Reader. New York: Grove Press.

Papaiounnou, Kostas
1969 "Marx and the bureaucratic state." Dissent 16 (May-June): 252–262.

Perlo, Victor
1957 The Empire of High Finance. New York: International Publishers.

Poulantzas, Nicos
1969 "The problem of the capitalist state." New Left Review (November-December): 67–78.

Schroyer, Trent
1971 "A reconceptualization of critical theory." Pp. 132–148 in Colfax and Roach (eds.), Radical Sociology. New York: Basic Books.

Sweezy, Paul M.
1942 The Theory of Capitalist Development. New York: Monthly Review Press.
1953a "The illusion of the managerial revolution." Pp. 39–66 in The Present as History. New York: Monthly Review Press.
1953b "The American ruling class." Pp. 120–138 in The Present as History. New York: Monthly Review Press.

Therborn, Goran
1971 "Jurgen Habermas: a new eclecticism." New Left Review (May-June): 69–83.

Tucker, Robert C.
1961 Philosophy and Myth in Karl Marx. Cambridge: Cambridge University Press.
1969 The Marxian Revolutionary Idea. New York: W. W. Norton.

Walton, Paul
1970 "From surplus value to surplus theories: Marx, Marcuse and MacIntyre." Social Research 37 (Winter): 644–655.

The Legacy of Max Weber:
A Non-Metaphysical Politics

DANIEL W. ROSSIDES
Bowdoin College

Science, said Weber, cannot provide truth (only knowledge) and it cannot validate values (only help to achieve them) since reason, fact, and value are separate and unconnectable realms. In taking this position, Weber sought to remove social science from the metaphysical tradition of the West (in which it is still mired). For Weber, man creates his own meanings in a meaningless universe, a possibly moral creature with neither natural nor supernatural absolutes to guide him. This perspective gave Weber a unique detachment against all views of society, whether Traditional, Marxian, or his own preference, liberal, a detachment which contains unparalleled benefits for the student of contemporary society and its politics.

KNOWLEDGE WITHOUT TRUTH

One of the interesting things about Max Weber (1864–1920) is that while he exerted great influence on social science he never became the fountainhead of a movement. I suspect that this is due to the absence in his thought of the metaphysical synthesis (or goal) that permeates (and vitiates) the thought of most Western social theorists. It was Weber's unique contribution to social science to disentangle it from both philosophy and natural science. To be non-metaphysical in social science, it must be understood, is not to go from social philosophy to American social science (or to English empiricism or to French positivism). However much post-medieval social science is obscured by the trappings of science, basically it is still a metaphysical quest (general, unified, systematic theory, systems analysis, behavioralism, etc.).

All this to say that Max Weber is the only non-metaphysical social scientist of modern times (except Montesquieu), the only one to develop a genuinely scientific social science. Viewpoints similar to Weber's have been expressed, of course, both in and outside of the scientific tradition. The traditionalist, the romantic, the existentialist, the phenomenologist, the philosophical relativist, and the social philosopher would all agree with much in Weber. But these various schools of thought start from premises which are quite different from Weber's and his thought departs from theirs quite widely. Social scientists of the most varied kinds have also said things quite similar to Weber but in the last analysis they too are worlds removed from the essentials of his thought.

What then is Weber's position in regard to the type of knowledge available to the social scientist?[1] Basically, his position is that science cannot lead to unified (or metaphysical) knowledge and that it cannot validate any system of values. It is this position which made him unique and which separates him from the essentially metaphysical tradition of modern social science (liberal as well as Marxian) as well as from all forms of religious and philosophical opposition to science and modernity in general.

The diffusion of Weber's thought to the United States (and to Canada and probably elsewhere) has been highly selective. It would make a fascinating exercise in the sociology of knowledge to see which parts of Weber's work were congenial to American social science and therefore accepted and which were not. It would not be too wide of the mark to say that Weber's ideas (bureacuracy; class-status-power; rational-legal, charismatic and traditional types of authority; the separation of values and methodology; multiple causation; religion and the rise of capitalism) are the stock-in-trade of almost every practicing sociologist. And yet I suspect that almost all of them would be very much surprised to learn that, by and large, he did not believe in truth, but was rather a reluctant "relativist," or perhaps better stated, a "stoic" and "existentialist" (not in opposition to but because of science), ultimately a moralist who did not believe in the validity of any set of morals.

It was not that Weber did not have strong convictions or that he was not a man of principle—actually he had views which he held passionately. But this is the point—his views were passions, not metaphysical abstractions or longings, and, more importantly, he knew it. To be metaphysical is to accept the assumption begun by the Greeks that the structure of the human mind corresponds to the structure of the natural and moral realms. To be metaphysical is to assume either that this correspondence allows the mind to fathom reality by itself (the deductive approach preferred by the Greeks and medieval philosophers) or that the mind must grapple with phenomena directly to find itself (the inductive temper of the post-Enlightenment world). To be metaphysical is to assume that the main characteristics of the human mind are unity and permanence and that because the natural and moral realms are rational (lawful) they too are unified and permanent.

That Weber rejected the metaphysical tradition of the West is sometimes obscured by the fact that he insisted on the role of ideal or normative elements in human behavior. Weber's view of ideal elements, however, was

---

[1] Weber's views on the epistemology of the social sciences are found in Edward A. Shils and Henry A. Finch, tr. and ed., *The Methodology of the Social Sciences, Max Weber* (New York: The Free Press, 1949), esp. chaps. 1 and 2; and in two well-known essays "Politics as a Vocation" and "Science as a Vocation" in H. H. Gerth and C. Wright Mills, tr., ed. and intro., *From Max Weber: Essays in Sociology* (New York: Oxford University Press, 1946), chaps. 4, 5.

far removed from the metaphysical idealism which makes up the bulk of Western philosophy. His view simply was that human beings live lives of meaning. In contemporary language, he would say that behavior is made up of values and norms and therefore social scientists should study social relationships as patterns of meaning. However, none of these meanings has any intrinsic validity.

Weber's anti-metaphysical position is probably also obscured by his wide use of ideal types and by his fertile creation of concepts in general. But in all this he was far from trying to impart to reality the nature of reason or to find it through reason for the very simple fact that for Weber there was no ultimate reality.

"The fate of an epoch which has eaten of the tree of knowledge is that it must know that we cannot learn the *meaning* of the world from the results of its analysis, be it ever so perfect; it must rather be in a position to create this meaning itself. It must recognize that general views of life and the universe can never be the products of increasing empirical knowledge, and that the highest ideals, which move us most forcefully, are always formed only in the struggle with other ideals which are just as sacred to others as ours are to us."[2]

Standing directly on the skeptic side of Hume (as filtered down through Kant, Windelband, Simmel, and Rickert), Weber made a sharp separation between the realms of value, logic, and fact declaring them not only separate but unconnectable. American social scientists, of course, say something superficially similar: a scientist must use concepts carefully, he must avoid bias and value judgments in his work, and he must relate his concepts to the facts accurately (sometimes a contemporary social scientist will say that the facts identify and speak for themselves and that the social scientist is better prepared for their message if he avoids excessive conceptualization). But Weber's insistence that these three realms are not connectable, not now and not in the future, immediately separates him from American social science. And it is a separation which is wide, much wider than we are aware. Actually the divergent paths which emerge at this point lead further and further away from each other.[3]

---

[2] Edward A. Shils and Henry A. Finch, tr. and ed., *The Methodology of the Social Sciences, Max Weber,* p. 57.

[3] One reason why Weber's divergence from American social science is not more widely known is that his work was introduced by Americans who were (quite legitimately) trying to extract the meaning which his writings contained for general theory (e.g., Talcott Parsons, *The Structure of Social Action,* 1937). Another is that a great many theorists acknowledge their debt to him, and then proceed to write works quite contrary to the spirit and substance of his thought (e.g., Seymour M. Lipset and Talcott Parsons). The American social scientist closest to the spirit of Weber's work in my judgment is C. Wright Mills.

One way to see this is to understand American social science as a continuation of the metaphysical quest begun by the Greeks. No understanding of contemporary empirical social science (which emerged during the eighteenth century and ripened in the latter part of the nineteenth) is possible unless one first sees it as the replacement of old metaphysical views with a new one. The craving for a metaphysical solution to the problem of human existence is uniquely Western. The history of social metaphysics in the West is briefly this: from Thales (600 B.C.) down to Socrates (450 B.C.), Greek philosophy arose and developed a teleological view of nature. This philosophic achievement developed into a world-view with Socrates who applied the teleological view of Greek natural philosophy to human nature (ethical and social theory) in an effort to bring about the unification of both natural and moral phenomena. This teleological world-view triumphed over its rivals and held sway over the Western mind until the rise of modern science from the fifteenth century or so on. But while modern science shattered the teleological view of the Greeks, the Greek mania for unifying all phenomena through abstraction and deriving a hierarchy of values in the process ("knowledge is virtue") continued into the modern period. With the triumph of the mathematic-mechanistic view of nature during the sixteenth and early seventeenth centuries, Thomas Hobbes played Socrates to Galileo's Thales by trying to incorporate society and psychology into the mathematic-mechanistic world which had ripened in the realm of natural science. In an act of genius, Hobbes dissolved the feudal-teleological social world into its last divisible unit, the individual human being (analytically living in a state of nature), and then went still further analytically to divide the individual into the basic building blocks of the universe, the irreducible material particles which make up the structure of all phenomena. What he was hoping for, of course, was to see if mathematical relations existed in this world of material particles and if they were the same as those that natural scientists had found in nature. Hobbes failed in this quest, of course—but he did succeed (or at least helped) in transmitting the Greek mania for unifying moral and natural phenomena (henceforth through the abstractions of mathematics) into the modern world of social science.

Deductive social science (guided by mathematics and Newtonian mechanics rather than teleology) prospered for a short period after Hobbes but gradually succumbed to the more empirical temper of the eighteenth and nineteenth centuries. But the craving for unified knowledge continued, the best example of which is evolutionary theory. Not only did evolution provide a master concept for unifying nature and for unifying human nature but the unification of both realms of subject matter was attempted by a wide range of liberal theorists (Social Darwinism) as well as theorists in the Hegelian-Marxist tradition.

Empirical social science has long since reacted negatively to the evolutionary view (though Talcott Parsons has recently embraced it[4]). In the momentous re-definition of social science which occurred in the late nineteenth century, social scientists not only rejected evolutionary theory but they effected a separation between nature and human nature (at least for the time being) reasoning as follows: while the empirical method is common to both natural and social science their subject-matters must be deemed different (at least for the time being) and separate unifications must be sought. Social scientists were certain, however, that the same type of laws found in the behavior of natural phenomena would be found in human behavior (and many felt that there was no reason why the same laws would not be found someday).

Contemporary social science has not worried much about the ideological functions which the history of social metaphysics has performed primarily because it is not aware that it too is metaphysical. One of the conventions of science is that it has (or is on the verge of getting) a self-correcting methodology which protects it against error (ideology), a view derived no doubt from a number of sources such as the alleged power of logic and perhaps most immediately from the liberal belief in the cleansing power of the competitive market (businessmen who make mistakes will be punished or eliminated; the political market will see to it that obsolete groups and interests fall by the wayside; the marketplace of ideas will insure the defeat of bad ideas). To say that neither social science nor American society has processes for correcting error or eliminating obsolete elements would receive much less of an argument today than it would have even ten years ago. Actually the United States is far from being an up-to-date, pragmatic, dynamic, utilitarian, achievement-oriented, universalistic society busily cleansing itself of the barnacles of the past. It is rather more like a Victorian attic filled with the relics of a hundred generations— except that we are not using it for storage but trying to live in it.

The metaphor of the Victorian attic will be referred to below when we turn to political analysis. For now its relevance for understanding Weber's divergence from American social science should be apparent. Despite lip service to empirical science (the separation of reason, fact, and value), modern social scientists invariably (and largely unwittingly) engage in metaphysics (even when they point to the need to do research and develop theory in the future). And it should also be apparent that by supposing that social science is searching for the as yet unknown reality lurking beyond our historical experiences, social science diverts attention

---

[4] Talcott Parsons, *Societies: Evolutionary and Comparative Perspectives* (Englewood Cliffs, N.J.: Prentice-Hall, 1966); *The System of Modern Societies* (Englewood Cliffs, N.J.: Prentice-Hall, 1971).

from the possibility that there is no reality to which human beings should refer their activities. Or put in Weber's terms, " 'culture' is a finite segment of the meaningless infinity of the world process, a segment on which *human beings* confer meaning and significance."[5] Or said differently, there is a world of difference between those who know and those who don't know that they are theorizing (or researching) not about Society but about Liberal society (the American variant).

American social science is still deeply affected (constituted?) by a large number of metaphysical relics from the past (as is American society). Perhaps the best way to see this is simply to talk of the *mores* of American society. From early liberal thought (Hobbes, Locke, etc.) we accept the reality of individuals and the ultimate lawfulness of their psychology and behavior. From Newton and the commercial age of capitalism (Adam Smith, Montesquieu) we accept the idea of a finished mechanical universe clanging creatively to protect us against sloth and error (our self-equilibrating economic markets) and to protect us against the tyranny of elites and masses alike (our self-equilibrating political markets). From the *philosophes* we accept the doctrine of progress and from Darwin the idea of evolution (the latter giving the former the unwarranted credence of science), a pervasive and powerful tradition which allows us to use the future to mortgage the present indefinitely and escape paying our creditors (blacks, reds, browns, yellows, women, the poor, workers, and ourselves) forever. And the methodological function of progress-evolution should be clear. Ever since the *philosophes* sensed that the empirical world could not be made rational since our basic mental frame is derived from experience, we have used the idea of scientific progress (the gradual accumulation of knowledge with tentative codifications leading to a grand theoretical climax in the future) as a way to avoid this epistemological dilemma. Alone among modern social scientists (always excepting Montesquieu) Weber accepted the idea of a world without truth. Social science as we understand it, in other words, is something that science (and Weber) says is impossible. Or put more simply, far from being a stripling which will ripen into a wise old age, social science, in Weber's words, has "eternal youth."[6]

Weber's separation of values and science has also been badly misunderstood. Simply put, what Weber said was that men cannot be "presuppositionless," they cannot avoid attaching meaning to whatever they do even in science. Their choice lies not in whether they will make value judgments but whether or not they make them consciously or unconsciously. Values are what prompt science (even science, said Weber, is a value

---

[5] Edward A. Shils and Henry A. Finch, tr. and ed., *The Methodology of the Social Sciences, Max Weber* (New York: The Free Press, 1949), p. 81.
[6] *Ibid.*, p. 104.

peculiar to our culture). Values are focussed and clarified by logical analysis and the means for attaining them are found by determining the causal sequences in the empirical world. But, of course, values cannot be based either on reasoning or factual determination for the simple reason that reason and facts have neither a necessary relation to each other or with values.

Weber derived his definition of "fact" from the historicist opposition to natural science (a definition first developed by Vico whose work has been neglected badly in the Anglo-American world). The facts of human behavior are not givens (data) but are rather the non-necessary creations of history. As phenomena which needn't be, facts are not sovereign either in relation to ideas or to values. The non-metaphysical social scientist need never accept facts in the way that a natural scientist must. Indeed, he can take a stance as to whether or not he accepts a given range of facts, something which can be done only in terms of values. To say that values should not be employed in social science is to say that the values implanted and sustained in the present factual social order are valid—a value judgment by inadvertence, a disguised *a priori* perpetuation and legitimation of social reality. Not to see all this is to engage in ideology, the partisan defense of a particular historical structure of fact (power) in the name of objectivity and neutrality.

Weber accepted aspects of Greek philosophy, of course. He accepted logic (but only as an analytical tool)—in fact so much so that to some extent his systematic sociology[7] was at odds with his historicism. And he

---

[7] Weber's attempt to systematize his sociology was interrupted by his untimely death. Major portions of this unfinished book, first published in 1922 as *Wirtschaft und Gesellschaft* (2 vols., Tübingen: J. C. B. Mohr) and in an extensively revised 4th ed. in 1956, have been translated under the following titles: *From Max Weber: Essays in Sociology*, tr., ed., and intro. by H. H. Gerth and C. Wright Mills (New York: Oxford University Press, 1946); *Max Weber: The Theory of Social and Economic Organization*, tr. A. M. Henderson and Talcott Parsons and intro. by Talcott Parsons (London: Hodge and Co., 1947); *Max Weber on Law in Economy and Society*, tr. Edward Shils and Max Rheinstein with intro. and notes by Max Rheinstein (Cambridge: Harvard University Press, 1954); *The Rational and Social Foundations of Music*, tr. and ed. Don Martindale, Johannes Riedel and Gertrud Neuwirth (Carbondale: The Southern Illinois University Press, 1958); *The City*, tr. and ed. Don Martindale and Gertrud Neuwirth (New York: The Free Press, 1958); *The Sociology of Religion*, tr. Ephraim Fischoff and intro. T. Parsons (Boston: Beacon Press, 1963). A full translation incorporating most of these earlier translations may be found in *Economy and Society: An Outline of Interpretive Sociology*, ed., rev., and partially trans. Guenther Roth and Claus Wittich with an intro. by Guenther Roth (3 vols., New York: Bedminster Press, 1968).

Weber's other major work, *Gesammelte Aufsätze zur Religionssoziologie* (Tübingen, Germany: J. C. B. Mohr, 1920–21, 3 vols.), containing his special studies and essays in religion has been translated in its entirety under the following titles or in the following books: *The Protestant Ethic and the Spirit of Capitalism*, tr. Talcott Parsons, 1930 (New York: Charles Scribner's Sons, 1958); *The Religion of China*, tr. and ed.

also accepted the Socratic value-idea that consciousness is desirable and useful—men may not be able to apprehend the world rationally or derive a hierarchy of good from cognitive processes but they can and should be conscious of the forces that act on them even if consciousness is a burden (which for Weber it was).

By and large Weber himself accepted liberalism but his was a conscious choice. Only the formal rationality of capitalist institutions, he felt, could escape the traditionalism of both the agrarian past and a socialist future. Obviously his liberalism was on the whole quite different from American liberal thought—for one thing he was aware he was a liberal (in the social sense of the term).

Social theory in the United States has always been superficial because there has never been much need to think about social structure or about any of the assumptions on which it is based. The liberal symbolic monopoly in the United States (Locke, Madison, Jefferson, William Graham Sumner, Lester Ward, Cooley, W. I. Thomas, Talcott Parsons, etc.) along with the liberal social and political monopoly (federalism, constitutionalism, representative government, the destruction of plantation capitalism by industrial capitalism, a rising standard of living and the modernization and stabilization of a corporate economy through continental and overseas expansion and political reform) have largely ruled out creative political or social thought in the classic sense (a discussion and evaluation of social alternatives). Great Britain and Canada (and continental Europe) are better off in this regard since liberalism never gained the monopolistic sway in those countries that it enjoys in the United States.

For Weber there was no scientific validity to liberalism and he was quite prepared to admit that its chances of success were limited since his ironic turn of mind (derived from his encyclopedic historical-comparative studies) saw the menace which formal rationality posed for social existence. All of which is to say that he did not put liberalism in the usual evolutionary frame of reference, a frame of reference in which capitalism is depicted as

---

H. H. Gerth (New York: The Free Press, 1951); *Ancient Judaism,* tr. and ed. H. H. Gerth and Don Martindale (New York: The Free Press, 1952); *The Religion of India,* tr. and ed. H. H. Gerth and Don Martindale (New York: The Free Press, 1958); "The Social Psychology of the World Religions", "The Protestant Sects and the Spirit of Capitalism", and "Religious Rejections of the World and Their Directions" in *From Max Weber: Essays in Sociology,* chaps. 11–13.

The above works contain many excellent commentaries and should be consulted. Of the many other good commentaries special note should be taken of Reinhard Bendix, *Max Weber, An Intellectual Portrait* (New York: Doubleday Anchor Books, 1962); Julien Freund, *The Sociology of Max Weber,* tr. Mary Ilford (New York: Vintage Books, 1969); Dennis H. Wrong, ed., *Max Weber* (Englewood Cliffs, N.J., 1970).

both the terminal stage of human development and as busily perfecting itself through gradual progress. Liberalism, for Weber, was simply an historical individual, a meaningful segment of a meaningless world process. Evolutionary thought, it will be recalled, is the main way in which bourgeois social theory has sought escape from the epistemological dilemma posed by the rise of empirical science. Unlike religion, science does not require at some point the "sacrifice of the intellect"—but, whether required or not, the evolutionary-progressive view based on the inherent validity of science and a technologically oriented social system is an act of faith, the laying of all eggs in one metaphysical basket. And just as the dilemmas of knowledge are warded off by this act of faith so too its magic works to ward off the structural dilemmas of the American social system.

Weber's multi-casual theory (associated with his analysis of the rise of capitalism and his opposition to Marx) has also been distorted in its incorporation into American social science. What he opposed fundamentally in Marx was "one-sidedness" or metaphysics (which in Marx's case took the form of economic determinism). In denying the validity of economic determinism, Weber proposed not only a multi-casual approach but a genuinely historical approach. Thus Weber was quite prepared to accept the economic factor as a primary cause in human history but as an historical variable sometimes all-important (as it became *after* the rise of capitalism) and sometimes subordinated to other causes (even if one thinks of them as economic creations, for example, religion or the state). Thus in showing the role of Protestantism (as well as economic factors, mathematics, law, political and urban values and beliefs, geography, etc.) in the rise of capitalism Weber went past the conventional question: What caused capitalism?, the question asked by Marx and by historians, economists, and sociologists alike to this day. Weber was interested not so much in developing a better causal (universal) explanation of capitalism but in exploring the possibility that no universal causality existed for social science to find. Weber's conclusion to this question has been overlooked by those who have struggled to answer the conventional question. On the basis of his historical and comparative investigations, Weber concluded that the rise of capitalism was a fortuitous coming together of a number of causes, fortuitous in much the same way as being a cannibal or a Zuni is a fortuitous event. Far from being related to human nature or to a universal causal process, liberalism is a gigantic socio-cultural accident: individualism, privacy, choice, equality, representative government, etc. are simply the results of a unique and (as we will see) probably ephemeral phase of history.[8]

---

[8] Weber's views about the rise of capitalism are succinctly expressed in his *General Economic History,* tr. F. H. Knight (New York: Collier Books, 1961), Part IV.

THE POLITICS OF A PROBLEMATIC UNIVERSE

It need not be repeated at any length that a political concept or paradigm, for Weber, does not have to be proven, it does not capture reality, and it does not lead to unified theory. For Weber paradigms are simply useful or non-useful tools (much like a broom or a hammer), a usefulness measured by the way in which they clarify value positions and illuminate the causal processes which stand in the way of realizing values (social problems). One can accumulate knowledge through paradigms but only in terms of the assumptions contained in them, that is, only in terms of the values on which they are necessarily based and the criteria which they establish for selecting facts.

Weber's fundamental stance toward politics is that political issues involve, in a different (non-scientific) form, the major pre-occupations of the social scientist. To avoid or to be aloof from politics, therefore, is to become irrelevant and pedantic. Indeed to remain aloof or to withdraw from the hurly-burly issues of the day is to run the risk of becoming a private person in the Greek sense of the word (an idiot) even while enjoying national and even international fame. But to engage in politics is to cease being a social scientist because politics entails value commitments and decisions. Thus both withdrawal and involvement in political life pose insoluble problems for the man of knowledge.

The problem of the relation between knowledge and politics was raised by the genius of Plato (*The Statesman*) who tried first to solve it by transcending history (*The Republic*) and then by accepting history (*The Laws*). It cannot be said though that Western secular theorists have been much concerned with this problem. For Weber, however, this was a centrally important issue. Those who write books like *The Republic* are objective partisans of a system they only partially understand whether it be Athenian aristocracy or American liberalism. Those who write empirical books like *The Laws* are letting reason and morality dissolve into the *status quo*. Either way the given social world receives intellectual legitimacy. For his part Weber wrote an equivalent of neither *The Republic* nor *The Laws*. His unparalleled contribution to the analytical and moral repertoire of political and social science was a result of the course he set between the shoals of both deductive and inductive metaphysics and his belief that moral action was far too important to be confused with either morals or knowledge.

Behind Weber's well-known political concepts lie a number of assumptions which are more important than the concepts themselves. For brevity's sake (and with considerable interpretive license) these can be listed:

(1) The beginnings of political analysis, for Weber, lie with a felt problem on the level of values (which include intellectual questions as values). Once a threat to a value is seen, sometimes by another value(s)

one holds, sometimes by somebody else's values, then a rigorous analysis (should) takes place in which one dissects the logic of his value position and clarifies its relation to a course of action. Then a factual analysis is undertaken to determine how to realize any given value-program or course of (moral) action and how to gauge its costs and its consequences. In short, public policy analysis would be a central concern of Weber and the beginnings of such an interest in current political science would have pleased him.

While science meant problem-solving for Weber, what he meant by this is something quite different from that technocratic meshing of experts which we associate with decision-making in our advanced enterprises (General Motors, Rand Corporation, hospitals, law firms, the Pentagon, etc.). It is not that Weber preferred the individual scholarly approach so much as the fact that the definitions of problems by such experts pre-suppose the validity of these enterprises and the society they serve. Above all Weber would link problem-solving to an examination of the socio-cultural structure which causes problems in the first place paying due regard to the fact that this structure itself is the foremost problem in social science. No one can say what questions would have interested Weber were he alive today. But his problematic mentality, or perhaps better stated, his capacity for seeing through *mores* would no doubt have led him to ask questions which might seem unnatural. What is the implication of the steady and continuous growth of economic concentration (market power)? What has representative government to do with democracy? Is there any equality of opportunity in any industrial society? Is there any equality of any kind? Is science and economic growth worth it on balance? Is an Urban-Industrial society really possible? And so on.

(2) The first law of social research is that no society does anything the right way. The second is that the best way to know your own society is to study somebody else's. Perhaps Weber might have added that societies which use universalistic symbols have found a new way to camouflage their existence and ought to be analyzed with special care.

(3) The state is not a universal feature of social life since society is possible without it, and perhaps more importantly, when the state does appear, it varies quite radically in the way in which it functions—in short, the state is an historical phenomenon.

(4) The state is connected inextricably with a social system, not with human nature (natural rights, human needs, the spirit of liberty, profit instinct, territorial imperative, reason, I.Q., etc.). The state (along with society) creates human nature or rather, whatever personality a society creates is called human nature. State and society do not reflect human nature because there is no such thing. Like most Germans Weber did not fall prey to the bio-psychological, individualistic explanations which de-

veloped in England. To the English such explanations appeared plausible since capitalism promoted individualism gradually and English theorists reversed the relationship and came (like their American cousins) to think that individuals created capitalism. The rise of capitalism in Germany was rapid and disruptive and it was quite apparent to all that it did not come from individuals.

(5) The state reflects the given distribution of power even when it disguises itself as a fiduciary system (monarchy, noblesse oblige, wisdom of the elders, independent regulatory commission, representative government, the government as an honest broker, etc.), that is, the state helps to identify the interests of the powerful with the general interest and helps to make sure that they are never merged. This is no vulgar conspiracy, however—power groups exercise their domination in terms of legitimating arguments and (especially in the case of the middle class) with sincerity.

(6) The analyst must never succumb to the facts of political behavior (groups, lobbies, voting patterns, due process) because to do so is to become a victim-lackey of the power structure he is studying. The greatest danger in objective social science is that the analyst himself becomes an object along with his subjects. The political theorist must always remain conscious of the fact that men (their personalities formed by and responding to socio-cultural systems) create their own facts and values and that there is no necessary reason why any order of facts (or values or beliefs) must exist. All this even while knowing that changing society is difficult (impossible?) and that one's personal values might (will) never be realized.

(7) This leads to another non-universal *a priori* of political analysis. In systems of any complexity the sources of instability and change lie not with any world process nor with a creative nor volatile nor sinful human nature but with the institutionalization of contrary values and beliefs and the deceptions and postponements needed to keep things going.[9] Complex society is moved by the tug-of-war between rival redemptory programs and no less when these are muted (or put into a Hierarchy of Meaning) by the surface sway of some monopoly be it Prussian authoritarianism or liberal democracy. In short, students and teachers seek redemption from education, the pious and clergy from religion, businessmen and workers from work and economic expansion, politicians and reformers from government, artists from art, intellectuals from social science, and Max Weber from nothing (except perhaps the call of a meaningless but satisfying duty to make his own choices rather than society's, something which only the existence of rival and meaningless redemptory programs allows him to do).

---

[9] Weber's view of cultural change as the product of contradictory cultural elements is a pervasive theme in his writings. An explicit formulation can be found in his essay "Religious Rejections of the World and Their Directions," H. H. Gerth and C. Wright Mills, tr., ed., and intro., *From Max Weber: Essays in Sociology,* chap. 13.

Only when these assumptions are understood can Weber's identification of the structures peculiar to capitalism (today he would no doubt include the U.S.S.R.) such as bureaucratic administration, the mass political party, the class system, and rational-legal authority be understood (and then only if the metaphor of the Victorian attic is used as a safeguard against unconscious utilitarianism and progress). Only then can one understand fully what Weber meant when he said that "men are not open books" and why he stressed irony ("unintended consequences") as a way of seeing the full range of consequences which flow from political and social actions. What politically involved citizen has not at one time or another agreed with Weber that "The final result of political action often, no, even regularly, stands in completely inadequate and often even paradoxical relation to its original meaning. This is fundamental to all history. . . ."[10]

While Weber's problematic view was a cause of considerable personal anguish he never made "a sacrifice of the intellect" to find comfort in the magic of metaphysics. He would have attacked relentlessly all such "illusions" and he would have continued the hunt for "inconvenient facts," especially the facts which went against party (metaphysical) positions.

THE POLITICS OF MATURE CAPITALISM

The relevance of Weber for contemporary political analysis goes beyond the unique detachment provided by his problematic world-view. In these concluding sections I will hazard a few remarks on the relevance of his political ideas for contemporary American politics. Needless to say that, as before, whatever is worthwhile in these remarks is his, whatever wrong-headed, mine.

Weber's uniquely ambivalent view of capitalism (I doubt that his name can be used to support an evolutionary view of contemporary society as Talcott Parsons has done recently) stemmed from his ambivalence toward rationalization, the relentless disenchantment of the world and its transformation into a causal mechanism by the spirit of formal rationality. Of course, the analysis and interpretation of the process of rationalization is the main thread running through the history of sociology. Unlike Weber other sociologists have applauded the emergence of this process though of course they have been of different minds as to its ultimate nature and meaning. By and large though, sociologists from Condorcet, Saint Simon, and Comte to Durkheim, Herbert Spencer, William Graham Sumner, Lester Ward, Vilfredo Pareto and so on were certain that science was good for mankind. Science for Weber, however, was far from an unmitigated good.

How exactly then did Weber view the process of rationalization, how

---

10 *Ibid.*, p. 117.

prophetic was his vision, and what political lessons and research follow-ups are contained in his general image of Rational-Legal society? For Weber formal rationality is the transformation of human action into means-ends relations. It is the scientific analysis of the means necessary to achieve goals and an assessment of the costs involved (ethic of responsibility). As such it is intimately connected with the central activity of capitalism, economic behavior, as well as with the central feature of the institutional structure of capitalism, its rich opportunities for choice and conflict. What disturbed Weber, of course, was the fact that the goals of a society which embodied formal rationality might eventually become much like the means. Or said differently, the goals of such a society might become vague abstractions devoid of meaningful content. Societies based on substantive rationality (ethic of absolute ends) invariably develop a rich body of concrete, par-ticularized, and accessible goals as well as goals which are placed beyond attainment through mere human effort. This careful specification of what is possible and what is not possible leads to Traditionalism. An expanding technological civilization cannot afford to have this happen and it there-fore makes many of its goals abstract and places their full realization in the secular future. In Parsons's terms we have the emergence of property and labor as "disposable facilities" and the "generalization" of values. In Mar-cuse's terms we have an irrational fixation on rational means (technology, economic gain) in a one-dimensional (Liberal) society. In the language of politics we have a speech by a presidential candidate.

The social expression of formal rationality is secondary interaction, in-dividualism, universal ambition and egoism, associational activity, func-tional specificity, voluntary behavior, politics, mobility (geographical and social), and so on. Its best known embodiment, of course, is bureaucratiza-tion but it is also the factory system, professionalization, economic and political concentration and urbanization. It signifies the decline of crafts-manship as a modal form of economic activity or possibility; the decline of patriarchical and/or sacred marriages and the growth of partnership mar-riages; it means black and women's liberalism; it means the loss of a sense of place; it means the decline of individualized justice by class and the rise of bargain-basement, administered justice by class; the decline of the entrepreneurial hero and the rise of the salaried manager; the decline of the clergyman, religion and the church-related school and voluntary organization; the decline of the versatile common as well as cultivated man and the rise of the expert; the decline of the independent professional and the rise of the hospital-based doctor, the firm-based lawyer, architect, etc.; the decline of the political entrepreneur and boss politics and the growth of administration and non-partisan government; and the decline of the in-tellectual and of political and social theory and the growth of social science. Perhaps the epitome of this process is the general expropriation of individual substantive rationality (whether found in the charisma of religious, military, political, or economic heroes) by corporate or bureaucratic (formal) rationality. Perhaps all this can be understood better by saying that all social functions are being industrialized as the New Middle Class supplants the Old.

For Weber formal rationality (an integral part of the Protestant-Bourgeois Ethic, itself the offspring of a capitalist economy and society) is a dessicating process which may (will probably) make society impossible. Formal rationality has enabled Western man to climb out of his agrarian slumber. But historical and comparative analysis told Weber that the motors of society are powered by sentiments: aggression, love, charity, salvation, doing the Lord's work, sensuality, magic, awe, fear, etc. and that formal rationality may eventually separate from its moral moorings, live for a while on borrowed moral energy, and incapable of generating its own sentiments, sink into the "icy darkness" of mindless calculation.

Weber's ideas were deeply influenced by his family experiences and by his membership in a society torn by conflicting world-views (Prussian authoritarianism, liberalism, socialism).[11] How his ideas would have developed had he applied them to American politics cannot be said. No doubt they would need modification to suit two novel social conditions which Weber as a German never experienced: the fact that the United States is a fully established society unchallenged from within and by the fact that it embodies an unalloyed liberalism. One thing that Weber might have noted with interest is that America's meanings (liberty, equality, progress, happiness, individualism, work, achievement) have remained intact as value-ideas over the course of two hundred years of national existence, one hundred years of industrialization, and fifty years of mature industrialization. These value-ideas represent America's version of substantive rationality (metaphysical beliefs and values) and they seem as secure today as before despite the pronounced use of formal rationality. Is it possible, Weber might have asked, that capitalism can create a set of goals immune to the corrosive force of formal rationality?

On a lower level of abstraction, what might Weber's eye for conflict and irony have seen in contemporary American society? Are there parallels to the great ironies of history—the monks who fled from material pursuits only to create the conditions of wealth; the Protestants who purified religion only to promote capitalism and secularization; the monarchs who promoted royal centralization only to further squeeze their nobility and help the rise of liberal democracy, and so on? What would Weber have said about American reform movements which protect society against change (Pro-

---

11 For a valuable analysis, see Arthur Mitzman, *The Iron Cage: An Historical Interpretation of Max Weber* (New York: Alfred Knopf, 1969).

gressive movement, New Deal, Great Society, etc.), about a social security system based on a heavy regressive tax which allows the upper classes not only to keep their own taxes low but to control the masses with their own money (by raising their benefits—and their taxes—before every election), about a technology which enslaves and degrades more than we are willing to admit (cotton gin, the assembly line, the laid-off worker of 45 who never works again), about progressive economic policies which amount to "re-actionary Keynesianism" (the private individual knows best how to spend his money, therefore, tax cuts are in the public interest), about economic growth which produces poverty and threatens (insures?) the demise of the planet? No one can say what Weber would have thought of such matters though my guess is that he would see them as "inconvenient facts" con-taining deep implications for America's "illusions."

All this is to say that Weber would not have taken society at face value. The extent of operational America's deviation from ideal America would no doubt have impressed him—how plantation types dominate Congres-sional chairmanships; how pre-industrial natural law lives in the breast of right-wingers and that something similar throbs in the heart of the New Left; how Oral Roberts can start an instant accredited university and how Billy Graham can make a good living denouncing evil without mentioning racism; how the War on Poverty fills the pockets of the well-to-do; how people go hungry while farmers are paid not to grow food; how govern-ment is absorbed into the economy and vice versa under the cover of progress, national defense, and the restoration of free enterprise; how pre-industrial vestiges linger to control (constitute?) our educational world; how millions have second homes while millions are ill-housed; how public toilets are hard to find; how equality of taxation between the upper and lower classes distorts our social system in the same way that the aristo-cratic refusal to pay taxes distorted the structure of feudal France; how women, blacks, and the young are coopted by an irrelevant vote and other civil rights; and how our professions, hiding behind the technocratic cloak of excellence and fiduciary responsibility, have developed labor practices more restrictive and more damaging than anything found in the lower classes.

Weber's response to all this cannot be predicted except that he would no doubt have noted that American society cannot possibly satisfy all of the many and contradictory values of its interest groups and that there-fore much of the foregoing deviation from ideals is a way to avoid waking up to the fact that America is a dream. And he would not necessarily see all this as leading to social decay or instability. Capitalism, Weber might conclude, is a tough old bird which will live much longer than right-middle-and-left liberals, social democrats, and communists think largely for the simple reason that intelligence and morality have a lot less to do with society than most (all?) people think.

But all this is relatively abstract. Could a Weberian approach provide something more specific about our political life? Weber's stratification theory, in my opinion, leads to some important conclusions and some important suspicions about American political life. The application of Weber's stratification theory[12] to politics has lagged (as Wiley points out in his perceptive article[13]) and its application in American sociology has been distorted to suit American predilections. Weber never intended that the dimension of Status (Honor, Prestige, Deference, the Warner school, The Protestant Establishment, social action as evaluation, etc.) was a substitute for Class or that it was more important than Class. In tackling the problem of inequality, Weber followed the main bent of his sociology which was to see human behavior as a system of relationships energized by meanings (values, norms, culture). Even though socio-cultural systems are irreducibly diverse and have no natural career or destiny, they nonetheless provide meaningful existences for the people in them. Weber never minimized the role of force and usurpation in human behavior but he did insist that at some point men come to clothe their naked aggression and possession in the garbs of authority and legitimacy. Thus the mere ownership of property is not an adequate explanation of social inequality. Economic assets are invariably turned into prestige assets (status or consumption groups) to complement (and sometimes oppose) Class position. Thus family life, marriage, self-adornment, residence, "socializing," recreation, manners, and consumption in general are institutionalized as hierarchies of differential honor and differential access to valued forms of interaction. Though status groups can be traced back to economic conditions they can exist in their own right and they can also run counter to the logic of the market (for example, when status considerations remove land from the market through entail or premogeniture, when occupations become hereditary, or when elites abstain from work). Depending on historical context, therefore, Class and Status can each be most important, they can function independently of each other, they can clash, or they can interpenetrate. Given this emphasis Weber can be said to depart from the monistic Marxian emphasis on Class.

Weber's definition of "Class" was also somewhat richer than Marx's. "Property and lack of property" are the basic categories underlying all class relations for Weber as for Marx. But for Weber property relations can be quite complex and class interests and struggles can take very different forms, specifically three: relations between creditors and debtors, between sellers and buyers, and between employers and employees (credit, commodity,

---

12 "Class, Status, Party" in H. H. Gerth and C. Wright Mills, tr., ed., and intro., *From Max Weber: Essays in Sociology,* chap. 7; widely reprinted.

13 Norbert Wiley, "America's Unique Class Politics: The Interplay of the Labor, Credit and Commodity Markets", *American Sociological Review* (August, 1967).

and labor markets respectively). Though Weber implied an historical evolution of these three market relations, it is best today to think of them as co-existing in our Victorian attic.

The importance of occupation in contemporary class structure was not stressed by Weber though it is somewhat implied in his emphasis on bureaucratization and specialization. He was quite aware, however, that economic and political inequality was being lodged in bureaucratic (occupational) hierarchies, the appropriation of the means of production finding its counterpart in the appropriation of the means of administration and violence. The importance of occupation for the derivation of income, personal identity, and power over others is of obvious significance for the student of inequality. However neither Marx nor Weber would have made the mistake of substituting occupation for class or seeing a managerial revolution against property. Managers may be better educated and/or more experienced than stockholders, and while these two groups may have their quarrels their fundamental class interests are identical when compared with lower level employees, consumers, and voters. And the same applies to the occupational system—doctors, lawyers, civil servants, professors, business executives, engineers, and so on may have their differences but fundamentally they have similar class interests in maintaining the enormous income, prestige, and power differentials they enjoy over their employees and clients. And perhaps most importantly access to occupation is massively controlled by class origin.

Weber's analysis of the role of political-legal forces in the class system is fragmentary. Though his sociology stresses the role of political factors in history he would not have been deceived into thinking that a franchise divorced from property or the formal right to hold public office or to be treated equally by the law were forces which counteracted the power of socio-economic class. As for civil service reform its meaning, for Weber, was clear—a decline in the influence of the masses and the rise of a powerful literati (holding positions by virtue of educational credentials which in turn are derived from class position). It was also clear to Weber that the capitalist enterprise needed a certain kind of legal order (one which provides maximum economic predictability either by ignoring moral, ethical, or political factors or by suppressing their interference with property relations) and he was quite aware that status groups invariably struggle to get the law and thus the state to enforce their demands for this or that type of honor.

All in all, Weber would not have doubted for a moment that the U.S. (like all industrial societies) had a class system in which, by and large, Status and Power were dependent variables. To deny that America has a class system because Americans are not class conscious is to argue with Marx rather than address the realities of contemporary society. Americans are not class conscious because the class system of mature industrialism prevents this form of consciousness from arising. The empirical jungle known as the American economy is so complex that its economic subordinates and victims are too diverse ever to think or feel in similar terms. To see that Status factors (race, religion, ethnicity, style of life, forms of association) further diversify economic classes is to increase our understanding of why Americans are not class conscious. But to complete our explanation we must also see the way in which the state (politics, government, legislation, our moral-political-legal equalitarianism) produces, perpetuates, hides, and legitimates class inequality.

Using Weber's theory of stratification, my own study of the American class system finds a deep absorption of Power (political-legal) by class.[14] Every aspect of American political behavior lends itself to class explanation provided we use Weber's definition of class and not Marx's. Our class system is a welter of conflicting, cross-cutting types of class interest (labor, commodity, credit markets), an attic full of various forms of economic rivalry and domination muted by fake fiduciary systems (including political and social science). Fundamentally the economic and social pluralism of American society is made up of and dominated by those who prevail in our various class markets (the middle class). Organized labor, representing a static 30% or so of the working class as a whole, is a small part of this pluralism (many organized workers live marginal material existences and organized labor has not even been able to get the federal minimum wage up high enough so that a family of four with a full time worker can live at the official poverty level of $4000). And of course there are ethnic, religious, and racial groups which occasionally break loose from their middle class moorings to assert themselves and avoid being left behind. In all this it is true that America's political and legal institutions are effective causal agents but as the following list shows they do not operate beyond the confines of our class system:

(a) Voting, the financing of political parties, political attitudes, political job-holding (whether elected or appointed) are directly and strongly related to class.
(b) Political representation is malapportioned and gerrymandered to favor the Old Middle Class and the New Middle Class. However it appears to make little difference in public policy (so far at the state level) if apportionment is fair or not, and the segregation of residence by class (and race) and thus political jurisdiction is now so far advanced that our political system appears to have been absorbed ("feudalized")

14 *The American Class System: An Introduction to Social Stratification* (Homewood, Illinois: The Dorsey Press, forthcoming).

into our class system (more than 75% of our congressmen, for example, come from homogeneous districts).

(c) Public policy whether in taxation, housing, education, medicine, social security, welfare, anti-trust, regulatory commissions, or in monetary-fiscal-wage-price-full employment policies is best understood as a preservation and modernization of the class system. Public policy cannot be said to be a force toward a more rational utilization of resources, toward more merit, or toward more equality (black Americans it should be understood are being brought into the class system at the bottom and so far they have made no significant progress within it relative to whites).

Basically our public policies make the most sense if they are thought of as ways in which government takes the heat off one class relation after the other in a never ending brokerage process which updates the *status quo* by smoothing the loss of relative position by declining class elements (for example, farmers, small business, independent professionals, unskilled labor). And interestingly enough, while government has grown the federal government has not (its civilian employees relative to the labor force, its budget relative to GNP), its debt has actually declined (relative to GNP), and almost all federal legislation is thwarted because it has to run the gauntlet of being administered by local government (the "feudalized" Old and New Middle Class).

(d) Far from being equal with problems of inequality our legal system is fundamentally unequal and has the problem of maintaining a façade of equality. Justice is basically an extension of the market system: lawyers have to be paid and expensive lawyers get you more justice than inexpensive lawyers, pre-trial detention and forms of punishment are deeply influenced by money, the adversary system assumes that competition is good and exists, what the upper classes do in breaking the law is not considered to be the same as illegal behavior by the lower classes, and different laws and different legal procedures exist for the upper and lower classes. The great constitutional decisions to extend rights to lower class criminal defendents (Gideon, Escobedo, Miranda) really amount to the bureaucratization of justice (over 90% of such defendants plead guilty and are serviced by a variety of professionals as they negotiate a conviction). Along with other reforms-without-change these famous decisions help to perpetuate the constitutional theme that the government is an enemy of the people, they help to legitimate a market-oriented legal system, and they divert attention from the question, Why crime in the first place, let alone rising rates?

Nothing illustrates the power of class and the weakness of American social science more than the widespread belief that the U.S. (and Canada, etc.) has either equality of opportunity or has made a good start in this direction. The common sense of the matter, of course, is that the U.S. does not have any equality of opportunity at all, has never had any, and never will (as long as it remains a capitalist society with deep, transmittable inequalities of income, wealth, occupation, and education). It is not that social scientists (including Parsons whose name will be around when the rest of us are forgotten) miscalculate the amount of equality or the difficulty of increasing it which is at stake. The interesting thing is that they should believe that such a thing exists or is possible in the first place. Of course some socialists and all communists know this but why is it that all Americans (liberals) do not? I think Weber is one of the few liberals who would have seen through the rhetoric of equality of opportunity probably by starting with the simple distinction that while the U.S. has enormous amounts of opportunity it has no equality of opportunity.

The confusion about equality of opportunity stems no doubt from liberalism's historic struggle to overcome feudal privilege—having defeated feudal absolutism in the name of abstractions (the people, freedom, equality, progress) the middle class succumbed to its own rhetoric. This was quite easy in the United States where the liberal world-view had no opposition to speak of from monarchists, fascists, anarchists, socialists, or communists. The American middle class, in other words, has lived in an unchallenged social universe in which its facile identification of itself with the cause of humanity has congealed into a cluster of *mores* beyond even the power of social scientists to penetrate (most of whom are Late Liberals struggling to overcome the legacy of Early Liberalism).

The only equality which Americans experience occurs within specified classes (and categories)—fundamentally the middle class competes largely against itself but even here the upper middle class has a distinct edge. Everything we know, for example, about education: attendance, years completed, I.Q., achievement tests, grades, prizes, diplomas, going to college, type of college, type of program in college, finishing college and graduate school are all related and heavily to class position. Even benefits from school lunch subsidies and enrichment opportunities seem to go to middle class youngsters more than to youngsters from the lower classes. And there appears to be a considerable amount of privilege—the less qualified middle class go on to college while high academic achievers from below do not, all in significant amounts.

The implications of all this for our achievement ethic and our professions cannot be gone into here (basically it means that we have no idea how good our best really are). Our present concern is with how all this affects our view of politics and the state. The class nature of education confirms the suspicion derived from evidence in all other spheres of public activity and policy that the liberal state is not an independent force. This can be seen most dramatically if we remember that public policy as it focuses on education does nothing to counter the ascriptive advantage of class birth. Education (the free school, amount of money spent, type of curriculum, teacher salaries, buildings, library, etc.) appears to have no effect whatever on differential academic success (Coleman Report). It is a mechanism which does not sort out the unfit. It is not even related to economic and political functions and cannot even be said to be keeping up with functional illiteracy. And from studies in California, Florida, and Wisconsin (and by implication all 50 states) our system of public higher education is a vast device to redistribute income from the poor to the rich. The present drive to equalize educational expenditures (implicit in the Serrano-Priest decision) even if successful will not provide equal opportunity. It may even make things worse. For example, our urban schools probably need much higher expenditures per student than middle class suburbs just to avoid falling behind. Public education is and will continue to be a legitimating device for ascriptive advantage, a vast subsidy to the middle class, and a way of modernizing our class system by providing limited and wasteful competition (according to class) and by providing limited opportunities for the lower classes (basically the upper working class) to rise in the class system to fill vacancies created by differential birth rates, economic and population expansion, war, etc.

Provided one does not confuse rising absolute levels of socio-cultural benefits with their relative distribution, the United States can be seen as a deeply stable system of class stratification which has made no progress toward equality or greater merit, or anything else. The dimension of Class (our Corporate economy) has elaborated congenial Prestige and Power (political-legal) dimensions which together work as an interlocked system to produce a society unique to human history. The touchstone to understanding American society is the absence of change. There exists a wide and stable difference in income and wealth going back as far as we have records (and as far as the data are available and comparable, back to colonial days) despite the Age of Reform, independent regulatory agencies, the progressive income tax, social expenditures, welfare, or the Welfare State. There are wide and steady Status differentials based on occupational prestige, styles of material and symbolic consumption, and voluntary behavior. And while Americans are better educated they are not more equally educated and rising levels of education have not given them more in common by way of belief or value than they had in the past.[15] Our universalistic perspective blinds us into confusing rising absolute levels in income, oc-

---

[15] Norval D. Glenn, "The Trend in Differences in Attitudes and Behavior by Educational Level," *Sociology of Education*, (Summer 1966).

cupational skills, education, etc. with a decrease in the relative distribution of these values and equating them with social progress.

Knowing this and seeing all aspects of political behavior as reflecting a deeply entrenched class system, Weber would no doubt have questioned whether political variables have any independent force in a liberal social system. In other words, he might well have modified the important causal role he attributed in general to political-legal institutions. Or put better he may have said that America's (and all industrial) political-legal institutions are incapable of counteracting the class system which spawned them though they are no doubt useful in helping it to solve its problems and modernize itself (and of course in disguising its existence). The basic lesson for political scientists in all this is that those who take American politics seriously have themselves been absorbed into the class system!

What are the basic trends in American political life which would have interested Weber? No one can say for certain. Most likely he would have been struck by the steady bureaucratization of political (and social) life. Would he have overlooked the fact that the strength of local government has thrown up a welter of public bureaucracies often in competition with each other and often working at cross-purposes? And would he have appreciated the difficulties that bureaucrats have with our populist tradition, with the way in which our interest groups by-pass legislatures and deal directly with government administrators? He may have noted the fraternal authority which has appeared at the upper levels of our bureaucracies (the committee system or the corporation as a technostructure, the collegial system in higher education and in other professions, managerial-fraternal authority in the military and government, and so on) but (unlike Parsons and others) he would have noted too, no doubt, that this was an upper middle class phenomenon (with a considerable traffic, coordination, and mutual respect among the upper reaches of these various elites) which actually insures the dominance of the upper middle class over the more traditionally bureaucratized lower reaches of society.

And Weber would have been interested no doubt in the way in which our stalemated society turns political questions into bureaucratic routines (the Institutionalized Presidency, government re-organization as political creativity, the growth of politically irresponsible regulatory commissions, public corporations, transportation, water, sewerage, etc., agencies, and our reliance on a politically irresponsible Supreme Court to settle all our major political issues). The growth of bureaucratic professionalism in public life is, of course, the counterpart of the pervasive growth of professionalized super-subordinated relations in the now difficult to distinguish private sector.

Indeed it may have occurred to Weber that all this represents his own fears come true—the deep technocratic streak permeating liberalism (found in its most explicit formulation in Saint Simon and Comte), which takes its contemporary form as the demand for autonomy and fiduciary trust on the part of contemporary elites, may have finally surfaced. It may even have crossed Weber's mind that, ironically, the liberal forces he supported against Prussian authoritarianism were not in such disagreement with Prussia after all.

To the extent that political science thinks of a system of interest groups held together by a referee broker government they are right to a point. But not to see the middle class as the main beneficiary of this "pluralistic" system is the major defect of American political (and social) analysis. Our political paradigms always contain implicit assumptions that this parallelogram of forces, this sordid business of interest groups, this structure of temporary imperfection is subject to higher forces: the Constitution, competition, universal norms and values, reapportionment, the national interest, rising education, strategic elites, reformism, evolution-progress. All these forces obviously exist and as socio-political processes they can be thought of as a functional system, as input-output processes, in terms of equilibrium models, and so on. They can even be said to provide opportunities for genuine political choice and thus moral action. But to see them as a social process which can yield objective social theory or to depict them as being in an Hegelian-like process of self-actualization are illusions of the first order.

American society works not because its functional requirements are being met (a tautology), or because it is a system based on shared values (it is not[16]), or because it is making progress toward realizing its values, or because it is meeting the dictates of human nature, natural law, or cosmic processes (evolutionary or otherwise). It works first because the American people have been so thoroughly persuaded that Liberal society is natural and in their interest that the question of what type of society is best rarely arises. More specifically, it works because the American economy is accepted as normal, that is, few dispute corporate concentration, deep gradations of income, wealth, and occupational prestige, and a national tax system that leaves income-wealth distributions pretty much intact. It works because no one can think in terms of imposing luxury maximums while most find it easy to think of an unemployment rate of 4% as full employment. It works in short because the upper and upper middle classes (roughly 10-15% of the population) are firmly astride the horses of power and social policies and problems are defined in term of their values and beliefs (work, economic expansion, technological and scientific advance,

---

[16] Michael Mann, "The Social Cohesion of Liberal Democracy," *American Sociological Review* (June 1970).

professional autonomy, competence gap derived from equality of opportunity and competition, etc.) even though these images are only tenuously
true about how society works.

It works too because the lower middle class (small business, small farmers, small town professionals, and local government officials) shares the
values and beliefs of the classes above it, and while it occasionally causes
trouble (progressive movement, prohibition, McCarthyism) it is a stable,
hard-working, conformity group.

It also works because the Working Class (roughly 50% of the population) has enough of its expectations met and enough of its disappoint-
ments explained to keep it within the liberal orbit. It works because the
Working Class aspires upward, is divided internally, and dislikes those
below it. It works because Working Class members who encounter problems solve them through non-revolutionary deviance, that is, they show
their acceptance of the liberal goal of success and its explanation of failure
by deviating into the ranks of Innovation, Ritualism, and Retreatism but
not Rebellion.

And it works because a Lower Class of miserable poor (roughly 20%
of the population) provides a lower boundary to society and thus helps to
preserve its identity and purpose. As a secular hell, it reaffirms society as
heaven and provides living examples of what the good should fear and
hate. It helps American society work because Lower Class deviance helps
to re-create continuously the sentiments and beliefs needed to keep straight
society going. Created by society and nourished by the welfare system
the main value of this group is that it helps to enforce the work ethic
among the marginal labor force.[17] In short without the Lower Class the
bottom would fall out of Liberal (every?) society.

All this might have intrigued Weber for implicit in it is the possibility
that formal rationality (and its class system) may have hidden itself in a
maze of metaphysical cliches (traditionalism) and may not be a threat to
social existence after all.

KNOWLEDGE AND ACTION WITHOUT TRUTH

Weber had what may be called a tragic, somewhat pessimistic view
of political and social life, an element in his thought that is as uncongenial
to the American temperament as his non-metaphysical politics. Tragedy
is a minor theme in American life having no deep roots in our history or
social life. An occasional American literary figure or theologian or philos-

---

[17] For a brilliant analysis of the welfare system as a way to legitimately quell civil
disorder and to legitimate "how some men are made to do the harshest work for the
least reward", see Frances Fox Piven and Richard A. Cloward, *Regulating the Poor:
The Functions of Public Welfare* (New York: Random House, 1971).

opher might see man as someone trapped by his own nature or by a social system derived from that nature or as someone who lives in an indifferent universe. On the whole, however, Americans believe that they live in a New Jerusalem and they are optimistic about their prospects for adding further to what they feel are their already weighty achievements.

One of the reasons for Weber's pervasive sense of unease was his poly-theistic value system. Unlike most of us, Weber was not anchored to any one culture and his values did not have the easy consistency that comes from living in the well-worn grooves of a single way of life. The empathetic or *verstehen* method that he used, in which one puts himself in the place of the thing to be studied, is not without its psychic dangers. Weber shows again and again a deep respect, if not outright liking, for many of the values of pre-industrial society—charismatic heroism, the grace and dignity of aristocratic life styles, eroticism, the sense of immediacy and "naive unambiguity" with which life was lived, and so on.

But of course Weber also placed great value on industrial culture. He valued ascetic Calvinism for promoting responsible individualism (and hated Lutheranism for promoting servility to the state). Actually there was much in Weber's complex and contradictory nature which was rooted in the petty-bourgeois (Anglo-American) stage of capitalist development. He believed in the liberal separation of institutional spheres because it pro-moted (and reflected) formal rationality. He believed strongly in the value of a free sector of voluntary groups. For Weber, the free, individually scaled arena of voluntary life promoted versatility and choice, a counter to his fear of bureaucratization and its remorseless "parcelling-out of the soul." It was here he felt that the individual could compete freely as an individual and that accurate judgments could be made about his capa-bilities.

Weber was also a German nationalist and he was very realistic about the compromises and expedients intrinsic to political life; and yet he espoused a personal ethic of brotherhood, he denounced the Kaiser during wartime, and supported parliamentary government as a counterweight to Prussian bureaucratic bungling.

As a liberal it is not surprising that Weber also set value on the formal rationality of liberal law. Unlike the diffused and personalized legal obli-gations of Traditional society, capitalism separates law from morality and attempts to govern itself through clearly defined legal norms, something which helps to make government predictable and responsible and pro-motes choice in general. And of course Weber was committed to science, to the intellectually honest kind of science which makes no claims unwar-ranted by its capabilities. All in all, Weber's liberalism rested on the belief that only a rich, complex, non-integrated culture based on formal rationality could provide choice and therefore genuine moral action (ethic of responsibility)—and above all else Weber's values centered on the supreme value of moral action itself, that is, the rendering of all values as problematic and thus subject to choice.

Given his comparative-*verstehen* method and his personal experiences in a society torn by rival world-views, it is not surprising that Weber found little inner peace. But for whatever reason, he was denied the comfort of conviction. Modern society was a rich congeries of choices and thus preferable to the immoral peace of agrarian and socialist existence. But it was also a congeries of conflict and contradiction with no roots in the universe to ensure its survival. Thus while he valued Liberal society above all others he could neither "sacrifice his intellect" to its illusions nor could he withdraw from it to the psychic security of a romanticized past or a utopian future.

Ultimately, Weber's tragic vision came from a view of science which destroyed all "illusions" including the belief that science is the gateway to truth and virtue. Unlike sociology (and liberal social theory in general) which attacked the metaphysics of feudal-absolutism in the eighteenth and early nineteenth centuries and then turned its fire on the new metaphysical enemy, socialism, Weber attacked all "convictions," liberalism's included.

Again no one can say what Weber would have questioned about contemporary American society. Beyond its rich and satisfying choices he might have focussed on the dilemmas it contained, the fact that it may never realize liberty *and* equality; efficiency *and* individualism; economic expansion *and* a respect for persons; grassroots democracy *and* enough public revenue to pay for civilized existence; private income differentials *and* equality of opportunity, and so on. He might well have seen much of what passes for progress as the standardization of life, as the blotting out of opportunities for heroic encounters, as the end of a manageable moral universe of diversity and tension. Above all he might well have considered the growing interpenetration of economy and state as the end of what limited pluralism early capitalism had managed to develop and/or tolerate and the beginnings of that "iron cage" of meaningless efficiency he feared so much.

It is for this reason that even in his own time he sensed the menace represented by the growing grip of capitalism over all spheres of life. The growing inner unity of Liberal society might have worried Weber on a number of levels. High on the list of his concerns might have been the question, Is Industrial Society a permanent half-way house providing some freedom for the few and mostly the illusion of freedom for the rest? So too he might have asked, How is it possible to narrow effective choice (moral action) through (not despite) the universalistic values of liberty, equality, progress, and so on? And of course, Weber would undoubtedly have gone further to face the possibility that none of capitalism's values could be achieved by anybody for any length of time. Formal rationality may well be destined to erode the sentiments which energize Liberal society and usher in "a polar night of icy darkness and hardness."

The supreme irony for Weber was that man had escaped bondage to magic, ignorance, naïveté, hunger, and disease by basing his life on science and methodical effort only to destroy the possibility of meaningful existence. His tragic presentiment, however, was not merely a belief that Liberal society was unworkable but that science had destroyed the possibility of any kind of society. Once eaten the apple of knowledge cannot be disgorged. For Weber the values of the past were lost forever, the values of the future were utopian (where they are not state capitalism in disguise) and a meaningful present was becoming less and less possible as the relentless march of bureaucratization turns means into ends and places life in a never-to-be-achieved set of abstractions (progress, perfectability, equality, happiness, etc.). Weber knew that his own work would contribute to the process of disenchantment and yet he wrote and not without a streak of Promethean defiance; and he would have regarded this essay as yet another blow at the illusions which men need to sustain them but he'd have wanted to see it written anyway, though of course much better.

A Man of His Time and Place:
A Selective Appraisal of S. M. Lipset's Comparative Sociology

COLEMAN ROMALIS
York University, Toronto

This article reviews S. M. Lipset's major works of comparative sociology, specifying their problematic assumptions and appraising their contribution to the cross-national study of political and social systems. It is made clear that Lipset's perspective has shifted over the years. The second part of the paper focuses on the changes that his views have undergone, and explains such alterations by examining certain aspects of Lipset's intellectual and professional life experiences.

Sociology is both an art and a science; it is subjective and interpretive as well as objective and factual, a blend reflected by the characteristically sociological debate, originally raised by Weber, over the notion of "value-free" analysis. Many have come to believe that no one can conduct a totally detached and objective social analysis; that social analysis cannot operate independent of the analyst's position in the social order, the path he took to get there, and a host of other social characteristics which define individuals and collectivities.

In some cases of sociological research, the problem is of such picayune dimensions or so remotely related to the core values of society that it is possible to evaluate the work largely on methodological grounds, or on the basis of where it fits into some research tradition, without giving particular emphasis to qualities of the sociologist who carried out the research. In other cases, however, the analysis is addressed to an understanding of the core values of the social system and/or is of such a broad scope that it becomes important to know the author in order to know his work. The writings of Seymour Martin Lipset pose just such a problem, since they are concerned with sweeping areal comparisons and with an explanation of the central "motive" values in societies comparatively considered.

This paper will, first, review Lipset's major works of comparative sociology, as they have appeared chronologically, specifying their key assumptions and appraising their contribution to the cross-national study of political and social systems. During the course of this review, it will be made

I wish to thank Steve Longstaff for the acute and thorough reading which he gave to a draft of this article.

clear that Lipset's perspective has shifted over the years. The second part of the paper will focus more explicitly on the changes which his views have undergone, and will attempt to locate the explanation for such alteration by examining some aspects of Lipset's intellectual and professional life experiences.

THE DEVELOPMENT OF A SOCIOLOGIST:
SOCIALISM IN SASKATCHEWAN

Lipset's first book, *Agrarian Socialism* (1968a; originally published in 1950), was remarkably good and demonstrated early his conversance with the classical sociological theorists, particularly Marx, Weber, and Michels, and his ability to join their thought to contemporary stratification and political issues. This orientation was enriched by the nearly fourteen months Lipset spent in the field (Saskatchewan) gathering his data. The thoroughness of his research, which combined interview, survey, and other quantitative and historical data, is remarked upon twenty years later by Bennett and Krueger in their contribution to the up-dated reissue of *Agrarian Socialism,* in which they note that their own article is primarily dependent upon the data originally presented by Lipset in 1950 (Bennett and Krueger, 1968). Furthermore, Lipset skillfully processed his quantitative data in the careful way imparted by Lazarsfeld and his colleagues to the students at Columbia, especially those working at the Bureau of Applied Social Research. It is indicative of this technical professionalism that Lipset even draws upon the "Lazarsfeld latent-attribute method"—a forerunner of factor analysis in the days when that technique was just being refined (1968a: 201). As has been widely recognized, *Agrarian Socialism* was technically excellent, methodologically thorough and innovative, and carefully argued. Part of the value of the book lay in its contribution to the then largely unstudied area of North American political movements and institutions. As an impetus to the development of a more than journalistic sociological literature on politics, the book was of the greatest importance.

From the standpoint of Canada, where little at that time was known and even less written about fundamental aspects of the sociopolitical processes in the country, *Agrarian Socialism* was a ground-breaking work. For one thing, Lipset's analysis of electoral support in the Province of Saskatchewan helped to dispel the popular Canadian myth that except in Quebec and Tory parts of Ontario, religion exerted little effect on party choice and support. Running cross-tabulations containing both religious affiliation and ethnic origin, Lipset showed the important stratifying function of religious affiliation with regard to political behavior, independent of income, occupation, or education. He was also able to shed light on the general association of the Conservative Party with the western Canadian Protestant and

English denominations, while showing that the Catholic elements tended to support the Liberal Party in federal politics. Despite the diffuse nature of these two parties ideologically, and their pragmatically opportunistic penchant for appropriating each other's attractive programs (not to mention those of the New Democratic Party [N.D.P.]—formerly the socialist Cooperative Commonwealth Federation [C.C.F.]), they continue to hold a clearly defined religious appeal roughly similar to that held by the American Democratic and Republican parties. This "religious" party support is even more marked when one turns to the minor N.D.P. and Social Credit parties—the Canadian Left and Right, respectively.[1]

Lipset's second finding of major importance in *Agrarian Socialism* deals with the actual or perceived colonialism which operates even in a country as developed as Canada. "Internal colonialism," although it is often considered under the heading of "regionalism," is also essentially a function of varying economic roles combined with superordination, subordination, and dependence; and in some countries (such as Mexico), "internal colonialism" may be composed of regional economic disparities reinforced by ethnic and cultural differences (see, e.g., González Casanova, 1965; and Stavenhagen, 1965). In somewhat diluted form, the whole of Western Canada has often considered itself a supplier of raw materials for the industrial East (usually thought of as the Toronto region), and it is conceivable that one of the explanations of splinter, "maverick", or third-party politics can be traced to feelings that only a local party will not sell out a Western province to Eastern political and economic interests. In British Columbia, for example, both the provincial Government and the official Opposition are minority parties (within the national context), while the Liberals and Progressive Conservatives are weakly represented and their parties are considered a graveyard—or better, a quicksand—for politicians with federal aspirations. Of course, the major party faithful may be rewarded by such federal appointments as judgeships or Senate seats; but within the sphere of elective politics, there is little movement between the national electoral arena of the two main parties, and those of the Western provincial organizations.

Lipset recognized that the C.C.F. Government in Saskatchewan was too dependent economically and constitutionally upon the federal government, indeed upon the rest of North America, to have full freedom in planning and operating the province along socialist lines. It is one of the great virtues of his book that he understood these implications, that he was able to view

---

[1] My own data, collected in a survey of the attitudes of the Montreal Jews toward French Canadian nationalism and separatism in Quebec, indicate that more than 90% of the voting age Jews in that city support the Liberal Party both in Quebec provincial politics and also nationally (Romalis, 1967). Traditionally, the Quebec provincial party, the Union Nationale, clearly has had specific French Canadian and Catholic appeals (McDonald, 1969).

Saskatchewan within its North American context. Yet, it seems that even *more* importance could be attached to this factor that Lipset attributes. Not only was the Saskatchewan C.C.F. Government unable to pass certain types of legislation without having it declared *ultra vires* by the Canadian Supreme Court, but the United States has also viewed with some measure of hostility this bridgehead of socialism on the North American continent. Among the consequences of this was the slackening of American investments in the province, as well as outright financial support for "anti-socialist" campaigns such as the doctors' strike of 1962.

The straight electoral analyses in *Agrarian Socialism,* and the hypotheses Lipset formulates as to the sources of cleavage and cohesion in Canadian society were all so thoughtfully worked out that current political studies by Canadian researchers have found little reason to criticize his work in any fundamental sense. However, in his Introduction to the Anchor edition of *Agrarian Socialism,* Lipset says that since writing the book he has altered his position with respect to the abilities of third parties to arise and sustain themselves in Canada, and now attributes a great deal more weight to constitutional arrangements for electoral support, and to the important constituency representation system of Canada, where there is no separate election for a supreme electoral post (such as a United States President). On the basis of research data centered on the dramatic rise of the Social Credit Party in Quebec during the 1962 and 1963 federal elections, Pinard argues that Lipset is over-estimating the effect of the varying electoral systems; although "formal" variables such as constitutional arrangements do clearly buttress and help to sustain certain types of political behavior, such as the emergence of third parties, they are not the main causes. These are still to be found in the structural, economic, and sociopolitical conditions characterizing varying geographic regions of the country (Pinard, 1967).

Pinard also makes the point, now acknowledged by Lipset, that radical third parties in North America can grow, independent of a "one class social structure" as Lipset characterized the Saskatchewan of the 1940s. Of course, occupational uniformity can easily be a facilitating factor in class-based action, but present-day Quebec is far too complex to be labeled "one class" and yet the Social Credit Party and *separatiste* Parti Quebecois have arisen there, while economically complex and highly differentiated Ontario and British Columbia have given consistently strong support to the New Democratic Party. Perhaps, as Lipset suggests, it is the flexibility of the Canadian electoral system which permits the emergence of third parties. But it is evidently also the case, as Pinard's data suggest, that extra-legislative *social* structural conditions underlie and bolster such third parties. The assignment of causal priority to formal electoral arrangements as opposed to structural conditions, in the emergence of third parties, has not a shred of empirical support.

POLITICAL MAN AND THE DEVELOPMENT
OF AMERICAN NATIONALISM

In *Agrarian Socialism,* Lipset had launched his career with an interest in how the United States is distinguished from other countries, especially with respect to social structure and politics, and he had selected Canada for his comparative research setting. The essays in *Political Man* (1963; originally published in 1960) continue this trend, and even more explicitly are based on comparative data drawn from Europe and from the developing nations. Precisely because the analysis of development is such a value-laden area, and because Lipset's attention was focusing more on what he called "the conditions of the democratic order", one of the important and fascinating parts of the book is the Introduction to the 1963 Anchor edition: important because, as Lipset says, it ". . . enables the reader or critic to locate the politics which accompany the analysis"; and fascinating because his ideological biases are so revealing.[2] For these reasons it is well to consider closely what Lipset has to say in his Introduction as he labors to make explicit his biases, among which is the peculiar remark that ". . . I consider myself a man of the left, but, I must add that I think of the United States as a nation in which *leftist values* predominate." To add strength to his assertion, he invokes the authority of Talcott Parsons, whom he cites as defining Lipset's as a non-dogmatic Marxist approach. Therefore, Lipset concludes, he could *hardly* be conservative.

Many of Lipset's assertions in his Introduction to *Political Man* are so naively nationalistic that it is tempting to quote at length from it. Any man who aspires to scientific objectivity, as does Lipset, and can at the same time celebrate American foreign policy in the following terms, is laying bare a nationalist orientation which has serious consequences for comparative political analysis.

> . . . anyone who seeks to understand American foreign policy must recognize that it has rested primarily on the commitment of the United States to extend democracy and to oppose political imperialism ever since the country overthrew its own rulers . . . .

As a case in point, his embrace of the domino theory is reinforced by a narrowly nationalist view of the Korean War:

> Stalin had been absolutely convinced that capitalist America would never allow the Communists to take over China. The fact that it did undoubtedly contributed to his willingness to unleash the Korean War, since it must have

---

[2] The lengthy Introduction to the 1963 Anchor edition of *Political Man* was written largely as a response to the variety of criticism which greeted the book's original publication three years earlier.

seemed obvious that a nation which would not fight for China in 1948–49 would hardly intervene in South Korea in 1950.

A brief selection of Lipset's views from his Introduction reveals his limitations for the comprehension of comparative sociology and international relations. For instance, Lipset's contention that ". . . in 1962 the Kennedy administration offered economic assistance to the Marxist and pro-Communist regime in British Guiana, asking only that it remain formally neutral in international affairs and democratic in its electoral system", is repudiated by former Premier Cheddi Jagan's own testimony that the United States and Britain put an unyielding squeeze upon British Guiana in the conduct of her affairs, forbade Jagan to trade with China and other Eastern bloc countries, and freely circulated C.I.A. men and money throughout the country to work for the overthrow of Jagan and the installation of the economically and politically more acceptable Forbes Burnham, meanwhile crying that the British Guiana conflict was both racial and "communist".[3] Once Burnham was in power, furthermore, the U.S. began to grant the aid necessary for road construction and other social overhead projects that had long been desperately needed by British Guiana. It is no secret that it is not only British Guiana's strategic position on the South American mainland, but also her rich bauxite reserves presently being exploited by North American interests, that have motivated the keen U.S. interest in the preservation of "democracy" (as Lipset calls it) in that otherwise insignificant country.

The quite extraordinary belief in America's righteousness which shapes Lipset's political understanding is again demonstrated by the following passage from his Introduction:[4]

> The United States has not made a serious effort to overthrow Fidel Castro by force, to a considerable degree because the American political tradition finds such behavior so repugnant. It is, of course, true that certain groups in the military and the Central Intelligence Agency have engaged in secret operations which clearly violate these assumptions. But the very fact that these are done secretly pays tribute to the political morality of most Americans, and it should be also noted that, with the exception of Guatemala, accusations by foreign critics of such efforts have pointed to supposed American failures, as in Laos, rather than successes in affecting affairs abroad.

It requires an exceedingly selective view to construe the extensive clandestine activities of the C.I.A. both externally and internally, as an expression of American political morality, and to characterize these activities as mere

---

[3] Jagan has given this analysis verbally, publically, and in seminar, in St. Lucia, British West Indies, during September 1967. Additional documentation is provided in Lewis (1969).

[4] Gideon Sjoberg and Roger Nett (1968) also cite this passage in their discussion of values and analysis.

good-natured bungling is ludicrous. It is this type of nationalist perspective which leads Lipset, as we will see later, to speak of the United States as a revolutionary society committed to the spread of egalitarianism, and faithful to the principles enunciated in the Declaration of Independence.

In trying to determine the conditions which facilitate a democratic order, Lipset relies largely on the argument that ". . . the chances for stable democracy are enhanced to the extent that groups and individuals have a number of crosscutting, politically relevant affiliations" (1963: 77), an argument first developed by Lipset, Martin Trow, and James Coleman in their fine study of the International Typographical Union, *Union Democracy* (1956: 13–16). The notion that crosspressures—or lines of conflict—at a lower level of the sociopolitical order can yield stability at a higher level of organization has a long history which can be traced through Simmel (1955); Berelson, Lazarsfeld, and McPhee (1954); Gluckman (1955); and Coser (1956), and is demonstrated in recent detailed field studies to be a useful analytic concept today (Frankenberg, 1957; Jayawardena, 1963). So Lipset has considerable academic agreement for his functionalist assumption that a stable equilibrium is frequently sustained by a diversity of conflict bases, and a lack of consensus on the goals of conflict groups. In fact, in the real world of politics this relationship has been well understood, receiving its Machiavellian application in the maxim: "Divide, to rule." Few things have pleased ruling classes or imperial powers more than seeing subordinates squabbling among themselves and working at cross-purposes, rather than concentrating their efforts on throwing out those at the top.

The mistake Lipset seems to make, however, is in confusing stability with democracy, and both with the United States. He writes, for instance:

> If crosscutting bases of cleavage makes a more vital democracy, it follows that, all other factors being constant, two-part systems are better than multi-party systems, that the election of officials on a territorial basis is preferable to proportional representation, and federalism is superior to a unitary state. (1963: 80)

If the distillation of stability and democracy is seen to be the United States, what does Lipset consider the greatest threat? The villain is communism, which ". . . cannot possibly be accorded the right of access to actual political power by a democratic society" (1963: 83). The reason for this is that "The Communists' self-image, and more particularly their ties to the Soviet Union, lead them to accept the self-fulfilling prophecy that they cannot secure their ends by democratic means" (1963: 83). In Lipset's view, the tragedy is that the communists actually seem to be in a position of increasing power:

> In Asia the left wing is now in power during a period of population explosion and early industrialization, and will have to accept responsibility for all the

consequent miseries. And, as in the poorer areas of Europe, the Communists, who capitalize on all these discontents in a completely irresponsible fashion, are currently a major party—the second largest in most Asian states. (1963: 84)

Accordingly, Lipset concludes in the next line, ". . . the prognosis for political democracy in Asia and Africa is bleak", ignoring totally the possible legitimacy of communism as an ideology of social change and development, not to mention the variability of communism and the national forms which it assumes (many of which are no less "democratic" than the non-communist political systems of numerous developing nations). In the Caribbean, for example, there certainly is greater popular participation of the population and sensitivity to its needs and wishes in Cuban communism than there is in Haitian non-communism; while the "communist" Government of Cheddi Jagan in Guyana was as "democratic" as that of non-communist Forbes Burnham or Trinidad's Eric Williams's. In another area, communist Yugoslavia is no less "democratic" than is Greece; and apparently the same relationship holds for communist Kerala and selected Indian non-communist states. The list could be extended; but the point is that Lipset's analysis is wrong largely because his ideological posture has led him to ignore counterevidence. Recently, for example, John Kautsky (1968: 184–206) has tested quantitatively the cross-national relationship between communism and economic development and finds, *contra* Lipset, that a definite curvilinear relationship exists between degree of economic development and Communist Party strength—not the inverse relationship claimed by *Political Man.*

Throughout *Political Man,* Lipset is strongest when limiting himself to the analysis of voting behavior and political attitudes and clarifying the roles of the major stratifying variables: income, occupation, education, age, religious affiliation, and ethnic origin. Where the book weakens badly is in those sections in which the author's American nationalism and anti-communism determine his view of social and political processes beyond the borders of the United States, especially in the underdeveloped countries.

THE PREOCCUPATION WITH VALUE ORIENTATIONS

Lipset's two most recent books dealing with comparative sociology and development, *The First New Nation* (1963) and *Revolution and Counterrevolution* (1968b) are comprised of collections of essays dealing with many similar or identical problems. Essentially, Lipset is concerned to demonstrate through a comparison of historical data and more contemporary structural information that the value systems of nations can be traced to their early histories, as the young countries transformed themselves from colonial dependencies to sovereign states. Unfortunately, he fails to make clear the extent to which these early experiences, such as the American

Revolutionary War and Declaration of Independence, became the "predispositions" which became the "value systems" of the countries under consideration, relative to the weight which should attach to: (a) the constant adaptations in values which societies make to bring themselves into line with altered structural circumstances;[5] and (b) the significance of contemporary data regarding social, political, and material interest-motivated behavior.[6] Instead, Lipset attempts to trace through history the geneses and constancy of present-day values, which are presumed to cause behavior.

While Lipset's purpose is thus clear, one of the more serious consequences of his approach is that it forecloses opportunities for consideration of contrary evidence. For example, we may note the absence of the American Negroes from Lipset's books, with all the questions and challenges which they pose for the American democratic system which Lipset has celebrated in so many hundreds of pages.[7] Indeed, the fact that they finally make an appearance in the Appendix to *The First New Nation,* and then only as a troublesome and anomalous afterthought, calls into question the selectivity of the data Lipset adduces to support his principal arguments. The Englishwoman Harriet Martineau seems to have been more concerned about the position of the Negro in the American society of her time, in the 1820s and 30s, than has been Lipset in his time.[8]

---

[5] This process of values realigning themselves to conform to behavioral changes, is just as, if not more, usual and significant than the reverse process. This is supported by general socio-psychological data, particularly in the area of minority group relations, and by the work of cognitive dissonance theorists, contrary to the implications of Lipset's books. One source is none other than "The Prejudiced Society," by Earl Raab and Seymour Martin Lipset, in *American Race Relations Today,* E. Raab (ed.), Doubleday Anchor, 1962.

[6] For an extensive discussion of both the above points, see S. M. Lipset & Irving L. Horowitz (1966). Horowitz argues, inter alia that ". . . Woodrow Wilson had more to do with making the United States a 'new nation' than did Washington" (p. 18).

[7] Ibid. In the debate Horowitz utilizes the absence of American militarism in much the same way that I use the absence of the American Negro, from the pages of Lipset's books. These "skeletons in the closet" seriously threaten Lipset's consensualist, democratic model of America. They also raise questions about the nature of American political stability, as well as the means by which it is maintained.

[8] Lipset has recently evened the balance somewhat by devoting an entire volume to right-wing extremism in America, which pays major attention to the bigoted movements since 1790 (Lipset & Raab, 1970). In the historical catalogue of movements which the authors analyze, anti-Negro movements occupy a large place, along with anti-Catholic and (especially) anti-Semitic ones. But, characteristically, Lipset and his co-author accept American democracy as a given, rather than treating it as problematic. They regard right-wing extremism as a persistent though unfortunate by-product of the democratic political system operating in the U.S., instead of viewing the system itself as basically conservative and preservatist, founded essentially on socio-economic interests. Within the American national polity, the general electorate and the organization of the two major parties are dominated by the few preeminently powerful elements within the system. And at the international level—as this paper argues further on—the extension of imperial domination and manipulation is again centrally based on economic interests.

The gravity of neglecting so important a phenomenon—a key variable in the comprehension of the American political and social system—is given by the fact that in comparative terms the United States can be conceived as a nation at war within itself, in which violence of scale and dispersion occurs regularly. It might be suggested that much of this tension, and the current explosion, can be traced to the coercive nature of the American sociopolitical system, in which much of the flavor of politics at *all* levels for over a hundred years has been directly or indirectly concerned with containing the actions and movements of Negroes in the country. The degree to which such racism *is* the American domestic political system, and increasingly as a national and not just a regional phenomenon, has still to be determined. All this has somehow escaped Lipset's notice. Avoiding the issue is a tactic by which the argument can be sustained that the U.S. is committed to freedom, egalitarianism, and achievement. At other points, idiosyncratic conceptualizations serve the same end, as the following sentence demonstrates: "Enlightenment or radical values which have predominated in the United States . . . foster policies of complete separation such as . . . the 'separate but equal' doctrine of the American South, or a massive moral struggle for real equality and integration as in the United States as a whole" (1968: 24). Lipset's view is a most peculiar twisting of data and theory. It leaves in doubt his competence to understand his own society, and calls into question the meaning of the "democratic system" that he would have other, "backward" nations emulate. It is the outcome of a conceptual sequence which places primary importance upon the stability and constancy of values, rather than emphasizing change, conflict, and coercion, in both the value and material interest spheres. The fierce and continuing struggle over fundamental values and interests within the United States should raise the question whether ambivalence on values is not the predominant American social condition. Or, even operating within Lipset's conceptual framework, the great weight of counter-evidence contradicting what Lipset asserts to be the central American values, should result in a quest for the "real" values of the United States. It might be countered that the predominant value patterns are indeed those claimed by Lipset, and that the seeming contrary evidence is merely the usual gap between the generalized values of a society and its specific empirical norms. But even if this argument were to be made, one would still have to examine the extent to which the counternorms are institutionalized, or are in the process of institutionalization.

This problem is further exemplified by Lipset's position regarding cross-national comparisons of social and economic development, particularly evident in his third chapter of *Revolution and Counterrevolution,* "Values and Entrepreneurship in the Americas". Here again, rather than focusing on such contemporary structural variables as the distribution of political and economic power, Lipset's preference is to locate the origins of entrepreneur-ism and economic growth in historically-rooted "value orientations". Thus, in explaining Latin American economic development or the lack thereof, Lipset's analytic emphasis falls not on the structural conditions of the area (although he explicitly recognizes their importance), nor on the relationship of the area to the developed countries, but on the "Latin" or Iberian value systems which are presumed to have functioned crucially in retarding development. The weakness of this approach is seen if we contrast it with the incisive studies of the anti-imperialist Paul Baran (1957) and his intellectual descendants, Andre Gunder Frank (1967) and James Petras (1970). These scholars, focusing on economic relationships—especially the role of capitalism—nationally and internationally, instead of on amorphous "value orientations" conveniently tagged "feudalism," "modernism," and so forth, bring a cutting edge to the analysis of underdevelopment. One of their principal arguments is that an underdeveloped economy cannot be understood in isolation, but only in relation to other, developed economies, i.e., in terms of the classic metropolis/satellite imperialistic relationship. Petras sums up the position well in his critical review of Latin American studies in the United States, in which he comments upon the use of unilinear conceptions of historical development:

> The First New Nation ideology, which transfers a given type of development from one period to another that is totally different, and which imposes the characteristics of the one on the other, overlooks the relations of domination and subordination which the first nations impose on the latter. More to the point, it overlooks the degree to which the development opportunities (colonies, export markets, etc.) which obtained earlier no longer exist for the developing nation, but have become positive advantages and weapons for maintaining dominance by the already developed country. The cumulative disadvantages of today's subordinate countries, in a context of established centers of industrial power, impose radically new patterns for development. (1970: 333)

The position of Baran, Frank, and Petras, so different from that of Lipset, reconceptualizes the problem in terms of the struggle between neo-colonialism (or "economic imperialism," as Latin Americans term it) and anti-colonialism, rather than as a strain between "modern" and "preindustrial" systems of values. While there is not the space in this article to fully demonstrate the extent to which the material interest position is more productive for the understanding of social and economic underdevelopment, nowhere in Lipset's work has he demonstrated the superiority of his approach.

CANADA AND THE PATTERN-VARIABLES

As in his first book, *Agrarian Socialism,* Lipset has been returning in his recent works to the puzzling ways in which Canada and the United States differ, and trying to understand how basic these are. To isolate and describe such variations, Lipset has resorted to a battery of Parsonian pattern-variables to which he has added an axis of his own: egalitarianism versus elitism. It need hardly be added that Lipset finds the United States more achievement oriented than most, more universalistic, more egalitarian, and more self-oriented, and that these turn out to be also the precise needs for economic development and thereby, stable democracy. It is Lipset's contention that if the explanatory utility of these pattern-variables can be demonstrated for the relatively insignificant structural and value differences between Canada and the United States, then their usefulness for the analysis of more widely varying nations will likewise be demonstrated. Aside from the fact that the second part of Lipset's argument does not necessarily nor even logically follow from the first part, the attempt itself seems to fail the test. Instead, what is proved is the leakiness of the pattern-variables for empirical analysis, their vagueness as concepts to be applied to data whose understanding requires precision, and the realization that their use is highly amenable to the subjective distortion of data.

It is true, as Lipset notes, that Canada is a more elitist and clearly stratified society than the United States; intellectuals and holders of higher degrees are more esteemed, perhaps because of their greater scarcity. But these characteristics may be confused with something else which David Reisman's schema may be closer to describing than Lipset's pattern-variable analysis: There is in Canada a greater compound of autonomous "inner direction" and conformist "other direction," a Gestalt which characterizes the society and particularly its elites. In many respects the Canadian elites are colonial fragments. They are unsure of their status relative to other national elites, and especially their reference elites in the United States and Great Britain; but they are very sure of their status with respect to the non-elite strata of Canadian society. This lends them the self-consciousness which characterizes most colonial elites, so that paradoxically they are simultaneously more autonomous and more conformist. In popular culture, for instance, Canadian television and radio networks sponsor pompous "panel" shows which are an amalgam of the B.B.C. and American types. Thus, "English" (mid-Atlantic) accents and inflections abound, as well as understatement, reserve, and dry puns. At the same time, the studio audience is requested to applaud and laugh at the appropriate places, but this "artificial" aspect of the program (possibly no less artificial than many of the "English" aspects) is somewhat intrusive and embarrassing to the panelists. It is not that Canadians are more British, elitist, and particularistic, that is of primary importance here; it is that they are more colonial. In common with those of other colonial cultures, English Canadians have built into their value system a fundamental duality with respect to their identity. They lack the cultural certainty which is the attribute of a non-colonial society.

Again, Lipset looks to the educational system to illustrate the differential valuation of elitism and equalitarianism. Yet the Canadian elementary and secondary school system (as he notes) fosters greater desires for individual creativity, "intellectuality," and scholarliness than does the American system, while the Americans are more concerned with "civic" values than are the Canadians. To conclude on this basis, as Lipset does, that the Canadian educational system is more elitist seems to obscure the more important issue, which is that there is more of a tendency toward self-orientation. If the Parsonian jargon is jettisoned and the sociologist confines himself to less generalized levels of observation and analysis, the differential behavior is brimming with interesting economic and political implications which have much more to do with consumption and production than with hazy dichotomous variations in societies. Canada operates on a distinctly lower economic plane than does the United States. There is not only less affluence, but it also takes longer to acquire, and the practice of university students largely paying their way through school by summers of physical labor is common—even in the middle classes, and particularly in the Prairie Provinces, the Maritimes, and British Columbia. Even though a much smaller proportion attends university than the proportion in the United States, the gulf between student life and non-student life, between "town" and "gown," is in this sense less pronounced in Canada. Anti-intellectualism is at a lower ebb, and it could even be argued that the greater respect for the intellectual-academic elites is a measure of the deeper embeddedness of universalism and achievement orientation in the Canadian value system than in the American value system, under what historically have been more trying and less open economic circumstances. That the same pattern-variables could be used to support this argument—which is the opposite of Lipset's—indicates the weakness and selective use of one of the main conceptual props for Lipset's recent work. In more technical terms, the pattern-variables have an exceedingly low coefficient of reproducibility, and can be employed and interpreted to serve any given purpose.

The theme that the United States is a revolutionary society and Canada a counterrevolutionary society is not original to Lipset, and he acknowledges that Canadian historians (particularly Frank Underhill) have been discussing it for years (Underhill & Fox, 1960). The argument rests essentially on the fact that the American Revolution violently threw off British domination and seized sovereignty, while the Canadian decision was to remain a British colony and peacefully evolve into a sovereign nation-state. Further, a consequence of the American Revolutionary War and its aftermath was an exchange of populations, the pro-British United Empire Loyalists (in Canada, now somewhat similar to the Daughters of the American Revolution) heading north to Canada while the pro-Republican elements in Canada migrated to the new United States. Lipset contends that in this way the fun-

224   PERSPECTIVES IN POLITICAL SOCIOLOGY

damental political and social radicalism of the United States was bolstered, while the conservatism of Canada was similarly strengthened, and that these patterns can be distinguished up to the present. And if I read Lipset right, he is also saying that these early historical experiences—the residues of them—continue to play a powerful role in the contemporary value systems of the two countries.

Lipset seeks to expand the U.S. revolution/Canada counterrevolution theme of Underhill. But what Lipset adds to the theme is of little use: merely an attempt to apply Parsons's vaguely defined pattern-variables to historical and contemporary data, with all the attendant methodological problems this entails. In order to make his analysis "work" Lipset is forced to manipulate some data in odd ways while completely ignoring other relevant data. An example of how strained his argument can become is furnished by the observation that "The decision to provide Canada with a strong central government, which unlike that of the United States would be able to veto or 'disallow' provincial laws, was designed to resist the democratic threat within and across the border" (1968b: 49). Lipset's selection of data and interpretation of them ignores the fact that during the years preceding Canada's confederation in 1867, the United States and its Civil War served as a federal model to be avoided. As well, Lipset is oblivious to the fact that the United States was at the time an armed, militaristic, and aggressive neighbor which had long indicated desires to expand territorially into British North America. Lipset is ideologically incapable of conceiving of his country, even a hundred years ago, as an interest-oriented militaristic threat. He prefers to characterize it as a "democratic threat," as the courier of democracy in the New World. It would appear that Lipset's ethnocentrism prevents him from being able to accord legitimacy to political commitments and decisions which run counter to the goals or values of the United States, and thus leads him to the conclusion that anti-egalitarian and conservative sentiments informed Canada's role during the American Revolution and later during the period of her own confederation. He does not consider the possibility that Canadian politicians might have regarded colonial status within the United States as no different, if not worse, than colonial dependency within the British Empire. At least Britain was on the other side of the Atlantic and could not maintain as close surveillance on Canada's activities as could her powerful neighboring state. The other possibility, of course, was complete absorption by the United States: the disappearance of Canada's independence.

UNDERDEVELOPED NATIONS AND "DEMOCRACY"

To conclude this appraisal of Lipset's last two books on comparative sociology, I will turn to his continuing concern with ". . . the emergence of one-party regimes with little respect for the rule of law in many of the new nations of Asia and Africa" (1968b: 363). Lipset pessimistically bemoans the fact that two- or multi-party democracy finds it so difficult getting established in the developing nations, and forecasts a gloomy future. Here again, his belief is that the types of formal provisions comprising U.S. democracy are necessary for the betterment of life and the advancement of political stability in other countries. In doing so, he fails to take full note of the historical antecedents of many of these countries' so-called "independence," i.e., the types of problems—social, cultural, political, and economic—left them by the departing colonial powers. Often even if the problem of national integration can be overcome (no small task after imperial rule), the economic dominance of the former colonialists continues to maintain the new country in a dependent status. Lipset also ignores the forms of new freedom and self-realization which many of these emergent countries now enjoy despite the absence of the formal niceties of parliamentary democracy, in the American image. In some new countries the problems of economic and social development are so critical that it is proper to ask not only whether formal political opposition should be high priority objective, but also whether there are sufficient able personnel to man more than a single national party committed to one general path of development. In some countries there is an absolute scarcity of talent, training, and technical advisors. Thus, single parties can be far more than just tools to mobilize votes at election time: they may also serve a continuing function as movements which mobilize the available social and human resources of countries in the process of development (Wallerstein, 1961; Horowitz, 1966: 225–46; Von der Mehden, 1964).

Lipset's argument that democracy can only be realized under conditions in which there is more than one party is susceptible to attack on another level also, for he fails to recognize that cleavages, crosscutting alliances, crosspressures on individuals and groups, and competitive struggles for the right to make decisions can all occur independent of the number of "official" political parties in a system. From this vantage point, such parties as the *Partido Revolucionario Institucional* in Mexico can be considered equivalent to the Republican and Democratic parties in the United States, taken together; and these latter, in turn, may be conceptualized as one, two, or four parties loosely aggregated under the two formal titles. A less complacent sociologist than Lipset, John Porter, has viewed the Liberal and Progressive Conservative parties in Canada as nearly indistinguishable (1965: 374), and these closely parallel the American Democratic and Republican parties, respectively. It may be a function of the sameness of the two major American parties that insignificant differences become magnified into the entire basis for electoral choice, e.g., personality of the candidates, appearance, religion, or accent. Lipset himself, in his general analyses of American politics, seizes upon small differences in order to claim that a real "choice" is presented to the American electorate through the operation of their two-party democratic system, and that real class interests are expressed in the process. As in many other instances, Lipset has mistaken here the form for the substance.

SUMMING UP

To recapitulate the argument of this critique, we have seen a growing conservatism and American nationalist bias afflict the work of Lipset over the years. From a concern with the structural bases of behavior in his early work, his focus has steadily shifted over to the constitutional and value orientational determinants of behavior. Such a shift in focus would not in itself have been so serious, had Lipset not tended to select, compare, and analyze cross-national data through such a narrowly American nationalist lens. Thus, even as Lipset was expanding the geographical base of his comparative investigations, he was simultaneously restricting his consideration of relevant data, and foreclosing possibilities for evaluating evidence which contradicted his hypotheses and assumptions.

It might be asked what influences have contributed to the molding of such comparative sociology. In the last part of this paper, I wish to suggest a few of them, and to indicate some possible relationships between the investigator's ideological posture and his scholarly perspective.

SOME REFLECTIONS ON PROFESSIONAL SUCCESS AND SOCIAL ANALYSIS

Any critique or analysis of Lipset's work is in part a study in the sociology of knowledge as well as a "detached" consideration of objective facts marshalled by Lipset to illustrate and support an "objective" interpretation of how the world is put together and what makes it move. And indeed, Lipset himself is well aware of the possible pitfalls in his approach, and of the criticisms which have been leveled at him on political grounds, as he makes clear in his preface to *Political Man*. Nevertheless, I want to move this analysis of his cross-national work beyond the earlier levels, and consider his political orientation within the context of a broader social orientation flowing from Lipset's origins and mobility, and his appreciation and celebration of the facts of this mobility and social environment—the free America in which such events occurred. It is noteworthy that Lipset's perspectives have changed as his social mobility and position changed, and that they appear to reflect accurately the rapidity of his academic and professional success.

It is exceedingly difficult to demonstrate causality within a sociology of knowledge framework—particularly given the limitations of a journal article.

This section is a preliminary formulation, suggestive of the approach a more thorough-going study might usefully undertake. As such, it rests on a general sense of what is relevant, rather than standing as an attempt to substantiate a complex hypothesis involving social structure, mobility, behavior, and ideology.

S. M. Lipset did his doctoral work in sociology at Columbia University and his first book, *Agrarian Socialism,* was published in 1950 as a re-worked version of his dissertation. During the years that Lipset was a graduate student at Columbia, the sociology department there was reaching toward its zenith as a power in American (indeed, world) sociology, and was establishing itself as what was to become known as the "Columbia School" of sociology as exemplified by the Bureau of Applied Social Research. Not only was the sociology department at Columbia becoming preeminent in the field during these years, dominating much of the style of social investigation in the United States and setting a model for the rest of the world, but sociology itself was rapidly becoming highly bureaucratized, professionalized, and institutionalized in American life. Lipset's career both coincided with and was a consequence of the general growth of sociology as a discipline, and of the Columbia department in particular.

Hailing from a Jewish, skilled craft worker's family in New York, Lipset was immersed in the intensely ideological and intellectual atmosphere of the Young Peoples' Socialist League (Y.P.S.L.).[9] in high school and as an undergraduate at City College of New York. Thriving in this competitive environment, Lipset moved on to do graduate studies at Columbia, where he absorbed theory from Robert Melton, methodology and techniques from Paul Lazarsfeld, and, from Robert S. Lynd, support for his concern with important problems. "Important problems," for the young Lipset, revolved very much around questions of social equality, particularly as embedded in the reconstructive potential of democratic socialism. Indeed, it was the concern with and commitment to socialism which prompted Lipset to undertake a study of the C.C.F. socialist success in Saskatchewan; and while writing up his Ph.D. dissertation and holding his first teaching position at the University of Toronto, he was associated with the socialist circle controlling the magazine *Canadian Forum.*

Shortly after graduating from Columbia, Lipset secured a post at the University of California at Berkeley. This was another department on the rise, soon to establish itself as the major sociological factory in the world,

---

[9] His father was a member of the International Typographical Union, which Lipset has discussed in his "The Biography of a Research Project: UNION DEMOCRACY" in Phillip E. Hammond (ed.), *Sociologists At Work,* New York: Basic Books, 1964. Other information is drawn from his engaging and candid autobiographical statement, "Socialism and Sociology" in I. L. Horowitz (ed.), *Sociological Self-Images: A Collective Portrait,* Beverly Hills: Sage Publications, 1969, pp. 143–175.

functionally differentiating itself into a labyrinth of institutes, and processing literally hundreds of graduate students. However, even as the Berkeley students began to react negatively toward the mass-production nature of their "multiversity" and country by becoming more critical and radical, the former young socialist Lipset was becoming increasingly complacent and conservative about the role of America in the world, and the character of American society, and began to conceive of it as the "good society" or "democracy" itself. In retrospect, it seems inevitable that he should have left Berkeley in 1965 for the traditional elitism of Harvard University.

How do the elements of Lipset's work relate to his biography, cursorily sketched above? Obviously there is no simple one-to-one ratio; nevertheless, it can be seen that as Lipset was transformed from a young Jewish New York socialist into a sociologist lionized by the profession, and finally into a prominent member of the American intellectual community, his admiration for and celebration of America kept pace. His ideological posture was frequently reflected in his selectivity of data, as well as the interpretations and analyses of them. In the short space of ten years, Lipset travelled the road from ideologist to sociologist and back to ideologist *cum* American apologist.[10]

By the time *Political Man* appeared in 1960, Lipset had already established himself as one of the most prominent American sociologists, while the department at Berkeley was well on the way to becoming the greatest bulwark of "sociology as a profession." With the publication of this volume (which won the 1962 MacIver Award), we have an explicit statement of Lipset's belief that the United States represents the highest point in the development of democratic and egalitarian societies, fundamentally guided by its revolutionary past.

This position is elaborated and extended comparatively in *The First New Nation* and *Revolution and Counterrevolution,* along with an increasing reliance upon the "pattern-variables" for explanatory purposes. That Lipset has become more Parsonian in his work is no surprise, since it fits well with both his general scholarly functionalist assumptions and the individual competitive success of himself and so many academics of his generation (Lipset,1969). For example, Lipset's confusion of stability with democracy is quite understandable if we remember that he works within a hallowed functionalist tradition, in which the "problem of order" has been a central concern for Comte, Durkheim, and especially Parsons. When this assumption was joined to the latter's voluntaristic model of man and society (ren-

---

[10] Lipset is obviously sensitive to criticisms of his political shift and increased conservatism. As he remarks in the last line of his autobiographical statement, "To some considerable degree, I would think, my own recent work represents a response to . . . changes in the political climate." (Lipset, 1969)

dered particularly persuasive to Lipset by his career experiences), it was inevitable that Lipset's focus should have devolved onto the problem of the adequacy of motivation which is based in the value and normative systems, since this is critical for the theoretical coherence of the voluntaristic model of society. Indeed, it might be argued that this is a model of social action which is not only attuned to the affluent post-War American society of the fifties and early sixties, but is peculiarly responsive to the smug rhetoric of national success which accompanied those years. During this period, the U.S. believed itself to be an abundantly endowed, open society, blessedly free from the poverty and instability of nearly all other countries. Within such a social and intellectual setting, it was only natural that the inclination of the liberal sociologist would be to spread the "good society" to those unfortunates standing on the outside. For Lipset and his liberal anti-communist intellectual generation, consensus prevailed that the end of ideology had finally arrived in the West, borne by the disillusionments of the past and the affluent stability of the present.

While the links between ideology and biography pointed to above are far from conclusive, they also cannot be lightly dismissed. From a sociology of knowledge analytic viewpoint, Lipset's drift from being a young socialist, to the position he now occupies as a bourgeois centrist, is strongly suggestive. It is worth considering the hypothesis that Lipset's political beliefs stem from and have been reinforced by his own success within the academic and social systems, his personal verification of the American Dream.

It is readily acknowledged that the relationships among an investigator's social position, his ideological commitments, and his research are far too complicated to have thorough treatment within the compass of a journal article. Still, the ideological pattern in Lipset's work appears to have coincided with his own success within an increasingly bureaucratized profession, and within American society generally. The reader can consider this suggested relationship to be an initial, tentative probe within a sociology of knowledge framework. Whether or not the argument would hold up under the painstaking attention to process that a thoroughgoing investigation would entail, it is still evident that Lipset's comparative sociology suffers from an undue nationalist bias. Despite Lipset's professional proficiency, he falls short of a model analyst of his own society, or of others, in historical and comparative perspective.

REFERENCES

Baran, Paul
1957   The Political Economy of Growth. New York: Monthly Review Press.
Bennett, John W., and Cynthia Krueger
1968   "Agrarian pragmatism and radical politics." Pp. 347–63 in Lipset (ed.), Agrarian Socialism. Updated edition. New York: Doubleday Anchor.

Berelson, Bernard, P. F. Lazarsfeld, and William McPhee.
1954   Voting. Chicago: University of Chicago Press.

Casanova, Pablo Gonzalez
1965   "Internal colonialism and national development." Studies in Comparative International Development, I, No. 4.

Coser, Lewis
1956   The Functions of Social Conflict. Glencoe: The Free Press.

Frank, Andre Gunder
1967   Capitalism and Underdevelopment in Latin America: Historical Studies of Chile and Brazil. New York: Monthly Review Press.

Frankenberg, Ronald
1957   Village on the Border. London: Cohen and West.

Gluckman, Max
1955   Custom and Conflict in Africa. Oxford: Blackwell.

Horowitz, Irving Louis
1966   Three Worlds of Development. New York: Oxford University Press.

Jayawardena, Chandra
1963   Conflict and Solidarity on a Guianese Plantation. London: Athlone.

Kautsky, John H.
1968   Communism and the Politics of Development. New York: John Wiley & Sons.

Lewis, Gordon K.
1969   The Growth of the Modern West Indies. New York: Monthly Review Press.

Lipset, S. M., and Earl Raab
1970   The Politics of Unreason: Right-Wing Extremism in America, 1790–1970. N.Y.: Harper & Row.

Lipset, S. M., Martin Trow, and J. S. Coleman
1956   Union Democracy. Glencoe: The Free Press.

Lipset, S. M., and I. L. Horowitz
1966   "The birth and meaning of America: A discussion of The First New Nation." Sociological Quarterly, 7 (Winter): 3–20.

Lipset, S. M.
1963   Political Man. New York: Doubleday Anchor; originally published in 1960.
1966   The First New Nation. New York: Doubleday Anchor.
1968a Agrarian Socialism. Updated edition. New York: Doubleday Anchor; first published by The Free Press in 1950.
1968b Revolution and Counterrevolution. New York: Basic Books.
1969   "Socialism and sociology." Pp. 143–175 in I. L. Horowitz (ed.), Sociological Self-Images: A Collective Portrait. Beverly Hills: Sage Publications.

McDonald, Lynn
1969   "Religion and Voting: A study of the 1968 Canadian federal election in Ontario." Canadian Review of Sociology & Anthropology, 6, No. 3: 129–45.

Petras, James
1970   Politics and Social Structure in Latin America. New York: Monthly Review Press.

Pinard, Maurice
1967   "One-party dominance and third parties." Canadian Journal of Economics and Political Science, 33, No. 3: 358–73.

Porter, John
1965   The Vertical Mosaic. Toronto: University of Toronto Press.

Raab, Earl (ed.)
1962   American Race Relations Today. New York: Doubleday Anchor.

Romalis, Coleman
1967   "The attitudes of the Montreal Jewish community toward French Canadian nationalism and separatism." Unpublished M.A. thesis, McGill University.

Simmel, Georg
1955   Conflict and the Web of Group Affiliations. Trans. Kurt H. Wolff and Reinhard Bendix. Glencoe: The Free Press.

Sjoberg, Gideon and Roger Nett
1968   A Methodology for Social Research. New York: Harper & Row.

Stavenhagen, Rodolfo
1965   "Classes, colonialism and acculturation." Studies in Comparative International Development, I, No. 6.

Underhill, F. H., and Paul Fox
1960   "The radical tradition: A second view of Canadian history." Toronto: C.B.C. Publications Branch.

Von der Mehden, Fred R.
1964   Politics of the Developing Nations. Englewood Cliffs, N.J.: Prentice-Hall.

Wallerstein, Immanuel
1961   Africa: The Politics of Independence, chap. 5. New York: Vintage.

Ideology and Mythology: Reply to Coleman Romalis (and Other Critics)

Seymour Martin Lipset
Harvard University

It is obviously difficult for any scholar to evaluate, or even to understand the direction of his own work. I am, therefore, grateful to Coleman Romalis for the time he has devoted to seeking to formulate the direction in which I have been going. Quite naturally, I must disagree with many of his conclusions. My major disappointment lies in the fact, that although he has clearly read much of what I have written, he has ignored most of it. As I see it, in his effort to describe a thread of consistent development (or retrogression as the case may be), he has ignored statements and findings that may contradict his theme. Rather than write an essay at this point presenting a general position, I will try to indicate the nature of my disagreement with some of the points he raises. I should note, however, that I have made a number of efforts to describe my underlying value premises, and to explain why I think, or thought, I engaged in various pieces of research, either as the prefaces to my books, or in two exercises in intellectual autobiography.[1] As I have frequently noted in these introductions, I have always contended that the values of investigators necessarily affect choice of research topics, variables dealt with, and interpretations of data. Consequently, it is incumbent on scholars to make whatever pertinent beliefs they hold public so that the readers of their works may be aware of these in evaluating any given work.

It is curious that many who polemicize against the notion of a "value-free" science frequently fight a straw-man, that is they refute a position which

---

[1] For the autobiographical essays, see S. M. Lipset, "The Biography of a Research Project: Union Democracy," in Philip E. Hammond, ed., *Sociologists at Work* (Garden City: Doubleday-Anchor, 1967), pp. 111–139; S. M. Lipset, "Socialism and Sociology," in I. L. Horowitz, ed., *Sociological Self-Images* (Beverly Hills: Sage Publications, 1969), pp. 143–176. I have also attempted to reply to various critics. See especially "Some Further Comments on the 'End of Ideology,'" *American Political Science Review*, 60 (March 1966), pp. 17–18; (with Irving Horowitz) "The Birth and Meaning of America: A Discussion of *The First New Nation*," *Sociological Inquiry*, 7 (Winter 1965), pp. 3–20; "Ideology and Political Bias—A Reply to Peck," *American Catholic Sociological Review*, 23 (1962), pp. 207–223; and "Working-Class Authoritarianism: A Reply to Miller and Riessman," *British Journal of Sociology*, 12 (1961), pp. 277–281.

233

few, if any, reputable scholars hold. Thus Max Weber who is often discussed as an exponent of the concept of value free scholarship explicitly enunciated the impossibility of such work. He argued that the very concept of ethical neutrality was a spurious one, and that those who maintained this "spuriously 'ethical neutral' " approach were precisely the ones who manifested "obstinate and deliberate partisanship."[2] It is interesting to note that the largest survey of the opinions of American sociologists, one conducted by Alvin Gouldner in 1964, found that those most involved in research, who published more, and had the greatest access to research funds were most disposed to reject the concept of value-freeness. As the one detailed report of this study of over 3,000 sociologists states "those who have little or no research funds tended to score high on Value-Freeness. . . . Those with least ability to affect their field productively hold strongly to the belief that sociology is, will be, and should be a value-free science."[3] These data would suggest that it is precisely those scholars who are most involved in research and publication who have been most aware of the difficulties posed for objective analysis by value preferences. And such awareness generally dictates a concern with *methods* of inquiry, with a desire to foster the competition of ideas and concepts, the only way to heighten the possibility of finding analytic laws regardless of who does the investigation. "For scientific truth is precisely what is valid for all who seek the truth."[4]

Not surprisingly, ideological evaluations have played an important role in affecting the "memory" of some scholars with respect to responsibility for statements which they like or dislike. Thus, a number of writers who disapprove of the concept of the "end of ideology," have sought to assign credit for the phrase to Dan Bell and myself. They have ignored the fact that the phrase first appeared in an article published in 1951 by H. Stuart Hughes, "The End of Political Ideology."[5] Professor Hughes, though stressing the idea picked up in subsequent discussions of the topic that disagree-

---

[2] Max Weber, *The Methodology of the Social Sciences* (Glencoe: The Free Press, 1949), p. 6. For an elaboration of my views on the subject in the context of a discussion of Weber, see S. M. Lipset, *Rebellion in the University* (Boston: Little, Brown Paperback, 1972), pp. 206–209.

[3] See J. T. Sprehe, *The Climate of Opinion in Sociology: A Study of the Professional Value and Belief Systems of Sociologists* (Ph.D. dissertation: Department of Sociology, Washington University, St. Louis, 1967; obtainable through University Microfilms, Ann Arbor, Michigan), pp. 449–450. This is the only available detailed analysis of the survey, originally conducted by Gouldner. The dissertation was completed under his direction. A comprehensive report on various surveys of sociologists from 1913 to 1969, which have basically reported findings comparable to the Gouldner-Sprehe study is S. M. Lipset and Everett C. Ladd, Jr., "The Politics of American Sociologists," *American Journal of Sociology*, 78 (July 1972), pp. 67–104.

[4] Weber, *op. cit.,* p. 84.

[5] H. Stuart Hughes, "The End of Political Ideology," *Measure*, 2 (Spring 1951), pp. 146–158. See S. M. Lipset, "Ideology, No End," *Encounter*, 39 (December 1972), pp. 17–22.

ments over methods had succeeded those concerned with ideological principles, had, himself, been active in the Henry Wallace 1948 campaign, describes his politics as "socialist," subsequently ran in 1962 in Massachusetts as a third party "peace" candidate for U.S. Senator, and was a founder and president of SANE. Subsequently in 1958, Barrington Moore, Jr., who comes closer to being an exponent of Marxist analysis in sociology than any other major figure in the field, wrote of American politics that "as we reduce economic inequalities and privileges, we may also eliminate the sources of contrast and discontent that put drive into genuine political alternatives. . . . There is, I think, more than a dialectical flourish in the assertion that liberty requires the existence of an oppressed group in order to grow vigorously. . . . Once the ideal has been achieved, or is even close to realization, the driving force of discontent disappears, and a society settles down for a time to a stolid acceptance of things as they are. Something of the sort seems to have happened in the United States."[6]

Two academic figures, Herbert Marcuse and Kenneth Keniston, who have been widely recognized as sympathetic spokesmen for the revival of student activism in recent years, both once were convinced that there was little or no possibility of widespread conflict in contemporary society. A recent analysis of Marcuse's work by the French Marxist sociologist, Lucien Goldman, noted the similarity between Marcuse's analysis and various less radical interpreters of the "end of ideologies." Goldman concluded that "it is still true that they all—Aron, Marcuse, Bell, Riesman—share the mistaken belief that Western society has been so stabilized that no serious opposition can be found within it."[7] Time and again in his writings and public lectures, Marcuse reiterated his belief that modern industrial capitalism through its ability to sustain abundance and entertainment had eliminated all but the slightest possibility for mass radical protest. Similar to Barrington Moore, he assumed that the class struggle in the West was all but over. In 1964, he commented that "In the capitalist world, there are still the basic classes [capitalists and workers] . . . . but an overriding interest in the preservation and improvement of the institutional status quo unites the former antagonists in the most advanced areas of contemporary society."[8] Marcuse's pessimism about the revolutionary potentiality of the working-class is, of course, well known. Far less publicized is the fact that he was so pessimistic about the role of blacks and students, that he openly opposed the participation of the first in the political process and of the second in the power system of the

---

[6] Barrington Moore, Jr., *Political Power and Social Theory* (Cambridge: Harvard University Press, 1958), p. 183.

[7] Lucien Goldman, "Understanding Marcuse," *Partisan Review,* 38, no. 3 (1971), p. 258.

[8] Herbert Marcuse, *One Dimensional Man* (Boston: Beacon Press, 1964), pp. xii–xiii.

university because the system is able to seduce both into basically conforming to the status quo. At a symposium in 1965 at Rutgers University, Marcuse stated that Negroes are brainwashed by American society and consequently follow middle-class norms in their political behavior:

> When asked which situation he preferred—one in which the Negroes were deprived of their civil rights, including the power to vote, and one in which they freely exercized the civil rights to choose "middle-class values" Marcuse replied: "Well, since I have already gone out on a limb, I might as well go all the way: I will prefer that they did not have the right to choose wrongly."[9]

Less than a month before the French "events" of May 1968, in an interview with *Le Monde* he stated: "Everywhere and at all times, the overwhelming majority of students are conservative and even reactionary. So that student power, in the event of it being democratic, would be conservative or even reactionary."[10] By 1969, Marcuse, like many others, had learned that he was wrong. In his essay, *On Liberation,* he identifies the American "ghetto population" and the student opposition as major disruptive forces. Yet it should be noted he still concluded that a liberating "revolution is not on the agenda" of the advanced western industrial states; that the combination of the necessary "subjective factor," political consciousness, and the "objective factor," "the support and participation of the class which is at the base of production," only "coincide in large areas of the Third World."[11]

Kenneth Keniston, though sympathetic to radical social change, has limited his writings largely to the field of student "alienation" and political behavior, a subject he began investigating in the late 1950s. Yet in spite of his political concerns and psychological depth analyses, Keniston also wrote of the "decline of utopia" and the "quiescence" among students.[12] His sustained conviction that American youth were inherently "predominantly apolitical" led him in 1963 to put "political revival" in quotation marks in the title of his article discussing "signs of increasing political activity on a number of campuses," and to devote most of the essay to analyzing the

---

[9] Leo Rosten, *A Trumpet for Reason* (Garden City: Doubleday, 1970), pp. 64–65.

[10] This interview published in *Le Monde* for April 11, 1968 is cited in "Upsurge of the Youth Movement in Capitalist Countries," *World Marxist Review,* 11 (July 1968), p. 8.

[11] Herbert Marcuse, *An Essay on Liberation* (Boston: Beacon Press, 1969), p. 56.

[12] See especially his book *The Uncommitted* (New York: Harcourt Brace, 1965), and his articles, "Alienation and the Decline of Utopia," *The American Scholar,* 29 (Spring 1960), pp. 1–40, and "American Students and the 'Political Revival' ", *The American Scholar,* 32 (Winter 1963), pp. 40–64. Both articles are included in his recent collection of essays, *Youth and Dissent* (New York: Harcourt, Brace, Jovanovich, 1971) in which Keniston allows his readers to share his changes in evaluations as the years progressed.

sources of "apathy." He suggested that it "almost appears that affluence and education have a negative effect on political involvement, at least in America."[13]

In discussing the work of a number of social scientists who have been identified with Marxism or whose scholarly writings include endorsement of various forms of left-wing activism as proponents of an extreme "end of conflict" variant of the "end of ideology" thesis, I do not mean to suggest that their work gives the thesis specific leftist ideological coloration. Rather, I want to call attention to the fact that writers of many diverse political persuasions have lent support to the idea. Raymond Aron, once a Gaullist; Herbert Tingsten, long time editor of Sweden's leading liberal newspaper; and Thomas Molnar, conservative American intellectual, are also among the elaborators of the end of ideology thesis.[14] Some have even suggested that one of its earliest formulations was presented by Max Weber in his analysis of the consequences of electoral democracy. Weber seemingly believed that the European type of ideological party, as represented before World War I by the Social Democrats, would ultimately come to resemble the American much less ideological one, because of the need of all parties to build a bureaucratic machine in order to maximize electoral support.[15] Ralf Dahrendorf, probably the best-known contemporary German sociologist, was elected in 1969 to the German Parliament as a leader of the Free Democratic (liberal) party. While still an active socialist in 1957 he described modern society as a "post-capitalist" one in which the industrial class conflicts between employers and workers no longer have much effect on political struggles, "that, indeed, the notion of a workers' party has lost its political meaning."[16] Writing as a historian and analyst of political theory, Judith Shklar, discussed the "decline of political faith," as a result of the fact that "utopianism is dead, and without it no radical philosophy can exist."[17]

In my own writings on "the decline of ideology," I elaborated on the themes originally suggested by the British sociologist, T. H. Marshall, that total ideological or revolutionary politics on the left were largely a phe-

---

[13] *Ibid.*, p. 82.

[14] See Raymond Aron, *L'Opium des intellectuels* (Paris: Calmann-Levy, 1955), pp. 315–344; Herbert Tingsten, "Stability and Vitality in Swedish Democracy," *The Political Quarterly*, 26 (1955), pp. 140–151; Thomas Molnar, *The Decline of the Intellectuals* (Cleveland: World Publishing Co., 1961), pp. 199–222; Edward Shils, "The End of Ideology?", *Encounter*, 5 (November 1955), pp. 52–58; Daniel Bell, *The End of Ideology* (New York: The Free Press, 1962), pp. 393–407.

[15] See Reinhard Bendix and Guenther Roth, *Scholarship and Partisanship: Essays on Max Weber* (Berkeley: University of California Press, 1971), pp. 248–250.

[16] Ralf Dahrendorf, *Class and Class Conflict in Industrial Society* (Stanford: Stanford University Press, 1959), p. 275, see also pp. 241–318.

[17] Judith Shklar, *After Utopia: The Decline of Political Faith* (Princeton: Princeton University Press, 1957), esp. pp. 218–219.

nomenon of the working class struggle for citizenship which resulted in industrialized countries in their incorporation as a legitimate partner in the resolution of issues through representation by party and trade-unions. I suggested that once "the workers have achieved industrial and political citizenship," and "the conservatives have accepted the welfare state," that this resulted in "a decline in the sources of serious political controversy" with respect to domestic issues.[18] This analysis, moreover, was presented in the context of arguing *against* the theses of Barrington Moore and others concerning the impact of these changes in reducing the class struggle. As I noted in 1960, "one wonders whether these intellectuals are not mistaking the decline of ideology in the domestic politics of Western society with the ending of the class conflict which has sustained domestic controversy. As the abundant evidence on voting patterns in the United States and other countries indicates, the electorate as a whole does not see the end of the domestic class struggle envisioned by so many intellectuals. . . . The predictions of the end of class politics in the 'affluent society' ignore the relative character of any class system."[19] In the same book, in discussing the decline of leftist sentiment among American intellectuals in the 1950s, I suggested that it was questionable "whether a permanent change in the [adversary] relationship of the American intellectual to his society is in process. In spite of the powerful conservatizing forces, the inherent tendency to oppose the *status quo* will remain. . . . Any *status quo* embodies rigidities and dogmatisms which it is the inalienable right of intellectuals to attack, whether from the standpoint of moving back to traditional values or forward toward the achievement of the equalitarian dream."[20] Curiously, though the tone and ideological content are seemingly quite different, C. Wright Mills reached almost identical analytical conclusions about the same time. Thus in his famous "Letter to the New Left," published in 1960, he stated: "generally it would seem that only at certain (earlier) stages of industrialization, and in a political context of autocracy, etc., do wage-workers tend to become a class-for-themselves, etc." He described the belief of some radicals in the revolutionary role of the working class in "advanced capitalist societies" as running "in the face of the really impressive historical evidence that now stands against this expectation . . . . a legacy from Victorian Marxism that

---

[18] S. M. Lipset, "The End of Ideology?" *Political Man* (Garden City: Doubleday-Anchor, 1963), pp. 442–443; S. M. Lipset, *Revolution and Counterrevolution* (Garden City: Doubleday-Anchor, 1970), pp. 268–270. Marshall's analysis is presented in his essay "Citizenship and Social Class," first published in 1949 and reprinted in his volume *Sociology at the Crossroads* (London: Heinemann, 1963), pp. 67–127. The American edition of Marshall's book published by Doubleday under the title of *Class, Citizenship, and Social Development* is out of print.
[19] *Political Man, op. cit.,* p. 444.
[20] *Ibid.,* p. 371.

REPLY TO COLEMAN ROMALIS (AND OTHER CRITICS)

is now quite unrealistic."[21] And Mills also suggested that the social group which was most likely, given its structural situation, to be a source of continuing anti-establishment struggle, is the intellectuals. "It is with this problem of agency [of change] in mind that I have been studying for several years now, the cultural apparatus, the intellectuals—as a possible, immediate, radical agency of change . . . . it turns out now, in the spring of 1960, that it may be a very relevant idea indeed."[22]

A further criticism posited against my writings on the "end of ideology," has been made by some who note the congruence between their own evaluation of erosion of ideological controversy among the major party protagonists in the western democracies and my own, but who argue that those who have proclaimed the "end of ideology" have failed to recognize that the concept is a conservative one, that it contributes to undermining efforts at radical change. Thus Stephen Rousseas and James Farganis have commented that "there can be little doubt that . . . [Bell's] arguments and that of Lipset on the decline, if not the end, of ideology as an operative force in the Western world are based largely on fact." They go on, however, and state further that "C. Wright Mills would agree that the end of ideology makes a fetish of empiricism and entails an ideology of its own—an ideology of political complacency for the justification of things as they are . . . ."[23] But such an insistence only reiterates a component part of my own analysis. My most comprehensive discussion of the sources and consequences of the "decline of ideology," first published in 1963 noted:

> Not only do class conflicts over issues related to division of the total economic pie, influence over various institutions, symbolic status, and opportunity, continue in the absence of *weltanschauungen,* but that the decline of such total ideologies does *not* mean the end of ideology. Clearly, commitment to the politics of pragmatism, to the rules of the game of collective bargaining, to gradual change whether in the direction favored by the left or the right, to opposition both to an all powerful central state and to *laissez-faire* constitutes the component parts of an ideology. The "agreement on fundamentals," the political consensus of western society, now increasingly has come to include a position on matters which once sharply separated the left from the right. And this ideological agreement, which might best be described as "conservative socialism," has become *the* ideology of the major parties in the developed states of Europe and America.[24]

---

[21] Reprinted in C. Wright Mills, *Power, Politics and People* (New York: Ballantine Books, 1963), p. 256.

[22] *Ibid.,* pp. 256–257.

[23] Stephen Rousseas and James Farganis, "American Politics and the End of Ideology," in I. L. Horowitz, ed., *The New Sociology* (New York: Oxford University Press, 1964), pp. 271–272, 274.

[24] S. M. Lipset, "The Changing Class Structure and Contemporary European Politics," *Daedalus,* 93 (Winter 1964), p. 296. This article has been reprinted in slightly revised form in S. M. Lipset, *Revolution and Counterrevolution, op. cit.,* p. 303.

Dan Bell has also discussed the ideological implications of the "end to chiliastic hopes, to millenarianism, to apocalyptic thinking"—what he means by ideology in his use of the famous phrase. And unlike, a number of others who have analyzed it, Bell saw the "end of ideology" in politics as making realistic discussions of utopia possible for the first time. "The end of ideology is not—should not be the end of utopia as well. If anything, one can begin anew the discussion of utopia only by being aware of the trap of ideology."[25]

The general methodological and ideological issues subsumed in the controversies concerning the implications and validity of propositions dealing with the supposed declining role of certain types of ideology have been the subject of a considerable literature dealing with many countries. Many of these articles have been reprinted in two collections on the subject.[26] The interested reader may go through these and judge for himself. This debate is particularly interesting in the present context of the growing literature dealing with the "sociology of sociology," much of which confuses ideological evaluations with questions of validity. As Rejai and others note in evaluating the literature dealing the hypothesis of ideological decline: "Perhaps the most alarming attribute of the anti-decline writers is their apparent willingness to disregard the empirical significance of the hypothesis in question and to rely, instead, on semantic justification."[27]

This long discussion of the way in which the empirical content of a concept like the "end of ideology" has commended itself to scholars of diverse ideological persuasions, and to being criticized as reflecting the selective biases of given orientations points up the immense confusion possible when men do not distinguish between the value orientations of the investigator and the propositions he enunciates. Whether a given statement is valid or not, whether different studies of the same topic come up with similar findings, has nothing to do with the biases of the scholar. And it is obviously necessary to differentiate between efforts at intellectual history or the sociology of knowledge which address themselves to tracing through the factors involved in the creation or reception of scholarly efforts and their validity. As Richard Simpson has noted recently, this separation has not been present in some works dealing with the "sociology of sociology." "A central idea . . . is that when we pin an ideological tag on a theory . . . we say something about the validity of the theory. This notion is alarming, for it would turn

---

[25] Bell, op. cit., p. 405.

[26] Chaim I. Waxman, ed., The End of Ideology Debate (New York: Funk and Wagnalls, 1968) and Mostafa Rejai, ed., Decline of Ideology? (Chicago: Aldine/ Atherton, 1971). See also Raymond Aron, "The End of Ideology and the Renaissance of Ideas," in his The Industrial Society (New York: Praeger, 1967), pp. 92–188.

[27] Mostafa Rejai, W. L. Mason, and D. C. Beller, "Empirical Relevance of the Hypothesis of Decline," in Rejai, ed., op. cit., p. 269.

sociology into substandard moral philosophy with the resonating of sentiments replacing reason and observations as the basis for constructing and judging theories."[28]

A similar argument has recently been made by the Marxist sociologist, Pradeep Bandyopadhyay, writing in the oldest continuous journal of Marxist scholarship in English, *Science and Society*. He strongly challenges the contention of contemporary university activists that a Marxist sociology of knowledge would deny the possibility of objective knowledge in the social sciences, and cites various comments by Marx himself which are directly relevant.

> The sociology of knowledge deals as much with the sources of truth as of error. Relative truth is what is obtained: this simply means that truth at a given time is partial and imperfect, and the search for it may be fallible. The corrigibility of our knowledge is what makes it relative rather than absolute, but we move from the objectively *less true* to the objectively *more true;* in no case is relative truth necessarily nonobjective truth. . . . By denying objectivity and its concomitants, radicals deny themselves the ability to refute and expose falsehoods and artificial limitations on reason.[29]

I raise some of these broad issues here because I believe that one of the weaknesses of Romalis's discussion is a failure to distinguish sufficiently between the matters of intellectual orientation, ideology, or bias, and validity. In dealing with his specific points, I will take them up in the order presented by him.

SOCIALISM IN SASKATCHEWAN

Romalis makes a number of flattering comments concerning *Agrarian Socialism* for which I can only thank him. He does, however, challenge my brief comment (in the "Introduction" to the revised paperback edition of the book published 18 years later) that the original work had underestimated the effect of the varying electoral systems of Canada (parliamentary single member district) and the United States (focus on choice of one man as President or Governor) in affecting the propensities for a multiple party as contrasted with a two party system. This comment was a brief summary of an earlier published detailed analysis of the relationship between electoral and party systems dealing with many countries.[30]

---

28 Richard Simpson, "System and Humanism in Social Science," *Science,* 173 (May 1971), p. 664.

29 Pradeep Bandyopadhyay, "One Sociology or Many: Some Issues in Radical Sociology," *Science and Society,* 35 (Spring 1971), pp. 17–18, 22. The relevant citations to Marx are in footnote 16, p. 18.

30 See S. M. Lipset, "Party Systems and the Representation of Social Groups," *European Journal of Sociology,* 1 (1960), pp. 50–85, included in an elaborated form as chapter 9 in Lipset, *The First New Nation: The United States in Historical and Comparative Perspective* (Garden City: Doubleday-Anchor, 1968), pp. 327–365.

In discussing the brief summary of my position in the 1968 Preface to *Agrarian Socialism,* Romalis states that my supposed "assignment of causal priority to formal electoral arrangements as opposed to structural conditions, in the emergence of third parties, has not a shred of empirical support." This is rather a strong statement, given the existence of literally hundreds of books and articles, some of them systematically quantitative by many leading political scientists in different countries which have attempted to demonstrate the proposition Romalis thinks has no "shred of support." Many of these works are cited in my discussion of the topic in *The First New Nation.* I will not argue against this statement of his because he is not polemicizing with me, but with some of these other analysts. In fact, Romalis is more accurate when he states while even implying that I *may* be right: "Perhaps, as Lipset suggests, it is the flexibility of the Canadian electoral system which permits the emergence of third parties." He goes on, however, to urge as an apparent disagreement with me that "it is evidently also the case, as Pinard's data suggest, that extra-legislative *social* structural conditions underlie and bolster such third parties." But, of course! What else is my analysis of the emergence of the CCF in Saskatchewan and its relative weakness in other provinces about? I am deeply puzzled as to why Romalis could possibly think that by making this point, he is challenging or adding to anything I wrote. In the Preface, I was elaborating on a point made in the original edition of *Agrarian Socialism* in which I contrasted the phenomenon of the wheat farmers of Saskatchewan and Alberta taking the third party route, while the equally or possibly even more radical farmers of North Dakota, whose left-wing organization The Non-Partisan League (NPL) was at least as socialist and class-conscious as the Saskatchewan CCF, took the road of participation as a faction in the Republican Party primaries. The almost identical "extra-legislative social structural conditions" of Saskatchewan and North Dakota produced two organizations, the CCF and the NPL, which formulated almost identical programmatic and ideological responses to their economic and social problems. But north of the border, the electoral system and the phenomenon of disciplined parliamentary parties, led to a third party, while south of it, the NPL won office through capturing the Republican Party primaries. Its leaders included men who had tried the Socialist third party route, and concluded that it would not work in the United States.[31] Romalis mentions Maurice Pinard's excellent study of Quebec politics. Quebec as many have suggested may be compared for certain purposes with the American South. In Quebec, the special conditions which set it apart from the rest of Canada, have resulted in a variety of "third-party" protest movements; in the South, local protest whether it be racist or black

---

[31] *Agrarian Socialism* (Berkeley: University of California; paperback, Revised Edition, 1971), pp. 28–32, 154–157, 261–263.

militant finds that the best road to electoral success for state office lies in the Democratic Party primaries. The factors which determine the *character* and *goals* of protest politics are social structural, the *form* which they take may be affected by electoral systems and constitutional arrangements.

POLITICAL MAN

In presenting some statements from my "Introduction" to *Political Man,* Romalis selects quotations which strike me, at least, as out of context and incomplete. In the part which he discusses, I was seeking to point out how the liberal or left self-image of Americans has led them to support for ideological reasons, opposition to totalitarianism and Communist imperialism, at the same time "that American conservatives and businessmen oppose Communism and socialism because they see these as threats to their own interests." I went on to note that "American business has had considerable power and influence in affecting government policy. But I would argue that such power would be ineffective were it not for the fact that Communism appears as an evil to the American left, unions, intellectuals and others . . . ."[32] I stand by this statement.

It is precisely the anti-imperialist liberal ideological position which characterizes the American self-identity that facilitates an activist foreign policy usually presented in terms of support for the rights of other peoples. I am not here discussing the underlying meaning of an actual act of foreign policy, but rather the fact that where other western nations see themselves acting for national self-interest, ideologically defined countries such as the United States, the Soviet Union, or Communist China, perceive their actions as designed to implement an ideologically motivated good. Recently, the left-wing political scientist, Wilson Carey McWilliams, who has been a major foe of the Vietnam War from its start, made a similar point in reviewing writings on that conflict. McWilliams argued:

> It is clear, after all, that Washington did not *think* it was planning an aggressive war. It believed it was acting to forestall "Communist expansionism" and to reduce the risks of nuclear war, the most criminal of all wars. Johnson told [Maxwell] Taylor that we must be prepared to make our case at the United Nations against North Vietnamese aggression.[33]

It should be understood that McWilliams is convinced that the United States was totally wrong in undertaking war in Vietnam. What is at issue is his conviction that the leaders of the government really believed at the time that they were acting to stop an expanding Communist empire, that this

---

[32] *Political Man, op. cit.,* "Introduction," p. xxvii.
[33] Wilson Carey McWilliams, "Washington Plans an Aggressive War," The *New York Times Book Review,* September 26, 1971, p. 5.

rather than the defense of America's business interest was primary. Lester Gelb, the director of the Task Force which produced the Pentagon Papers, regretfully concluded: "Vietnam is what happened when our values, international and domestic were pushed to their logical extreme."[34] In my judgement, the main dynamics behind the expansionist interventionist phases of American foreign policy, certainly in this century, have reflected a Wilsonian liberal to left commitment to reform the world, to extend self-determination, to eliminate colonial empires, more than the efforts of business interests to enhance their profit position. With few exceptions, the latter need can be met without sending American troops abroad, the former often could not be. Seeing the American liberal creed as a source of an aggressive foreign policy is not to praise American efforts abroad; it is to attempt to explain them in terms which make understandable what a narrow economic motivation analysis fails to account for. The concern of businessmen to maximize international trade and profits has often served, as Wilson pointed out at the end of his Presidency, to frustrate the reformist objectives of the politicians and intellectuals who advocated intervention.

This thesis may be illustrated by post World War II events since it is clear that an activist interventionist American foreign policy has largely been fostered by liberal Democratic administrations, urged on by left intellectuals and the trade-union movement. Thus, the Korean War, the Bay of Pigs intervention in Cuba, the Dominican affair, and the Vietnam War were all initiated and pressed by Democratic administrations, based electorally on those segments of the population which in most countries support the left. A look at the institutions backed covertly in the anti-Communist fight by the C.I.A. indicates that most of them were liberal-left to socialist in their political sympathies. After the lists were made public, Senator Goldwater and the *National Review* complained bitterly that *their* friends and organizations received little or no help from the C.I.A. This apparent "leftist" bias may be related to the suggestions made by some informed commentators that the C.I.A. had been staffed in the early 1950s by refugees from (Joe) McCarthyism. By moving from State or other departments to the C.I.A., men with leftist records vulnerable to McCarthyite attack were protected from Senatorial inquisition.

The Republican, business-dominated, conservative administrations have, on the other hand, been characterized by a much less interventionist foreign policy. Eisenhower promised to end the war in Korea and he did so. In spite of the loud out-cry against Communism by John Foster Dulles, the Eisenhower administration did not intervene in Germany during the June 1953

---

[34] Lester Gelb, "On Schlesinger and Ellsberg: A Reply," *New York Review of Books,* 17 (December 2, 1971), p. 34.

uprising in East Berlin, and the prolonged strike in the Communist zone. Rather, American troops in Berlin were used to hold back West Berlin Social Democratic demonstrators from aiding their comrades in the East. In 1954, the U.S. refused to aid the French in Indo-China with pilots, troops, or tactical nuclear weapons to prevent a Communist victory. Again in 1956, under Eisenhower, no American aid was given to the Hungarian Revolution. In the same year, the United States joined with the Soviet Union in forcing the Israelis, British, and French out of the Sinai and the Gaza Strip. Most recently the Nixon administration has shown much greater flexibility in dealing with Communist nations or radical movements from Indo-China, to China, to the Soviet Union, to Chile than its Democratic predecessors. The one major force in America which still maintains some support for an activist posture in Indo-China is the American labor movement, led by George Meany.

The general point concerning the variation in partisan (and ideological) responsibility for "hard" and "soft" periods in post-war American foreign policy has been effectively made by Gaddis Smith, Yale diplomatic historian, in his review of the 12 volumes of the "Pentagon Papers." As he points out the policymakers of the Truman administration were convinced "that if only the United States had the opportunity to apply enough money, intelligence, and military force to Vietnam it could destroy the enemy," that they adhered to " 'the domino theory,' by which expulsion of Western influence from Vietnam was equated with the collapse of the Free World."

> It is reasonable to speculate that had the Truman Administration been in power in 1954, at the time of the French defeat at Dienbienphu, the United States would have intervened militarily. But Dwight D. Eisenhower was then President, and he held the hawks on a tight leash, as the documents in the Government edition (but omitted from the Gravel edition) amply illustrate. In 1961 President Kennedy brought many of the veterans of the Truman years back into positions of power . . . . They then took the opportunity to do what, had they been able, they might have done years before.[35]

To shift to another part of the world, Guyana, Professor Romalis challenges my example of American policy there as an instance of the United States support of a "leftist" regime. Although I am not as acquainted with the inside politics of that country as he is, I would note that its Premier, Forbes Burnham, does present himself as a Socialist, that his formal politics are at least as radical as that of the New Democratic Party in Canada, and, in some ways, more so. The latter point has been illustrated by the current relations of Guyana with China. As a *Washington Post* dispatch from there

---

[35] Gaddis Smith, "United States-Vietnam Relations, 1945–1967," *New York Times Book Review,* November 28, 1971, p. 30.

indicates: "Communist China chose Guyana as a logical land for negotiating the first bilateral trade agreement in the Caribbean area. It calls for $15 million of trade each way over the next five years on a quid pro quo basis, with China providing one or two textile plants as a starter and Guyana shipping alumina ore, timber and possibly sugar." The fact that Guyana can maintain friendly relations with both the United States and China is viewed with alarm by the pro-Russian Communists. "Burnham's arch political rival, Cheddi Jagan, . . . sees it as a dark and devious plot hatched in Washington. In a parliamentary debate and in a lengthy interview, Jagan insisted that he did not oppose dealings with Peking but that it is a subterfuge 'to drive another wedge between China and the Soviet Union.'" On July 15, 1971, the Burnham government nationalized the country's largest industry, the bauxite mines owned by Alcan Aluminum, Ltd. And an article in the business section of the *New York Times* noted that "The Government's domestic economic policies have not set well with local business interests."[36]

In the remaining discussion dealing with research material from the body of *Political Man* as distinct from the manifest statement of political orientation in the Preface, Romalis wanders between commentary on empirical findings and political exhortation, the purpose of which I find confusing. Thus he links my generalizations about "cross-cutting cleavages" to the maxim: "Divide to rule." This maxim may be valid, but the empirical issue is whether or not reinforcing cleavages make for more intense ideological politics while cross-cutting ones make for greater moderation, or even as I suggest, greater apathy. I think that Romalis agrees with the empirical proposition; what he dislikes is my using the term "democracy" in conjunction with the United States. A discussion of our differing conceptions of democracy might clearly be worthwhile; to somehow drag in the empirical analysis of the cleavages seems somewhat irrelevant.

Romalis does not, however, choose to elaborate on the issue of what is democracy; rather he criticizes me for "ignoring totally the possible legitimacy of communism as an ideology of social change and development, not to mention the variability of communism and the national forms which it assumes. . . ." I must plead guilty to thinking that communism is not a progressive movement, that in the long run the institutional structure, the monopoly of economic and political power in state and party, which it creates will result in a highly retrogressive (steeply stratified) system. There is, of course, no question that most of the regimes of the Third World are also dictatorial, that no one may speak of them as more democratic than communism. But I never have done so, though Mr. Romalis seems to infer that I do. In analyzing variations among Latin American governments in *Political*

---

[36] Irwin Goodwin, "China-Guyana: a trading 'coup'", *Boston Globe,* January 3, 1972, p. 24. "Guyana: Wider Markets," *New York Times,* January 28, 1972, p. 66.

Man, I differentiate between more or less stable, *not* more or less democratic, in part for this reason. Beyond this, I did not rule out governments in which communist parties participate or dominate as necessarily undemocratic by the purely operational criteria of the presence or absence of institutionalized opposition. The Chilean Popular Front government is still a democratic government, it permits opposition groups and press to operate. The Popular Front governments of Finland have been democratic in this sense. Romalis seeks to make me a defender of the Haitian system; I must decline the invitation, since it is clearly a monstrous authoritarian one. Nothing that Fidel Castro can do in Cuba will improve Haiti's position on a comparative scale of democratic governments. Why bring in this red herring? Romalis tells us that "communist Yugoslavia is no less 'democratic' than is Greece." Where have I ever said anything contradictory? (At the moment, I happen to be involved on the national committee of the main American organization campaigning for freedom in Greece.) Or where did I discuss "communist Kerala" (it is not communist) as less democratic than selected non-communist states in India? In *Political Man* (pp. 119–121), I analyzed the differences between the composition of Communist voters in Kerala, where the party was then strong, with those in the rest of India. There is not the slightest mention or inference made on these pages concerning the relative degree of democracy in Kerala as compared with any other place. Does Romalis question my research evidence and conclusions concerning the differential character of Communist voters in places where the party is small and large? This is all I addressed myself to, although he does not mention the topic.

Romalis does raise a genuine challenge to one proposition in *Political Man.* He reports that John Kautsky has tested the "cross-national relationship between communism and economic development" and finds, *contra* Lipset, that a definite curvilinear relationship exists between degree of economic development and Communist Party strength." Romalis introduces this report with the comment that "Lipset's analysis is wrong largely because his ideological posture has led him to ignore counter-evidence." This is a grievous charge, if true. But the only study mentioned that I have supposedly ignored that by Kautsky was published in *1968. Political Man* was published in *1960.* I know some people think I have assorted gifts, but such foresight is unfortunately not one of them. In any case, Kautsky, in the study to which Romalis referred dealt with underdeveloped countries, I dealt only with European ones. The issue of the relationship between levels of economic development and political forms and movements is much more complicated than is suggested in my original work (the first on the subject and necessarily the most primitive). There are literally dozens of highly technical publications on the topic, some of which reach quite varying results, depending on conceptualization, systems of classification, and quantitative methods employed.[37] I fear that I am acquainted with much more supportive as well as counter-evidence on the subject than Romalis.

VALUE ORIENTATIONS: THE FIRST NEW NATION AND REVOLUTION AND COUNTERREVOLUTION

Romalis's main complaint about these works is that they do not deal with Negroes. I must acknowledge that he is right in the main, although as he notes, there is some discussion of the subject. But I must here report that I have dealt with problems of racism, prejudice, bigotry, and discrimination in two other works which I have written with Earl Raab.[38] The first work is not mentioned by Romalis, while the second is passed over in a slighting footnote.

Romalis, of course, may still argue that I should have also treated the race situation in depth in the two books he chooses to discuss, since American racial practices totally contradict the values dealt with there. The fact of the contradiction is obvious. I discuss some of the implications in *The First New Nation* pointing up the fact that

> American egalitarianism is, of course, for white men only. The treatment of the Negro makes a mockery of this value now as it has in the past. During the nineteenth century, when European leftists and liberals were pointing to the United States as a nation which demonstrated the viability of equality and democracy, America was also the land of slavery. The trauma of slavery is deeply rooted in the American psyche. The contradiction between the American value system and the way in which the Negro is treated has, if anything, forced many Americans to think even more harshly of the Negro than they might if they lived in a more explicitly ascriptive culture. There is no justification in an egalitarian society to repress a group such as the Negroes unless they are defined as a congenitally inferior race. Therefore, Americans have been under pressure either to deny the Negro's right to participate in the society, because he is inferior, or to ignore his existence, to make him an "invisible" man.[39]

Thus as should be clear from the above statement, I have argued that Blacks have been held down in the United States even more than they might

---

[37] Some of these papers have been included in Charles F. Cnudde and Deane E. Neubauer, eds., *Empirical Democratic Theory* (Chicago: Markham, 1969), esp. pp. 143–235; in Hugh D. Graham and Ted R. Gurr, eds., *The History of Violence in America* (New York: Bantam Books, 1969), esp. pp. 570–687; and in James C. Davies, ed., *When Men Revolt and Why* (New York: The Free Press, 1971), esp. pp. 203–313. For a revised discussion of this topic including reference to the literature which has appeared since 1960, see S. M. Lipset and William Schneider, "Political Sociology," in Neil Smelser, ed., *Sociology* (New York: Wiley, 1973, in press).

[38] See our publications: *Prejudice and Society* (New York: Anti-Defamation League, 1959) and *The Politics of Unreason* (New York: Harper and Row, 1970). See also S. M. Lipset, *Group Life in America* (New York: American Jewish Committee, 1972).

[39] *The First New Nation, op. cit.,* pp. 379–380.

have been, given various structural arrangements which followed on emancipation, *because* of the value system, not *in spite* of it. This phenomenon, however, does not rule out an analysis of the implications of the value system for various aspects of the society, some of which may be viewed as positive and others as negative. For example, I also discuss the pressures derivative from the American value system, for more violence of all kinds, for greater crime, and for higher rates of corruption than in comparably developed countries. The assumption that much about American life may be understood by assuming a greater acceptance on equalitarianism as a value, in spite of the denigration of the black population, has been made in many works about American society which have influenced me, including those of Harriet Martineau, Alexis de Tocqueville, Karl Marx, James Byrce, Gunnar Myrdal, and Louis Hartz, among others. And, except for Martineau and Myrdal, the others wrote about its implications without focusing on the problems of the Negroes.

Since Romalis notes that I explicitly recognize "the structural conditions" which determine the situation of Latin America, I see no reason to go into detail in a discussion of his opinions about my chapter on Latin America in *Revolution and Counterrevolution*. I would note, however, that the reviewer of the book in the *American Sociological Review*, himself an authority on Latin America, drew politically different implications from his reading of my chapter:

> In the context of [discussing] predominant values that are dysfunctional to socio-economic development, Lipset provides counsel to social policy: ". . . [T]hose concerned with Latin American economic development . . . might best devote themselves to an analysis of the conditions for *revolutionary transformation of class relationships*. . . . Presumably, the quickest way to initiate major changes in values is through (social) revolutions which remove those dominant strata which seek to maintain their position and traditional values." The point is well taken.[40]

It is curious that a recurrent criticism of "behavioral scientists," i.e., sociologists, social psychologists, and anthropologists, who concern themselves with concepts such as value patterns, "achievement orientations," or the cultures of specific groups or nations in accounting for varying aspects of economic behavior, is that they do not engage in the same sort of analysis as economists. Thus, the sociologist writing about the Third World is challenged for highlighting non-economic factors. The critics, often sociologists who think themselves to the left of a given writer, argue that the total explanation for the difficulties of Third World nations lies in the economic relations between the United States or other developed nations and the less

---

[40] F. B. Waisanen, review of *Revolution and Counterrevolution, American Sociological Review,* 35 (May 1970), p. 561.

developed countries. There is no doubt that exploitative and unequal economic relationships between developed and underdeveloped regions contribute to the failure of the latter to develop rapidly or at all, but that clearly does not account for all of the story. How did Australia, New Zealand, and Canada become much more wealthy than various Latin American nations with comparable economic resources and relations with metropolitan countries, sometimes as in the case of Argentina, Chile, and Uruguay with the same one? Surely, no country has ever been as much at the economic and political mercy of another as Japan after 1945; yet while occupied and controlled, it developed rapidly into a major competitor with its occupier and chief trading partner. The post-war West German story is similar. Within the Soviet Union and Yugoslavia, national units vary enormously in their capacity to take advantage of the same economic system. Disparate rates of development characterize multi-national communist countries. The problem this poses for the Soviet Union has been pointed up in a dispatch from Baku, the capital of the Azerbaijan Soviet Socialist Republic, which discusses the way in which the "Azerbaijani style of life, reflecting centuries of Moslem influences, refuses to conform to the Communist model":

> No less a figure than Geldar A. Aliyev, the Communist party chief, has been complaining about nepotism, forced child marriages, corruption on a grand scale, the urge for private ownership and the penchant for private trading— "plundering of socialist property for mercenary reasons," he called it—and the practice of bribing examiners at universities for entrance or graduation. . . .
> The clannishness of the Azerbaijanis, their skill at arranging deals under the table and their general undisciplined ways have long been a problem for Communist leaders—apparently at a greater scale than in many other regions. Some local Communists blame centuries of Moslem domination over this southern territory. . . .
> "Islam is more aggressive and more reactionary than other religions," asserted Gasham Asianov, editor of the Communist youth paper Yunost. . . . "This religion teaches people to think about themselves and their families. . . . We lived about 1,300 years by this religion, by this ideology," he explained. . . . "We have lived under Soviet power only 50 years. During 50 years it is very difficult to change human nature."[41]

Clearly, assuming some rational division of labor in analyzing developments in both communist and non-communist nations, it would seem to be the job of the sociologist to analyze the non-economic variables which affect the varying propensities of culturally distinct groupings to fulfill certain

---

41 Hedrick Smith, "Islamic Past of Azerbaijan Republic Frustrate Moscow's Marxist Plans," *New York Times,* December 13, 1971, p. 2. For a report on a study which demonstrates the continued effect of sharp differences in values among the Yugoslav ethnic groups on various forms of behavior, see Gary K. Bertsch, *Nation Building in Yugoslavia* (Beverly Hills: Sage Publications, 1971).

REPLY TO COLEMAN ROMALIS (AND OTHER CRITICS)

roles. The origins of such variations may often lie in historically separate and unequal economic experiences, but whatever the source of the differences and whatever moral judgement may be applied to them, there is some reason to believe that it is worth elaborating and testing the hypotheses concerning variations in achievement that are rooted in cultural and social structural analysis.

It is important to note here that Marxism, as East European sociologists and economists are well aware, does not have conceptual variables to deal with these issues. Rather in a theory of long-term historical change from one level of technology and accompanying class relationships to another, Marx focused on the role of position in the productive apparatus as the prime determinant of other patterns of behavior. Such an emphasis, however, is not very illuminating for any effort to explain the range of variation within similar social systems, as characterized by class relationships. It is obvious that there are enormous differences in inter-class relationships, in types of status and political power systems, among capitalist and communist countries. And while some of these variations may be accounted for by reference to levels of economic development, many others may not be. Thus, although recognizing the significance of structural factors derivative from levels of economic development as determinants of behavior (Talcott Parsons once referred to my work as a variant of "Marxism," for this reason, others more recently have described it as carrying on the tradition of structural analysis of C. Wright Mills), it seems to me that contemporary sociological theory, particularly aspects of the work of Parsons, has suggested a number of concepts, such as the pattern variables, which are useful in analyzing social differences among comparable economic systems.[42] Thus, to my mind any effort at systematic comparative analysis should draw theoretical inspiration from the compatible analytic frameworks of Marx, Weber, and Parsons.

Some would argue that the approaches of Marx and Parsons are incompatible because the first was primarily concerned with specifying the conditions for social change, while the second has devoted much of his analysis to dealing with problems of social cohesion. It should be obvious, however, that both interests are among the primary concerns of sociology, that any effort to deal with one is at the same time a contribution to the other. William Goode in a recent essay dealing with, among other things, the "cognitive errors" of the radical student critics of sociology notes that one of them is:

> . . . the notion that if the social analyst works from a conception of society as some kind of equilibristic system, he cannot use that system to analyze social

---

[42] References to various articles and books which have placed my work in a Marxist or C. Wright Mills's tradition of analysis may be found in the "Preface" to the Anchor Edition of *Revolution and Counterrevolution, op. cit.,* pp. xi–xiii.

change or conflict, or even to admit its failings. Since all developed sciences do in fact use different types of equilibristic conceptions, but also analyze how these systems change and break down, it is clear that conception itself contains no assertation that present-day structure is a good one [or is stable.][43]

Romalis's amplification of my discussion of the differences between Canada and the United States is interesting and useful. Although, he strains to present it in the context of a sharp disagreement with me, I do not find it contradictory with my analysis. As he notes, and as I made clear in my analysis, my writings on the subject are largely derivative from those of a number of distinguished Canadian scholars, including in particular those of that magnificent historian, Frank Underhill, and my friend and former colleague, S. D. Clark, but in addition, Kaspar Naegele, Dennis Wrong, A. R. M. Lower, W. L. Morton, Harold Innis, Claude Bissell, and many others. What I tried to report to a predominantly non-Canadian audience was a consensus among many Canadian sociologists and historians concerning the nature, and the genesis, of some important differences between Canada and the United States, differences which when added up consistently illustrate some assumptions about continued variations in values between the two North American states. Romalis seems to agree concerning these variations. He disagrees, to some minor extent, as to the way they should be conceptualized, and to some greater extent with interpretations of historical events. Thus, he objects to my not mentioning the fear Canadians had concerning the possibility of invasion and annexation by the United States after the Civil War. I am certainly aware of this anxiety, a concern which paralleled the desires of many Americans to end any trace of monarchy and British rule on the continent. But the matter in question, the insertion by Canadian Conservatives into the Canadian constitution of a clause which permitted the Federal government to veto any act passed by a provincial legislature, was addressed to the fear of populism, to a desire to enable the federal government to prevent experimentation by a radical provincial government, not to worry about American soldiers entering Canada. Romalis seeks to emphasize that I do not appreciate the desire of nineteenth-century Canadians to avoid being dominated by American imperialism, that they preferred the British because they were further away. This may be so, but it is also a fact, as S. D. Clark and Frank Underhill have shown, that the pro-British groupings in British North America tended to be the Conservatives, who opposed majority government, while the pro-American elements, those who wanted to break with Britain, and possibly join the United States, tended to be the more liberal and radical forces, those who favored majority rule.

---

[43] William J. Goode, "Must Sociologists Be Revolutionaries?" (Unpublished paper, Department of Sociology, Columbia University), p. 16.

DEMOCRACY AS OBJECTIVE AND MEANS

Romalis concludes his discussion with a renewed criticism of my supposed formalistic views about democracy. All I can do is once again try to briefly reiterate the relevant portions of my political credo, by saying again as I did in the Introduction to *Political Man* that I regard myself as within the democratic left. Briefly, this means that I believe in the necessity to reduce inequality of all kinds as much as possible within the confines of a complex human society. I would reiterate my underlying assumptions and action implications in the precise terms to which I replied to a comparable set of criticisms almost a decade ago:

Essentially it [my philosophy] consists of the belief that while a system of stratification (differences in the distribution of status, income, and power) is inherent in the nature of any complex social system, such inequality is basically punitive and discriminatory. The lower strata in all societies are punished psychically and often physically for being in an inferior position. Stratification advantages or disadvantages cumulate in a self-supporting cycle. And since I feel that inequality though inevitable is *immoral*, I support all measures which would serve to reduce its extent, or which would bring the utopian goals of "equality of status and opportunity" closer to reality. My commitment to democracy as a political system does not rest solely on the belief that free debate and institutionalized conflict among opposing groups are the best way for society to progress, intellectually as well as materially, but also on the assumption that only a politically democratic society can reduce the pressures endemic in social systems to increase the punitive and discriminatory aspects of stratification. I believe with Marx that all privileged classes seek to maintain and enhance their advantages against the desire of the underprivileged to reduce them. I agree with Plato that the family necessarily fosters inequality, that parents and others tied by the affective values basic to kinship, must seek to give to their children and others to whom they are tied by familial sentiments all the possible advantages they can. And consequently, ruling strata under all economic and social systems will try to institutionalize their superiority so that their kin may inherit. This tendency is as true for the Soviet Union as it is for the United States, as strong in Communist China as in France or Japan.

If it is true, as I assume, that pressures toward inequality and status ascription are basic to human society, then it follows that those who would reduce such reactions as much as possible, must seek for institutionalized means of restraining them. And I know of no means to do so which are superior or even approach the method of conflict. The only groups which have an "interest" to modify and reduce inequality are the underprivileged. But the underprivileged can only impress their concerns on the social system in a polity in which they are free to organize in unions, parties, cooperatives, and the like. The only effective restraint on the power of the dominant class is counterpower. The primary weapons of the lower strata, of the exploited classes, are the ability to organize, to strike, to demonstrate, and to vote rulers out of office. In any given society at any given time in history, the lower classes may not use these weapons effectively, they may not recognize their interests, but there is no other way. Hence, a society which denies the masses such rights is not only undemocratic politically, it also fosters the increased privileges of the ruling groups.[44]

These assumptions lead me to favor the maintenance and extension of all institutional practices and structural conditions which facilitate opposition by non-elites to those who dominate. Where power is monopolized by a tiny elite as it is in all one-party or other authoritarian systems, whether they describe themselves as leftist or rightist, Communist, Populist, nationalistic, or religious, the great mass will have little or no way to prevent those who control the economy, institutions of force, organs of communication, or the state, from dictating the way they shall live. Hence any movement, regardless of its manifest objectives, which undermines existing institutions that facilitate opposition to power-holders, however, inadequately, is a force for authoritarian rule, and for increased rather than reduced inequality. Wherever small elites command the resources of society and polity, and they do in diverse ways in nations ranging from the Soviet Union, China, Cuba, Greece, and Spain, to the United States, Japan, Germany, and Britain, they can only be restrained from using, from exploiting, the non-elite, by the ability of segments of the latter to bring pressure to bear on those in power. The non-elite, the less privileged, may only protect themselves through their ability to form parties and other mass organizations, and to demonstrate, strike, and vote against those in authority.

These issues are, of course, as much political as they are matters for scholarly inquiry. And from the days when as a young Socialist in college, I was convinced that Robert Michels's analysis of the sources of oligarchy was a better discussion of the problems of a post-capitalist society than anything written by a Marxist down to the present, these concepts have informed my politics and my sociology. Politically, I reiterated them at a conference of the Socialist party in 1971, at which I argued that a socialist program "could only ameliorate, never solve, the problem of continued inequality of power and status."

> On the other hand, revolutionary ideologies have attempted total solutions to the problems of inequality, but we know that the revolutionaries have failed even more dismally than the reformers, by putting a tiny elite in power. In China, even with the "cultural revolution," the program of sending students back to the farms for manual labor does not extend to party members and children of party members. The problem of inequality cannot be solved, but the struggle to limit inequality is an endless struggle. One must advocate struggle against inequality, not the belief in a total solution to the problem.[45]

---

[44] S. M. Lipset, "Ideology and Political Bias. . .", *op. cit.,* pp. 214–215.
[45] "SP-USA Conference: Program for America," *New America,* June 26, 1971, p. 6. This article includes a report on my talk to that conference.

Societies which are democratic are better than those which are autocratic precisely because democratic systems are based on the assumption that internal conflict is legitimate, proper, necessary, while autocratic systems, communist or other, operate on the assumption that consensus is proper. Since all complex societies, whether pre-industrial, industrial, or post-industrial, capitalist, communist, or socialist, give power to small ruling elites, the issue remains, regardless of the form of ownership and control of economic institutions, as to how to limit the power of the elites, how to reduce their efforts to enhance their power, and consequent status and privilege. A political ideology which defines a social system as a "people's" one serves to prevent the people from opposing those who govern, for the latter are enabled to define all opposition as antagonistic to the people's will. Ironically, it is precisely those, who in western democratic societies criticize defenders of democratic political institutions as advocates of consensus, who are themselves the believers in consensus politics. Democratic institutions are not epiphenomena, are not means to be used or even destroyed in the process of attaining economic ends. Rather they are an absolutely necessary condition for any effort to systematically reduce the differences in power, status, and privilege. From my perspective, therefore, those who would weaken democratic institutions are themselves advocates of an elitist system, no matter how much they subjectively believe that when they are in power they will reduce or even eliminate inequality.

The history of most past revolutions has demonstrated the extent to which the revolutionary advocates of equality have repeatedly created more autocratic, more concentrated, and therefore more inequalitarian power systems than those which they overturned. As Albert Camus noted: "All modern revolutions have ended in a reinforcement of state power." The great German-Polish revolutionary, Rosa Luxemburg, understood this danger and predicted long before Stalin that the Russian Revolution would wind up creating a totally repressive society "in which only the bureaucracy remains as the active element."[46] As she noted: "it is a well known and indisputable fact that without a free and untrammelled press, without the unlimited right of association and assembly, the rule of the broad masses of the people is entirely unthinkable."[47] A somewhat similar position was presented much earlier by Leon Trotsky in opposing Lenin's efforts to create a party organization dominated from the top. In 1903, he accused Lenin of talking socialism, but actually modeling himself on the dictatorial bourgeois revolutionary, Robespierre, and planning to set up a "pseudo-Jacobin dictatorship over the masses," which would end with the use of the "guillotine" to

---

[46] Rosa Luxemburg, *The Russian Revolution* (Ann Arbor: University of Michigan Press, 1961), p. 76.

[47] *Ibid.,* pp. 66–67.

eliminate dissidents. Trotsky prophetically stated that the upshot of a Leninist seizure of power would result in a situation in which:

> The Organization of the Party takes the place of the Party itself; the Central Committee takes the place of the organization; and finally the dictator takes the place of the Central Committee . . .[48]

It should be noted that in taking these positions Trotsky and Luxemburg were closer to the classic Marxist one than was Lenin. Thus, Friedrich Engels had explicitly written: "If anything has been established for certain, it is this, that our party and the working class can achieve rule only under the form of the democratic republic. This is even the *specific form* for the dictatorship of the proletariat, as the great French revolution has already shown."[49] There is some indication in Lenin's writings that he was aware of the contradiction between his own views and those of Marx's co-worker concerning democracy. In *State and Revolution,* Lenin commented on the precise statement of Engels, quoted above: "Engels repeats here in a particularly emphatic form the fundamental idea which runs like a red thread throughout all Marx's work, namely, that the democratic republic is *the nearest approach* to the dictatorship of the proletariat."[50] It is clear that Lenin changed Engels's formulation so as to be able to deny that the specific form of a state dominated by the workers should be a democratic republic, a fact Stalin was glad to acknowledge.

Non-Marxist radicals had, of course, long warned that a revolution which intensified state power and placed a party controlled by a self-annointed intellectual elite in power would result in an even greater level of domination over the masses than existed in capitalist or pre-industrial societies. This was a major theme in the writings of the anarchist theoretician, Michael Bakunin, who predicted that the Marxist revolution would ultimately result in the substitution of "a new class, a new hierarchy," which would be retro-

---

[48] Reported and cited in Bertram D. Wolfe, *Three Who Made a Revolution* (Boston: Beacon Press, 1955), p. 253.

[49] See Karl Marx and Friedrich Engels, *Writings on the Paris Commune* (New York: Monthly Review Press, 1971), p. 235 (emphasis mine). For detailed evidence that the term "dictatorship of the proletariat" meant "class-rule" through democratic means in the writings of Marx and Engels, see Hal Draper, "Marx and the Dictatorship of the Proletariat," *New Politics,* 1 No. 4 (1962), pp. 91–104 and Michael Harrington, *Socialism* (New York: Saturday Review Press, 1972), pp. 37–40, 49–54.

[50] (Emphasis mine). Published in a section in Karl Marx and Friedrich Engels, *Correspondence 1846–1895* (New York: International Publishers, 1934), p. 486. I cite this edition because it is a translation of the collection published under the auspices of the Marx-Engels-Lenin Institute of Moscow, with an introduction by its then director, V. Adoratsky. The clearly erroneous reference by Lenin to Engels's statement is published together with the original on page 486. Stalin also pointed to Lenin's "revision of traditional Marxist views about democracy." See *Political Man, op. cit.,* p. xxxv.

gressive.[51] Subsequently, at the turn of the century, a Polish former Marxist and revolutionary leader, Jan Machajski, paralleled the interpretation which Marxists presented of the role of populist and equalitarian slogans of the American and French Revolutions in legitimating bourgeois class rule in his analysis of the consequences of a Marxist triumph in the Czarist empire. Like Bakunin, he argued that it would bring about a society controlled by the mandarins, the educated classes. And Machajski suggested, predating the similar thesis of Robert Michels, that concepts of participatory democracy, of control of the machinery of complex industrial society by the masses, were utopian and would only serve to conceal the fact that dictatorial socialism would be severely stratified with respect to power and privilege. Hence, he argued that the only honest position for any one interested in improving the position of the masses was to protect their right to resist those in power through mass organizations independent of the dominant party and state.[52]

As might be expected, Machajski's writings have not been allowed to circulate in the Communist world, but there is some reason to believe that his analysis and predictions bothered the leaders of the Soviet state long after the Revolution. Machajski and his teachings were subject to vitriolic attack in *Pravda* in 1926 when he died, and again in 1938, when they were condemned as "outrageous, hooligan, and dangerous to the Soviet state."[53]

Since the break-up of Stalinist absolutism, various writers and scholars have reported in considerable detail the patterns of considerable inequality with respect to privilege and opportunity (mobility) in the Soviet Union and other eastern European states. Among other things now documented by sociological investigations is the fact that the children of the intelligentsia form a disproportionately large segment of the university student population, suggesting that almost all their offspring enter these institutions and so qualify for the upper rungs of Soviet society; the workers are consequently heavily underrepresented, while relatively few children of the peasantry are involved in higher education. Although almost half the Soviet population lives in rural areas, a 1966 Russian report indicated that "the percentage of students from the country is ten times lower than students from the town."

---

[51] See *The Political Philosophy of Bakunin* (Glencoe: The Free Press, 1953), pp. 283–289.

[52] Unfortunately little of Machajski has been translated into English. For a brief sample from his book, *The Intellectual Worker*, see V. F. Calverton, ed., *The Making of Society* (New York: Random House, 1937), pp. 427–436. Max Nomad has been Machajski's main American disciple, and has summarized and applied his teachings in *Aspects of Revolt* (New York: Noonday Press, 1961), pp. 96–117; *Dreamers, Dynamiters and Demagogues* (New York: Waldon Press, 1964), pp. 103–108, 201–206; and *Political Heretics* (Ann Arbor: University of Michigan Press, 1963), pp. 238–241. See also Paul Avrich, "What is 'Machaevism'?", *Soviet Studies,* 17 (July 1965), pp. 66–75 and Marshall Shatz, "Jan Waclaw Machajski: The 'Conspiracy' of the Intellectuals," *Survey,* No. 62 (January 1967), pp. 45–57.

[53] Shatz, *op. cit.,* p. 57; Nomad, *Aspects . . . op. cit.,* p. 117; Avrich, *op. cit.*

Given these findings, it is not surprising that the results of Soviet studies of occupational prestige are strikingly similar to those in non-Communist countries, and that investigations of the occupational aspirations of school children indicate that few want to be workers or peasants.[54]

Sociologists in Russia and eastern Europe generally have discussed the continued existence of stratification as an endemic characteristic of Communist society. "Some [Russian scholars] have even argued that those who are professionally engaged in administrative social functions constitute a separate social group. And some have even viewed the Party, not in the original Leninist terms, as the vanguard of the working class, but as an instrument for resolving conflicts of interest among different social groups."[55]

Communist societies, which are multi-ethnic or religious, face the problems of economic, political, and social discrimination related to ancestry comparable to those of non-Communist nations. An unpublished sociological survey of the population of a major Yugoslav city found a strong correlation between skin color and occupational position. As in many other countries, the lighter the skin color the more privileged the status. The denial to Russian Jewry of cultural and religious rights given to other Soviet ethnic and religious groups, and the efforts to impose *numerus clausus* with respect to admission to universities and other sources of privilege, are part of a well documented story and need not be repeated here.[56] Less well known are the Polish events of 1968, when following on the repression of prolonged student demonstrations and strikes in March of that year, the regime and party turned on the historic national scapegoat, the Jews, and viciously persecuted the remaining small group of them, including some people searched out because of half or even quarter Jewish ancestry, as agents of foreign Zionist and capitalist conspiracies. The Communist regime was able to complete the Nazi program of making Poland *Judenrein*. All this was done in the absence of any protest from other segments of Polish society, except for some intellectuals, and those who protested left Poland, together with the remnant of the Jews. The absence of democratic rights in the Communist world means, of course, that minorities may be mistreated with few outside

---

[54] For a report on the findings of Soviet social science, see Zev Katz, "Hereditary Elements in Education and Social Structure in the USSR," (University of Glasgow, Institute of Soviet and East European Studies, 1961); "Soviet Sociology: A Half-Way House," (Russian Research Center, Harvard University, 1971), and S. M. Lipset, "Social Mobility and Equal Opportunity," *The Public Interest* No. 29 (Fall 1972), pp. 90–108.

[55] Daniel Bell, "The Post-Industrial Society: The Evolution of an Idea," *Survey*, 79 (Spring 1971), p. 150. This article contains a detailed set of references to Soviet and other east European publications dealing with stratification, see pp. 149–155.

[56] For a discussion of contemporary anti-Semitism in different contexts see S. M. Lipset, "The Return of Anti-Semitism," in Irving Howe and Carl Gershman, eds. *Israel, The Arabs and the Middle East* (New York: Bantam Books, 1972), pp. 390–427.

their ranks being aware of the situation, or in a position to assist them.[57] Similarly, the suppression of the massive 1968 Polish student revolt brought few repercussions or expressions of support, either within Poland or outside, given the ability of the regime to conceal knowledge of the events while they were occurring.

The existence of democratic rights is no guarantee that the power of the dominant strata will in fact be restricted or challenged in any given area of the society. The underprivileged are often too weak or disorganized to affect the decision structure. Yet a comparative look at the way in which various nations have dealt with weak foreign countries or colonies since World War II points up some consequences of varying political systems. Britain, France, and the United States each faced considerable internal opposition to efforts to retain or assert their power over other peoples. In France and the United States concerted efforts by students, intellectuals, and others to their wars in Algeria and Vietnam clearly influenced their governments' decisions to withdraw their troops. The domestic politics of both countries were badly bedeviled by these unpopular military efforts. The Soviet Union, on the other hand, was able to invade both Hungary in 1956 and Czechoslovakia in 1968 without concern about domestic reactions. We know of no voiced criticism to China's invasion and occupation of Tibet. Other parts of the Communist world have cooperated with or endorsed these occupations (Castro has praised the 1968 occupation of Czechoslovakia) without meeting with internal unrest.

The most recent effort to suppress a revolutionary socialist movement occurred in Ceylon in April 1971. And as an article in the British journal, The *New Left Review* attests: "Within a few weeks of the outbreak of the insurrection, the Ceylonese bourgeois state had received military aid from the U.S., Britain, Australia, Russia, Yugoslavia, Egypt, India and Pakistan; and economic and political approval from China."[58] This mass revolt which is described in an editorial in the same issue as "the highest form that the international phenomenon of a radicalized youth movement has yet taken: the only one, hitherto, that has achieved the dimensions of an autonomous mass uprising," upset the preservatist interests of the ruling elites of a very heterogeneous set of nations and they united in suppressing it. Chou En-Lai and the Chinese government strongly denounced the "Guevarist" revolt. I know of few efforts to aid the JVP (People's Liberation Front) of Ceylon, but all that I have heard of are from radical and civil libertarian groups in western countries. And these groups have secured their news of what has

---

[57] For a detailed documented account of the persecution of Jews in Poland and Czechoslovakia see Paul Lendvai, *Anti-Semitism Without Jews* (Garden City: Doubleday, 1971).

[58] Fred Halliday, "The Ceylonese Insurrection," *New Left Review,* No. 69 (September-October 1971), p. 56, see pp. 55–91.

260 PERSPECTIVES IN POLITICAL SOCIOLOGY

happened in Ceylon from the *New York Times,* the *Times* (London), *Le Monde* (Paris), the *Guardian* (Manchester and London), *Nouvel Observateur* (Paris), the *Washington Post,* the *Daily Telegraph* (London), the *Hindu* (New Delhi), and the *Financial Times* (London), to judge from the footnotes in articles. There is no news or reports or pro-Liberation Front activities from China, the Soviet Union, or any other Communist country.

The United States and China in different ways strongly supported the Pakistani military dictatorship's effort to suppress the efforts of the elected representatives of East Bengal to create the People's Republic of Bangladesh. An active movement (of which I was a part) emerged to oppose the policy of the American government, and it appears to have had some success in restraining Nixon from sending a flow of arms and other aid to Pakistan. As far as any outsider knows, there was no opposition within China to its policy.

It has been my contention that the most positive aspects of any social system including the American are the factors within it that generate critical opposition. As I have noted in my most recent book which deals with student activism, "the passion unleashed by the antiwar movement is strongly related to basic aspects of the American value system. To decry war, to refuse to go, is at least as American as apple pie." And I document the fact that there has been large-scale opposition to *every* war in which the United States has engaged with the single exception of World War II.[59] In an "Introduction" to the work of the early feminist, socialist, and sociologist, Harriet Martineau, I offered the comment that Martineau who had analyzed the future of America of the 1830s in terms of the working out of the egalitarian creed, would look favorably on America today as a nation which inherently generates protest.

> She would see in the continuing strength of the American Creed, in the reforms attained since her death, evidence that America still offered hope to the world, provided there *remained a resolute group of radicals willing to risk antagonizing public opinion in order to fight for more pervasive equality,* thus bringing ever-increasing harmony between America's values and its reality. This struggle would take the form of a continuing fight against large-scale capitalism. For she argues: ". . . [E]normous private wealth is inconsistent with the spirit of republicanism. Wealth is power; and large amounts of power ought not to rest in the hands of individuals."[60]

---

[59] Lipset, *Rebellion in the University, op. cit.,* pp. 12–14.

[60] *Revolution and Counterrevolution* (New York: Basic Books, 1968), pp. 361–362. The essay on Martineau together with two other biographical ones are not included in the Anchor paperback edition. I did, however, include this passage in the "Preface" to the Anchor edition, published in 1970, see p. xvii. This article was first published as "Harriet Martineau's America," the introduction to my edited edition of Harriet Martineau, *Society in America* (Garden City: Doubleday-Anchor, 1962), pp. 5–42.

In various analyses of "extra-parliamentary social movements" in the United States, I have stressed the extent to which "reliance on extremist methods has played a major role in effecting change through much of American history."

> [M]any of the major changes in American society have been a product of violence, a result of the willingness of those who feel that they have a morally righteous cause to take the law into their own hands to advance it. By its extreme actions, the moralistic radical minority has often secured the support (or acquiescence) of the moderate elements of the community who come to accept the fact that change is necessary to gain a measure of peace and stability. . . .
>
> Any realistic appraisal of the process of political change in America must recognize that violence, extremism, and the resort to extra-legal and extra-parliamentary tactics, are a major part of the story.

In seeking the account for the propensity of Americans to foster such movements, which have also included a labor movement which historically has been more militant (strike-prone) and violent than those of Europe, I have suggested in various writings that the source lies in unique elements in the American value system. These include "the emphasis on the attainment of ends, on the one hand, and the strong hold of religious moralism, on the other."

> American extremism may be seen as another example of the propensity to seek to attain ends by any means, whether legitimate or not.
>
> Moralism is also a source of extremism. Americans tend to be a moralistic people, an orientation which they inherit from their Protestant sectarian past. This is the one country in the world dominated by the religious traditions of Protestant "dissent," Methodists, Baptists, and the other numerous sects. The teachings of these denominations have called on men to follow their conscience, in ways that the denominations that have evolved from state churches (Catholic, Lutheran, Anglican, and Orthodox Christian) have not. . . .
>
> The American therefore, as political and religious man, has been a utopian moralist who presses hard to attain and institutionalize virtue, or to destroy evil men and wicked institutions and practices.[61]

This analysis ties in with the earlier discussion of aggressive aspects of American foreign policy. The American propensity to define foreign relations and international wars in moralistic terms, good versus evil, God against Satan, *and* the fact that there has been more resort to conscientious objection and other forms of anti-war activity by Americans during war time than in any other country, can only be explained in value terms. As Harriet Martineau recognized, the moral passion of American radicals has been

---

[61] These quotes are taken from S. M. Lipset, "On the Politics of Conscience and Extreme Commitment," *Encounter,* 31 (August 1968), pp. 66–71. I have elaborated on them in subsequent books dealing with right-wing extremism and with student activism cited earlier.

uniquely American. The student activists of 1965–1972 illustrate the continued vitality of these aspects of the American value system, not its breakdown.

> Such extreme behavior by moralistic reformers has made the task of running this country extremely difficult. Those in authority have often found themselves in the position of President Johnson, denounced as wicked men who sponsor evil and corrupt policies. Consensus politics has never been an effective answer to moralistic politics. As a result, the moralistic reformers have often obtained their objectives. . . .[62]

A SUMMARY OF A POSITION AND A REBUTTAL

The editor of this symposium has asked me to include a statement of my general analytic framework with respect to the issues discussed here. My previous efforts to do so in response to critical comments have only resulted in more controversy with respect to what I really meant or stood for. Fortunately, the socialist economist, Robert Heilbroner, in reviewing *Revolution and Counterrevolution* did me the rare courtesy of summarizing my work in that book, which is a collection of essays written over a number of years, by specifying a number of "large-scale generalizations." These strike me at least as accurate and I would, therefore, close my discussion of scholarly issues by citing Heilbronner at length.

> *The essential building blocks of political stability are social rather than economic.*
> This does not deny the enormous moving force of economic change. Rather it implies that economic changes operate through social motivations. Thus poverty in itself does not lead to social restlessness any more than affluence alone leads to social harmony. The existence, or the narrowing, of economic gaps does not necessarily offset motivations born of status, tradition, ethnicity, etc. Hence the search for the causes of social stability or change must always include matters of status and value as well as questions of economics:
> "The prolonged intensity of class conflict in many continental nations," Lipset writes, "was owing to the overlap of economic class conflict with 'moral' issues of religion, aristocracy, and status. Because moral issues involve basic concepts of right and wrong, they are more likely than economic matters to result in civil war or at least class cleavage."
>
> *The basic movement of Western society is toward industrial-bureaucratic societies in which traditional class conflicts are lessened.*
> Social unrest, as Lipset sees it, is primarily a product of social change. Hence we must expect to find it in its most exacerbated form when change is most acute as in the case of the Third World or in the West, in those nations and eras when the industrial transformation was most rapid. Conversely, the gradual surmounting of the dislocation of industrialization opens the way for the emergence of a pragmatic rather than polarized politics. This is not to

---

[62] *Ibid.*, p. 71.

maintain that conflict ceases in such an environment. As Lipset notes,

"All democratic countries, from the lands of the Mediterranean basin to Sweden, Australia, or the United States, remain highly stratified societies in which access to education, economic opportunity, culture, and consumption goods is grossly unequal." Hence conflict necessarily continues, even in the most advanced nations. But the conflict becomes institutionalized and muted, as the values of industrial society triumph over those of the pre-industrial.

A new ideological consensus begins to unite the formerly opposed classes, but fails to include all elements or to bridge the gap between the industrialized and nonindustrialized world.

As bureaucratization softens the views of the upper class vis-a-vis the lower, and the slow rise in living standards lessens the gap between the lower and the upper, a consensus begins to emerge around a view that Lipset calls "conservative socialism." This clearly heightens the change of social peace insofar as this is threatened by economic conflict. Yet the new ideology fails to include both the extreme Right and the far Left, including the student body, and it fails as well to seem relevant to the leaders of the underdeveloped world. Thus, as so often before, this generation finds that it has achieved extraordinary social progress by comparison with the last—and yet discovers to its discomfiture that social harmony is no nearer. Like preceding generations, it fails to perceive that the very act of raising standards also changes them. The old frictions are lessened, but new ones arise. The acceptance of industrialism brings a new ideological center, but not an end to ideological or economic conflict.[63]

This summary of my position, as contained in various essays which were written in the mid-sixties, suggests a point of view which is somewhat different from the caricature of my analyses sometimes presented by New Left critics in the context of refuting it. It is a well known debater's trick to enhance one's own arguments by knocking down an exaggerated "straw-man." In concluding my effort to clarify, I would like to briefly turn to some writings, which Romalis does not criticize, those contained in the book, *The Radical Right*. Various New Left writers have attacked the position presented by me and other contributors to that volume, on the grounds that we have misrepresented the social base of (Joe) McCarthyism, as "Populist," and lower class, in order to bolster a conservative pluralist ideology. The most systematic and empirical effort directed at *The Radical Right* is that of Michael Rogin, who on the basis of electoral analysis, concluded that *The Radical Right* authors were wrong to see McCarthyism as rooted in the status-stricken or among the midwestern agrarian populists. His evidence suggests McCarthy was backed by conservative Republicans feeding on prevalent anxieties about Communism and the Cold War. But if one turns to my summary of the empirical findings, which Rogin is supposedly refuting, they read as follows:

---

[63] Robert L. Heilbroner, "Societies and Change," *The New Republic*, 159 (July 13, 1968), pp. 27–28. I had previously included these quotations from the Heilbroner review in the Anchor Edition of *Revolution and Counterrevolution, op. cit.*, pp. xix–xx.

From a political standpoint, he [McCarthy] recruited most heavily from the conservative groups, from Republicans, backers of right-wing policies on domestic issues, isolationists, and those most concerned with the need for a "tough" anti-Russian policy. . . . The studies analyzed here do not validate the assumption [concerning the impact of status strains] with respect to objective sources of status strain (high education and low economic position, for example). The evidence bearing on the belief that McCarthy appealed to the traditional "populist" ideology . . . also produces contradictory or ambiguous results.[64]

PROFESSIONAL SUCCESS AND SOCIAL ANALYSIS

I find it distasteful to discuss the matters raised under this heading by Romalis. I will limit myself to noting a few points about which he is wrong or totally ignorant. I do not think my basic view of America or the nature of democracy changed from 1945 to the present, but that is for others to judge. I should note for the record that I was a member of the Executive Committee of the Socialist Party in Berkeley, at the time I wrote *Political Man*. I was one of the founders of the Teachers Union local in Berkeley in 1963. I was faculty advisor of the Young People's Socialist League (YPSL) unit at Berkeley until I left. I have been faculty advisory of the Harvard YPSL since I have been here. The selective reading of my works which has led some, like Romalis, to criticize me as a celebrant of the American way of life, and as a conservative, has led others to describe me as a "Marxist," as the foremost exponent in sociology of C. Wright Mills's conflict approach, and to criticize me as an "exponent of totalitarian statism," as "a Social-Democrat," as a supporter of the "extreme left in the United States," as including "revolutionary directives" in my writings about student activism, and to denounce my politics for backing student activism and antiwar protest.[65]

I have been reluctant to discuss in print my reasons for leaving Berkeley, particularly since they have been the subject of occasional published gossip. Since they are raised here, and sufficient time has gone by to make the matter of little interest or consequence to people at Berkeley, I will note a few items for the record. First, I did not leave Berkeley because of reactions to the Berkeley Revolt of 1965. I had made arrangements in the Spring of 1964 with David McClelland, then head of the Social Relations Department

---

[64] S. M. Lipset, "Three Decades of the Radical Right," in Daniel Bell, ed., *The Radical Right* (Garden City: Doubleday, 1964), p. 420. The attack on this work, which in fact reiterates its empirical findings, is Michael Paul Rogin, *The Intellectuals and McCarthy: the Radical Specter* (Cambridge: MIT Press, 1967).

[65] For those interested in references to such exotica, see the "Preface" to the Anchor edition of *Revolution and Counterrevolution* and the "Introduction" to *Rebellion in the University*.

at Harvard and with Talcott Parsons, to go to Harvard a year later in the Fall of 1965. The arrangement long predated the campus troubles at Berkeley. My decision to leave Berkeley was linked to a controversy I had with the campus administration there involving policies followed by the Institute of International Studies of which I was Director, concerning distribution of internally-controlled research funds. Without going into details, the dispute essentially revolved about a policy adopted by the Institute after I became Director which served to increase the availability of funds to junior faculty and the consequent rejection of applications from a number of senior faculty who had been receiving grants year after year without demonstrating continued research activity. This matter became an issue; the administration refused to resolve it, and I decided to leave. The affair was as simple as that.

The decision became more complex the following year, for after the Berkeley Revolt developed, the new campus administration which took office in January 1965, learning of my decision, made strong efforts to get me to change my mind. I finally agreed to put off any formal resignation from Berkeley, in part, to avoid giving the impression that I was leaving because of the campus tension. The administration was concerned that knowledge of my resignation in the context of the turmoil, might affect the decision of others who were considering resigning. As a result, I went to Harvard in the fall of 1965 as a visiting professor, and did not formally take office as a regular member of the faculty there until January 1, 1966.

In commenting about the relationship of professional success to political views among academics and intellectuals generally, it is important to note also that Romalis is wrong in his assumption that such achievements are associated with conservative opinions. A large number of surveys of academic attitudes, from before World War I to the recent period, *all* find that the more successful or distinguished a scholar, the better the university he is at, the more critical or left his views. As various analysts of the subject have suggested, there appears to be a clear relationship between creativity in intellectual activities and propensity for hetrodoxy in other areas, including religion and politics. Since I have written amply on this subject, elsewhere, I will not comment further here.[66]

---

[66] See S. M. Lipset, "Academia and Politics in America," in T. J. Nossiter, ed., *Imagination and Precision in the Social Sciences* (London: Faber, 1972), pp. 211–289; and S. M. Lipset and Richard B. Dobson, "The Intellectual as Critic and Rebel: With Special Reference to the United States and the Soviet Union," *Daedalus*, 101 (Summer 1972), pp. 137–198.

Political Values and Sociological Analysis: Some Further Reflections

COLEMAN ROMALIS

One of the consequences of this exchange with Professor Lipset is that I have become increasingly aware of certain contradictory aspects in his work, as well as realizing afresh the pitfalls entailed in a lack of political and value self-consciousness on his part as a comparative analyst. In these pages I will therefore concern myself with examining Lipset's discrepant conception of himself as a citizen and repository of social values, and the analytic stance he has adopted as a professional sociologist.

It would be well to begin with Lipset's puzzlement that my earlier paper comments favorably upon the approach and execution of his 1950 study, *Agrarian Socialism,* and then goes on to deal critically with his Introduction to the 1968 updated edition, and in particular with his elaboration of the conditions which allow third parties to arise and sustain themselves in North America. In the original monograph, the focus was quite properly on social structural conditions, a perspective carried through in the analysis of the emergence of third parties. Eighteen years later, however, we find the author publishing a statement in which he revises his view: now, "the big difference between the United States and Canada, in their relative propensities to throw up third parties, lies in their varying electoral systems" (1968: xiii). I do not deny a role to formal electoral arrangements—or to varying value systems; that position has been well-developed not only by Lipset, but also by serious critics of his methodology and supportive evidence (e.g., Truman, 1971). But to now claim that the "big difference" is the formal electoral system and not the social structure strikes me as the expression of an altered sociopolitical perspective—a drift toward a more conservative perspective, if you will. That is why, I suggest, Lipset's earlier work in Saskatchewan is more satisfying than his later reflections upon it.

Lipset is also exercised by my equation of conservatism and belief in the decline of ideology, and produces evidence that many analysts across the spectrum of political persuasion have entertained a belief in the end of ideology.

But in abstracting certain superficial shared observations from various works, it seems to me that a kind of distortion occurs. This is particularly so in the case of writers on the "left," and notably in the case of Herbert Mar-

267

268 PERSPECTIVES IN POLITICAL SOCIOLOGY

cuse, where there is a general misreading by Lipset of their central analyses and conclusions. In my understanding of the writings of the radical or Marxist authors, and especially of Marcuse's work, the decline of ideological fervor on the part of what Marcuse terms the proletarian sector of society is conceptualized as a problem of "false consciousness" induced by affluence and a type of bogus "pluralist democracy" which paralyzes subjective awareness and collective action (Marcuse, 1964). When Marcuse writes of the homogenization of class interests in advanced industrial society, he refers to not all interests and values, but simply to those which uncontrolled technology and its associated system of ideas have utilized in order to sate an oppressed population. His focus is not on the meeting of common needs through an equalization of access to the rewards of society, but to the manipulation and oppression of a major portion of the population—a totalitarian system in which societal and individual needs are blended into one, so that the genuine human needs go unmet. The steam is taken out of this potentially revolutionary situation by seducing the exploited classes into a blind alley of "wrong choices." This neo-Marxist argument rests, of course, upon such notions as the fetishism of commodities and the manipulation of the ideological superstructure by elites who control the productive system.

The above analysis bears a surface similarity to some of Lipset's approach, especially if matters are stretched to accept his characterization of "*the* ideology of the major parties in the developed states of Europe and America . . . (as) . . . conservative socialism." While the data which Lipset and the radical critics utilize appear to be much the same, they part company in their interpretation of the situation.

The radical critics have tended to frame their explanation around the linked concepts of manipulation and oppression. In their view, control of the structure of advanced industrial society is in the hands of the leading bourgeois elements. The productive system, the educational institutions, the agencies for social welfare, communication, and entertainment are all dominated by the elites or their agents. Through their control of the technostructure and "political" institutions of the social system, they produced a condition of stable internal oppression supported by economic and political external oppression (imperialism). As domestic conditions underwent change, however, the radical critique increasingly has emphasized the potential for social transformation inherent in the flames of internal rebellion (especially among university students and ghetto populations), and tied together globally through a "Third World" rhetoric all oppressed peoples. Though their position has shifted and awareness grown gradually over the years, the radical critics' attitude has consistently been one of rejection of the central aspects and goals of advanced industrial society. Whether it was an apparent suffocating stability or the perception of widening seams of discontent which excited their analytic imagination, their stance was never complaisant.

A wholly different diagnosis of the situation has existed in the work of Professor Lipset. His conclusion is that many of the inequalities in American society have been reduced or erased, in both the economic and socio-political areas. His *feeling tone* about the society is one of major satisfaction with its character and what it has already accomplished; as a democratic model, it approaches more closely than any other nation-state the model of the "good society" itself.

Consonant with Lipset's value predispositions (to employ his language), he published in 1959 a full statement on his intellectual orientation in political sociology, in a volume officially commissioned by the American Sociological Association (Lipset, 1959). Batting clean-up on the sociology all-star team—behind Merton, Parsons, and Lazarsfeld—Lipset notes with approval the resolution of the intellectually immature separation of the "state" and "society" in the work of contemporary social analysis, and goes on to specify social stability and cohesion as a new and important study focus for sociology, replacing the earlier fixation on conflict and cleavage. As he says:

> The basic issue of much of contemporary sociological analysis is the problem of order. This concern for the conditions of social stability seeks to integrate under one theoretical rubric the functions fulfilled by the nuclear family and those satisfied by the economic system or the central value system. If the stability of society is a central issue for sociology as a whole, the stability of a specific institutional structure or political regime—the *social* conditions of democracy—is the prime concern of political sociology. (1959: 91–92)

Lipset here is speaking as the leading exponent of American political sociology, and its most prominent practitioner. The voice is that of the objective social analyst. But for all his remarks *as a citizen* endorsing democratic socialism and condemning social inequality, he has felt compelled in his *professional* role to employ a functional perspective which regards inequalities in the distribution of power, prestige and privilege as inevitable and necessary in any social order. This position—despite Lipset's disclaimer that it runs counter to his personal social and political values—is reinforced by his Schumpeterian elitist concept of democracy. Schumpeter's model defines democracy in terms of the competitive struggle for the people's votes as a basis for the power to make decisions; and yet, as Lipset recognizes, the functionalist view of society has a built-in contradiction to this position, since in kin-linked societies there is an unequal distribution of social advantage and access to the levers of societal power, and an impulse to lineally transmit a material inheritance. But, he shrugs, again this is an inevitability. He would like the model to work, and it is the one he cherishes . . . . but it can never *really* work. Moreover, when this democratic conception is translated into comparative analytic terms it imposes on all societies a western bourgeois model of contervailing interest groups prepared and able to compete for scarce rewards.

For Schumpeter's formulation of democracy to be at all meaningful, conditions must exist whereby some sort of equality is made to obtain within the sphere of political and economic competition. Clearly, however, this is not the case nor not to be: for not only is Schumpeter's formulation rigidly formal (ignoring the subtleties of the social and political process), it is also firmly elitist in that it neither accommodates nor welcomes a broadly based participation in the decision-making process. It envisions a system in which those who are advantageously situated compete for the power to make decisions, while the vast majority are ruled by the decisions thus made. If this is, objectively and analytically, a *Realpolitik* position, do we find that Lipset the citizen is distressed by it?

In fact, his position has not been well thought through, so that at first it gives the appearance of a schizoid embrace of all positions at once. The implicit suggestion is that of a dialectic composed of two contradictory models locked in a competitive relationship: within a fair and open social system buoyed up by a plethora of Tocquevillian voluntary associations, a political elite holds sway. Both systems are to coexist; the broadly based participatory political system, resting upon a fundamentally egalitarian base, is seen in a struggle for supremacy with an elite-dominated system which has a mainly passive electorate at its base. Upon closer inspection, however, this conflict model is revealed as illusion, since one of the two partners in the dialectic can never really exist. About that, Lipset has *no* illusions. As he puts it in *The First New Nation,* "I have urged the view that *realistically* the distinctive and most valuable element of democracy in complex societies is the formation of a political elite in the competitive struggle for the votes of a mainly passive electorate" (1966: 238). From a functionalist standpoint, no system of full equality can ever be; every social order is characterized by unequal life chances and influence (see Lipset's view, p. 253–54). In short, Lipset does not believe that a truly egalitarian democracy is possible, so that the very core of the dialectic ceases to exist. There are not two models, after all . . . just one; and that is the elitist one.

Formal electoral democracy without economic democracy is hollow, even in advanced industrial states. In countries where the economic system is underdeveloped and (usually) malformed, it is irrelevant. In such cases, the overriding task is to even out some of the grosser inequities—especially with respect to the productive system—and to develop the kind of economic and educational base that will give substantive meaning to "democratic" political procedures. As was noted in my earlier paper, the most effective instrument for accomplishing such aims may be "national" parties which, in their most responsive form, accommodate diverse interest groups within the state's boundaries. Frequently in underdeveloped societies portions of the non-elite population are so overwhelmingly disadvantaged in formally "democratic" systems that they may as well not be considered a part of the national political process. For example, in Jamaica where a well-entrenched two-party democracy prevails, substantial portions of the population are totally disinherited, living in conditions of abysmal poverty and expressing their alienation largely through a massive consumption of marijuana ("ganja") in a millenarian movement known as the Rastafarians which ignores a political system regarded as impervious to their needs.

Such situations are not unknown in advanced industrial states, and in fact the analysis may apply in some way not just to the obviously disinherited North American minorities such as Blacks, Indians, Eskimos, Chicanos and so on, but as well to major segments of the majority population, particularly among the youth, who have been disenchanted by a society and system of values which they regard as repugnant, unresponsive, and irrelevant. Given the general malaise in the advanced industrial states, and the very serious obstacles to Third World development, it is surprising that Lipset can speak with such assurance of an elite-controlled democracy being the good society itself.

If this were not enough, Lipset acknowledges the intellectual paternity of Robert Michels's analysis of the oligarchic impulse inherent in organization and the ability of an organized minority to control the unorganized majority. As he says in his reply to my critique, ". . . from the days when as a young Socialist in college, I was convinced that Robert Michels's analysis of the sources of oligarchy was a better discussion of the problems of postcapitalist society than anything written by a Marxist down to the present, these concepts have informed my politics and my sociology."

What irony that a citizen and sociologist governed by models of behavior drawn from Schumpeter and Michels should come to bemoan the existence of social inequality and to view with dismay the single-party states in the underdeveloped world as "offering bleak prospects for democracy." Ravaged as they have been by colonialism and imperialism, and beset with grave cultural, linguistic, tribal, and class divisions, Lipset would have them abandon the few political alternatives which offer a possibility of transforming conditions. The suggestion is that they should substitute for the most important such mechanism—charismatic single-party organization—a "democratic" system which is based upon a model that is both Western (a shared national culture, widespread literacy, and organized interest groups) and fundamentally elitist. The prospects are indeed bleak.

The capacity to transcend one's own time and place in history seems to be blunted in Lipset, with the result that he tends to view certain present institutions as somewhat changeless. Nowhere is this more clearly evident than in his treatment of democracy. His conception of democracy is that it is not only universally relevant and desirable but also in some essential sense timeless. What is good for the United States is equally good for Ghana, Guatemala, and Guyana.

It is a paradox of his work that even though it is so broadly comparative and addresses itself to historical materials, it is also ethnocentric and static in its underlying conceptions. This deficiency in what C. Wright Mills has called the "sociological imagination" is clearly seen if we examine the views on democracy of the economic historian, Joseph Schumpeter, from whom Lipset has liberally drawn in his own formulation of democracy. Primarily conservative though Schumpeter was, he nevertheless possessed sufficient sociological imagination to recognize the mutability and impermanence of established social arrangements. Though he affirmed the importance and positive social value of western democracy, he was able to discuss it as an historically-specific phenomenon. In a famous passage in his *Capitalism, Socialism and Democracy,* Schumpeter noted that the ideology and practice of democracy are of bourgeois origin, arising "along with capitalism and in causal connection with it" (1950: 296). The democratic method was the political tool "by which the bourgeoisie reshaped, and from its own point of view rationalized, the social and political structure that preceded its ascendancy." He then went on to question whether democracy is one of the products of capitalism which will die out with it, and "how well or ill capitalist society qualifies for the task of working the democratic method it evolved."

> As regards the latter question, it is clear that capitalist society qualifies well in one respect. The bourgeoisie has a solution that is peculiar to it for the problem of how the sphere of political decision can be reduced to those proportions which are manageable by means of the method of competitive leadership. The bourgeois scheme of things limits the sphere of politics by limiting the sphere of public authority; its solution is in the ideal of the parsimonious state that exists primarily in order to guarantee bourgeois legality and to provide a firm frame for autonomous individual endeavor in all fields. . . .
>
> Bourgeois democracy is certainly a very special historical case and any claims that may be made on behalf of it are obviously contingent upon acceptance of standards which are no longer ours. . . . as its colors fade it is all the more important to recognize how colorful it was in the time of its vitality; how wide *and equal* the opportunities it offered to the families (if not to the individuals); how large the personal freedom it granted to those who passed its tests (or to their children).

In selecting a definition and analytic approach for democracy largely from Schumpeter's work, it is quite clear that Lipset left behind the former's sweeping historical perspective and detached view of the class base and bias of contemporary democracy. It would seem that as part of the process of abstracting the perspective on democracy from Schumpeter (and others), Lipset also gave the conception a thorough laundering to insure that it would have universal and permanent application. This is not an idiosyncratic procedure peculiar to him, but rather an expression of general functionalist ahistoricity which tends to freeze institutions into an "all times and all places" mold.

Due to space limitations, it will be possible to deal with only one other issue raised by Lipset in his paper: his characterization of American self-identity and foreign policy. He reaffirms his position that "the American left, unions, intellectuals and others" consider Communism "an evil" because of their "anti-imperialist liberal ideological position." I suggest a contrasting interpretation: these strata have accepted the conservative private enterprise ideology of the American business and political community in defining the legitimate terms for the analysis of domestic and international competition.

There are two roots to the underlying assumptions about such legitimacy. One is that for straight national interest and competition, "ideological" constructions serve conveniently. The second is the essentially anti-statist position of the American public, which draws its strength from the wellspring of a widely dispersed commitment to laissez-faire. American economic and political conservatives have traditionally urged the primacy of the private sector in economic matters and maintain that it is to the mutual benefit of both government and business that the former refrain from "intervention" in the economy (for the speciousness of this position, see Cook, 1962). This laissez-faire ideology is not confined to economic matters nor to businessmen and politicians, but has diffused through such other sectors of American society as the educational and public service structures. Presumably "the American left, unions, intellectuals and others" also partake of this particular cultural mythology, since the belief in private enterprise capitalism is a deeply ingrained component of the national ideology.

This suggests that it is a predominantly conservative ideology favoring entrenched political and economic interests, and not an "anti-imperialist liberal ideological position" which characterizes the United States. From that viewpoint, Soviet and East European government involvements in the economy of Cuba are looked at askance, as are the efforts of the Allende Government to control the Chilean economy, since these offer a challenge to U.S. economic domination as well as constituting, in themselves, a violation of the principle of laissez-faire. These are immoral "statist" actions, as opposed to the "private enterprise" activities of the (American) "multinational" corporations operating in the advanced industrial areas and the underdeveloped countries of the Third World, alike (for two studies which are politically divergent, but analytically convergent in opposing American economic and cultural imperialism, see Levitt, 1970, and Servan-Schreiber, 1969).

Is there evidence of the "liberal to left commitment to reform the world, to extend self-determination, to eliminate colonial empires" that in Lipset's judgment has been "the main dynamic behind the expansionist interventionist phases of American foreign policy in this century"? Apparently not, since a review of U.S. military or C.I.A. interventions since World War II indicates that it is a specific type of political change which invites such American intervention: that which appears to threaten "the efforts of business interests to enhance their profit position" . . . despite the comparatively minor role Lipset would assign to this factor. In assessing the relative causal importance of ideology or material interests in shaping American foreign policy and behavior, it is plain that the latter weighs more heavily. Thus, it is the Cuba of Castro, not Batista; the Dominican Republic of Bosch, not Trujillo; the Guatemala of Arbenz, not Castillo Armas, which are all invaded; while the Somozas, the Duvaliers, and other supports for stable U.S. economic and political hemispheric hegemony are permitted to prosper.

I must confess to a sense of absolute incredulity upon reading Lipset's suggestion that since "a look at the institutions backed covertly in the anti-Communist fight by the C.I.A. indicates that most of them were liberal-left to socialist in their political sympathies . . . (this) . . . may be related to the suggestions made by some informed commentators that the C.I.A. had been staffed in the early 1950s (by) . . . men with leftist records." For fantasy, this statement is equalled only by Lipset's earlier remarkable interpretation of the role and values of the C.I.A. and the American public, published in the already mentioned Introduction to the Anchor edition of *Political Man*. That Lipset should again choose to reassert his position in these even more striking and absurd terms indicates that his former views on the liberal cast of the C.I.A. and the American nation, far from being a lapse, are a continuing and seminal key to his thought.

REFERENCES

Cook, Fred J.
1962   The Warfare State. New York: Macmillan.
Levitt, Kari
1970   Silent Surrender: The Multi-National Corporation in Canada. Toronto: Macmillan of Canada.
Lipset, S. M.
1959   "Political sociology." In R. K. Merton, Leonard Broom, and Leonard S. Cottrell (eds), Sociology Today. New York: Basic Books.
Marcuse, Herbert
1964   One-Dimensional Man. Boston: Beacon Press.
Schumpeter, Joseph
1950   Capitalism, Socialism, and Democracy. Third Edition. New York: Harper and Brothers.
Servan-Schreiber, Jean-Jacques
1969   The American Challenge. New York: Atheneum.
Truman, Tom
1971   "A critique of Seymour M. Lipset's article, 'Value differences, absolute or relative: the English-speaking democracies'." Canadian Journal of Political Science, IV, No. 4, December.

Structural-Functionalism, Exchange Theory, and the New Political Economy: Institutionalization As a Theoretical Linkage

TERRY N. CLARK
The University of Chicago

Any serious consideration of alternative approaches to the study of political phenomena must clearly deal with structural-functionalism, and for many purposes this consists of the work of Talcott Parsons. His many writings since the 1930s have played a central role in reorienting the discipline of sociology as well as of political science, anthropology, and parts of psychology. It is correspondingly difficult, often, to disassociate the distinctive contribution of Parsons from those of others around him.

Much sociological writing falls short of the criteria used to designate theory in the natural sciences, and this remark holds for most work by Parsons.[1] We clearly are not dealing, for the most part, with hypothetico-deductive theory, an interrelated set of propositions, and the associated conditions under which they hold. But if the Parsonian corpus falls short of the coherence of a paradigm in the Kuhnian sense, it still represents an important collection of orienting ideas, of thoughtful typologies, and a generalizing framework applicable to such a wide variety of phenomena.

Structural-functionalism in general and Parsons in particular have borne the brunt of much criticism in recent years. Indeed, one cannot escape the impression that more pages have lately appeared intending to criticize the structural-functional perspective than have been published with the intention of extending it. Unfortunately the bulk of this criticism has been so naive and irresponsible as scarcely to deserve the attention of serious persons.[2] Many critics, however, responsible and irresponsible alike,

I am grateful to Charles Bidwell, S. N. Eisenstadt, Victor Lidz, and Talcott Parsons for discussion and comments. This is research paper #27 of the Comparative Study of Community Decision-Making, generously supported by the Barra Foundation and the National Science Foundation (GS-1904, GS-3162).

[1] In recent years a number of provocative efforts have been moving toward more coherent theories in sociology, but we must unfortunately agree with Edward Shils that much of sociology "at present is a heterogeneous aggregate of topics, related to each other by more or less common techniques, by a community of key words and conceptions, by a widely held aggregate of major interpretative ideas and schemes." (Shils, 1970: 760)

[2] See the trenchant critique of Gouldner's recent work by Lipset and Ladd (forthcoming).

have called attention to Parsons's underemphasis of political and economic conflict, the structural bases of social change, and more generally "manipulative" behavior unregulated by values and norms. Structural-functionalism, and most of Parsons's writings, seem inadequate in their formulations concerning (1) the relationships between institutionalized and non-institutionalized behavior, and (2) the processes by which institutionalization takes place.

But to suggest that Parsons has been imperfect in these matters is not to imply that a superior alternative exists. On the contrary, insofar as critics of structural-functionalism have operated from some explicit theoretical framework, they seem to have fared little better than structural-functionalism in these respects. The major theoretical alternatives seem to fall under three general headings. Marxism is the oldest alternative and the one most frequently considered by critics as well as proponents of structural-functionalism—even though it has been observed more than once that many elements are shared by the two perspectives (Merton, 1957: 19–84; Stinchcombe, 1968: 57–148). The second is exchange theory, which we will seek to show in this paper is more complementary to than contradictory of structural-functionalism. Our argument concerning analytical complementarity also applies to the third perspective, one that has become quite important in economics and political science in recent years, and seems now to be growing among sociologists; it has been designated with such labels as public choice, the new political economy, and collective decision-making (see, for example, Lipset, 1969: xiv–xxii, 101–137, 137–162; and recent issues of the journal *Public Choice*). What distinguishes all three of these alternatives from structural-functionalism is a tendency to deemphasize values and norms, and often, institutions, in contrast to other variables.

The central thesis of this paper is that each of the four theoretical approaches is incomplete, and that a crucial point of intersection, and potential linkage, among them is the process of institutionalization.[3] In developing this argument, we consider first the analysis of institutionalized behavior, especially from the structural-functional perspective, then turn to processes of institutionalization. The third section presents an Institutionalization Theorem based on interchanges of resources among actors. Fourth, activation probabilities and the conditions leading to coalitions among actors are considered. Some empirical findings from American cities are then briefly discussed. Finally, the paper concludes with a discussion of the complementary aspects of certain theoretical perspectives currently in use in the social sciences.

---

[3] It will soon be clear, however, that these remarks relate more to exchange theory and the new political economy than they do to Marxism.

THE ANALYSIS OF INSTITUTIONALIZED BEHAVIOR

To say that behavior, or social action, is institutionalized generally means for structural-functionalists that this behavior is regulated by social norms and values. The most basic norms define the content of roles and statuses, the building blocks of formal organizations as well as those aspects of informal organization which are socially structured. The term institution is thus often used to designate reasonably delimited and interrelated sets of statuses and roles because it is not restricted to formally structured organizations. Roles, statuses, and institutions comprise the major elements of social structure, or what Parsons often refers to as social systems. Such systems of action may be distinguished analytically if not empirically on the one hand from cultural systems supplying the underlying values and beliefs which buttress particular social systems, and on the other from the personality systems of specific individuals whose regulated interactions comprise the social system. Institutionalization thus refers to a process involving primarily the social system, but it inevitably shades into the cultural and personality systems as well. It normally begins with the repetition of certain patterns of interaction which exhibit sufficient consistency to become defined as culturally distinctive. Institutionalization may thus consist of the creation of new normative standards by which behavior is subsequently regulated. But as the most firm normative standards are in turn grounded in values, as institutionalization proceeds we would expect that new norms would become articulated with basic values, and/or new values would be created to support the norms. Since the distinction between values and norms is necessarily analytical and in any case somewhat arbitrary, norms and values are best viewed as different points on a continuum, values being the more fundamental, more general, and more basic standards which apply to a variety of distinctive social situations, norms the more specific regulators of interactive situations. As the institutionalization process proceeds, then, norms and values should be created or redefined so that they articulate and are consistent with one another.

It seems almost paradoxical to suggest that a weakness of the Parsonian approach is its lack of concern for institutionalization and non-institutionalized behavior, as Parsons has pointed to the great analytical importance of the institutionalization process many times.[4] Despite these admonitions,

---

[4] See Parsons (1937: esp. 753 ff.). Indeed at one point Parsons even went so far as to define sociological theory as "that aspect of the theory of social systems which is concerned with the phenomena of the institutionalization of patterns of value-orientation in the social system" (Parsons, 1951: 552).

however, little has been formulated in the way of specific propositions. And Parsons has followed a reasonably consistent tendency to hold analysis within the confines of institutionalized structures.

This tendency becomes especially salient in works concerned with politics. The articles dealing with power and influence (Parsons, 1969: 352–438) are remarkable in their attention to basic structural relationships centering on the political process and in mapping interchanges among leading social units. The analysis of power as a circulating medium in the political system analogous in many respects to money in the economic system is most suggestive. And the implication of this analogy, that the volume and rate of circulation may vary, and that relationships involving power thus are often not zero-sum games, suggests in turn that a number of earlier formulations about power and the political process were at best incomplete if not directly misleading. We could proceed with the merits of the Parsonian contribution at some length, but as the purpose of this paper is to suggest how these ideas might be placed in broader context, we shall curtail our compliments.

It is again paradoxical that one of Parsons's earliest discussions of the inappropriateness of a zero-sum conception of power was contained in an article devoted largely to C. Wright Mills's *The Power Elite* (Parsons, 1969: 185–203—originally published in 1960.) While this article and the subsequent more refined discussions tended in general to move toward a more fluid, pluralistic, and complex portrayal of power and the political process than that of Mills, by working with concepts presupposing institutionalized behavior, Parsons maintained in this one important sense a more rigid conception of political processes than did many other writers. In this particular respect, Parsons came to assume a position with regard to the long-debated problem of the existence and importance of power structures closer to the "elitists" Floyd Hunter and C. Wright Mills than to the pluralist Robert Dahl (cf. Dahl, 1961; Clark, 1968:45ff.).

By cross-tabulating the four media—commitments, influence, power, and money—with "codes," "messages," (Parsons, 1969: 403), and "resources and their utilization" (Parsons, 1971), differing degrees of institutionalization are usefully classified. But just to use such concepts as "codes" and "messages," and to draw analogies between social behavior and genetic control and the control hierarchy of structural linguistics (Parsons, 1970; 1970a) indicates the degree to which behavior that is not patterned, and thus to a large degree controlled, by the hierarchy of media grounded in value commitments is simply not included in the analysis. Where such non-institutionalized behavior is considered explicitly, it tends to be treated as virtually Hobbesian. A major example is the discontinuity of institutionalized patterns across distinct political units:

"In the case of a 'national' political organization, however, its territorial boundaries ordinarily coincide with a relative break in the normative order regulating social interaction. . . . In other words, the danger of war is endemic in uninstitutionalized relations between territorially organized collectivities" (Parsons, 1969: 368). Theoretically more significant than viewing such non-institutionalized behavior as socially precarious, however, is the tendency to assume that it is not amenable to systematic analysis. However, much of politics, unfortunately perhaps, is simply not structured by established norms and values—much of the bargaining among political representatives, interest group activity, and decisions emerging from fragile coalitions largely escapes analysis within an institutionalized framework. A theoretical framework for political analysis should at least articulate in a consistent manner with such non-institutionalized behavior.

INSTITUTIONALIZATION PROCESSES

Even if one works primarily with such an institutionalized system, however, one must still inquire how it is perpetuated over time. Posing the problem of the relationship between institutionalized and non-institutionalized behavior in this manner leads to the obvious question of how new arrivals— immigrants, the young, etc.—become in some manner incorporated into an on-going social system and eventually become members of that system. The basic answer to this question which Parsons has tended to provide is socialization. Especially the young, but also adults under certain circumstances, internalize an attachment to cultural elements through mechanisms that operate largely on neo-Freudian principles (e.g. Parsons, 1964).[5] Although it need not be the case altogether, this solution tends toward treating social structure as given and unchanging; individuals adapt and become incorporated into it. There are two basic weaknesses here. First, variations from established cultural patterns by individuals or groups tend to be treated as "deviant" rather than incorporated into the theoretical structure in some way as embodying the germs of social change, the basis for institutionalization of new cultural elements. Second, although again not necessarily the case, the unit of analysis where change takes place tends to remain the individual.[6] It would be desirable to be able to specify a

---

[5] Obviously other principles of socialization could be introduced. The general body of ideas referred to as learning theory certainly comprise an alternative approach to institutionalization. Most work based on learning theory tends to follow an individualistic approach, but this need not necessarily be the case. Alker, for example, has analyzed decisions in the United Nations, invoking "successful" resolution of crisis as an explanation for subsequent repetition of the same adaptation pattern (Alker, unpublished).

[6] It should be made clear that these tendencies are most characteristic of Parsons's work prior to the 1960s and to the concern for evolutionary processes stressed in Parsons (1966 and 1971a).

process whereby social groupings as well as individuals help generate new normative patterns.

There is of course a vast empirical literature that deals with various patterns of institutionalization; and certain of these works formulate useful middle-level theoretical principles.[7] Nevertheless, the interpretations offered in most such literature tend to be reasonably ad hoc and are seldom articulated with more general principles of institutionalization. In an earlier paper (Clark, 1968a) we sought to order a number of reasonably descriptive analyses of change in universities in terms of four general models: organic growth, diffusion, differentiation, and a combined-process model incorporating the first three processes. Variations of these have also been employed on occasion by Parsons. Such models are clearly of some assistance for analysis of situations in other contexts, but they tend to remain somewhat descriptive models in the sense that they do not include a dynamic element as an intrinsic force for institutionalization.

A third approach to institutionalization, which doubtless applies to a number of empirical situations, is that the values underlying a particular normative structure may be redefined to apply and to legitimate new and different emerging norms. The linkages between most values and normative structures are sufficiently loose that a good deal of adaptation of this sort is possible. But simply to state that such redefinition of the situation may occur is hardly an adequate theoretical explanation for its taking place. Let us consider, then, a fourth alternative which may be of more general analytical utility.

A MODEL OF RESOURCE INTERCHANGES

Parsons's interpretation of relationships among political actors through systemic interchanges was a most suggestive insight. Its weakness, from the perspective of the present paper, was that it did not carry the analysis far enough—in terms of incorporating non-institutionalized behavior. Consider the portrayal of interchanges in Figure 1. It suggests that the fundamental systemic interrelationships among the four actors in a social system may be captured in six double interchanges. The content of these interchanges involves one or more of the four symbolic media: money, power, influence, and commitments. What elements of this framework would have to be changed if we begin to qualify the assumption of institutionalization? It might be that "deflation" would result in the circulation of the symbolic media as the trust built up in the system began to erode. We need not go

---

[7] Two of the most sophisticated examples of such analyses are Lipset and Rokkan's (1967) discussion of the formation of political party loyalties and Ben-David's (1971) work on the evolution of university structures.

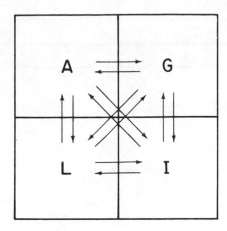

Figure 1. *Basic Interchange Model*

so far as to assume complete non-liquidity of resources, however, as in the situation of a barter economy. Rather, it would seem more useful to consider the situation involving relationships among actors who have not developed norms regulating their specific interactions, but who nevertheless act within a social system where extensive networks of norms and values are already present.

Consider, for example, a lobbyist who enters the office of a mayor. Although there may be few norms established to regulate their specific interaction as lobbyist and mayor, they still are constrained by a variety of values and norms specific to the country and time period: general standards defining "bribery," the role definition of the mayor with respect to the degree to which he will publicly and privately advance the cause of a particular interest group, etc. But within this framework of norms and values, a great deal remains, at least at the outset, uninstitutionalized: there is considerable room for bargaining between the two individuals, for coalitions to develop with other actors, and for relative types of interchanges and amounts of different resources to be exchanged.

Perhaps the situation briefly depicted here might be represented better by Figure 2 than by Figure 1.[8] The lobbyist and mayor may trust one another hardly at all, at least initially; but as they are actors within a larger

---

[8] Figure 2 is still not entirely appropriate as it does not depict the interchanges as involving *both* institutionalized and non-institutionalized behavior. The norms and values should be viewed as interspersed among the elements of non-institutionalized behavior.

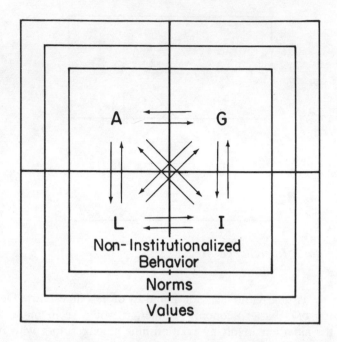

Figure 2. *Interchange Model Including Non-Institutionalized Behavior*

system, the system maintains the legitimacy and value of certain symbolic media (the value of money, for example) totally apart from what transpires between these two particular actors.

At this stage in the discussion, however, it seems useful to specify the basic elements of a model from which we will seek to make certain generalizations. The model consists of a social system S, comprised of actors A_1 ... A_k who achieve certain collective decisions through a subsystem designated the polity, P. As in Figure 2, there are certain institutionalized norms N, which regulate a good portion of interaction among the actors. But there is also much non-institutionalized behavior which we will seek to characterize more specifically. Those elements of non-institutionalized behavior which we will deal with here concern relationships between any individual actor A_i and the other system members insofar as they are organized through the polity, P. We may characterize the basic relations between A_i and P in terms of the inputs I_i which A_i contributes to P, and the outputs O_i which A_i receives from P. We define the content of politically significant interchanges between A_i and P as resources, R_i ... R_n. A resource exists, and takes on a given value, solely by virtue of the demand for it by members of a social system. Examples of basic resources are money, knowledge, and personnel (cf. Clark, 1968 and Coleman, 1971 for further discussion.) Resources may be utilized by an actor in two fundamental ways. They may be exchanged for other resources in wholesale transactions. And they may be applied toward a number of specific goals; the major goal we focus on here is institutionalization, as defined above. An actor in need of a particular bundle of resources to achieve his goals with respect to institutionalization may exchange resources he possesses for others which he does not. If we could measure each of the resources in an unambiguous manner, we could devise prices for each resource in the wholesale and retail markets. But because many resources impinging on the political arena are much less liquid than money, there are in some instances considerable transaction costs. Further, because of interaction effects between the personal characteristics of certain individuals and particular resources (e.g. more educated persons are more adept at applying technical knowledge), even the prices, especially in the retail market, inevitably vary to some degree for different individuals. A number of further complications concerning resources could be introduced, but for the moment these can suffice.

Although such resource exchanges may develop purely among individuals, the major exchanges of resources we consider here are those which impinge on the polity of a collectivity (social system). Considering again our actor A_i in terms of his relationships to others through the polity, we may characterize his net flow of resources in terms of the ratio of his outputs (payoffs) received from the polity to his inputs to the polity; this ratio we designate the payoff coefficient, PC.

$$PC_i = O_i/I_i$$

In keeping with our earlier discussion of the partially institutionalized aspects of a social system, we may suggest that although many elements of resource interchange in a social system remain unregulated by norms, many social systems will tend to institutionalize a payoff coefficient, which we may designate by the subscript I, PC_I. Once the PC_I has been defined, a number of consequences follow. Indeed, the PC_I as a system parameter plays the role of a constitutional provision as discussed by Buchanan and Tullock (1962). Let us consider three alternative normative and empirical definitions for a PC_I.

Perhaps the most common is the *parity norm,* the situation where $PC_I = 1$. The idea that each individual should receive benefits from others proportionate to the contributions he makes to the collectivity has been widely accepted (Gamson, 1964). This is the essence of the tradition where isolated individuals are treated in similar manner in collective situations irrespective of their social and economic characteristics, and of their previous interactions. Clearly an important line of social and ethical theory, this tradition has led to such manifestations as the legal institution of the social contract, the normative-legal arrangements surrounding many economic market transactions, and such theoretical formulations as the solution set of von Neumann and Morgenstern (1944) and what Homans has called distributive justice (1961). A number of writers have even seemed to imply that the only acceptable PC_I in terms of established ethical standards, and as an adequate description of empirical social behavior, is the parity norm.[9] Even if this institutionalization of the parity norm is ethically and empirically sufficient for a number of social systems, it is still important to consider possible alternative arrangements.

A second normative pattern might be termed the *social altruism norm*. This in fact represents a family of norms that have in common $PC_d > 1$, where A_d is a deserving actor; and $PC_a < 1$, where A_a is defined as an altruistic actor, who supports the more deserving actors of the collectivity via disproportionate contributions through the polity. In a system where the social altruism norm is shared by most actors, we may say in economic terms that the utility function of A_a includes as one of its elements the utility of A_d; there is an interdependence of utilities (Becker, unpublished). But this still leaves unspecified the manner in which the value of PC_i is to be defined. Although it has a certain teleological ring, one solution is to define the PC_i (in particular PC_a and PC_d) in terms of the basic values of the social system. More specifically, the crucial norms for these purposes tend to be those which relate to the minimal socially acceptable standard of living of the social system at that point in time. In some cases this may be low enough to permit starvation; in others it may represent a much higher threshold. A number of further complications could be introduced concerning the allocation of tax costs and benefits, redistribution effects, etc., but for purposes of the present discussion it is sufficient to establish that a social altruism norm is a very real parameter for certain social systems.

An individual variation of the social altruism norm states that the pay-offs to individual members of the social system should be consistent with the "needs" of each individual. This of course is the essence of the famous Marxian definition of the PC_I under communism: from each according to his abilities, to each according to his needs. Despite work by psychologists such as Maslow, however, there seems to be so little consensus as to how such a conception of "needs" may be objectively defined as to render

---

[9] Indeed, insofar as the norm of distributive justice is institutionalized among Homans's Persons and Others, then Homans is not dealing with *completely* non-institutionalized behavior—certain of his remarks to the contrary. On the other hand, to assert that distributive justice in the form of $PC_I = 1$ represents a social parameter of such universality as to remain constant across cultural systems seems, at this point, either foolhardy or ethnocentric.

the concept of meager scientific importance. But of course this does not diminish its importance as an ethical standard for certain groups.

A third conception of a payoff coefficient may be termed the *institutionalization value*. Here the intuitive idea is that the payoff to any individual is proportional to his overall balance of inputs and outputs to the social system in question, over the entire period of his relationship to that system. That is,

$$O_{ni} = (O_t/I_t)(I_n)$$

where O_{ni} is the output of resources to A_i for transaction n, O_t is the total output to A_i over the course of his relationship to the system, I_t his total input, and I_n his input for transaction n. But why should this equation be discussed under the heading of institutionalization value? The answer is based on considerations best made explicit at this point.

These considerations may be stated in an Institutionalization Theorem:
Where the PC_{ni} for A_i in any transaction n is not equal to PC_I, the result is a social imbalance, SI, where

$$PC_I = \frac{O_{ni} - SI_{ni}}{I_{ni}}, \text{ or } SI_{ni} = O_{ni} - (PC_I)(I_{ni}).$$

This SI is corrected through the institutionalization of cultural elements. Those elements represented by the A_p (individual or collectivity) whose $PC_{nq} > PC_I$ will gradually become accepted by the others, the A_q whose $PC_{nq} < PC_I$. In either case the amount of cultural elements projected or accepted by any actor is equal to his SI_{ni}.[10]

A few implications of the Theorem deserve consideration. At any given point in time a particular actor A_p (the proletariat, Bluebeard, capitalist employers) may relate to other sectors of the society through a particularly disadvantageous (in terms of some ethical system) PC_I. Our Theorem points out the directions of change, however, irrespective of the identity of the specific actors involved. The Theorem takes the particular PC_I as given and specifies the conditions under which "the rich may exploit the poor," or "the poor exploit the rich"; subordinates may become further subordinated through the same process that superordinates may find their authority eroded. We are thus dealing with a quite general and powerful principle. And although we have introduced such terms as "exploit" perhaps too loosely, it should be clear that far more is implied than momentary advantage: institutionalization means creation of an enduring normative relationship which can legitimate and maintain a position of power over

---

[10] It should be observed that one possible cultural element represented by A_p is a new PC_I. Our theorem thus includes in it the conditions under which the PC_I becomes defined and may be redefined.

time. Doubtless many competing actors have seized the essence of our Theorem and acted accordingly: the potlatch of the Kwakiutl, traditional charity associated with *noblesse oblige,* and corporate public relations are often directed toward the institutionalization and maintenance of certain values of the donor (Mauss, 1954; Levi-Strauss, 1969; Blau, 1964).

RESOURCE ACTIVATION AND COALITION FORMATION

These familiar examples, however, suggest the context of reasonably autonomous actors.[11] When we consider the potential impacts of the decisions taken by the polity of a large social system, another type of variable needs more careful consideration: the creation of coalitions by various actors in order better to achieve their goals. From the standpoint of the individual actor, if he can enjoin others to act in concert with him, he may be able to improve his net balance of inputs and outputs from the polity more effectively than by acting as an individual. Under what conditions, then, is it likely that actors will tend to create coalitions with each other and thus affect the PC_i, and subsequently, according to our Theorem, the PC_I?

To answer this question with precision, we need a theory of coalition effects which specifies the manner in which payoffs to an entire coalition are divided among its members. We cannot go into this matter in detail at this point, but let us attempt to develop a few implications of the above analysis in terms of the situations under which an individual actor might join a coalition.

Crucial in many instances is the configuration of resources at the disposal of the individual actor. But as any careful consideration of the problems of power soon makes clear (cf. Dahl, 1961), actors disposing of numerous resources may not choose to utilize them in collective decisions; the power structure of a social system is by no means identical to its decision-making structure (Clark, 1968: chap. 3).

It is thus useful to introduce the concept of an activation probability, AP_{ni}, the probability that A_i will activate resources at his disposal in situation n. We may then write the simple equation

$$R_{ti} \times AP_{ni} = R_{ani}$$

where R_{ti} is the total resources available to A_i, and R_{ani} the resources activated by A_i in situation n. Of course

---

[11] Our major focus in the present paper is on the relationships between social actors and the polity, but despite the lack of illustrative material provided here, the Theorem and propositions would seem to be generally applicable to interaction in most social systems. It is difficult to be more precise about the limits of our generalizations; perhaps subsequent work can help clarify this matter.

$$R_{ani} = I_{ni}$$

and since

$$PC_{ni} = O_{ni}/I_{ni}$$

then

$$I_{ni} = O_{ni}/PC_{ni}$$

and

$$R_{ti} \times AP_{ni} = O_{ni}/PC_{ni}$$

which, solving for AP_{ni}, yields

$$AP_{ni} = \frac{O_{ni}}{(R_{ti})(PC_{ni})}$$

At this point, however, coalition effects may enter to influence the outputs accruing to any individual actor. That is, the overall PC_I may be defined as a system parameter according to the parity norm or another such rule; and the PC_I may hold for the overall balance of inputs and outputs involved in the particular transaction n. But PC_I need not equal PC_{ni}; the internal division of inputs and outputs among members of the various coalitions involved may not proceed according to the same rules. Some actors may be more adept than others at forming coalitions, and certain aspects of coalition formation may favor some actors over others.

What additional information might then be of use in developing a theory of coalition formation? In many situations involving politics in the traditional sense one important factor may be the ideological outlook of the various actors.

1. *The greater the similarity in ideological outlook among a subset of actors, the greater the likelihood of their joining one another in a coalition.* Clearly the importance of ideology varies with the political situation; if it is impossible to create an ideologically congenial coalition large enough to influence an outcome, the ideological criterion will have to be relaxed or the actor must refrain from participating in a coalition. Where there are sufficient numbers of actors available to create several winning coalitions, however, ideological proximity can take on greater importance (cf. Leiserson, 1970).

The problems of maintaining within-coalition control and of allocating resources are often such that there would seem to be a tendency for coalition members to seek to maximize their control over the coalition itself. One means to this end is to limit the number of persons involved. Hence,

2. *The smaller the number of actors involved in a potential coalition, the more likely is an actor to join the coalition.* Proposition 2 implicitly

tends to assume, however, that other things are equal; one particularly important variable which may well vary independently of the number of actors is their relative control over resources. Hence to encompass the situation where each actor's control of an outcome is not directly proportional to his individual vote, we may suggest that

3. *The larger the proportion of resources which an actor can contribute to a coalition, and the more likely he is to activate these resources, the more likely he is to join the coalition.*

Two further propositions relate to the character of the inputs and outputs of the coalition.[12] If, as is often the case, potential coalition joiners are not in a position to control the exact nature of the political output which will result from their activities, they can still seek to influence it within a general range. The degree of control which actors may have over an output varies in part as a function of the type of output. One classification of outputs is in terms of their "publicness."

4. *When the outputs approximate public goods, the more similar are the outputs desired from the political system by a single actor to those desired by other potential coalition members, the more likely he is to join the coalition.* The concept of public goods is drawn from Samuelson (1954) and refers to the situation where an output must be shared by all members of the social system. National defense is the archetypical public good which is non-divisible among members of a social system, and from which no member may reasonably be excluded; mosquito control is a reasonably public good at the local community level. A significant point in coalition situations is that not only will a pure public good be shared equally by all members of the winning coalition, it will also be available to those outside the coalition (even if they may define it as a public bad). A slightly less pure, or we may say, more separable good, is amenable to division among the members of the system, and the coalition, in keeping with various decision rules.

Of course, insofar as ideology defines the nature of desirable political outputs, Proposition 4 is similar to Proposition 1. But as ideology may encompass both more and less than the nature of specific political outputs, it is worthwhile to include Proposition 4 as a separate principle.

In the case of more separable goods, it seems that

5. *When the outputs approximate separable goods, the more complementary are the outputs desired from the political system by a single actor to*

---

[12] These propositions concerning the nature of inputs and outputs are essential for analysis of many empirical situations, but tend to be ignored in discussions of coalition theory building on the game theoretic tradition (e.g. Shubik, 1964). This seems to be due to the fact that most of this work assumes that the only resource involved in the coalition game is money, or a monetary equivalent; hence problems concerning transaction costs of exchanging resources or the publicness or separability of inputs and outputs are ignored.

those desired by other potential coalition members, the more likely he is to join the coalition. Complementary outputs are those which may be sought by different members of a single coalition and which do not per se generate internal coalition problems, for example by appearing inconsistent to other significant actors in the social system. (Such significant actors might be voters if the coalition joiners were their elected political representatives.) One form of non-complementarity could derive from ideological inconsistency—if one output corresponded to a leftist and another to a rightist ideology. Another form, however, derives simply from the budgetary constraint. Insofar as many political outputs demand funding, and funding is limited, selection of these outputs must proceed as an essentially zero-sum game. The less close that one is to a zero-sum game, the greater is the complementarity as discussed in Proposition 5. In an ideal situation, complementarity would be of the sort that created a clear positive interaction effect. This would be the case, for example, where one actor sought to increase governmental spending in order to decrease unemployment, and a second sought spending for an extensive public transportation program.

Finally, the character of the resources available to various actors is significant.

6. *The more complementary are the inputs at the disposal of a potential coalition member to those of other coalition members, the more likely he is to join the coalition.* If the transaction costs of exchanging resources were negligible, Proposition 6 would not hold; but as we have pointed out, such costs may be considerable. It therefore is often more economical for a nascent coalition to expand its membership to include an actor who disposes of resources needed as inputs to P than it would be for the coalition to acquire the resource directly.

COALITIONS AND RESOURCES IN AMERICAN CITIES

Most of the above ideas are presented in terms general enough to apply to several different substantive areas. The theorem and propositions could be tested in many ways, and although at this point we can do no more than provide some very fragmentary evidence which bears on the theoretical formulations, this seems worthwhile if only to encourage others to do so more thoroughly in the future. The major empirical data to which we refer concern the configurations of leadership in a national sample of 51 American cities. Details concerning the sample, data collection procedures, etc. have been dealt with elsewhere (see Clark, 1971) and will be passed over here.

Two general findings are interesting to consider. The first relates to the power structure of the communities, operationalized using an issue-specific reputation series with the following format:

290 PERSPECTIVES IN POLITICAL SOCIOLOGY

"Is there any single person whose opposition would be almost impossible to overcome or whose support would be essential if someone wanted to . . ." followed by five different endings, each relating to a specific issue area: *"run for/be appointed to the school board in (city)?; organize a campaign for a municipal bond referendum in (city)?; get the city to undertake an urban renewal project?; . . . essential for a program for the control of air pollution in (city)?; run for mayor in (city)?"* From this series a power index was created for each of the major actors.[13] The basic results are shown in Table 1. The most striking finding is the consistent importance of the mayor and the newspaper as leading community actors across all five issue areas.

Second, an ersatz-decisional series of questions was used to gauge the decision-making structure of these same communities, i.e. to tap the actual influence exercised by specific actors in past decisions rather than their potential influence as measured in the earlier series. In the issue area of the mayoral election, generally the most important issue area in terms of its impact on subsequent decisions, the seven most important actors were those shown in Table 2. Businessmen and business organizations were of more importance here than on the power index, and the newspaper dropped slightly. (The mayor was not listed in the issue area of his own election.)

How may we interpret these results? Caution, clearly, should be exercised. We do not have information about actual coalitions in the sense of explicit agreements among actors—although this may be less a matter of inadequate measurement than a reflection of the amorphous configurations of groups supporting mayoral candidates in American cities.

We know from ancillary sources,[14] however, that a frequent coalition is that of business groups and the newspaper. The coalition is a natural one in terms of our coalition propositions. The ideology of many newspaper publishers tends toward that of the business community; indeed publishing is to a large degree a business (Proposition 1). The coalition appeals from the standpoint of restricting the number of actors involved to a manageable number (Proposition 2). The business sector tends to have access to more financial resources than any other single sector in most American communities, while control of the mass media is a resource of considerable importance for local politics as well (Proposition 3). Considered as the output

---

[13] The index consisted of

$$P_s = \sum_{i=1}^{7} \sum_{a=1}^{5} \frac{S_{ia}}{T_{ia}}$$

where P_s is the power of a given actor (status), i the seven informants, a the five issue areas, s_{ia} the mentions for a single status and t_{ia} the total number of statuses.

[14] Our major sources of information here are fieldwork in two of the 51 communities nearby Chicago and a qualitative reanalysis of our interview schedules.

Table 1

Leading Statuses on Power Index, P_s,
in Five Issue Areas

		$P_s \times 100$
I.	School Board Election	
	1. Newspaper	21.0%
	2. Mayor	20.0
	3. Members of Local Boards, Committees & Commissions	6.8
	4. Other Municipal Officials	6.0
	5. Officers of County Adm. Agency	4.3
II.	*Municipal Bond Issue*	
	1. Mayor	31.3%
	2. Newspaper	22.7
	3. City Councilman	4.2
	4. City Manager	3.5
	5. Executives of banks & other financial institutions	3.2
	6. City Council	2.8
III.	*Urban Renewal*	
	1. Mayor	48.0%
	2. Newspaper	15.3
	3. Director of Urban Renewal	5.8
	4. Executives of banks & other financial institutions	3.8
	5. City Manager	3.6
	6. City Councilman	2.7
	7. Senator or Congressman	2.5
IV.	*Air Pollution*	
	1. Mayor	29.6%
	2. Newspaper	12.6
	3. Health Officer	9.8
	4. Industrial Executives & Organizations	7.2
	5. City Manager	3.8
	6. Chamber of Commerce	3.5
	7. Other Federal, State or County Government Offices	3.4
V.	*Mayor Election*	
	1. Newspaper	24.3%
	2. Mayor	9.5
	3. Other Political Parties	7.3
	4. Leading members of local Democratic Party	6.8
	5. City Council	6.7
	6. Democratic Party, unspecified	3.5

of a mayoral election, the mayor of a community is a reasonably public good. Certain rewards may be offered to his supporters in the campaign, but it is often more effective to offer rewards (payoffs) in the form of broad policies than it is to provide more separable payoffs. It is also generally

Table 2

Leading Actors in the Mayoral Election
on the Influence Index

1. Businessmen and Business Organizations	.169
2. Labor Officials and Organizations	.096
3. Newspapers and other Mass Media	.091
4. Ethnic and Religious groups	.091
5. Democratic Party	.079
6. Republican Party	.071
7. Blacks	.065

considered more honest, or at least consistent with the civic culture of most American cities. The similar outputs (Proposition 4) desired by business and newspapers seem to be low taxes, efficient government, "social peace," business district improvements (often through urban renewal), and balanced economic growth. The major inputs (money and publicity) which the two actors can provide are also nicely complementary (Proposition 6).

On the other hand, neither of the two actors tends to be able to control directly very many votes; to exercise influence, at least in mayoral elections, these two actors must rely heavily on value commitments shared with the rest of the populations. The best way, following our theorem, to institutionalize and maintain such commitments is by contributing a surplus of inputs to the collectivity in general and to the polity in particular. In fact if one considers the identity of leading donors to community chest-type drives as well as to political campaigns, these often tend to be businesses. Although to quantify the ideological contributions of a newspaper to its collectivity in meaningful fashion is highly complicated, several studies to date (see Clark, 1969) seem to suggest that the general style of American city newspapers is to remain "non-partisan" in the sense of avoiding divisive issues. Newspapers frequently seek to champion causes which are salient to many citizens and will contribute to perceived community well-being but arouse minimal resentment (the definition of a successful "crusade"), and generally encourage community economic and population growth. These substantial inputs, which tend to exceed those of other actors in many American cities, would seem to contribute to a social imbalance as the term was used in our Theorem; the result, we would expect, would be maintenance of the legitimacy and continuing support of the civic values represented by the business and newspaper groups. This seems to have been the case in many American cities at least until the mid-1960s, and especially so in middle-sized and smaller cities, and in cities of the Southwest and West. Seattle, Phoenix, San Diego, Los Angeles, and Fullerton, California seem to have represented this tendency rather nicely. Data from national polls also suggest that the citizens of communities in the West and especially the Southwest, compared to those in other regions, tend disproportionately to support values that are congenial to business groups (Patterson, 1968). To establish causality in these matters is clearly most difficult, but at the very least these few pieces of evidence do not seem inconsistent with our theorem and propositions. Far more evidence could and obviously should be examined; however, as empirical materials cannot prove a theory, but can serve as useful ammunition with which to refute one, perhaps we are justified in leaving further consideration of empirical materials to others.

Three problems related to more precise operationalization and testing of these ideas might at least be listed, however, even if we have no very satisfactory solutions to them at present. First is the basic issue of measuring resources and cultural elements (norms and values) with sufficient precision that empirically-based measures could be introduced into our equations. The Comparative Study of Community Decision-Making is currently investigating these matters using data from the national sample of 51 cities and has developed some tentative measures for leading actors in American cities. (Early results are reported in Clark, 1969.) Still, these measures are far from being as complete as would be desirable.

One approach to obtaining more satisfactory information is that followed by the experimental social psychologists. Allocating fixed quantities of resources to different actors, and bringing them together under highly structured conditions, is an appealing solution for its general precision. It is likely, however, to be difficult to develop important enough resource exchanges, over a sufficiently long time period, to witness substantial changes in norms and especially values in such experimental situations. Nevertheless, the experimental approach is no doubt worth following as long as it seems fruitful. Alternatively, intensive observation by a sensitive observer of a legislature, city council, or mayor's office could be used to estimate values for resources and cultural elements; if several experts could offer their interpretations of the same situation, their results could be compared and combined. Another procedure would be to work with heavily documented historical decisions; in this manner several judges could be asked for independent assessments and not only could reliability measures be computed, judges could be asked for clarification at points of disagreement with one another, and the original documents consulted where necessary; some approximate measures of validity could thus also be developed. (See Axelrod [1971] for an effort in this direction.)

A second problem concerns the specific cultural elements which are to be institutionalized. Our theorem is stated at a general enough level as to leave unspecified the particular cultural elements which A_p represents. Doubtless some values and norms are more easily accepted than others. A proposition complementing our theorem is *the closer the values and norms offered for acceptance to those already institutionalized, the more readily will they be accepted.* This idea, discussed in a number of situations (cf. Clark, 1969a), is still quite difficult to make more precise; it is quite troublesome to specify the distance of different values from one another. The same basic problem arises in discussing ideological proximity (Proposition 1), but is amenable to solution in many political situations where participants operate with a reasonably unilinear (generally left-right) conception of ideological differences. It would seem appropriate to consider that the cultural elements institutionalized would be those which A_p most stressed in interaction with A_q. In complex and enduring interactive situations, to isolate such cultural elements may be most difficult; it is still perhaps most appropriate to consider as leading candidates for institutionalization those elements which persons in the interactive situation would consider that A_p was most concerned with seeing adopted by A_q. We might consider that SI represents a sort of liquid resource, credit which A_p holds with A_q. The credit may be used to institutionalize different cultural elements, although prices clearly vary across elements as well as individuals. If we had firm measures of SI, and prices for the different cultural elements, we could specify how far institutionalization would proceed. The many variables which we have introduced into the analysis at this point make it complicated enough that the most tractable empirical solution would probably be to ask experts in a situation to provide estimates of the different variables.

The third problem, even more than the last, involves fundamental conceptual issues as well as measurement difficulties. It relates to the fact that resource interchanges are often highly symbolic; this basic point is an important insight for which we are indebted to Parsons. But not only is money (and influence, power, and commitments) a symbolic medium, in many interchanges even the medium may not itself change hands; its mere presence, implicit or explicit, may be sufficient to influence the outcome of the interaction significantly. If a businessman known to be affluent asks a mayor for a favor, the mayor need not request immediate monetary recompense; and in cases where the resource in question is less immediately and directly quantifiable than money, for example political support, measurement problems are even further compounded. Nuttall, Scheuch, and Gordon have discussed this problem perceptively (Nuttall et al., 1968), but without offering very specific solutions. We have no simple resolution to the problem here, except to suggest that in the present state of theory we might do better to ignore some of the most complex empirical problems in order to concentrate on those with which we can deal more effectively. In this particular instance this suggestion might imply working only with resources, symbolic or material, which actors in the situation could generally agree were being exchanged. Of course in a highly structured experimental situation this problem would only arise to a minimal degree.

CONCLUSION

If we began by stressing the degree to which structural-functionalism overemphasized institutionalized behavior, perhaps it is appropriate to conclude by suggesting that the largely non-institutional approaches to social theory should consider certain institutions more seriously. The term institution is not popular with economists, nor is it with certain others building on such traditions as game theory, parts of the new political economy, and much of exchange theory. Most of the resistance to the study of institutions by economists, however, was less directed against institutions per se than against a descriptive and narrowly empirical approach to social science. The concept of institution as used in the present paper would not seem to present such a barrier to the development of social theory. Indeed, insofar as our framework makes theoretically explicit a process by which institutions develop, change in orientation, and decline, our framework subsumes particular institutional arrangements in a manner that makes possible the articulation of institutional arrangements with several bodies of social science theory.

In particular, the conceptualization of the payoff coefficient as a variable system parameter opens the way to reinterpreting certain results of earlier theorizing which have not been consistently supported by empirical work to date. It is conceivable that the predictions of von Neumann and Morgenstern, Gamson, and Riker concerning the size of a "minimal winning coalition" may be empirically incorrect. But mere presentation of a few negative findings (e.g. Browne, 1971) need not jeopardize their efforts, especially when such negative results are unaccompanied by an alternative interpretation. Rather it seems more advisable to subsume expectations concerning minimal winning coalitions under a more general interpretation which takes as a variable the norms governing inputs and outputs to various actors, and in particular the payoff coefficients that are institutionalized in the particular system.

Our theorem suggests two areas where attention should be focused in future empirical research on coalition formation, areas which seem to have been largely ignored to date. First, if we are correct that the specific payoff coefficient in a social system becomes institutionalized only following a history of social imbalances of inputs and outputs, then as a preliminary step to further work, careful attention should be directed to measuring the specific payoff coefficient in effect at any given point in time. Such possible variation seems to have been ignored in the empirical work to date in this area. Second, where the size of empirical winning coalitions exceeds that implied by the institutionalized payoff coefficient, the result should not be simply conceded to irrationality. Rather, the precise size of the SI should be gauged and an effort made to ascertain the effects of persistent social imbalances on the norms and values of the decision-making institution.

Future efforts at theorizing, we might also suggest, could benefit by seeking at least to articulate with other bodies of emerging social theory. In the division of intellectual labor, theorists should obviously seek to avoid duplication. But such division of the task in no way implies that alternative perspectives need be, or should be presented as, mutually incompatible. Indeed, if theorists would more often seek explicitly to articulate their activities with one another (as well as—always laudable—with middle-level propositions and empirical findings), new and suggestive lines of research, such as the new political economy at present, might be able to advance with more confidence and more general support from intellectual neighbors. And exchange theory, which too frequently has been offered as an iconoclastic theoretical outlook, belongs more appropriately among the interstices of institutions focused on by structural-functionalists.

Indeed, we might suggest that theorists who do not engage in empirical research to test their ideas—and there is no reason why they all should—might nevertheless assume as a scholarly obligation the occasional task of developing an explicit set of mechanisms by which their particular ideas could be theoretically articulated with alternative perspectives. If future theorists are sufficiently confident of their own presentations to the scientific community to follow this suggestion rather than engage in loud declamations of their complete distinctiveness, we shall be on the way toward a new stage in social scientific theory.

REFERENCES

Alker, H. R., Jr., and Cheryl Christensen
Unpublished   "From causal modeling to artificial intelligence: the evolution of a U.N. peacemaking simulation."

Axelrod, Robert
1971   "Psycho-algebra: a mathematical theory of cognition and choice with an application to the British Eastern Committee in 1918." Presented at Advanced Research Seminar in Mathematical Theory of Collective Decisions, Harbor Town, South Carolina.

Becker, Gary S.
Unpublished   "A theory of social interaction." The University of Chicago.

Ben-David, Joseph
1971   The Scientist's Role in Society. Englewood Cliffs, N.J.: Prentice-Hall.

Blau, Peter M.
1964   Exchange and Power in Social Life. New York: John Wiley.

Browne, E. C.
1971 "Testing theories of coalition formation in the European context." Comparative Political Studies 3 (January): 391–412.

Buchanan, J. M., and Gordon Tullock.
1962 The Calculus of Consent. Ann Arbor: The University of Michigan Press.

Clark, T. N.
1968a "Institutionalization of innovations in higher education: four models." Administrative Science Quarterly 13 (June):1–25.
1969 "A comparative study of community structures and leadership." Presented at annual meeting (September) of The American Political Science Association, New York, N.Y.
1971 "Community structure, decision-making, budget expenditures, and urban renewal in 51 American communities." Pp. 293–313 in C. M. Bonjean, T. N. Clark, and R. L. Lineberry (eds.), Community Politics. New York: Free Press.

Clark, T. N. (ed.)
1968 Community Structure and Decision-Making: Comparative Analyses. San Francisco: Chandler.
1969a Gabriel Tarde on Communication and Social Influence. Chicago: The University of Chicago Press.

Coleman, J. S.
1971 Resources for Social Change. New York: Wiley Series in Urban Research.

Dahl, R. A.
1961 Who Governs? New Haven: Yale University Press.

Gamson, W. A.
1964 "Experimental studies of coalition formation." Pp. 82–110 in Leonard Berkowitz (ed.), Advances in Experimental Social Psychology. Volume 1. New York: Academic Press.

Homans, G. C.
1961 Social Behavior. New York: Harcourt, Brace and World.

Leiserson, Michael
1970 "Power and ideology in coalition behavior: an experimental study." Pp. 323–335 in Svend Groennings, E. W. Kelley, and Michael Leiserson (eds.), The Study of Coalition Behavior. New York: Holt, Rinehart and Winston.

Levi-Strauss, Claude
1969 The Elementary Structures of Kinship. Boston: Beacon Press.

Lipset, S. M. (ed.)
1969 Politics and the Social Sciences. New York: Oxford University Press.

Lipset, S. M., and Ladd, Everett
Forthcoming "The politics of sociologists."

Lipset, S. M., and Rokkan, Stein
1967 "Cleavage structures, party systems, and voter alignments." Pp. 1–64 in Lipset, S. M. and Rokkan, Stein (eds.), Party Systems and Voter Alignments. New York: The Free Press.

Mauss, Marcel
1954 The Gift. Glencoe: The Free Press.

Merton, R. K.
1957 Social Theory and Social Structure. New York: The Free Press.

von Neumann, John, and Morgenstern, Oskar
1944 Theory of Games and Economic Behavior. Princeton: Princeton University Press.

Nuttall, R. L., E. K. Scheuch, and Chad Gordon
1968   "On the structure of influence." Pp. 349–382 in T. N. Clark (ed.), Community Structure and Decision-Making: Comparative Analyses. San Francisco: Chandler.

Parsons, Talcott
1937   The Structure of Social Action. New York: McGraw-Hill.
1951   The Social System. Glencoe: The Free Press.
1964   Social Structure and Personality. New York: The Free Press.
1966   Societies: Evolutionary and Comparative Perspectives. Englewood Cliffs, N.J.: Prentice-Hall.
1969   Politics and Social Structure. New York: The Free Press.
1970   "On building social system theory: a personal history." Daedalus 99 (Fall): 826–881.
1970a   "Some problems of general theory in sociology." Pp. 27–68 in John C. McKinney and E. A. Tiryakian (eds.), Theoretical Sociology. New York: Appleton-Century-Crofts.
1971   Unpublished Seminar Notes, The University of Chicago.
1971a   The System of Modern Societies. Englewood Cliffs, N.J.: Prentice–Hall.

Patterson, S. C.
1968   "The political cultures of the American state." Pp. 275–291 in Norman R. Luttbeg (ed.), Public Opinion and Public Policy. Homewood: Dorsey.

Riker, William H.
1962   The Theory of Political Coalitions. New Haven: Yale University Press.

Samuelson, Paul A.
1954   "The pure theory of public expenditures." Review of Economics and Statistics 36 (November): 387–89.

Shils, E. A.
1970   "Tradition, ecology and institution in the history of sociology." Daedalus 99 (Fall): 760–825.

Shubik, Martin (ed.)
1964   Game Theory and Related Approaches to Social Behavior. New York: John Wiley

Stinchcombe, A. L.
1968   Constructing Social Theories. New York: Harcourt, Brace and World.

Commentary on Clark

TALCOTT PARSONS
Harvard University

Perhaps I may start with a mild double complaint. Clark, like many other writers, tends to keep repeating the term "structural functional*ism*" and calling persons identified with it as "structural functional*ists*." On the other hand, in his title he refers to "exchange theory," note not "exchang*ism*" and the "new political economy," note not "new political econom*ism*." I find it rather difficult to understand why I, Merton, and others have to be identified with the label "ism" whereas others somehow escape this. I remember Merton on one notable occasion protesting against this. If I remember correctly, the structural was not stressed, but he said, "For heaven sake, why can't we talk about functional analysis and not functional*ism*."

There is another item of mild complaint. I have often wondered why I have never been identified with exchange theory. Going back to *Toward A General Theory of Action,*[1] certainly the analysis of interaction presented there dealt most conspicuously with exchanges and in another phase which began with the book *Economy and Society,*[2] which I co-authored with Neil Smelser, exchange is the very center of the analytical picture. Yet Homans and Blau are exchange theorists and apparently Smelser and I are not. This seems a bit illogical.

On the very first page there is another problem raised, namely, the question of "the criteria used to designate theory in the natural sciences," and continuing two lines later, reference to a "hypothetical deductive theory, an interrelated set of propositions and the associated conditions under which they hold." I am aware that I have put forward the desirability of this type of theory on a number of occasions, but I think my enthusiasm for it has rather considerably declined. One of the reasons for this change has been an increasing interest in the relations between biological theory and that in the social sciences. I have had the increasing impression that the kind of theoretical analysis which has become established in a great deal of biology is very similar, indeed, to that which sociologists and anthropologists and some kinds of psychologists use. It is very different from that used in economics and a great deal of physics, particularly as deriving from the classical mechanics, in both of which cases the ideal has been a deductive system of

---

[1] Talcott Parsons and Edward A. Shils (eds.), *Toward a General Theory of Action.* New York: Harper & Row, 1962 (First Edition, 1961).
[2] Talcott Parsons and Neil J. Smelser, *Economy and Society.* New York: The Free Press, 1969 (First Edition, 1956).

differential equations. It is my strong impression that the kind of mathematical models which will prove to be most fruitful in our field will not consist in systems of differential equations but will derive from quite different branches of mathematics. Put a little differently, it seems to me that biologists are inherently "structuralists," with reference to which they tolerate a great deal of qualitative descriptive analysis. They are also "functionalists" and for some curious reason there is no bitter argument about the legitimacy of functional analysis in the biological fields. I wonder why such a conspicuous difference?

Clark at the top of page 276 raises the old questions of "underemphasis" on political and economic conflict, the structural bases of social change, and more generally, "manipulative behavior unregulated by values and norms." On the first point, it seems strange how infrequently critics raise the question of underemphasis on political and economic conflict in *what context* with reference to *what problems!* By no means every social system in every aspect is shot through with political and economic conflict. Furthermore, even where one can make a case for its importance, the problem the sociologist is concerned with may often be better handled without going out of his way to emphasize political and economic conflict because these are only part of the phenomena of social systems. It therefore seems to me that Clark ought not to make these sweeping statements about underemphasis without specifying just what particular kinds of political and economic conflict in what kind of situations have been underemphasized.

By "the structural basis of social change" I presume he means those features of social structure which have built in factors tending to bring about change. Later in the paper Clark does refer to certain changes of emphasis associated with my concern in recent years with problems of social and cultural evolution. I would frankly find it a curious judgment that my recent little book, *The System of Modern Societies,*[3] underemphasized the structural bases of social change. Its point of view is of course not Marxian; but the followers of Marx do not have a monopoly on the analysis of social change.

Perhaps then I can take another example. In recent years I have devoted a great deal of attention to the analysis of the development of higher education, including research, in modern societies. I have treated this as part of what I have called the Educational Revolution to which I have given a status of importance fully equal to the famous Industrial and Democratic Revolutions. One of the most important features of the development of higher education is that it carries with it a very definitely built-in structural basis of social change and I surely have not been neglecting that structural basis.

---

[3] Talcott Parsons, *The System of Modern Societies.* Englewood Cliffs, N.J.: Prentice-Hall, 1971.

Both the growth of knowledge as such and the development of competence in individual persons, including both higher levels of competence and the wider spread of the same levels within a population, are processes which inevitably lead to structural change at the social system level, as well as that of the cultural system and the individual personality.

To take one more concrete example, Gerald Platt and I have devoted substantial analytical attention to what we consider to be essentially a new phase of the process of socialization of the individual which we have called "studentry," a neologism which we have introduced to make the distinction from adolescence quite clear. This seems to us to be a function of the development of mass higher education which is an entirely new phenomenon. The modern undergraduate college with its inclusion of such a greatly enhanced proportion of the age cohort is a first-rate example of a structural change which in turn will prove to be the basis, for the most part, of incalculable further structural changes.[4]

Finally, Clark uses the phrase, "more generally manipulative behavior unregulated by values and norms." He sometimes also refers to it as non-institutionalized behavior. It seems to me that this is an exceedingly problematical concept and should be handled with great caution. A first question is what aspect or parts of a set of behavioral phenomena are to be treated as uninstitutionalized. To take Clark's own example of the lobbyist calling on a mayor in his office: surely the office of mayor is not in any radical sense uninstitutionalized. Presumably it is because of certain powers of that office that the lobbyist is interested in seeking out the mayor in the first place. Suppose then that what the lobbyist seeks from the mayor concerns money, either some control of the use of municipal funds, or on the other side, the offer by the lobbyist even of illegal payments which would constitute bribery. As a medium of exchange in the wider society, money surely is not uninstitutionalized. Therefore, with respect to money, the interaction of mayor and lobbyist surely is part of an institutionalized system.

More generally, one of the most important consequences of institutionalization is the creation of areas of freedom within which individuals and subgroups can make their own choices at their discretion. The range of discretion which a mayor has by virtue of his office is the focus of the power he is in a position to exercise and to a considerable degree also of influence. Where actors interact within the range of such freedoms, the action may under certain circumstances correctly be called "manipulative," though there is somehow a vague connotation of illegitimacy in this term. Whether or not the attempt on both sides of such interaction to have an effect on the behavior or decisions of the other is illegitimate is however an entirely em-

---

4 Talcott Parsons and Gerald M. Platt, "Social Structure and Socialization in Higher Education," *Sociology of Education,* Winter 1970, Vol. 43, No. 1.

pirical question; in some cases it may be, in others not. Even the term "lobbyist" with its pejorative connotations does not mean that every time a lobbyist talks to a mayor, he is "manipulating" him in an illegitimate way.

Finally, apart from the legal institutionalization of offices such as that of mayor or of media like money we can certainly speak of informal institutionalization of which a notable historic example had been the political machine. Merton has written a famous article on the "positive functions" of the urban political machine which certainly meant that the development of such a machine was a mode of institutionalization of values and norms. To be sure, these values and norms might be in conflict and often have been with the legal system, for example, of the larger society. But this does not mean that they are not values and norms. One could go on, but I hope I have made clear the grounds for my skepticism of the validity of any sweeping statements about uninstitutionalized and/or manipulative behavior.

It seems to me that there is in Clark's statement an undercurrent suggesting belief in a kind of "state of nature" of the Rousseau variety and therefore an unrealistic either-or contrast between institutionalization and its absence. I regard such a contrast, implicit or explicit, of highly dubious validity, and the question of institutionalization a highly *relative* matter.

Clark's main thrust, however, concerns the process of institutionalization. So far as I have grasped his formal notation scheme and its implications, the general purport of the theorem he states on page 285 seems to me to be acceptable. I would in particular agree that new processes of institutionalization constitute one possible outcome of states of imbalance, as he calls them, in a social system. The institutionalization of the modern American-type university, to which I referred above, is a grand scale example. Its relative recency is one particularly notable fact concerning it. Before the end of the Civil War, as is pretty well known, there was no such thing as a university in the modern sense on the North American continent, but within a relatively brief period what is probably not only quantitatively but qualitatively the most notable university system in the world developed here. The fact that it has been undergoing severe crises in the last decade does not mean that it is not institutionalized; I should say it very definitely is institutionalized. And my personal belief, based on a good deal of study, is that its main outline will survive the recent and current crises. Since, however, this is a prognosis, I am of course not in a position rigorously to prove this proposition.

However that may be, I should like to register an objection to Clark's statement on page 277 that the distinction between values and norms is "somewhat arbitrary" and his inference that they are best viewed as different points on a continuum. I have not discussed this problem in print for some time, but perhaps this is an opportunity to state what I hope will prove to be a clarification. In a forthcoming analysis of the American university and with special reference to its function of training for the applied professions I have emphasized the importance of a familiar distinction between the "basic" sciences or "pure" intellectual disciplines and knowledge and competence that is primarily "clinically" oriented. The terminology, of course, comes from medicine. The phrase, "the science of medicine," does not refer to an intellectual discipline like physics or biochemistry, but to any and all knowledge in terms of its relevance to the problems of the health care of the individual. It includes knowledge taken from physics, chemistry, many branches of biology, psychology, sociology, and so on.

I should treat the distinction between values and norms, which of course, as Clark says, is analytical, as parallel to this distinction. Values constitute the "pure" commitments to patterns of normative orientation. Norms, on the other hand, are the "clinical" applications of values to complex practical situations. The necessity for the distinction lies in the fact that workable norms in the present technical sense cannot be derived from any one pattern of values, but must be derived from combinations of several. There is no one-to-one correspondence between value pattern and regulation of cases of concrete behavior.

It is at this point, that is, in the linking of the new complex with parts of the society outside its originating group that the development of norms precisely as distinguished from values is particularly important. Thus during and following the Industrial Revolution major changes in the legal institutions of property and contract occurred, including at a fairly late stage the limited liability corporation and general incorporation acts which did not require an act of the legislature to set up a single new corporation.[5] Interestingly a very large part of this change in the normative structure occurred through processes of business practice and judicial decision rather than by legislation, though of course there was some legislation. In the case of the institutionalization of research which I have used for illustration, there has also been a considerable development of regulatory norms, some of which of course are informal custom rather than formalized rules. There has, of course, been a great deal of discussion of the ethical problems involved in the conditions under which research is done and the uses to which its findings are put. This is a set of phenomena which I would definitely put under the heading of the development of new norms broadly as distinguished from values.

I think it very important, for example, that the logic of this distinction directly parallels one which has now become accepted in biology. This is to say there is no one-to-one correspondence between a gene and a character of the phenotype of the particular organism. It took biological thinking a

5 See J. Willard Hurst, *Law and the Conditions of Freedom*. Madison, Wisconsin: University of Wisconsin Press, 1956.

long time to get over the presumption that there was indeed such one-to-one correspondence. The logic of the relation between genes and the determinants of phenotypes, however, is a *combinatorial* logic and not a matter of a gradation between components of the gene pool on the one hand, characters influenced by environment on the other. The parallel distinction in the theory of action seems to me to be fundamental and Clark's proposal to ignore it seriously obscures the analysis of institutionalization.

One can define institutionalization either as a state or as a process. As a state, it is the situation where normative components of the system, that is, normative with reference to the "regulation" of action, define not only an ought, that is, a mode of action which is held in Kluckhohn's important term, to be *desirable,* but also a pattern of action which is (again to quote Kluckhohn) "desired," which one may generalize to the statement which is felt by acting units, individual or collective, to be in *their* interest. To take an example which may appear to be trivial but in its implications is not, in general it is not to the interest of units engaged in economic exchange to refuse to accept what is normatively defined as "good" money. This may take the form of what is legally defined as legal tender or by a series of gradations, cashiers checks, travelers checks, and so on, to the point of checks on personal bank accounts. As I have said above, money is deeply institutionalized in modern society. An index of its state of institutionalization lies in the fact that it is indeed to the interest of participating actors to accept money as a legitimate medium of exchange and base their planning and calculations on the expectation that others also will accept its legitimacy. To be sure, money, like other media, is subject to disturbances which we think of in such terms as inflation and deflation and extreme situations of runaway inflation, of course, make it virtually impossible to act in this way. I would call such situations, for example, as the German inflation of 1923, a case where the institutionalization of the medium had broken down.

I would suggest that as process, institutionalization must go through a series of several stages. As an initial condition, there must be in the value system what might be called an "orientational disposition" to treat an essentially new mode of the patterning of action as *desirable.*[6] A good example would be the positive valuation of the advancement of knowledge through research. For example, Merton's analysis of the relevance of the values of ascetic Protestantism as delineated by Weber to the field of cognitive advancement describes a kind of paradigm.[7] This particular Puritan version was by no means isolated in the history of the Western value system,

---

[6] It has seemed appropriate on various occasions to call this a "value pressure" in the direction of implementation of the relevant value patterns.

[7] Robert K. Merton, "Puritanism, Pietism and Science," in *Social Theory and Social Structure.* Illinois: The Free Press of Glencoe, 1949. Chapter XIV, pp. 329–346.

as Ben-David's comprehensive survey has shown,[8] but it was a somewhat intensified form. Part of the relevant value system which involves certain elements of norms would then be some of the kinds of freedoms which in the United States had become institutionalized in the Bill of Rights. This included something which could be called in a broad way intellectual freedom which included a kind of freedom of inquiry that clearly was not institutionalized in the same way in the European Middle Ages nor even so late as the Renaissance and part of the Reformation Period. The case of Galileo is paradigmatic. And this suggests that, for new institutionalization, a value pattern system must be capable of generalization *beyond* its previous boundaries of obviously institutionalized application and that the normative structure of the society in which this takes place must be sufficiently hospitable at least not to impose crippling prohibitions on the relevant types of activities.

In the case of the Industrial Revolution new types of activity in the field of economic production were the conspicuous innovations. These, of course, encountered a whole range of types of opposition which Weber, for example, summed up under the heading "traditionalism." The case of advancement of knowledge through research is comparable in that it also has encountered many modes of traditionalistic opposition. For example, alleged undermining of religious faith. We need remember only the furor caused at one time by the Copernican revolution with respect to the geocentric conception of the solar system and, two centuries later, the Darwinian revolution with respect to the man-centered conception of the world of living systems.

In order to overcome this type of opposition, which I think we can say develops in relation to any incipient major innovation whether it be cultural or social, it is necessary that there should be a mobilization of "interests" of acting units, be they individual or collective, to whom pursuing the innovative path "makes sense." Ben-David has strongly suggested that successful institutionalization in the field of research has required the development of a kind of "critical mass" of interested investigators in a broadly defined field. These people can effectively communicate with each other in the respective areas and their mutuality of communication can form a protection against the indifference or opposition of people who do not share their interests. Once the output of such a group then has reached sufficiently impressive levels, it can begin to bid for positive attention from quarters outside itself. Thus, perhaps, in England, as analyzed by Merton,[9] a particularly important step was the establishment of The Royal Society. Even though its

---

[8] Joseph Ben-David, *The Scientist's Role in Society: A Comparative Study.* New Jersey: Prentice-Hall, 1971.

[9] Robert K. Merton, *Science, Technology and Society in Seventeenth Century England.* New York: H. Fertig, 1970.

founders, Boyle, Newton, and the others, were engaged in privately esoteric investigations which could hardly have attracted very much direct technical interest in the Royal Court, they were somehow able to get royal sanction; otherwise they could not have used the title "The Royal Society." I think it fair to say that both aspects are entirely essential to the achievement of this sort of status. There must be, that is, a group who in the activity in question have achieved a strong enough position so that they are both protected from negative forces and able to "make an impression" beyond their own membership. At the same time it is necessary for institutionalization that there be a source of legitimation that extends beyond the initiating and innovating group. Surely the formula of "The Royal Society" symbolizes this as well as anything could.

When I speak of the impressiveness of the output of such a group or type of activity I am exemplifying a concept which I have used a great deal and called "adaptive upgrading." It must be an output like the case of economic production in the Industrial Revolution or of advancement of knowledge in the various phases of the scientific and educational revolutions which is able to validate claims to superiority over what had previously been done or might be done without this type of contribution. As such, innovative output of this character must be valued beyond the circle of the innovators themselves. The cotton textile output of the Industrial Revolution clearly had to sell and could not be confined to the esoteric interests of Lancashire manufacturers alone. The obvious inducement for selling, of course, was a combination of acceptable quality with a drastic lowering of previous prices.

The case of advancement of knowledge may raise certain difficulties. One possible "selling point," of course, is technological application, but it seems, at least to me, that it is easy to exaggerate the importance of this, particularly in the earlier stages of such developments. I am inclined to think that rather more important have been the sheer senses beyond the technically qualified circles that something had come to be understood on a level on which it could not be said to be so understood previously.

From a certain point of view, then, the end of the series of phases is the process that I have liked to call "inclusion." This refers to the pattern of action in question, or complex of such patterns, and the individuals and/or groups who act in accord with that pattern coming to be accepted in a status of more or less full membership in a wider solidary social system. There are many historical examples, but one which should be familiar to social scientists, may perhaps be especially illuminating. It is well known that the discipline of economics, which originated primarily in Great Britain, was for a long time entirely or almost outside the university system. Adam Smith, who was perhaps its most important single founder, was a professor of moral philosophy, not of political economy or economics, and at the University of Glasgow in Scotland, not in England. David Ricardo was a stockbroker who retired early and bought a seat in Parliament and was a special kind of country gentleman. John Stuart Mill, the third most important figure of the founding group, was a quasi-civil servant employed by the East India Company. It was not until the appearance of Alfred Marshall, whose seminal book was published in 1890, that the new discipline really found a solid footing in the English universities, in his case at Cambridge. Now, of course, no self-respecting university with any claim to general standing certainly in the Western world, would not have economics as a well-established discipline fully integrated into the university organization. Even in Great Britain and in continental Europe, there would be not just one chair of economics, but probably several in an important university. This pattern, which has been generalized in the present century, is what I mean by inclusion. Professor Clark's important study of the Durkheimian episode in the history of sociology in France is a case of partial inclusion which did not fully succeed, at least in that generation.

In this reference,[10] inclusion as I have used the concept means that the *new* component which has been relatively recently differentiated from an older "matrix" *both* retains its recently achieved "identity" *and* is accepted as a legitimate part of a broader "solidarity" which *also* includes the older components in their changed state. Thus economics as a discipline became included—some would say "established"—as structurally distinct from "moral philosophy" but both have been included in the *same* university organization.

The paradigm of institutionalization which I have outlined has a history. A first version of it was developed in collaboration with Neil Smelser and published as Chapter 5 of our joint book, *Economy and Society*.[11] It dealt a little more elaborately with seven steps or phases of the process of change. Smelser, in turn, developed this further and used it extensively in his own study of social change in the Industrial Revolution.[12] I myself went off on a slightly different tack.[13] This formulation in turn was considerably modified before it emerged as the paradigm of what I have called a phase of progressive structural change which clearly must imply the emergence of new structures generally by the process of differentiation from related older ones and eventually completion of the process of institutionalization.

It will not have escaped Professor Clark that the paradigm in terms of

---

[10] Another usage of the concept concerns the sense in which previously "excluded" groups have become or seem to be in process of becoming included in a solidary system. Cf. Parsons, "Full Citizenship for the Negro American?" in Parsons and Clark (eds.) *The Negro American*. Boston: Houghton-Mifflin, 1966.

[11] Talcott Parsons and Neil J. Smelser, *op. cit.,* pp. 246–294.

[12] Neil J. Smelser, *Social Change in the Industrial Revolution.* Chicago: University of Chicago Press, 1957.

[13] See especially Talcott Parsons, "Some Considerations on the Theory of Social Change," *Rural Sociology,* Vol. 26, No. 3 (September 1961).

PERSPECTIVES IN POLITICAL SOCIOLOGY

which I have been discussing the phases of an institutionalization process is one which I have been using for a number of years. It has been particularly set forth in connection with my two small books on societies in comparative and evolutionary perspective. The four basic categories are value generalization, differentiation, adaptive upgrading, and inclusion. Differentiation is the process by which new patterns are somehow developed by innovating groups within a society. Value generalization is an outcome, and its potentiality in the structure of the relevant value system is a necessary condition for the innovations to be institutionalized. Adaptive upgrading I take to be a necessary condition of the acceptance of the innovations within the society beyond the limits of the innovating originators. Finally, inclusion is, as it were, the seal of fully successful operation of the institutionalization process.

As I have said, I think by and large that I accept Professor Clark's broad formula and the relevance of his theorem. I fail, however, to see anything strikingly original about it or even to see how exchange theory and the new political economy can make a major contribution in aspects of the problem of institutionalization which have been neglected by so-called "structural functionalism."

One final remark. At the pole of my continuing concern with parallels between biological theory and that in the sciences of human action I have become increasingly impressed by the resemblance between the process of institutionalization as I have outlined it here and the processes of organic evolution by which new species have come to be established. It is surely well known to most social scientists that the evolutionary process requires processes of variation in the genetic constitution of the relevant groups of organisms, that is in what is now technically called the gene pool. These sources of variation *must* be basically independent of specific environmental influences, especially as these operate on what biologists call the phenotype. The other equally essential set of factors which produce evolutionary change are summed up under the concept of *natural selection* which has undergone considerable modification since Darwin's time. I suggest that the normative elements which I have outlined centering on the value system are the parallel in our type of theory to the gene pool and the processes of variation in the gene pool which makes a genetic basis of new speciation possible. The processes of natural selection, however, are parallel to those of the establishment of an integration of the interests of acting units and groups of them in the maintenance of action patterns and the strengthening of their position in a total action system which we call institutionalization.[14]

---

[14] A very full exposition of the relevant biological theory is given in Ernst Mayr, *Populations, Species and Evolution*. Cambridge, Mass.: Harvard University Press, 1970.

Institutions and an Exchange
with Professor Parsons

TERRY N. CLARK

Apologies are in order if "structural functionalism" was perceived as an offensive label. Somehow, it seems, the term has become institutionalized, although I will not seek to interpret the details of the process with a single theoretical framework. In any case, no offense was intended.

No doubt other writers have become more directly identified with exchange theory than has Professor Parsons, but one of the basic concerns of my paper was to make very clear that there is no essential conflict between structural-functional and exchange-oriented analyses. Even if Professor Parsons and others have seldom claimed the label of exchange theory, the discussions of interchanges in four-function paradigms and elsewhere quite obviously locate exchange at the center of Parsonian analyses. Certainly exchange theory is too important to leave just to the exchange theorists, narrowly defined.

As to types of theoretical models in sociology, I will not seek to predict the future in detail. If we consider simply the current situation, however, we do find a number of areas in the social sciences, and sociology in particular, where quite coherent sets of deductive propositions have been developed and linked with empirical materials. In other areas the theoretical structures are much less tight. Whether or not a successful general theory can be cast in such a deductive framework, I must agree with Professor Parsons, is an entirely open question. But whatever progress may be made on the level of general theory, we continue to see additional subfields of sociology codified in sets of deductive propositions, and in some instances, in systems of equations. If we do not have a single Kuhnian paradigm in sociology, we do have several more limited paradigms, in specific subfields —of organizational analysis, community decision-making, voting behavior, etc.[1] I see no reason to expect a reversal of this trend, at least as far as lower and middle-range theorizing is concerned. But this of course does not necessarily conflict with Professor Parsons's remarks.

I regret having introduced "manipulative" if it implied illegitimacy. Perhaps "voluntaristic" would have been a better choice. The fundamental point in any case was that much of social action is not *specifically* regulated

---

[1] See Raymond Boudon, *La crise de la sociologie* (Geneva: Droz, 1971), pp. 9–40 for a lucid discussion of this point.

309

by norms or values. Clearly the general outlines of most social action are "morally regulated," but only in a very general sense. If we define institutionalized behavior as that which is regulated by values and norms and non-institutionalized behavior as the behavior which remains, doubtless something generally remains. The discussion here frankly seems to resemble the old question about whether the glass is half full or half empty. As I stated, and Professor Parsons restated, in the mayor-lobbyist situation, money and the basic content of the roles are indeed institutionalized. But to know of these general values and roles provides no more than a very superficial understanding; obviously they cannot tell us the outcome of every visit involving a mayor and lobbyist, or very much about the dynamics of interaction.

If, for example, actions of the mayor and lobbyist were coded into some 1,000 categories during a half hour conversation, only a small percentage of these elements would be directly predictable from preexisting values or norms about mayors and lobbyists in general. No theory is likely to subsume every empirical datum, but perhaps some elements of the interaction left uninterpreted by a focus on general norms and values could still be productively analyzed using the Theorem and associated propositions of the above paper. The Theorem and propositions could thus *extend* the range of empirical situations amenable to interpretation in structural functional terms. This was the point which I sought to make about the complementarity of theoretical perspectives. If one litmus paper works better for the full half of the glass, perhaps another test can be applied to the empty half. And the results of both tests may potentially be integrated in a single more general theory.

Every theorist is free to define his own concepts, and there is little point to disagreement over definitions per se. Enough disagreement about definitions of "value" is found in the literature to make redefinition for one's own usage almost essential. The fact that in Professor Parsons's definition, several values may be linked with a single norm, and that considerable looseness characterizes the relationship between any value and norm, need not, however, exclude the possibility that values and norms, to some degree and on some occasions, may be conceived as different points on an analytical continuum. This is simply to suggest that my definition of value and that of Professor Parsons overlap to some degree.

The reason that I prefer to stress the empirical as well as the theoretical interpenetration of values, norms, and non-institutionalized behavior is that this makes explicit the possibilities for change in all three areas—the amount and degree being amenable to analysis using the framework set forth in the above paper.

The four-stage institutionalization scheme of Professor Parsons seems to me, like much of his work, to offer a very useful mapping of general variables and logical arrangement of stages. But it would seem that this scheme could be usefully complemented at least at two points by our framework. First the scheme seems to contain no provision for changes in values. It seems to understand by institutionalization almost exclusively the erection of normative patterns consistent with pre-existing values. This is no doubt adequate some of the time. Our framework, on the other hand, provides for this type of institutionalization as well as for implanting of new sets of values. It can thus subsume some of the many empirical examples of institutionalization which involve changes in values subsequent to changes in norms and behavior—for example the secular republican values which Durkheim helped diffuse throughout French society.[2]

Second, our framework helps specify the conditions under which Parsons's process of "making an impression" can be brought about, as it must be before "adaptive upgrading" may proceed. We know empirically that many potential institutions are arrested in their development; they do not proceed logically through all four of Parsons's stages. More careful theoretical attention might thus be directed toward specification of the dynamic mechanisms operating at each stage of the institutionalization process, and the conditions under which they continue to move the process ahead or cause it to stop. One important such dynamic mechanism would seem to be a series of exchanges involving social imbalances as analyzed in the above paper.

We have suggested that our framework can significantly complement the institutionalization scheme of Professor Parsons at at least two points. Perhaps these brief examples may serve to illustrate some of the ways in which one theoretical scheme can be extended by articulation with another. It may be fitting to close with a plea for more such eclecticism in the social sciences. Or should we say eclectic analysis?

---

[2] See Terry N. Clark, *Prophets and Patrons: The French University and the Emergence of the Social Sciences* (Cambridge: Harvard University Press, on press).